TRANSYLVANIA
The Roots of Ethnic Conflict

Transylvania

THE ROOTS OF ETHNIC CONFLICT

edited by
John F. Cadzow
Andrew Ludanyi
Louis J. Elteto

THE KENT STATE UNIVERSITY PRESS

Library of Congress Catalog Card Number 82-23354
ISBN 0-87338-283-8
Manufactured in the United States of America

Library of Congress Cataloging in Publication Data
Main entry under title:

Transylvania: the roots of ethnic conflict.

A collection of papers, some of which were presented at the Symposium on Transylvania, held on May 18–20, 1979, at Kent State University.
Includes index.
1. Transylvania (Romania)—Ethnic relations—Addresses, essays, lectures. 2. Transylvania—(Romania)—History—Addresses, essays, lectures. 3. Minorities—Romania—Transylvania—Addresses, essays, lectures. I. Cadzow, John F. II. Ludanyi, Andrew. III. Elteto, Louis J. IV. Symposium on Transylvania (1979: Kent State University)
DR279.8.T73 1983 949.8'4 82-23354

ISBN 0-87338-283-8

Contents

Introduction

When Americans read or hear about Transylvania, they immediately think of vampires, cemeteries, a mysterious, gloomy, and fog-covered countryside, lonely and terrorized people overawed and overshadowed by the castle and eery personality of Count Dracula. Bram Stoker and Hollywood have succeeded in relegating a real place, with real people and real problems, into a storybook creation, a never-never land for movies and television audiences. Once Transylvania became a fiction in the popular mind, it received the faddish attention of certain writers who capitalized on the interest by becoming scholars of the fiction. Thus, even the scholarly world has contributed to the perpetuation of the fog that engulfs Transylvania. For a while, even the Rumanian government promoted the confusion, to encourage its tourist trade. It ran advertisements—picturing a mysterious-looking castle—in the *New York Times* (and elsewhere) headlined "Yes there is a Transylvania."

The prevalence of these stereotypes compounds the problem of those who wish to deal with the real Transylvania, because although much more fascinating than the fictional one, the real land is not a refuge from the world's problems, but rather a microcosm of them.

The present volume seeks to provide students of ethnic affairs and of Eastern European history, politics, society, and culture with a scholarly, interesting, and up-to-date insight into the fascinating life and development of this multiethnic area. Transylvania is indeed a microcosm of our world; it is a seething, restless, exciting place, one with numerous problems waiting for solution.

The problem that stands out above all others is the quest for peace, unity, and order in a setting characterized by diversity, discontent, and a legacy of conflict. In Europe, Transylvania is the potential setting for one of the most troublesome ethnic minority crises of the current age. Although the question of the Hungarian and German minorities has not been as prominent since World War II as have the problems in Northern Ireland, the Basque-inhabited corner of Spain, or on Cyprus, it involves the destiny of many more people and ultimately the "structure of peace" that was created after World War I, reasserted after World War II, and reiterated at Helsinki as recently as August, 1975.

In Transylvania, the very foundations of this world order are challenged by the confrontation that has prevailed there at least since 1918 between the Rumanian, Hungarian, and German inhabitants. In the last fifteen years, or since the 1968 Warsaw Pact invasion of Czechoslovakia, the developments in the relations of these peoples have again created cause for concern. The revelations of abuses in the treatment of minorities through the Károly Király letters in the summer and fall of 1977 have broadened awareness of the Transylvanian question and documented the broken promises of the new Communist order in this area.

The collection of studies in this volume provides an analysis of the roots of the conflict, the description of its evolution to the present, and some reflections on possible future solutions.

Ethnic diversity and its close concomitant, minority problems, are now a global concern. Actually they have always been that, but in our time they have been brought to the forefront of our awareness by the attempt to make nation-states the guardians of the principle of "self-determination of peoples." The end of World War I saw the creation of new states in Eastern Europe that claimed to be based on self-determination. Similarly, after World War II the disintegration of vast colonial empires was achieved with reference to this principle. In actual fact, the creation of real nation-states based on the self-determination of a specific people was the exception rather than the rule. Both in Eastern Europe after World War I and throughout the world following World War II the pattern has been to impose the nation-state system on multinational settings. Instead of realizing the ideal of self-determination of peoples this has simply led to multinational states masquerading as nation-states. At the same time it has brought extreme pressure to be exerted on minorities to conform to the language, culture, and institutional order of the dominant majority or plurality peoples. At any rate, the process has generally led to more rather than less trauma and persecution regarding cultural matters as compared to the more haphazard practices of past colonial administrations and imperial bureaucracies.

As Walker Conner (*World Politics,* April, 1972) has pointed out, of the roughly 132 states in the world in 1972, only 12 percent were monoethnic "nation-states." All others had at least one significant ethnic or national minority, but most had two, three, or more. In 1982 when there are over 155 states in the world this percentage is almost certainly higher. This means that worldwide, mankind must come to grips with the problems of diversity and majority-minority relations. The Transylvanian experience provides a rich storehouse of information in this area about the past and present, the positive and negative approaches to coping with this global fact. Sometimes the failures of others may be as instructive as their successes; they can provide guideposts regarding what should be avoided as well as what should be attempted.

Transylvania is also an ideal laboratory for examining interethnic and internationality relations because the Hungarian (c. 2.4 million) and German (c. 350,000) minorities are large, self-conscious groups. They are not mere ethnic minorities, but significant linguistic and cultural blocks that differ from the majority population in historical and religious traditions as well. Furthermore, Rumania's reaction to the presence of minorities is intimately related to its conduct of foreign affairs. In the interwar years, this applied to all significant minorities in Rumania. Since World War II, it has been a factor primarily regarding the Hungarians and to a lesser extent the Germans. In terms of majority-minority relations, then, the Transylvanian setting provides lessons regarding almost every conceivable combination of problems and solutions. Finally, the ideological context also provides exceptionally interesting opportunities for comparative analysis, because Transylvania has experienced both the "bourgeois nationalist" and "Leninist-Stalinist" solution of the minority problem.

This volume approaches the problem of majority-minority relations in a four-step analysis. Step one includes studies that trace the history of emerging national consciousness in Transylvania. The Domonkos, Elteto, and Király essays focus primarily on the prenationalist phase of interethnic relations, outlining the factors that set the stage for this development among the various inhabitants of Transylvania. The second step relates to the emergence of modern nationalist orientations. The Held, Deak, Bődy, Stroup, and Vardy studies focus on the period during which Rumanians, Hungarians, and Germans became polarized politically. Step three examines the impact of international relations in the twentieth century on the Transylvanian setting. The studies by Pastor, Fisher-Galaţi, and Kertesz trace developments from World War I to the Paris Peace Treaty of 1947. Step four includes studies that outline the major features of contemporary Rumanian nationality policies in Transylvania. The Ludanyi, Illyés, and Veress analyses describe the cultural, educational, legal, and political context of majority-minority relations in Rumania.

Finally, the editors have provided four brief introductions and a conclusion to the studies. The volume also includes a chronology of Transylvanian history and appendices. The chronology enables the readers to get an overview and it also provides a grid on which each study may be placed. The Appendix includes a listing of Transylvanian place names in all relevant languages. (Although a concerted effort has been made to include place names in the three languages in the text, the listing at the end provides a convenient reference.) A table on the population of Transylvania provides an additional appendix that the reader can consult. There are also appended to the volume a series of memos issued during the diplomatic give-and-take at Paris in 1946, and the text of Paul Auer's speech at the Paris Peace Conference. Furthermore, the book includes the relevant maps to which the individual contributors make reference.

Many of the papers included in this volume were presented at the Symposium on Transylvania held May 18–20, 1979, at Kent State University. However, the editors have, where possible, solicited additional studies to make the collection as well-rounded as possible. They have also encouraged the writers of the original studies to revise or expand their contributions. Some have done so, others have not. This explains, in part, the differences in length and documentation of the various essays.

The studies have retained their individualism in other ways as well. The editors have left to individual author preference the designation of Rumania (Romania) and reference to the Székelys (Szeklers or Seklers). Regarding the latter, "Szekler" has been popularized in the West by German scholarship. It is a distortion of the Hungarian designation, "Székely." But since both spellings have been accepted in English-language sources, the editors have left its spelling to the discretion of the individual authors.

The designation of Rumania (Roumania, Romania) is a more sensitive issue. It is related to the whole question of historical claims concerning the origin and destiny of Rumania in Eastern Europe. As such it is also directly tied to the emergence of the Rumanian people as a self-conscious, state-building community. It is controversial, because historical claims to Transylvania are based on prior settlement, which in turn depends on whether or not present-day Rumanians are recognized as descendants of Trajan's Romans who conquered the Dacians in A.D. 106. Those who do not accept the Daco-Roman theory of Rumanian continuity are more likely to spell the national designation with a "u."

The preference for the "u" is based on the popular ethnic self-definition of the Rumanians as "Rumîni" (plural) or "Rumîn" (singular). This self-definition predates the actual creation in 1859 of a Rumanian state, which came into being as a consequence of the unification of the provinces of Wallachia and Moldavia. Until then, all the other peoples of Eastern Europe referred to the Rumanians as *Wlach, Vlah,* or *Oláh,* for which the English rendition is "Vlach." The latter term originally referred to the nomadic shepherd peoples of the Balkans. Consequently, those who think the Balkan Vlachs the precursors of the present-day Rumanians prefer to write the name with a "u." They assume that the popular "Rumîn" or "Rumîni" self-definition is based on the prevalent Ottoman Turkish designation for the Balkans (or the Byzantine empire covering that area) as the land of the "Rum" (i.e., Rome or Eastern Roman Empire).

Of course, not everyone who prefers "Rumanian" rather than "Romanian" is against the Daco-Roman theory, or vice-versa. At any rate, since the end of World War II, the official Rumanian spelling has been "Romania," and this has also been the spelling used for publications sent to English-speaking countries. However, in the West most English-language scholarly publications have spelled the name "Rumania" from World War II to the 1960s. Since about the middle of the 1960s, English-language publications in the West have used either Rumania or Romania. In German, the official designation has been Rumänien, while in French it has been Roumanie. Of all Rumania's neighbors, ironically, only Hungary writes "Románia" with an "o." Whatever the case may be, whatever the reason for the preference of each individual author, the editors have felt that the issue is sensitive enough that the acceptance of diversity is preferable to a uniformity that might be resented by some of the contributors. However, Roumania (still acceptable but now somewhat archaic) has been changed to Rumania or Romania, again based on author preference.

Still another designation that causes unease for advocates of standardization and uniformity is reference to the territories of pre-World War I Rumania. Some authors have called it the "old" kingdom (including Wallachia—today Muntenia and Oltenia—and Moldavia), while others have called it royal Rumania and still others the "Regat." Again, the editors have allowed for diversity as long as consistency has been maintained in the individual essays.

In relation to the use of the designation Magyar as opposed to Hungarian, some degree of standardization has been necessary to avoid confusion. Where possible the editors have used the more general term Hungarian. However, in some cases where not only national affiliation was discussed but the cultural and ethnic affiliation as well, Magyar has been preferred. Other, more controversial designations, which have been left to individual preference, have been references to the Treaty of Trianon and the Second Vienna Award. Some of the contributors have referred to one or both as "Diktats."

For the sake of consistency and clarity the editors have tried to standardize the use of place names and personal names. In the case of personal names, the standard has been to write the name of the individual according to national background (e.g., Cloşca, Dózsa). An exception has been made for first names. English equivalents for Hungarian, Rumanian, and German first names have been used interchangeably, again on the basis of the individual preferences of the authors. Furthermore, following the English practice, first names are given before last names even though in the case of Hungarian names the reverse would be accepted practice.

In relation to place names, the rule that the editors have followed is to present the name of the location in the language of the people that had control over it at the time of reference. Thus, if reference is made to a Transylvanian city prior to 1918, it will be in Hungarian. Cities mentioned in the period since 1918–20 will be in Rumanian, unless the mention refers to cities in northern Transylvania in the period of Hungarian jurisdiction between 1940–44. In either case, however, after a place is mentioned for the first time, the names of the place in the other languages are included in parentheses, e.g., Cluj-Napoca (Kolozsvár, Klausenburg). With respect to that city (the most important cultural center in Transylvania), there are some special problems concerning its Rumanian name. Recently, since the re-Dacianization craze overwhelmed the Rumanian party leaders, they have renamed some of the cities in the country. Thus the city of Kolozsvár (Hungarian) or Klausenburg (German), which was renamed Cluj by the Rumanians after 1918, has again been renamed and since the middle of the 1970s is officially called Cluj-Napoca. Within the present volume, the latter designation will only be used when reference is made to the city in terms of the past half-dozen years.

One other standardization has been attempted; to put the essays into third person, active voice. Again there have been some exceptions to this, where the personal testimony of the writer has been an important consideration. In the case of the Kertesz study, the first person has been retained because the author is not merely a scholar of those events, but was an active participant in them. In fact, it is through his assistance that the editors obtained copies of the Paris Peace Treaty memos and the Paul Auer speech that are included as appendices to the present volume.

Finally, the editors would like to express their appreciation to all those who made this volume possible. First and foremost, they would like to thank Mrs. Renee Harris, Mrs. Barbara Roberts, Miss Judith Szabo, and Mrs. Julianna Ludanyi for the typing and retyping that goes with any undertaking of this nature. The editors would also like to thank all those who contributed by providing moral or material support at important stages in the book's early evolution. Mr. Marton Sass, Dr. Enikő Molnár Basa, Dr. August Molnar, Mr. Tibor Cseh, Mr. William Koteles, Mr. Béla Lipták, Mr. László Bőjtös, Dr. Louis Szathmáry, Dr. John Palasics, Mr. John Venczel, Mrs. Narcissza Layton, and Ms. Agnes Bodnar deserve special mention. The editors also received constructive criticism and scholarly advice from their colleagues and friends in numerous academic disciplines. They are particularly grateful to Dr. Anne Lippert of Ohio Northern University for reading the French original of the Auer speech and its English translation to make sure that the latter was an effective and accurate rendition of the former. Along these lines, the editors also wish to say special thanks to Dr. Enikő Molnár Basa and Mary and András Boros-Kazai for checking Rumanian census data at the Library of Congress and the Indiana University Library, respectively. For the maps included in this volume the editors want to express their gratitude to Mr. Tamas Frecska, whose language skills and historical awareness guaranteed maps that are accurate as well as attractive. They also want to say thanks for the suggestions and assistance or intellectual stimulation of Dr. Peter J. Fliess of the University of Massachusetts, Dr. David C. Saffell and Professor Mary Hammond of Ohio Northern University. Finally, for the attractive pen drawing on the jacket they would like to thank Vígh, István. Of course, for the opinions expressed in each one of the essays the responsibility belongs to the individual contributors. On the other hand, for any shortcomings that this joint effort may contain, the editors accept full responsibility.

The editors are confident that *Transylvania: The Roots of Ethnic Conflict* will fill a gap in the English-language scholarly world on the affairs of Rumanians, Hungarians, and Saxon-Germans in an important corner of Eastern Europe, and by providing a clearer perception of the area's past and present, they hope they have also contributed to a better future for *all* the inhabitants of Transylvania.

J.F.C.
A.L.
L.J.E.

Contributors

PAUL BŐDY is a specialist in nineteenth-century Central European revolutionary and social movements. His published works include *Joseph Eőtvős and the Modernization of Hungary, 1840-1870.*

JOHN F. CADZOW is the director of the Ethnic Heritage Program at Kent State University and organizer of the conference from which the present volume emerged. He is the author of *The Lithuanian Americans and Their Communities in Cleveland.*

ISTVAN DEAK is professor of history at Columbia University, former director of Columbia's Institute on East Central Europe, and past chairman of the American Association for the Study of Hungarian History. Among his books on East European topics is *The Lawful Revolution: Louis Kossuth and the Hungarians, 1848-1849.*

LESLIE S. DOMONKOS is professor of history at Youngstown State University. His speciality is medieval and renaissance history, and he has served several terms as visiting senior scholar at the Hungarian Academy of Sciences.

LOUIS J. ELTETO is chairman of the Department of Foreign Languages at Portland State University. His research in religious movements and church history have particular emphasis on the Unitarians in Transylvania. He is editor of *Itt-Ott* [Here-There], a bilingual periodical of social and literary criticism.

STEPHEN FISCHER-GALAŢI is professor of history and director of the Center for Slavic and East European Studies at the University of Colorado. He is the author of numerous books and articles on Eastern European history and international affairs and is editor of *East European Quarterly* and *East European Monographs*.

JOSEPH HELD is former chairman of the History Department of University College, Rutgers University and, at present, Dean of the College of Arts and Sciences at Camden. His latest book is *The Modernization of Agriculture: Rural Transformation in Hungary, 1848-1949.*

ELEMÉR ILLYÉS, now living in West Germany, is a frequent contributor to Hungarian language periodicals in Europe, largely on topics of minority problems in East Central Europe. His major work is *Erdély változása* (Metamorphosis Transylvaniae), a study of nationality policies in present-day Rumania.

STEPHEN D. KERTESZ is professor emeritus of Government and International Studies at the University of Notre Dame. Before emigrating to the United States in 1947, he served in the Foreign Ministry of the Hungarian government and was for a time first secretary of the Hungarian legation in Bucharest with responsibility for the Hungarian minority in southern Transylvania. He has published extensively on Eastern European political questions.

BÉLA K. KIRÁLY took a leading role in the Hungarian Revolution of 1956. Now professor of history at Brooklyn College, he is also chairman of the East European Section, Center for European Studies of the Graduate School at CUNY. He has written and published widely on Hungarian history and Eastern European politics.

ANDREW LUDANYI is professor of political science at Ohio Northern University and associate editor of *Itt-Ott.* His research and writings have dealt with ethnic relations in the American and Eastern European settings.

PETER PASTOR, professor of history at Montclair State College, is the author of *Hungary Between Wilson and Lenin: The Hungarian Revolution of 1918-1919* and other works in modern Eastern European history.

EDSEL WALTER STROUP, author of *Hungary in Early 1848: The Constitutional Struggle Against Absolutism in Contemporary Eyes,* is currently working on his dissertation on the government of Count Lajos Batthyány at the University of Akron.

STEVEN BELA VARDY, current president of the American Association for the Study of Hungarian History, is professor of history at Duquesne University. He is the author of a political biography of Joseph Eőtvős and several works on Hungarian historiography.

BULCSU VERESS holds a law degree from Eőtvős University of Budapest and a degree in international relations from Columbia University. He is presently staff assistant to Senator Christopher Dodd of Connecticut and has written numerous position papers on Eastern European ethnic relations.

A Chronology of Transylvanian History

120,000–100,000 B.C.	Neanderthal man appears on the territory of the future Transylvania*
8,000–5,000 B.C.	Archaeological evidence from Péterfalva (Petreşti), Erősd (Ariuşd), and elsewhere indicates that the Stone-Age stage of development has been reached in Transylvania.
1,700 B.C.	People of the Wietenberg culture with rudimentary political organization inhabit this territory.
500 B.C.	Herodotus mentions that Transylvania is inhabited by Agathyrs, Scythians, and Celts.
60 B.C.	Burebista's Getic-Dacian domain includes the future Transylvania.
106 A.D.	Roman emperor Trajan destroys the Dacian domain of Decebalus, and its territory becomes a Roman province for the next 165 years. (all subsequent dates will be A.D.)
271	Emperor Aurelian evacuates the Romans from Dacia, and the Goths gain possession of its territory.
376	The Huns push the Goths out and establish their own dominance.
453	Attila, ruler of the Huns, dies and his empire disintegrates. For a brief period the territory of Transylvania is controlled by the Gepids.
567	Khan Bajan of the Avars pushes the Gepids out of this area. Besides the Avars, traces of Slavic settlements appear after this date.

*The designation Transylvania means "the land beyond the forest" in Latin. It is a name that became popular during the Middle Ages to designate the easternmost province of the Hungarian Kingdom. The name also received international recognition by the treaties of Nikolsburg (1621) and Linz (1645) which recognized Transylvanian independence. The Hungarian name for Transylvania is Erdély (wooded land); the Rumanians call it Ardeal; the Saxon-Germans always refer to it as Siebenbürgen. This Transylvanian chronology is based on András Bodor and Elek Csetri (eds.) *Történeti Kronológia* [Historical Chronology] (Bucharest: Kriterion, 1976) vols. I-II; Constantin C. Giurescu, Horia C. Matei, Marcel D. Popa, et al. (eds.), *Chronological History of Romania* (Bucharest: Editura Enciclopedică Română, 1972); Peter Gunst, László Benczédi, et al. (eds.), *Magyar Történelmi Kronológia* [Hungarian Historical Chronology] (Budapest: Tankönyvkiadó, 1970).

797 — Near Tulln the Franks defeat the Avars. According to the Kézai Chronicle it is at this time that the Székely remnants flee east and settle in Transylvania.

812 — Bulgarian influence replaces Avar rule as Khan Krum pushes the frontiers of his domain all the way north to the Tisza (Tisa, Theiss) River.

896 — As the seven Magyar tribes sweep into the Carpathian Basin, the tribe of the *gyula* (military warlord) and the tribe of the *kende* (titular ruler) occupy the area that will become Transylvania. The *gyepű* (military frontier) defense system is established and henceforth Transylvania becomes the organizational center of defense activities against threats from the East. Military pressure from the Petchenegs is its first challenge.

895–1091 — The Petchenegs control most of the area immediately east and south of Transylvania. These territories will in the future become Moldavia, Wallachia, and Dobruja (Dobrogea).

997–1038 — The reign of István I (Saint Stephen) transforms the Hungarian kingdom into a centralized state and imposes Western Christianity on the inhabitants.

1002–08 — Saint Stephen establishes the bishopric of Gyulafehérvár (Alba Iulia, Karlsburg), consolidates his hold over Transylvania, and defeats the decentralizing efforts of the Transylvanian leaders Gyula and of Ajtony.

1091 — Cumans (Kumans) in alliance with Byzantium defeat the Petchenegs and acquire dominant control over the lowlands east and north of the Danube and south and east of the Carpathians. Cuman control over this area lasts until the great Mongol (Tatar) invasion of 1241. Cuman incursions into Transylvania occur sporadically after 1068 but are unable to wrest the area from Hungarian control because László I decisively defeats the Cumans near Orsova (Orşova) in 1091.

1111 — Hungarian documents mention for the first time the title vajda (voivode) of Transylvania, specifically "Mercurius princeps."

1143 — Géza II (1141–62) invites Saxon (German) settlers to populate those areas of Transylvania that are important to the defense of the kingdom and are not yet peopled by the Székelys and Magyars.

1202 — The Monastery of Kerc (Cîrţa) is founded in Szeben (Sibiu) County.

1209 — In the Fogaras (Făgăraş) area of southeastern Transylvania, the existence of Vlach (Rumanian) settlements is mentioned in royal documents for the first time.

1211 To counter Cuman incursions, Andrew II (1205–35) settles Teutonic Knights in the Barcaság (Bîrsa) area of southeastern Transylvania.

1224 The Székely population migrates from southeastern Transylvania to the eastern corner of Transylvania. Their former area of settlement in southeastern Transylvania is now settled by Saxons (Germans) who are guaranteed certain privileges, autonomy, and exemptions by the Andreanum of 1224.

1225 Andrew II of Hungary expels the Teutonic Knights from Transylvania after they attempt to set up a state within a state. However, the other German settlements continue to receive royal support and extensive rights to autonomy.

1227 Mention is made of the establishment by Prince Béla of the first Cuman bishopric with its center at Civitas Milcovie (Odobeşti today) east of the Carpathians in Moldavia.

1234 Papal bull mentions that in the southern part of Moldavia and the eastern part of Wallachia there is a significant Vlach (Rumanian) Orthodox population.

1241–42 The Mongol (Tatar) invasion sweeps through Transylvania, devastates the land, and depopulates the countryside. The invasion also destroys and scatters the Cuman settlements south and east of the Carpathians.

1247–91 Saint Michael's Cathedral is constructed at Gyulafehérvár; it is one of the most important Romanesque-style structures in Transylvania.

1266 Székelys repopulate the Aranyos (Aries, Aranyosch) area and Saxons repopulate the area of Medgyes (Mediaş, Mediasch) to compensate for Tatar devastations.

1279 Cumans are permanently settled along the Körös (Criş), Temes (Timiş, Temesch), and Maros (Mureş, Mieresch) rivers as well as the Hungarian plains between the Tisza (Tisa, Theiss) and the Danube rivers.

1284–85 A Tatar (Mongol) incursion sweeps through Transylvania.

1288 First mention is made of a general conclave of the nobility *(congregatio generalis)* in Transylvania.

1291 Andrew III holds a meeting at Gyulafehérvár, (Alba Iulia, Karlsburg) where for the first time Vlachs (Rumanians) are also present besides the Hungarian nobility and the representatives of the Székelys and the Saxons.

1301	Andrew III, last king in the line of Árpád, dies.
1344	The general conclave *(congregatio generalis)* of the Székelys in eastern Transylvania is first mentioned in royal documents.
1348–49	The plague devastates Transylvania and other parts of the Hungarian kingdom.
1352	The Crimean Tatars make an incursion into Transylvania but Vajda (Voivode) Endre Lackfi defeats them.
1354–1444	Saint Michael's Church is constructed at Kolozsvár (Klausenburg, Cluj). It is one of the most important Gothic-style structures in Transylvania.
1366	Louis I begins a campaign to convert the Vlach (Rumanian) population to Roman Catholicism.
1420	First major Ottoman Turkish incursion into Transylvania.
1437	Antal Budai Nagy leads a major peasant revolt at Bábolna (Bobîlna). In response to this social strife the Hungarian nobility, the Saxons, and the Székelys establish the Union of Three Nations *(Unio Trium Nationum)*.
1441	János Hunyadi becomes vajda (voivode) of Transylvania and in this same year he defeats the Ottoman Turks near Marosszentimre (Sîntimbru), Gyulafehérvár (Alba Iulia), and Nagyszeben (Hermannstadt, Sibiu).
1446	János Hunyadi becomes regent of Hungary.
1456	János Hunyadi stops the Ottoman Turks led by Mohammed II at Nándorfehérvár (Belgrade).
1467	Matthias Corvinus (Hunyadi) crushes the revolt of the Transylvanian nobility.
1479	The Battle of Kenyérmező (Cîmpul Pîinii) takes place where the armies of István Báthory and Pál Kinizsi defeat Ottoman forces.
1482	The Saxons establish their own self-governing institution, the *Saxon Universitas*.
1490	Matthias Corvinus dies.
1493–95	Ottoman incursions devastate some areas of Transylvania.
1499	Wladislaw II issues a letter of exemptions in which he reaffirms the freedoms and privileges of the Székelys in eastern Transylvania.

1505 Székely conclaves in Agyagfalva (Lutiţa) and Székelyudvarhely (Odorheiu) establish the rules of appeal within the Székely judicial system.

1510 János Zápolya becomes vajda (voivode) of Transylvania.

1514 The peasant rebellion led by György Dózsa sweeps through central Hungary and has reverberations throughout Transylvania. János Zápolya, voivode of Transylvania, decisively defeats the peasant army near Temesvár (Timişoara) and has Dózsa executed.

1523 The first significant Orthodox bishopric in Transylvania is established at Rév (Vadul Crişului).

1526 Suleiman II (the Magnificent) defeats the Hungarians in the Battle of Mohács. Louis II, king of Hungary, and many of the nobility and higher clergy lose their lives in the battle. Consequently, the Hungarian kingdom is opened to Ottoman conquest and depredation. The defeat also sets the stage for years of internal strife as the struggle for the succession pits János Zápolya, voivode of Transylvania, against Ferdinand II of the House of Habsburg.

1538 The Treaty of Várad ([Nagyvárad], Oradea, Grosswardein) temporarily terminates hostilities, leaving western Hungary under Ferdinand, while Zápolya controls eastern Hungary and Transylvania.

1540 János Zápolya dies.

1541 Buda falls to the Ottoman Turks. The Hungarian kingdom is divided into three parts, with the Habsburgs controlling the west, the Turks controlling the central plain, and Transylvania becoming semiautonomous under Hungarian princes beginning with János Zsigmond (1541–51, 1556–71) son of János Zápolya. Henceforth the rulers of Transylvania attempt to maintain their independence by accepting Ottoman supremacy. They transform Transylvania into the main center of Hungarian culture and national development until at least 1690.

1544 The national convention at Torda (Turda, Thorenburg [Thorda]) announces the union of Transylvania with the Partium (the Hungarian plains east of the Tisza and to the west of Transylvania).

1546 A paper mill is set up in Kronstadt (Brassó, Braşov) to supply the needs of the fledgling publishing activities in Transylvania. Many of the works that appear reflect the religious ferment of the time and the tremendous impact that the Reformation has had on Transylvanian intellectual development.

1556 The Diet of Transylvania proclaims that every person has the right to follow the religion of choice. Transylvania thus becomes the first state in Europe to declare a policy of religious toleration.

1567 Ferenc Dávid publishes "Rövid Magyarázat" ("A Brief Exposition") at Kolozsvár (Cluj, Klausenburg) and thereby establishes the Hungarian version of Unitarianism.

1568 The Diet of Transylvania decrees the "accepted" status of the Roman Catholic, Lutheran, Calvin Reformed, and Unitarian faiths.

1571 István Báthory becomes prince of Transylvania until 1581.

1575 István Báthory becomes king of Poland.

1581 István Báthory founds a Jesuit academy that becomes the precursor of contemporary higher education in Kolozsvár (Cluj, Klausenburg).

1581 Zsigmond Báthory becomes prince of Transylvania until 1597. He embroils his state in the Fifteen Years' War on the side of the Habsburgs against the Turks (1591–1606). The bloodshed and chaos that ensue enable the Wallachian voivode, Mihai Viteazul, to invade Transylvania.

1599–1600 Mihai Viteazul obtains control over Transylvania in October, 1599, and holds sway until September, 1600. Although this interlude is less than a year, it has been presented in recent writings by Rumanian historians as the first "unification" of the "Rumanian countries." His rule is followed by the brutal Habsburg incursion of George Basta, who terrorizes Transylvania from 1599 to 1604.

1604–06 The popular uprising led by István Bocskai finally re-establishes order. Bocskai defeats the Habsburg forces and is able to re-establish Transylvanian independence. He is also successful in terminating the Fifteen Years' War with the signing of the Treaties of Vienna (June 23, 1606) and Zsitvatorok (November 22, 1606).

1608–13 Gábor Báthory becomes prince of Transylvania and for a short period also claims to be voivode of Wallachia.

1613 Gábor Bethlen becomes prince of Transylvania and retains this position until his death in 1629. His reign is the "Golden Age" of independent Transylvania. Commerce, construction, education, and culture flourish. Transylvania plays an important role in the Thirty Years' War.

1621 The Treaty of Nikolsburg recognizes Transylvanian independence.

1630 György Rákóczi I becomes prince of Transylvania and reigns until 1648.

1639 Maize begins to appear as an important crop in Transylvania.

1643 Transylvania again becomes embroiled in the Thirty Years' War as an ally of Sweden and France.

1645 The Treaty of Linz terminates Transylvania's involvement in the conflict on favorable terms, ceding to it seven counties of the Partium. The treaty also confirms the terms of the Treaty of Nikolsburg with the further stipulation that religious toleration should also apply to the serfs.

1648 With the sponsorship of György Rákóczi I the first complete Rumanian translation of the New Testament (Noul Testament) appears in Gyulafehérvár (Alba Iulia, Karlsburg).

1648 György Rákóczi II becomes prince of Transylvania and reigns until 1660.

1653 The *Approbatae Constitutiones Regni Transilvaniae* is published. It becomes the legal framework of Transylvania for the next 200 years.

1657 January–July György Rákóczi II undertakes his ill-fated war to obtain the Polish crown. Although he successfully captures Krakow and Warsaw, the defection of allies and the stretched supply lines lead to his defeat and the capture of his army by the Tatars.

1657 Zsuzsanna Lorántffy, the widow of György Rákóczi I, establishes a Rumanian school in Fogaras (Făgăraş).

1658 The Turks and their Tatar allies unleash a punitive expedition against Transylvania. It devastates and depopulates the Szamos (Someş) Valley and leads to the sack of such cities as Gyulafehérvár.

1660 Várad ([Nagyvárad], Oradea, Grosswardein) is captured by the Turks. They also defeat György Rákóczi II in the Battle of Szászfenes (Floreşti) and again devastate extensive areas of Transylvania. Rákóczi dies from the wounds received in the battle.

1661 Mihály Apafi becomes prince of Transylvania with the support of the Turks. He reigns until his death in 1690 as the last ruler of an independent Transylvanian state.

1675 Transylvania's Orthodox Church Synod at Gyulafehérvár (Alba Iulia, Karlsburg) decides to suspend clergy who officiate in Slavonic rather than Rumanian.

1677 In Warsaw, Imre Thököly, rebel *(kuruc)* leader from northeastern Hungary, engineers an alliance with Apafi's Transylvania and Louis XIV of France against the Habsburgs.

1686–87 Habsburg imperial troops invade Transylvania.

1690 Upon the death of Apafi, the Transylvanian Diet elects his son Mihály Apafi II. However, the Habsburgs have by this time consolidated their position and they begin to incorporate Transylvania into the empire. The *Diploma Leopoldinum* of October 15, 1690, is the legal termination of Transylvanian independence. The Ottoman Turks sponsor Imre Thököly as prince, but he cannot wrest control of the land from the Habsburgs.

1697 The synod convened in Gyulafehérvár (Alba Iulia, Karlsburg) by Orthodox Metropolitan Teofil between March 27 and April 6 accepts "Union with Rome," and many Transylvanian Orthodox Rumanians thereby become Greek Catholics or Uniate Catholics. This decision is also reconfirmed in October by Metropolitan Atanasie Anghel and thirty-eight archpriests. The Union with Rome is seen as the way to obtain equality with the accepted religions.

1703–11 The *kuruc* rebellion led by Ferenc Rákóczi II attempts to reestablish an independent Hungarian state. In 1704, Rákóczi is elected prince of Transylvania. However, he loses a battle at Zsibó (Jibou) and this begins to undermine his influence and power in Transylvania.

1711 The Treaty of Szatmár (Satu Mare) ends hostilities and consolidates Transylvania and Hungary within the Habsburg empire.

1717 A Tatar incursion sweeps through Transylvania.

1718 The Treaty of Passarowitz brings to an end Ottoman Turkish control over territories in the Carpathian Basin, specifically their last stronghold in the Bánság (Banat) of Temes (Timiş, Temesch). The areas depopulated by the Turkish occupation are now recolonized by Swabian settlers, Serbs, and Vlachs (Rumanians). Hungarians are specifically excluded from these former Hungarian territories by the Habsburg policy of colonization and reconstruction.

1722 The Transylvanian Diet confirms the *Pragmatica Sanctio* and thereby the legitimacy of succession by Maria Theresa (1740–80) to the Habsburg throne.

1729 Ion Inocenţiu Micu-Klein is appointed Uniate bishop of Transylvania. Under his leadership (until 1751) the Vlach (Rumanian) population acquires its first effective spokesman for the recognition of their growth in numbers and of the changed political circumstances. He effectively utilizes the "Union" with Rome as a political weapon for enhancing the power of the Rumanians in Transylvania.

1754 The establishment of a Uniate Catholic primary school, high school, and theological seminary at Balázsfalva (Blaj, Blasendorf), transforms it into a center of Rumanian self-consciousness and organization.

1762–68 Habsburg efforts to formalize the organization of frontier defense in the Székely regions and in three Vlach-inhabited counties leads to widespread resistance in the region of Beszterce (Bistriţa, Bistritz) and in the Székely counties. The Habsburgs crush the resistance with the brutal massacre at Mádéfalva (Siculeni) on January 7, 1764. Many Székelys cross the Carpathians to Moldavia and settle there at this time. They are the so-called Csángó Hungarians of present-day Rumania.

1765 Maria Theresa raises the status of Transylvania from principality to "Great Principality of Transylvania."

1769 On November 11, the "Bizonyos punctumok" ("Special Points") are issued by Maria Theresa to regulate the duties of bondsmen.

1769 Maria Theresa issues a decree of toleration by which the Orthodox church is legally recognized by the Habsburg monarchy.

1774–85 The Bánffy Palace is constructed at Kolozsvár (Cluj, Klausenburg); it is one of the most important exmples of Baroque architecture in Transylvania.

1775 The Institute of Surgical Medicine is established at Kolozsvár (Cluj, Klausenburg).

1777 The publication of the *Ratio educationis* provides a general reorganization of the educational system for children between the ages of seven and thirteen at both Catholic and non-Catholic schools. Instruction is to be in German and in the mother tongue of the respective nationalities on the basis of Austrian textbooks.

1778 Maria Theresa orders the reannexation of the Bánság (Banat) of Temes (Timiş, Temesch) to the kingdom of Hungary. It is organized into the counties of Torontál, Temes, and Krassó (Caraş).

1778 Samuil Micu writes the first study on the history of the Rumanians that represents the Transylvanian School's effort to prove the Roman and Dacian origins of the Rumanian people. This is followed by Micu's publication of the "Prayer Book for the Piety of the Christian" in 1779. The latter is printed in Latin characters and is the first public assertion of the Transylvanian School's ideology. This is followed a year later (1780) by the publication of Samuil Micu's and Gheorghe Şincai's *Elementa linguae daco-romanae sive Valachicae* (Vienna), which is the first printed grammar of the Rumanian language setting out to prove the Latin origin of the Rumanian language. It advocates the adoption of Latin letters and the enrichment of the vocabulary with Latin words.

1780 Maria Theresa's death brings to the throne Joseph II whose reign lasts until 1790. He is an "enlightened" despot. However, his zeal for efficiency, modernization, and centralization produces unrest in many parts of the empire.

1784 On May 1, Joseph II calls for the first official census of the empire, including Transylvania. According to the data published in 1787, this census shows the overall population of Transylvania to be 1,440,986.

1784 On May 11, German is declared the official language of the empire in Hungary and Transylvania as well as in the western provinces. German is to become the official language of instruction in all schools of the empire within three years.

1784 The centralizing tendencies and certain raised expectations contribute to the unrest of the population in Transylvania and spark the Rumanian peasant rising led by Horea, Cloşca, and Crişan. The uprising begins on October 31 and lasts until the end of December when the ringleaders are captured. Crişan commits suicide in prison, while Horea and Cloşca are executed in Gyulafehérvár (Alba Iulia, Karlsburg) on February 28, 1785. Present Rumanian historiography sees this as both a social and national uprising of great importance. While the conscious national sentiment of the Rumanian peasants is questionable, it is clear that their wrath was directed mainly against the Hungarians and others who did not adhere to the Rumanian Orthodox religion. The pillaging and bloodletting is particularly extensive

	in Fehér, Hunyad (Hunedoara), Torda, Kolozs, and Zaránd counties.
1784	The Saxon *Siebenbürger Zeitung* begins publication in Brassó (Kronstadt, Braşov).
1788	The first German-language theater is established at Nagyszeben (Hermannstadt, Sibiu).
1789	The Hungarian *Erdélyi Magyar Hírvivő* begins publication in Kolozsvár (Cluj, Klausenburg).
1790	Emperor Joseph II revokes (January 28) most of his reform decrees with the significant exception of those that relate to religious toleration and the freedom of movement of the serfs. He dies soon thereafter and is succeeded by Leopold II on February 20.
1791	The Transylvanian Diet declares that it wants Transylvania's reunification with Hungary and the acceptance of Hungarian as the official language of the land. Emperor Leopold's response is to continue separate chanceries for Hungary and Transylvania.
1791	Rumanian Orthodox Bishop Gherasim Adamovici and Uniate Catholic Bishop Ion Bob submit to Leopold II the *Supplex Libellus Valachorum,* in which they request equal status for the Rumanian people with the three officially recognized "nations" (i.e., Magyars, Székelys, and Saxons) and in addition representation in the Diet in proportion to their share of the population. The petition is rejected by the emperor.
1792	Leopold II dies on March 1 and is succeeded by Francis I. The former's short and stormy reign contributes greatly to a deterioration of relations between Hungarians, Saxons, and Rumanians, since he openly plays them off against one another.
1792	The submission on March 30 of the *II. Supplex Libellus Valachorum.* It, too, is rejected by the new emperor, Francis I.
1792	The Hungarian Theater Society is organized at Kolozsvár.
1798	Ignác Batthyány establishes the Batthyanaeum Library at Gyulafehérvár.
1802	Chancellor Sámuel Teleki opens the Teleki Library at Marosvásárhely (Tîrgu Mureş, Neumarkt).
1806	Samuil Micu completes his study *Istoria, lucrurile şi întîmplările românilor* (History, Deeds and Events of the Rumanians) on the history of the Rumanians. It is followed closely by Gheorghe Şincai's Rumanian history *Hronicul românilor şi a mai multor*

neamuri (Chronicle of the Rumanians and of Several Other Peoples) in 1808 and Petru Maior's historical analysis of 1813 entitled *Istoria pentru începutul românilor în Dachiia* (History of the Beginning of the Rumanians in Dacia), all published at Buda, Hungary. These works constitute the core of the historiographical work of the Rumanian Transylvanian School and the attempt to trace the origins and the development of the Rumanian people.

1813–17 An extensive drought in Transylvania produces widespread famine.

1814 The Hungarian *Erdélyi Muzeum (Transylvanian Museum)* begins publication under the direction of Gábor Döbrentei.

1815 The first Rumanian-language play is performed in Transylvania at Brassó (Braşov, Kronstadt).

1817 The Bruckenthal Library is founded at Nagyszeben (Sibiu, Hermannstadt).

1825 Samuil Micu and Petru Maior publish their *Lexicon romanescu-latinescu-ungurescu-nemţescu* (The Romanian-Latin-Hungarian-German Dictionary), which is the first etymological and explanatory dictionary in Rumanian and marks the beginning of modern Rumanian lexicography.

1833 János Bolyai publishes an appendix to his father's (Farkas Bolyai) study *Tentamen*. This *Appendix* provides the foundation for non-Euclidean geometry.

1834 On January 11, the Transylvanian Diet is called into session after not having been consulted since 1811. It challenges the activities of local Habsburg officialdom and appeals to the Hungarian Diet at Pozsony (Pressburg) and to the emperor for redress. The complaints are not considered by the emperor, and he has the Transylvanian Diet dissolved on February 6, 1835. Parallel to the activities of the Hungarian, Saxon, and Székely representatives in the Diet, the Rumanians become active under the leadership of the Orthodox and Uniate Catholic bishops of Balázsfalva (Blaj, Blasendorf). They reiterate their demands of 1791.

1838 The Habsburgs sentence Miklós Wesselényi, the Transylvanian reformer, to three years in prison.

1838 Under the direction of George Bariţiu the first overtly political Rumanian journal is published as *Gazeta de Transylvania*. However, instead of working toward some modus vivendi with the other nationalities, it strikes an alliance with Vienna.

1840 The monarch pardons Louis Kossuth and Miklós Wesselényi.

1841–43 The Transylvanian Diet meets at Kolozsvár (Cluj, Klausenburg) to consider proposals for making Hungarian the official language of Transylvania. The Saxons and Rumanians oppose this. In 1842, Stefan L. Roth summarizes the goals and the position of the Saxons in *Der Sprachkampf in Siebenbürgen.*

1843–47 Katalin Varga organizes peasant unrest in the Transylvanian Érc Mountains (Muntii Metaliferi, Erzgebirge).

1847 László Kővári publishes his study *Erdély statisztikája* (Transylvanian Statistics).

1848 On March 15, the anti-Habsburg revolt erupts in Pest and starts the 1848–49 revolution in Hungary. By late March, mass meetings in Transylvanian cities express solidarity with the Hungarian Revolution. Cities like Kolozsvár (Cluj, Klausenburg) Nagybánya (Baia Mare), Marosvásárhely (Tîrgu Mureş), Udvarhely (Odorhei), Arad, and Nagyvárad (Oradea) are the scenes of enthusiastic support for the twelve points of the Hungarian Revolution, including the demand for reunification of Hungary with Transylvania. The Rumanian intelligentsia gives its qualified support, with reservations on the question of reunification. The Saxons are divided both on the question of support and the question of reunification.

1848 On April 18–30, a Rumanian mass meeting at Balázsfalva (Blaj, Blasendorf) demands freedom for serfs and national rights. On May 2–14, a second Rumanian mass meeting reiterates the demands of the first meeting and adds the demand that no decision should be made on the question of union without consulting the Rumanian people. The meeting selects delegations to convey this position to both the government in Vienna and the Transylvanian Diet at Kolozsvár.

1848 On May 29, the Transylvanian Diet declares union with Hungary and frees the serfs.

1848 On September 15, the third Rumanian mass meeting at Balázsfalva (Blaj, Blasendorf) declares that it does not recognize the union of Transylvania with Hungary and calls for the arming of the Rumanian people and the setting up of fifteen Rumanian legions to fight the Hungarian Revolution.

1848 During October 16–17, the Székely mass meeting at Agyagfalva

(Lutiţa) declares its support of the revolution, and calls for interethnic solidarity and a united front against Habsburg reaction. Habsburg forces defeat the Székelys near Marosvásárhely (Tîrgu Mureş, Neumarkt) on November 4 and occupy most of the Székely counties. However, during the winter months, stiff Székely resistance confronts them under the leadership of Áron Gábor.

1848 On November 28, Kossuth appoints the Polish general József Bem to lead Hungary's Transylvanian Army. A series of brilliant campaigns clears most of Transylvania (with the exception of Gyulafehérvár and Déva) of imperial troops by March 20, 1849. However, Avram Iancu's anti-Hungarian Rumanian forces retain their position in the Érc Mountains (Muntii Metaliferi). Pro-Hungarian Rumanians attempt to negotiate a separate peace with Iancu between April 22 and May 6. The talks break down as fighting is renewed.

1849 On May 27, talks take place at Debrecen between Louis Kossuth and Nicolae Bălcescu, which lead to an agreement called "Projet de pacification" on July 14 at Szeged. This agreement promises some administrative decentralization and extensive cultural and linguistic rights to the Rumanians.

1849 On June 19, the czarist Russian forces break through the Tömösi Pass (Pasul Predeal) and enter Transylvania on the side of the Habsburgs.

1849 On July 31, czarist forces defeat General Bem at Segesvár (Sighişoara, Schássburg). Sándor Petöfi dies in this battle.

1849 On August 13, the main Hungarian army under Arthur Görgey surrenders at Világos (Şiria) and the forces under Lajos Kazinczy surrender at Zsibó (Jibou) on August 26. This is followed by Transylvania's immediate subjugation to imperial absolutism, centralization, and punitive military occupation.

1849 On October 6, imperial authorities execute thirteen Hungarian generals at Arad.

1853 The first telegraph line is completed between Vienna and Temesvár (Timişoara).

1859 Moldavia and Wallachia unite and become the new state of Rumania. Henceforth the Transylvanian Rumanians have an independent state concerned with their fate.

1860 The "Diploma of October" diminishes the centralization of the empire and returns some autonomy to Transylvania (October 20).

1861 Transylvanian Rumanians found the Transylvanian Association for the Literature and Culture of the Rumanian People (ASTRA) with the objective of defending the cultural interests of the Rumanians of Transylvania and of having them recognized as a "politically independent nationality" with the right to use Rumanian in all aspects of public life.

1862 On May 18, Kossuth (in exile) publishes his plans for a multinational Danubian Federation.

1863–64 The Transylvanian Diet at Nagyszeben (Sibiu, Hermannstadt) proclaims three official languages: Hungarian, Rumanian, and German.

1867 On February 12, the Compromise of 1867 establishes the Dual Monarchy of Austria-Hungary. It also leads to the reunification of Transylvania with Hungary on February 17.

1868 On December 6, Francis Joseph I approves the nationalities law no. 1868:XLIV, which guarantees the Rumanians as well as other minorities extensive rights within the Hungarian kingdom. Unfortunately, legislation to implement it is not forthcoming.

1872 The Francis Joseph University is founded at Kolozsvár (Cluj, Klausenburg).

1872 On July 3, the leaders of the Transylvanian Rumanians meet at Balázsfalva, (Blaj, Blasendorf) and issue a memorandum requesting that Rumanian be declared the second official language of Transylvania.

1879 On September 15, the Székely National Museum is founded at Sepsiszentgyörgy (Sfîntul Gheorghe).

1881 During May 12–14, the Rumanian National party of Hungary and the Banat unites with the Transylvanian Rumanian National party and adopts the latter's name. In its program it calls for Transylvanian autonomy and the right to use the Rumanian language in administration and in legal proceedings.

1883 In May, the law on instruction in high schools (1883:XXX) requires for the first time that in national minority schools Hungarian history and Hungarian literature be taught in Hungarian. The adoption of this law leads to demonstrations in Nagyszeben, (Sibiu, Hermannstadt), Déva (Deva, Schlossberg), and Balázsfalva (Blaj, Blasendorf).

1884 Temesvár (Timişoara, Temeschwar) becomes the first European city to have its streets lit by electricity.

1884 The Transylvanian Party of moderate Rumanians is organized. It accepts the dualistic order of Austria-Hungary.

1888 The Hungarian Transylvanian Literary Association is founded and its periodical *Erdélyi Lapok* (Transylvanian Pages) begins publication.

1890 On December 7, the Social Democratic party of Hungary is organized with the participation of all nationalities in Transylvania.

1891–96 The Iron Gates are made navigable for large sea-going vessels.

1892 The Rumanian National party (of Transylvania) sends a memorandum to Emperor Francis Joseph with the political demands of the activists. Francis Joseph forwards the memorandum to Budapest. The authors are then put on trial (May, 1894).

1892–95 Sándor Márki writes the history of Arad county and city *(Arad vármegye és Arad város története).*

1895 On January 14, under the new Prime Minister Dezső Bánffy, a special office is established to handle minority nationality problems.

1895 On August 10, the minority nationalities hold a convention in Budapest to protest various aspects of the government's policies. In part, this contributes to Francis Joseph's amnesty for those who have been convicted in the "Memorandum trial."

1896 Hungary celebrates the 1,000th anniversary of its existence. In Transylvania, a significant event during this year is the establishment of an artist's colony in Nagybánya (Baia Mare) by Béla Iványi-Grünwald, Károly Ferenczy, and others.

1898–99 The first railway links between Hungary and Rumania are constructed, via the Vöröstorony (Turnu-Roşu) and Gyimes (Ghimeş) passes through the Transylvanian Alps.

1898–1904 ASTRA sponsors the publication of three volumes of the *Rumanian Encyclopedia (Enciclopedia română)* at Nagyszeben.

1901 Extensive strike activity spreads from the mining center of Resica (Reşiţa) to other cities in Transylvania, including Kolozsvár.

1902 János Fadrusz completes his Matthias Rex memorial in Kolozsvár and his Wesselényi memorial at Zilah (Zalău).

1903 *Erdélyi Munkás* (Transylvanian Worker), the Hungarian Social Democratic periodical, begins publication at Kolozsvár and the *Adevărul,* the Rumanian language periodical of the Social Democrats, is founded at Budapest.

1905 On January 10, the Rumanian National party meeting at Nagyszeben decides to turn to activism rather than continue passive resistance.

1905 On November 5, Rumanians hold a mass meeting at Lugos (Lugoj, Lugosch) to protest nationality policies and demand increased opportunities for the use and development of the Rumanian language.

1906–07 The construction of the University Library is completed at Kolozsvár (Cluj, Klausenburg).

1907 A new educational law is adopted to regulate the language of instruction in state-supported schools. The "Lex Apponyi," as it is called, is viewed by the national minorities as a threat to their existing educational opportunities in parochial schools.

1909 István Apáthy founds the Zoological Institute at Kolozsvár.

1910 The last Hungarian census is administered on the total territory of Transylvania.

1912 During May 29–June 11, a Rumanian mass meeting at Gyulafehérvár (Alba Iulia, Karlsburg) protests church-state relations in Hungary, particularly as they affect Uniate Catholics.

1913 Jenö Janovics begins Transylvania's film industry at Kolozsvár.

1914 On October 1, Russia and Rumania sign a secret pact according to which Russia recognizes Rumania's territorial integrity and agrees to protect the same. It also includes Russia's support for Rumanian territorial claims against the Austro-Hungarian Empire in return for Rumanian neutrality.

1916 On March 17, the Secret Agreement of Bucharest is signed by Rumania and representatives of the Entente powers regarding Rumania's involvement in hostilities against the Central Powers. This is followed on August 17 by a Treaty of Alliance signed by Rumania and the Entente representatives of Great Britain, France, Russia, and Italy. For entering the war on the side of the Entente, Rumania is promised the Rumanian-inhabited parts of Austria-Hungary. In line with this agreement, Rumania declares war on Austria-Hungary on August 25 and Rumanian troops attack Transylvania. At first the Central powers retreat, but a concerted counter-attack leads to the defeat of the Rumanians and the capture of Bucharest on December 6, 1916.

1918 On January 8, President Woodrow Wilson enunciates his Fourteen Points. The stipulation under point 10, for the "self-determination of peoples" has a particularly electrifying effect on all the nationalities living in Transylvania.

1918 On April 8, the leaders of the national minorities of the Austro-Hungarian Monarchy hold a joint conference in Rome where they declare their desire to separate themselves from the monarchy.

1918 On May 8, at Bucharest, Rumania and the Central Powers sign a peace treaty terminating hostilities.

1918 On June 3, the Entente powers officially recognize the demands of the nationalities conference held in Rome in April.

1918 On October 12, at its meeting at Nagyvárad (Oradea, Grosswardein), the Transylvanian Rumanian National party declares that the Transylvanian Rumanians also want to exercise their right to self-determination.

1918 On October 18, Woodrow Wilson declares to the Monarchy that the Fourteen Points have been made moot by events. On the same day, Vajda Vojvoda declares in the Budapest Parliament that the Rumanians of Transylvania have committed themselves to self-determination and unification as a separate nation.

1918 During October 30–31, the Hungarian National Council under Mihály Károlyi comes to power. It declares Hungary to be a republic on November 16.

1918 On November 1, the representatives of Austria-Hungary sign an armistice with the Entente at Padua.

1918 On November 13, Oszkár Jászi negotiates unsuccessfully with Rumanian leaders at Arad. On this same day, the Hungarian government signs the military convention with the Entente at Belgrade, which defines the lines of military demarcation to the south and southeast.

1918 On December 1, the Rumanian mass meeting at Gyulafehérvár (Alba Iulia) declares that the Transylvanian Rumanians want to be united with the Rumanian state south and east of the Carpathians. Although this is a unilateral declaration of the Rumanians, Entente support makes it prevail over the wishes of Hungarians, Székelys, Saxons, and Swabians.

1918 During December 2–3, the Entente permits Rumanian troops to cross the Mureş (Maros, Mieresch) River, beyond the first lines of demarcation established by the Belgrade military convention.

1918 On December 25, the Hungarian government establishes an autonomous region for the Ruthenians in eastern Hungary, named Ruszka-Krajna.

1919 On January 19, the mass meeting of the Hungarians at Cluj (Kolozsvár, Klausenburg) is dispersed by Rumanian troops; more than 100 Hungarians are killed. This meeting was not allowed to declare its "self-determination," unlike the one at Alba Iulia (Gyulafehérvár, Karlsburg) on December 1, 1918.

1919 On March 20th, Colonel Vyx presents Mihály Károlyi with the new Entente lines of military demarcation. This establishes a neutral zone that requires even further territorial losses for Hungary. The Hungarian government resigns in protest.

1919 On March 21, the power vacuum is filled by Béla Kun and his Communist supporters, who declare Hungary to be a Council (i.e., Soviet) Republic.

1919 On April 16, the Entente encourages Rumania to undertake whatever military action necessary to overthrow the Béla Kun regime. With French military advisers Rumanian troops cross the latest lines of military demarcation. On April 23, Rumanian troops capture Debrecen.

1919 On August 1, the Council Republic collapses and Rumanian troops occupy Budapest until November 14.

1919 On November 16, Nicholas Horthy enters Budapest. He becomes regent of Hungary on March 1, 1920.

1920 In March, all Hungarian street signs are replaced by Rumanian signs and markers throughout Transylvania.

1920 On June 4, at Versailles, Hungary is compelled to sign the Treaty of Trianon ceding Transylvania, part of the Banat (Bánság), part of the Tisza plains, and part of Maramureş (Máramaros) to Rumania. This means that Hungary loses more territory (102,787 square kilometers) to Rumania than it has left for itself (91,114 square kilometers). At the same time 1.7 million Hungarians are placed under Rumanian jurisdiction.

1921 The Magyar Szövetség (Hungarian Federation) is formed to provide the Hungarians of Transylvania with a representative political organization.

1921–22 Construction of the Rumanian Orthodox Cathedral in Alba Iulia (Gyulafehérvár, Karlsburg). It is an example of the neo-Byzantine style based on the church built much earlier at Tîrgovişte in the Regat.

1922 The Országos Magyar Párt (National Hungarian party) is formed to provide the Hungarian minority with an electioneering organization.

1923 The Rumanian government carries out a "land reform" that takes land mainly from Hungarian and non-Rumanian landowners and redistributes it mainly among Rumanian peasants. A total of 2,218,146 acres are distributed in this discriminatory fashion.

1924 The Erdélyi Szépmives Céh (Transylvanian Artist Guild) is organized and becomes the major cultural agency of the Hungarians.

1924 The Rumanian government requires Hungarian shopkeepers to pay extra taxes if they continue to advertise in Hungarian as well as in Rumanian.

1925 A new wave of Rumanianization closes many Protestant and Catholic parochial schools.

1926 The Peasant party unites with the Transylvanian "Rumanian National party" to form the National Peasant party (Partidul Naţional Ţărănesc), providing the Transylvanian Rumanians with their main vehicle of influence in national politics.

1926 The publication *Korunk* (Our Age) appears at Cluj (Kolozsvár, Klausenburg). It becomes the major journal of the populist and left-oriented elements of the Transylvanian Hungarians. In 1929, Gábor Gaál becomes its editor.

1928 The *Erdélyi Helikon* (Transylvanian Helicon) begins its cultural mission for Hungarian linguistic survival against the growing excesses of Rumanianization.

1928 The League of Nations is presented with a long list of minority grievances concerning Rumanian policies in Transylvania. Nothing is done to ameliorate minority conditions.

1930 The Little Entente (Rumania, Yugoslavia, and Czechoslovakia) holds meetings to establish a united stand in support of the territorial status quo.

1930 *Erdélyi Fiatalok* (Transylvanian Youth) begins publication and *Erdélyi Múzeum* (Transylvanian Museum) reappears to serve the cultural and literary needs of the Hungarians.

1933 Under Petru Groza's leadership, the Ploughman's Front is organized at Deva (Déva).

1933 On February 16, the Little Entente meets in Geneva to formalize its alliance against territorial revision.

1933	Construction of the Rumanian Orthodox Cathedral in Cluj (Kolozsvár, Klausenburg). It is a representative neo-Byzantine structure.
1934	In January, the main issue of the electoral campaign in Hungary is revisionism. Both Gyula Gömbös and István Bethlen take a stand for the unconditional return of Hungarian-inhabited territories and for the establishment of an independent Transylvania.
1934	On Feburary 9, the Balkan Pact is signed. It reinforces the objectives of the Little Entente against Hungary as well as Bulgaria.
1934	The MADOSZ (Hungarian Workers' Federation) organizes as the political agency of the Hungarian left in Transylvania.
1934	On October 15, the Csángó Hungarians in the Ghimes (Gyimes) Valley revolt. Retribution is swift and brutal.
1935	On December 6, the MADOSZ, the Ploughman's Front, the Independent Socialist party, and the Democratic Bloc agree to present a united front against the threat of fascism.
1936	Iron Guard anti-Semitic and anti-Hungarian excesses take place in Braşov (Brassó, Kronstadt), Aiud (Nagyenyed, Gross-Enyed), and Cluj (Kolozsvár, Klausenburg).
1936–46	Construction of the Rumanian Orthodox Cathedral in Timişoara (Temesvár, Temeschwar).
1937	On October 2, the Conclave of Vásárhely (i.e., [Marosvásárhely] Tîrgu Mureş) brings together most of the Hungarian intellectuals of the left to map their strategy vis-a-vis the growing pressure from the right. They agree on joining forces with democratic Rumanian elements. The conclave is followed on November 14 by an important MADOSZ congress at Braşov (Brassó, Kronstadt).
1938	On February 10, King Carol II ends parliamentary politics and introduces his royal dictatorship over Rumania. On March 31, he has all political parties disbanded, including the organizations of the national minorities.
1939	On March 23, the German-Rumanian Commercial Treaty transforms Rumania into an economic dependency of the Third Reich.
1939	During September 1–4, Woermann and Ribbentrop exert pressure on the Hungarian government to desist from further anti-Rumanian and revisionist policies.
1940	On May 27, the German-Rumanian Petroleum Pact is signed.

1940	On June 26, the Soviet Union delivers an ultimatum to Rumania to evacuate Bessarabia and Northern Bucovina. Soviet troops move into these areas on June 28.
1940	During August 16–24, Rumanian-Hungarian negotiations are held at Turnu-Severin concerning the fate of Transylvania.
1940	On August 30, the German-Italian arbitral award divides Transylvania into two parts, returning Northern Transylvania to Hungary while leaving Southern Transylvania under Rumanian jurisdiction. This Second Vienna Award continues the polarization of Rumania and Hungary. Hungarian troops move into Northern Transylvania between September 5 and 13.
1941	During June 11–12, the German-Rumanian agreement is negotiated to go to war with the Soviet Union. The attack begins on June 22.
1941	On June 26, the Kassa (Košice, Kaschau) bombing incident is followed by Hungary's declaration of war on the Soviet Union.
1941–44	Animosities continue over Transylvania. The German-Italian Commission supervising the implementation of the Vienna Award documents numerous violations of minority rights.
1944	On March 19, German forces occupy Hungary.
1944	On August 21, Soviet troops reach Iaşi in Moldavia.
1944	On August 23, Ion Antonescu is overthrown; Rumania switches sides and attacks German forces on Rumanian territory. Soviet troops reach Bucharest on August 30–31.
1944	During September 5–8, the German-Hungarian counterattack into Southern Transylvania is repulsed and a Soviet-Rumanian offensive reaches Makó on September 24. Between October 4 and 25, most of Transylvania falls under Soviet control. However, Rumanian atrocities in Northern Transylvania convince the Soviet Union not to return the area to Rumanian administration right away.
1944	On September 12, Rumania signs the armistice agreement with the Soviet Union. The agreement includes a reference to the cession of Northern Transylvania to Rumania.
1945	In January, the Hungarian-language Bolyai University is established at Cluj (Kolozsvár, Klausenburg).
1945	On February 6, the "Nationality Statute" is made public that guarantees all individuals equal rights without regard to race, nationality, language, or religion.

1945 On March 6, Petru Groza comes to power and establishes a People's Democracy with the Communists obtaining key political positions. The Soviet Union rewards the Rumanian shift leftward by turning Northern Transylvania over to the new Rumanian administration.

1945 On March 22, the "land reform" is implemented that has particularly devastating consequences for the Saxon and Swabian areas of Transylvania. Again, minority nationalities lose land to the majority nationality.

1945 On November 8, the Medical and Pharmaceutical Institute is established at Tîrgu Mureş (Marosvásárhely, Neumarkt).

1946 On December 20, the Hungarian journal *Utunk* (Our Way) begins publication under the editorship of Gábor Gaál.

1947 On February 10, Rumania and the Allied Powers sign a peace treaty at Paris. Rumania retains its state frontiers of January 1, 1941, with the exception of the Rumanian-Hungarian frontier, in which the Vienna Award of August 30, 1940—which divided Transylvania (between Hungary and Rumania)—is annulled.

1947 On December 30, King Michael abdicates and Rumania is declared a "Republic."

1947 At Bucharest the *Romániai Magyar Szó* (Rumanian Hungarian Word) begins publication; after 1953, it becomes the daily *Előre* (Forward).

1948 On January 24, Rumania and Hungary sign a Treaty of Friendship and Mutual Assistance.

1948 The Hungarian Opera again begins to function at Cluj.

1949 Religious persecution begins in earnest and the minority denominations again bear the brunt of the repressive measures. Lay leaders, ministers, and priests of the Roman Catholic, Calvinist, Lutheran, and Unitarian churches are imprisoned or sent to forced labor camps in large numbers. At the same time the Uniate Catholic church is completely liquidated by "reintegrating" it into the Rumanian Orthodox church.

1952 An "Autonomous Hungarian Region" is established—under Soviet pressure—in the Székely area of Transylvania with Tîrgu Mureş (Marosvásárhely, Neumarkt) for its capital. While its "autonomy" exists mainly on paper, it does provide some benefits, such as bilingual street signs and inscriptions.

1952 László Luka, Anna Pauker, and other minority cadres are purged from the Rumanian Workers' party.

1953 The literary periodical *Igaz Szó* (True Word) begins publication at Tîrgu Mureş.

1956 On October 23, the Hungarian uprising in Budapest leads to extensive unrest in Transylvania with demonstrations in most of the large Hungarian-inhabited cities. Mass arrests, imprisonments, deportations, and many executions follow. The events of 1956 are later used to justify anti-Hungarian measures throughout Transylvania.

1957 On April 15, a Soviet-Rumanian pact is signed defining the status of the Soviet troops stationed in Rumania.

1958 Petru Groza dies on January 7. He was the Rumanian leader who attempted to overcome nationalistic policies and to normalize Rumanian-Hungarian relations.

1958 In June, Soviet occupation troops are withdrawn from Rumania.

1959 On March 5, the Hungarian-language Bolyai University is compelled to merge with the Rumanian Babeş University at Cluj, (Kolozsvár, Klausenburg), becoming the Babeş-Bolyai University. The merger becomes the first step in the Rumanianization of Hungarian higher education in Transylvania. Three Hungarian professors commit suicide to protest the merger, including the writer László Szabédi.

1960 The overall administrative reorganization of Rumania provides the opportunity for gerrymandering the Hungarian Autonomous Region out of existence. Purely Hungarian areas are detached from it while Rumanian-inhabited areas are attached to it to dilute its compact Hungarian character. The name of the region is also changed to reflect this erosion. It is henceforth called Mureş-Maghiar Autonomous Region.

1962 The University of Timişoara (Temesvár) is established without a Hungarian or German section, even though Timişoara has many Hungarian and German inhabitants.

1964 During April 15–22, the Rumanian Workers' party issues its famous "April pronouncement" on the relations of Communist parties and states. The document is a clear statement of revived Rumanian nationalism, primarily rejecting the integrationist efforts of COMECON economic plans.

1965	Gheorghe Gheorghiu-Dej dies on March 19. He is succeeded as first party secretary by Nicolae Ceauşescu on March 22. Both leaders committed Rumania to a nationalistic orientation.
1965	At the IXth Party Congress (July 19–24) the Rumanian Workers' party changes its name to Rumanian Communist party. This is followed on August 21 by the declaration that Rumania is no longer a peoples' republic, but has now become the Rumanian Socialist Republic.
1967	On February 28 is the premier of the film "Dacii." This begins the extensive popularization of the interwar commitment to a nationalistic self-definition via the "Daco-Roman" assumption of national origins.
1968	On February 14, the administrative reorganization of Rumania eliminates the Mureş-Magyar Autonomous Region and replaces it with the counties of Mureş, Harghita, and Covasna.
1968	During August 15–17, Nicolae Ceauşecu visits Czechoslovakia. The visit is followed shortly by the Soviet and Warsaw Pact invasion of Czechoslovakia. Rumania does not participate in the invasion and issues a strongly worded declaration on national sovereignty, independence, and the principle of noninterference in domestic affairs (August 21–22). These events set the stage for a brief (1968–73) thaw in majority-minority relations in Transylvania.
1968	The Hungarian Nationality Workers' Council and the German Nationality Workers' Council are established to serve as agencies for the articulation of minority needs and interests. However, their roles remain symbolic.
1970	On July 7, the Soviet-Rumanian Friendship and Mutual Support Treaty is renewed and signed at Bucharest.
1971	On October 12, a University is established at Braşov (Brassó, Kronstadt) without a Hungarian or German section, even though Braşov has many German and Hungarian inhabitants.
1972	On February 24, the Rumanian-Hungarian Friendship and Mutual Support Treaty is renewed and signed at Bucharest.
1972	On May 16, the Iron Gates Power and Shipping System is officially opened by Tito and Ceauşescu.
1973	On May 11, Decree Law 278 requires the presence of a minimum of twenty-five students at the grade school level and thirty-six students at the high school level to maintain instruction in a minority language. In small towns, this makes it very difficult

or even impossible to maintain instruction in the minority nationality languages.

1974 On September 20, the Trans-Făgăras (Fogaras) highway is opened linking Transylvania with Muntenia/Oltenia (Wallachia) and Bucharest.

1974 On October 6, joint Rumanian-Hungarian commemorations are held for the 125th anniversary of the execution of the thirteen generals at Arad. They had been executed for their role in the 1848–49 revolution.

1974 During October 15–November 2, Act No. 63 on the protection of the national cultural treasures and Decree Law 207 (1974), amending Decree Law 472 (1971) on the National Archives, opens the door to the legal confiscation of all "documents, recordings, official and private correspondence, diaries, manifestos, posters, sketches, drawings, engravings, imprints, seals, and like material" over thirty years old from the possession of religious and cultural institutions or private citizens. This tool for legally confiscating historically significant items makes it possible for the nationalistic Rumanian regime to eradicate or at least erase and/or censor the history of the Germans, Hungarians, and other nationalities in Transylvania.

1975 In Helsinki, Finland, in August, the Final Act of the "Conference on Security and Cooperation in Europe" is signed by thirty-five states. Rumania enthusiastically endorses the Final Act for its commitment to the territorial status quo, while Hungary supports it for the protections it may provide to its minorities in Transylvania and elsewhere.

1976 On November 8, Decree Law 372 is issued amending Decree Law 225 (1974), which had prohibited the accommodation of non-Rumanian citizens in private homes with the exception of immediate family members. The law of 1976 continues the objective of the earlier legal restriction by discouraging Hungarian tourism and contact between the Hungarians of Transylvania and their conationals in other parts of the world.

1977 The census of February shows that, out of Rumania's total population of 21.5 million, c. 1.7 million are Hungarians. These figures, as do those of 1966 and 1956 (as well as earlier censuses), underrepresent the actual Hungarian population of Rumania. According to objective outside analysts, the Hungarian population is probably closer to 2.4 million in Rumania in 1977.

1977 On June 2, Károly Király, former first party secretary of Covasna County, member of the Party Central Committee, alternate member of the Politburo, member of the Grand National Assembly, and member of the Council of State writes his first letter to Ilie Verdeţ (Politburo member responsible for ideological matters and nationality policies), raising the shortcomings of Rumanian nationality policies. After he fails to receive any response he writes János Fazekas in August and János Vincze in September about this same problem. Instead of receiving a hearing, he is called to Bucharest in October and is accused of having no faith in the Party leadership.

1978 In January, the Károly Király letters are published in major newspapers throughout the West. He is harassed and forced to leave his home town of Tîrgu Mureş (Marosvásárhely, Neumarkt) and to go into "internal exile" to the small town of Caransebeş (Karánsebes). Soon after he speaks to three Western correspondents about minority conditions in Rumania he is also deprived of his post as vice president of the Hungarian Nationality Workers' Council.

1978 On December 21, a new law on Education and Instruction is enacted. Although it is supposed to supercede Decree Law 278, the new law does not rectify the discriminatory practices of the 1973 law. In effect it perpetuates the discriminatory policies by remaining silent about the real needs of minority instruction.

1980 During August 10–17, the International Conference of Historians is held in Bucharest. The timing of the conference and the Rumanian celebrations of Burebista's founding of the Dacian state is utilized as the occasion to propagate the Daco-Roman theory on an international forum.

The Dawn of National Consciousness 1

The roots of ethnic conflict in Transylvania go back at least as far as the collapse of the feudal kingdom of Hungary on the blood-soaked plains of Mohács. This battle against the Ottoman Turks in 1526 resulted in the division and depopulation of the once powerful and prosperous kingdom of Matthias Rex (1458–90). The Hungary that had provided stability for Eastern Europe for over 500 years was now subjected to depredations from both East and West. Transylvania, which had been an integral part of this kingdom, henceforth faced an uncertain future as the Habsburgs and the Ottomans attempted to consolidate their hold over northwestern and central Hungary respectively.

The defeat at Mohács opened an age of constant conflict. The Hungarian population was dramatically and drastically reduced in the ceaseless military struggles. Many sections of the former kingdom were totally depopulated. It was during these critical years of the Turkish wars that Transylvania gained added significance for the peoples of Eastern Europe. The Hungarian princes who governed it from 1541 until the end of the seventeenth century provided continuity to the quest for Hungarian independence. At the same time, Transylvania became a haven for the Rumanian populations of Wallachia and Moldavia.

The study by L. S. Domonkos provides an ethnic profile of the medieval kingdom of Hungary on the eve of the Battle of Mohács. It sketches the ethnic composition and the prevailing state order of which Transylvania was an integral part. Domonkos also shows that the relations between these diverse groups were not confrontational along ethnic lines.

The study by Louis J. Elteto focuses on the beginnings of the disintegration, which in the long run produced some of the nationality conflicts of the future. Elteto's analysis reflects on the period that follows the Battle of Mohács, its main concern being to outline the impact of the Reformation on the national consciousness of the Hungarians, Saxons, and Rumanians of Transylvania. This period represents for all the peoples of Transylvania an important phase in the differentiation of their respective self-definitions.

Béla K. Király's study is concerned with the role of Transylvania in the seventeenth and eighteenth centuries in fostering or hindering the concept of independence for the kingdom of Hungary. As noted above, the Battle of Mohács signalled the end of independence for Hungarian statehood. Its division into Habsburg and Ottoman-occupied parts meant that the remainder, i.e., Transylvania, was now the only hope for the preservation of Hungarian liberty and the only political entity that could work toward the reestablishment of the kingdom of Hungary.

Together these three studies provide the broad background for the developments that led to the emergence of modern nationalism in Transylvania.

I. MEDIEVAL HUNGARY AND TRANSYLVANIA, XV-TH CENTURY

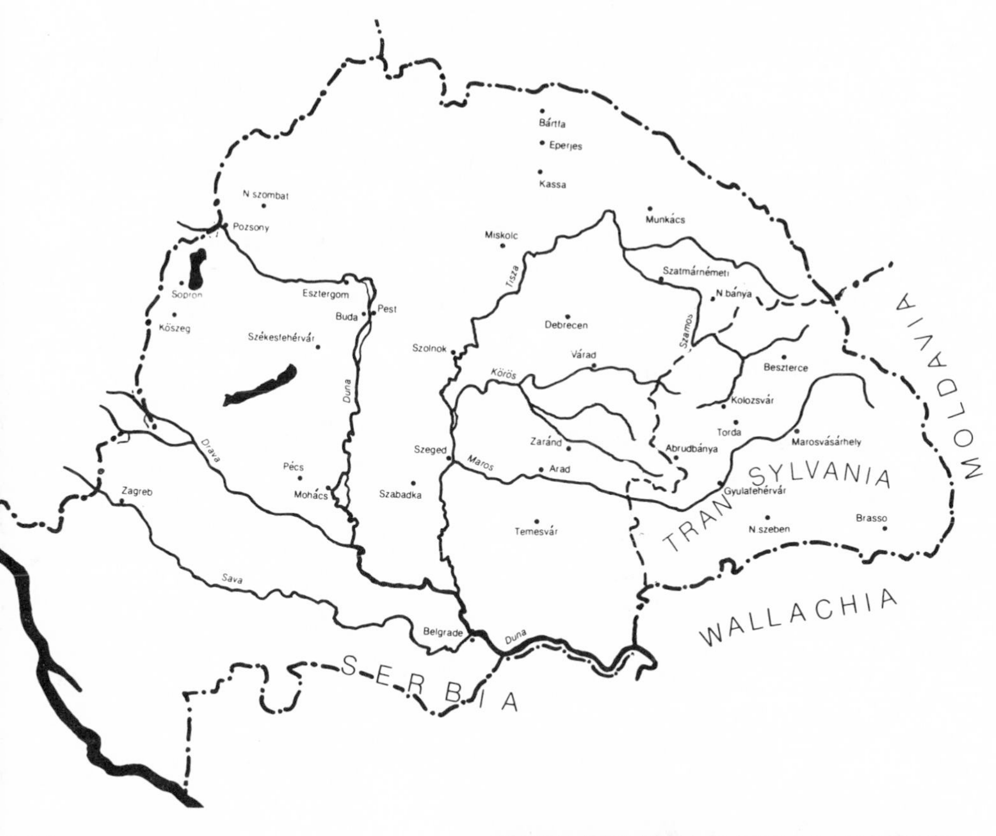

GEND:

- International Borders
- Border of Transylvania
- Kingdom of Hungary
- Holy Roman Empire
- Ottoman Empire
- Kingdom of Poland
- Other States

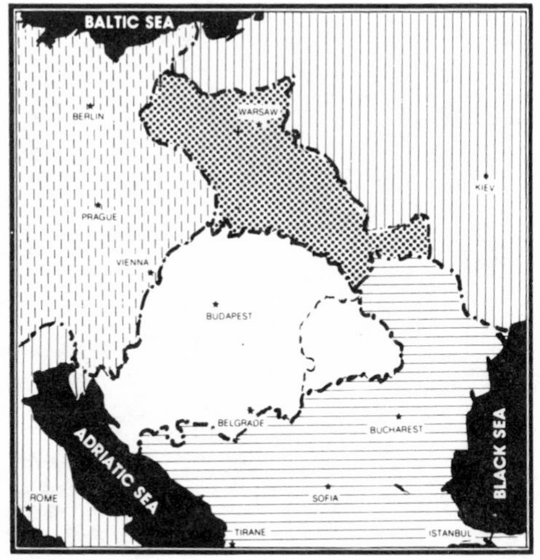

II. THE PRINCIPALITY OF TRANSYLVANIA BETWEEN OTTOMANS AND HABSBURGS, 1606

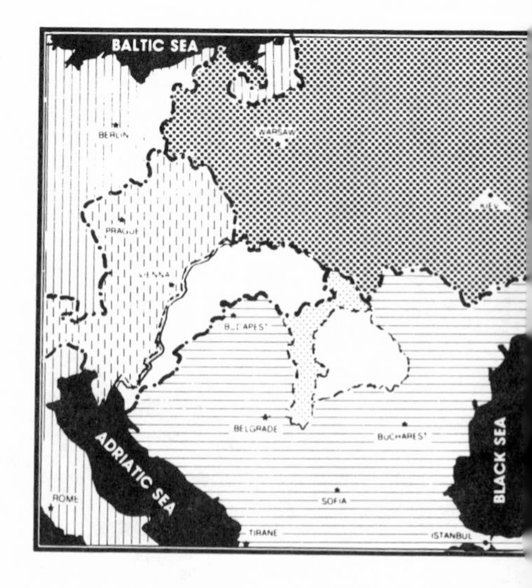

The Multiethnic Character of the Hungarian Kingdom in the Later Middle Ages

L. S. DOMONKOS

THE NATIO HUNGARICA

The Hungarian kingdom in the late Middle Ages was not a national state in the modern sense of the word, but a multiethnic political unit in which the Magyar nobility held the dominant position. In this respect Hungary is not unique, for the medieval period does not offer examples of national states. Hungary had within its borders a large number of non-Magyar inhabitants in the fourteenth and fifteenth centuries who were nevertheless members of the "Natio Hungarica" or "Natio Hungarorum," irrespective of the ethnic background. The terms of "Natio Hungarica" or "Natio Hungarorum" should be viewed basically as indicators of geographic and not ethnic origin. An individual belonged to the "Hungarian Nation" if he or she resided under the authority of the king of Hungary, i.e., in the lands of the Hungarian crown.[1] Probably the clearest illustration of this point can be drawn from late medieval university practices. A large number of students from the Hungarian kingdom attended the University of Vienna in the fifteenth century, where the scholars were divided into four "nations," following the model of the great University of Paris. These nations were the Austrian, which also included Italy; the Rhenish, comprising the Rhineland and Western Europe; the Hungarian, with the Slavic areas added; and the Saxon, to which belonged students from northern and eastern Germany, Scandinavia, and England.[2] If, for example, a student from one of the Transylvanian Saxon towns enrolled at the University of Vienna, as Thomas Altenberg of Szeben (Hermannstadt, Sibiu) did in 1453, he was inscribed into the registers of the Hungarian Nation[3] and not the Saxon Nation, for the simple reason that he came from a territory of the Hungarian crown. The fact that Thomas Altenberg spoke German and might have felt more at home in the Austrian, Rhenish, or Saxon nations at the University does not enter the picture at all. He was, because of the geographic location of his home, a member of the Natio Hungarica.[4]

The Hungarian kingdom in the fifteenth century comprised a geographic entity bounded by the Carpathian Mountain range in the north, east, and southeast, and by the Danube and Száva (Sava) rivers in the south and southwest. The western border with Austria did not follow any major geographical barrier or line. The area of the kingdom was about 300,000 square kilometers (or 124,000 square miles) and included the regions of Hungary proper, Croatia-Slavonia, and for a time the coast of Dalmatia. The population of fifteenth-century Hungary (including Transylvania but excluding Croatia-Slavonia), has been estimated to have been between 3.4 and 4 million inhabitants. The more conservative figure given by Erik Molnár,[5] who based his calculations on a family unit of four members, is probably more nearly correct than the estimates of István Szabó, who took a five-member peasant family as the norm.[6] It is interesting to note that in 1720, almost 200 years after the Battle of Mohács, the population of the same area is still 3.5 to 4 million.[7] This gives some indication of the devastation caused by the Turkish wars. Under the authority of the Hungarian crown, the areas of Transylvania and Croatia-Slavonia enjoyed a degree of autonomy in their political and administrative life but were parts of the *regnum Hungariae*. The kingdom was subdivided into counties, of which fifty-seven were in Hungary proper, seven in Transylvania, and seven in the Slavonian area. South of the Száva River frontier were a number of military districts (bánságok), which were buffer areas against Turkish expansion and scenes of a number of campaigns against the Ottomans during the early period of the reign of Matthias Corvinus.

In the early sixteenth century, Miklós Oláh (1493–1568), humanist scholar, friend of Erasmus, and later archbishop of Esztergom—and as his name indicates, of Rumanian origin—composed an important geographic treatise entitled "Hungaria,"[8] in which he gave an invaluable description of the kingdom as it was before the Turkish devastation. Oláh's work has been studied with care by art historians, but it is also important to us because in Chapter XIX of "Hungaria" Oláh enumerated the various inhabitants found in Hungary during his own lifetime. He describes these as follows: "The territory of the Hungarian kingdom contains in our time diverse nations, [namely] Hungarians, Germans, Bohemians, Slavs, Croatians, Saxons, Székelys, Vlachs, Serbs, Cumans, Jaziges, Ruthenians, and most recently Turks."[9] Oláh mentions twelve "nations" who resided under the sovereignty of the Hungarian crown. These same twelve groups were present during the 200 years prior to the Battle of Mohács, which is the period on which we plan to focus. It is well known that Mohács brought about the destruction of the medieval Hungarian monarchy and ushered in great changes that also effected the subsequent ethnic composition of the state, to the detriment of the once dominant Magyar element. Following roughly the outline presented by Oláh, let us examine the twelve "nations" and their major characteristics during the fourteenth and fifteenth centuries.

The Magyar Element and the Székelys

The first mentioned "nation" were the Magyars, who were the dominant ethnic group in the Hungarian kingdom in the late Middle Ages. Not only were the Magyars the politically significant element, but they also constituted the vast majority of the population. By the end of the fifteenth century, the kingdom was more thoroughly Hungarian than it ever was until the post-Trianon era of the twentieth century.[10]

Our most reliable, although unfortunately incomplete, sources of information concerning the wealth, size, population density, etc. of the late medieval Hungarian state are the taxation records of 1494–95. These were prepared during the tenure of Zsigmond Ernuszt, bishop of Pécs and treasurer (thesaurarius) of the realm, who in 1496 was accused of having stolen a sizeable sum from the treasury. In order to clear himself, Ernuszt prepared elaborate accounts for the period 1494–95, which are an invaluable source for the study of the social and economic conditions of the period.[11]

Elemér Mályusz, one of the most renowned Hungarian medievalists, estimated on the basis of taxation documents that 77.25 percent of those employed in agricultural pursuits in the fifteenth century were Magyars. This is based on the analysis of the names of the taxpayers. Mályusz also found that about 17 percent of the names were such that it is impossible to determine the ethnic group to which the individual belonged. Some of these were undoubtedly also Hungarians, which would push the percentage up further, to about 80 percent.[12]

The Magyar population was concentrated in the lower-lying regions of the Carpathian Basin, in the plateau areas, and in the river valleys. Since there was, for a long period, an ample land reserve, the less desirable areas were left to others or remained unoccupied. Particularly strong were the settlements in the counties of Baranya, Tolna, Bács, and Bodrog. Towns and villages in the valleys of the Körös, Szamos, and Maros in eastern Hungary were inhabited predominantly by Hungarians. The same is true of the lower valley of the Vág and Nyitra rivers in northwestern Hungary. The evidence presented by surviving charters and other documents from the fourteenth and fifteenth centuries is overwhelming: the place names are predominantly Hungarian, indicating that the majority of the population was in fact Magyar.[13]

If one were to draw a map showing ethnic distribution in Hungary, the more mountainous regions would show the presence of Slovak, Rumanian, or Ruthenian inhabitants in large areas. This, however, should be viewed with a certain amount of caution because of the great differences in the density of the population between the counties on the plain and in the Carpathian or Transylvanian regions. Mountains and forests can give livelihood to much smaller numbers of people; consequently, settlements were of more modest proportions in these regions. Furthermore, since many of these mountain settlements were of more recent foundation, they were also less populous.[14] To illustrate density of population, we must again turn to the tax lists of 1495, which measure the number of *porta* (tax-paying units) per county. There were 15,000 *porta* in Baranya, 11,000 in Somogy, and 10,000 in Tolna County. At the same time there were 300 *porta* in Árva County, 790 in Liptó, and 1,420 in Zólyom,[15] all located in the mountainous areas of northern Hungary. It is clear that the population of the Magyar-inhabited plains counties was several times the number of inhabitants that could be found in the border counties, which were generally more sparsely inhabited and where the Hungarian population was a smaller proportion of the total.

Of the fifty-seven counties that made up Hungary proper, twenty-two counties formed a coherent block of Magyar-inhabited areas. Around this core were twenty-six counties where other "national" or ethnic groups were present in larger or smaller numbers. And, finally, there was a number of counties in which the Magyar element was probably less than 20 percent. Seven of these were in the northernmost part of the kingdom: Trencsén, Árva, Turóc, Liptó, Zólyom, Szepes, and Sáros. Two, Máramaros County in the east and Pozsega in the southwest, had few Hungarian inhabitants, although even there the nobility was predominantly Magyar.[16]

In general, we can say that the weight of the Hungarian population was to be found in the south, in those regions that fell under Turkish domination first and remained subjugated for the longest. It is there that the tragedy of Hungarian history can be found. While the southern counties would be depopulated, the northern would be able to grow relatively unimpeded. In 1495, there were 2.75 *porta* per square kilometer in Tolna County and .80 *porta* per square kilometer in Trencsén County. Yet, in 1870, Trencsén County had 258,000 inhabitants, Tolna 222,000.[17]

Two areas under the Hungarian crown but with some degree of autonomy were the Croatian-Slavonian region and Transylvania. The number of Hungarians in Slavonia was small. Except for a few members of the nobility, the percentage of Magyars in this region was insignificant.

In Transylvania, the situation was quite different. There were three administrative units in Transylvania: the Saxon region (Szászföld), the Székely region (Székelyföld), and the Seven Counties (Belsőszolnok Doboka, Kolozs, Torda, Küküllő, Fehér and Hunyad). The Saxon region was obviously German; the Székelys were Magyars; and in the seven counties the total population was about two-thirds Magyar, and one-third Rumanian (Vlachs, Wallachians).[18] In some areas, the number of Vlachs (Wallachians) was probably higher.

We have until now been concerned mainly with the peasantry, which, after all, was the bulk of the population. Let us now examine briefly the other segments of the Magyars, namely the nobility and the urban dwellers. The "political nation" was made up of the nobility, secular and ecclesiastic, which constituted about 5 percent of the total population. The vast majority of these belonged to the petty or lesser nobility, which was almost exclusively Magyar. Among the barons and prelates, however, there were many who rose to prominence although of non-Hungarian ancestry. Random examples of this can be seen in the case of the Cillei (Cilli) family, the powerful competitors of the Hunyadis. The Croatian-Slavonian Frangepán and Vitrovec families were also considered barons of the Hungarian kingdom.[19] Although some Hungarian historians have tried to disprove that the Hunyadi family was of Vlach (Wallachian) origin, the overwhelming evidence supports the view that they indeed were not Magyars, but rose in the service of the Hungarian king, received nobility, intermarried with Magyar noble families, and thus rose to prominence.[20] A large number of others were also able to make this transition, among them the famous Drágffy, Majláth, and Nádasdi families.[21] Similarly, leaders of the Slovak, Ruthenian, and Saxon communities made their way into the ranks of Hungarian nobles. There are, however, instances where the reverse situation was also evident. Magyar nobles living in predominantly Slovak-inhabited areas became linguistically assimilated to their subjects, as is evident from their correspondence by the sixteenth century.[22] Generally, it was advantageous for any person, regardless of ethnic background, to join the ruling class rather than to be part of the exploited segment of society.

Among the prelates there was also a number of important men who rose to prominence in the Hungarian state, although they were ethnically not Magyars. Excellent examples of this are provided by the careers of Archbishop János Vitéz of Esztergom and of his nephew, the great humanist-poet Janus Pannonius, bishop of Pécs (Fünfkirchen). The Vitéz family was of Slavonian origin and had intermarried with Magyar nobility.[23] Vitéz was one of the most loyal supporters of Hunyadi, and under Matthias was eventually rewarded with the offices of chancellor and primate of Hungary. Janus Pannonius was a member of the Royal Council and privy chancellor. It was obviously ability that determined the rise of these men and not the question of whether they were Magyar or Slavonian. Other examples abound: the successor of Janus as bishop of Pécs was Zsigmond Ernuszt, whose family originated from Austria and who was probably partially Jewish. György Szathmári, bishop of Várad (Oradea, Grosswardein) and later of Pécs, was born of German parents in Kassa (Košice, Kaschau) while Johann Filipecz, bishop of Várad, was a Moravian. László Vingárdi Geréb, bishop of Transylvania, was a member of a Saxon family that made the transition to the Magyar nobility in the course of the fifteenth century. All these men served the Hungarian kingdom without being of Magyar ancestry and had a strong attachment to the "Natio Hungarica," of which they were an integral part.

When we examine the backgrounds of the heads of the "political nation," namely the kings, we find that the Hungarian kingdom was ruled by men who were, for the most part, non-Magyars. The list of rulers for the fifteenth century presents a curious picture. Sigismund (1378–1437) was of the House of Luxembourg. Although a stranger in Hungary at first, by the end of his reign he often wore Magyar dress, swore in Hungarian, and was buried next to his hero, Saint László, at Várad. Albert (1437–39) was a Habsburg, Wladislaw I (1440–44) a Pole. János Hunyadi, regent (1446–52), was of Rumanian ancestry; László V (1444–57) lived most of his life abroad and probably knew little if any Hungarian. The only "true Magyar" king was Matthias (1458–90), succeeded by the Polish Wladislaw II (1490–1516). The ethnically predominantly Magyar kingdom of Hungary was ruled by non-Hungarian kings through most of the fifteenth century.

Turning our attention away from nobles, prelates, and kings, we find that the population of the urban centers was predominantly non-Magyar. Hungary was slow to develop cities. The growth of towns before the Tatar invasion was minimal, and even in the fifteenth and sixteenth centuries the number of true cities was very small.[24] The Decree of 1514 enumerated those cities *(civitas)* that by virtue of their privileges could be counted as genuine urban centers. Altogether there were only twenty-four in the whole kingdom, the most important of which were the free royal cities of Buda (Ofen), Pest, Kassa, Pozsony (Bratislava, Pressburg), Nagyszombat, Bártfa, Eperjes, and Sopron (Ödenburg).[25] By 1500, however, there were about 750 market towns *(oppidum, mezőváros)* throughout the land.[26] It is an interesting Hungarian phenomenon that from the second half of the fifteenth century onward the growth of the *civitas* stagnated, while the number of *oppida* increased considerably.[27] The population of the market towns was often made up of German settlers (*hospites,* guests) in the early fourteenth century. During the course of the next 100 years, however, large numbers of Magyar and Slavic settlers took up their residence in the market towns. In the areas inhabited predominantly by Hungarians, the *oppida* became mainly Magyar, while in areas where the Slavic population was the majority, their movement to the market towns made those particular settlements Slavic.[28] Our information about the development of *oppida* in the Transylvanian area is fragmentary. The almost complete monopoly of the Germans as urban settlers was eventually broken down by the movement of both Magyar and Slavic populations into the cities and towns.

This urbanization trend was a general European phenomenon and is not peculiar to the Hungarian kingdom. Two obvious results of this population movement were the abandonment of villages in many formerly inhabited areas[29] and the increase of Magyar and Slavic elements in the urban centers. The fact that many towns had increasingly mixed populations made it possible to weaken the ethnic identity of the non-Magyars, especially of the Germans. This led in some instances to the "Magyarization" of some individuals, just as others lost their German identity and became part of their Slovak environment. In Buda, for example, the Ohnwein family became Bornemissza during the course of the fifteenth century.[30] In Eperjes, the entry of Magyars into town life and their growing influence has been demonstrated by the study of Béla Iványi.[31] Towns such as Székesfehérvár and Esztergom were almost completely Magyar by 1500, although they had had large French, Flemish, and Italian populations in the previous centuries. Szeged and Óbuda were always Magyar. Pest was changing from a predominantly German to predominantly Hungarian town. In Buda, the German-speaking population was still very strong. Only in the fifteenth century were the Hungarians able to force the Germans to agree to the rotation of the judgeship *(judocus)* so that one year the incumbent was German, the next Hungarian.[32] The German preponderance at Buda can best be seen in the organization of the parishes on Castle Hill. The Hungarian parish was the Church of Saint Mary Magdalena, a simpler, smaller structure. The German parish church, named after Our Lady (today

Matthias or Coronation Church), was a far more imposing and larger structure than the parish of the Magyars. The laws of the capital city of Hungary were written in German and are known as the *Ofner Stadtrecht.*[33] Buda became a Hungarian city only in the twentieth century.

Before leaving the subject of the Hungarian element, let us turn briefly to the examination of the Székelys (Siculi, Seklers). In origin and language, they were Magyars and lived as a compact block in the eastern part of Transylvania called the Székelyföld. All the Székelys were considered noble and as such owed military service but paid no taxes to the king.[34] The royal representative in the region was called the ispán *(comes sicolorum),* whose primary function was to lead the Székely military units in case of war. Their social organization still reflected the vestiges of the clans that made up the "Székely nation." Originally, there were seven territorial units based upon these clans, each of which was called a *szék*. From these, several subunits *(fiuszék)* were formed in the course of time. At the head of each *szék* there was an elected captain *(hadnagy,* later *kapitány)* and a judge.[35] Together, all the Székelys formed the *Universitas Sicolorum,* one of the three administrative units of Transylvania. The population was originally divided into two major classes based upon the type of military service that they performed; i.e., those who fought on foot were called *darabant* and those who fought on horseback, *lófő*. In 1473, Matthias Corvinus reorganized them militarily and created three classes, namely the *primor,* who led a troop of Székelys into battle; the *primipilatus,* composed of the *lófő,* who constituted the cavalry; and the *pixidarius,* made up of those who fought on foot.[36]

This autonomous block of Magyar-speaking inhabitants in Transylvania was able to retain its language, customs and institutions throughout the late Middle Ages and for centuries thereafter.

The "Saxon" and German Elements

A wide variety of Germans migrated to Hungary during the course of the Middle Ages. Five important groupings of these settlers can be identified. Let us begin with the people who are usually referred to as the Saxons of Transylvania.

The first major influx of German settlers into the region occurred during the reign of Géza II, who issued a call for colonizers in 1141. These first settlers were mainly from the areas of Saxony in northern Germany, and, although subsequent people came from all parts of the Holy Roman Empire and Flanders, the term "Saxon" came to denote all Transylvanian Germans. The Germans received a major set of privileges from king András II in 1224 in a document usually referred to as the *Diploma Andreanum.*[37] Although this gave them autonomy in most local matters, they were still subject to the authority of the count *(comes)* of Szeben (Sibiu, Hermannstadt). Following the Tatar devastation, the Saxons were able to free themselves from the *comes* and had similar immunities to those that governed the life of free cities. Eventually, the area developed further administratively, with complete local judicial autonomy. By the fourteenth century, there emerged the so-called Seven Seats *(Stűhle, sedes),* to which two other "seats" were later added.[38] Other important Saxon centers were the cities of Beszterce (Bistriţa, Bistritz) and Brassó (Kronstadt, Braşov), which were able to gain, by the fifteenth century, the same tax privileges as the other Saxon seats.[39] The Saxon settlements in Transylvania were obliged to pay a set sum of taxes to the royal treasury, to be delivered on Saint Martin's Day.[40] They also contributed an agreed-upon number of soldiers to the royal army.

When the first German settlers arrived, they found the environment hostile to the growth of towns; but as they prospered, urbanization set in, and soon the villages were subordinated to the rising towns. The areas settled by the Saxons were only sparsely occupied by Hungarians, and thus it was possible for the Germans to create large, coherent blocks of territory almost exclusively inhabited by their own people. Penetration of Magyars and later of Rumanians into these units was slow. The first mention of Vlachs in the Saxon cities comes in 1404.[41] It is interesting to note that a number of the judges among the Saxons, known as *Gräve,*[42] made the transition to Magyar nobility, intermarried with Hungarian families, and advanced in the administrative or ecclesiastic field. The Saxons formed the *Universitas Saxonum* (or *Saxonorum*) and were one of the three elements (together with the Székelys and the Magyar nobles) who made up the *Universitats Trium Nationum.*[43]

The second major concentration of Germans was in the area of Szepes (Zips) and Sáros in northeastern Hungary, on the important trade routes between Poland and the Hungarian plains. These settlements originated mainly from the period following the Tatar invasion. The first major charter of privileges was issued to the settlers in 1271 by István V.[44] The newcomers, many of whom came from the region of Flanders, settled in among the existing Magyar and Slovak villages, forming not a continuous unit of territory such as existed in Transylvania, but a mosaic of settlements bound together by their common privileges. These newly-arrived Germans soon emerged as the dominant ethnic element in the cities of Kassa, Lőcse, Késmárk, Bártfa,

Eperjes, and others.[45] Their numbers were reinforced by continuous new migrations, especially from Silesia. The cities prospered under the commercial advantages granted to the settlers and steadily rose in importance throughout the fourteenth and fifteenth centuries. To further protect their privileges from possible erosion, a confederation under the leadership of Bártfa came into existence in the fifteenth century. This bound the northeastern cities together in common defense of their interests in national and international matters. Every second year they held conferences to develop a unified policy on major issues. This development reached its peak in 1485 with the signing of a far-reaching promise of cooperation among the cities.[46]

The third major group of Germans settled in the north-Hungarian mining towns in what is today central Slovakia. Most of the immigrants came following the Tatar invasion, from the areas of Thuringia and Nűrnberg. In these mining regions, the German settlers found a mix of Slovak and Magyar inhabitants. The towns were predominantly German, although some movement from the countryside into the cities is evident.[47] The language, culture, and even architectural style in these towns were predominantly German. The Slovak and Magyar elements were not among the leaders of these municipalities.

The fourth area of German domination can be seen in the various towns throughout the Hungarian kingdom. We have already mentioned the strong German influence on the life of the capital city, Buda. The same situation prevailed in other towns such as Pozsony and Sopron. In both cities, the town council was usually dominated by the German element, and the majority of the correspondence and city council documents were in German.[48] Nagyszombat (Tyrnava) was also founded with special privileges granted to German colonists by king Béla IV in 1238[49] and grew into a major trade center on the highway leading to Brűnn (Brno) and Prague from Esztergom and Buda. The town became one of the free royal cities with extensive privileges and immunities. In Transylvania, the town of Kolozsvár (Cluj, Klausenburg), which became a free royal city in 1316, was at first a Magyar settlement. By the beginning of the fifteenth century, the German element had become dominant. There was, however, a constant influx of Magyars into the city, and by the second half of the century the Hungarians had made major advances.[50] In 1458, a compact, or union, between the Magyars and the Saxons was established. Half of the town council had to be made up of Germans, the other half of Magyars. Likewise, the judgeships *(Richter)* also had to be rotated, with one German and one Hungarian serving his term. Although this meant considerable political progress for the Magyar population, the Germans managed to retain their economic superiority well into the next century.[51]

Finally, one more area of German settlement needs at least passing attention, namely, the region on the western borders of Hungary with the Austrian lands. In the area that is now part of the Burgenland, there were extensive Magyar settlements in the period before the thirteenth century. Subsequently, however, a shift in populations occurred, and a number of new settlers from other parts of Austria were brought here and established their homes in the area of the Neusiedlersee (Fertő Tó), in a southwestern direction. The Hungarians were progressively pushed from this region in the fifteenth and sixteenth centuries.[52]

To sum up, we can say that the German settlers in Hungary, although a small minority compared to other ethnic groups, exerted an influence that was far greater than their numerical strength would indicate. The fact that they were mainly urban dwellers and possessed extensive privileges and immunities helped to insure their prosperity. Their presence in Hungary was a definite economic and cultural advantage and helped to raise the general level of society in the kingdom.

Rumanians, Vlachs or Wallachians

The most difficult task facing the historian in dealing with the ethnic character of the medieval Hungarian kingdom is the problem concerning the origin of the Rumanians. This has been debated and disputed, and much ink has been spilled on all sides in heated and acrimonious debates that have not resolved the basic issues satisfactorily. Our study focuses on the ethnic elements that made up the Hungarian state in the fourteenth and fifteeneth centuries; we can therefore avoid getting involved in the question of Daco-Rumanian continuity and thus eliminate at least one major controversy. With strict reliance on documentary evidence, we shall try to trace the increasingly important role that the Rumanians played in Transylvania in the period under discussion.

There is no written evidence for the presence of Rumanians in Transylvania prior to the beginning of the thirteenth century, although we must emphasize that all documentation for this generally underdeveloped area is meager. From the location of the first settlements it seems probable that the Rumanian migration into Transylvania began sometime in the twelfth century, first as a trickle. Later, when the situation in Wallachia and the Balkans became more threatening due to the Turkish expansion in the fourteenth and fifteenth centuries, the trickle became a steady stream.

The Vlachs first appeared in the vicinity of Hátszeg (Haţeg) and Fogaras (Făgăraş) around 1206–09.[53] These were small settlements, and until the middle of the thirteenth century there is no evidence of any major group of Vlachs living in Transylvania, for the examination of all geographic names, mountains, rivers, towns, and villages shows a preponderance of Magyar, some Slavic, a few German, but no Rumanian names.[54] Following the Tatar invasions and especially in the late thirteenth century, a number of royal fortifications were established in the southern border areas. Subsequently, the kings of Hungary employed large numbers of Vlachs in these frontier defense areas. Other settlements followed. With the authorization of László IV, sixty Rumanian families were settled on the lands of the bishop of Transylvania.[55] Other early settlements were established mainly in Bihar (Bihor) and Hunyad (Hunedoara) counties and in the districts of Brassó (Braşov, Kronstadt) and Szeben (Nagyszeben, Sibiu, Hermannstadt). Even with these settlements, in 1301 there were only nine places in all of Transylvania where the habitation of Rumanians can be proven by documentation.[56] In the following 100 years, the number of places with Rumanian names increased considerably. In the charters and documents from 1301 to 1350, there were 820 place names mentioned, of which 641 are Hungarian, 36 Rumanian, and the others Slavic or German. Fifty years later (1400), the known town and village names had risen to 1,757, of which 1,355 are Hungarian and 76 Rumanian. While we must be careful not to put too much credence in these numbers, simply because place names alone do not necessarily reflect the exact character of the populations, still, we cannot ignore the significance of these statistics. It is quite clear that prior to 1300 the number of Rumanians in Transylvania must have been small, and even in the mid-fourteenth century the numbers do not reveal a massive population block.[57] It is important to remember that the fact that many Rumanians still followed a seminomadic existence, herding their flocks in mountainous regions, makes any estimate of their true numbers difficult.

The social organization of the Rumanians who settled in Transylvania was relatively simple. The various groups of wandering herdsmen and soldiers were under the leadership of a voivode and of a *knez* or *kenéz*. These local leaders were the major official contact between the Rumanians and the Hungarian political or ecclesiastical authority.[58] Generally the *kenéz* offered the services of his people to the captain of a royal fortification or to a feudal lord. The condition of the Rumanian population does show a marked difference between those who were in royal service and those who lived on the lands of secular or ecclesiastical lords. The Vlachs on royal estates or fortifications were more likely to keep their freedom and were often granted extensive privileges and immunities by the kings. The Rumanian inhabitants of the great feudal estates, on the other hand, often sank to the level of exploited serfs.[59] This explains why a large number of the Rumanian peasantry took part in the great Peasant Revolt of 1437 in Transylvania. Many Rumanians found themselves on the lower level of the socioeconomic ladder and were probably even more exploited than the Magyar-speaking peasantry and townspeople. To the downtrodden Vlach peasantry the relief promised by the leaders of the revolt was something worth fighting for. Rumanians were present at the signing of the first Treaty of Kolozsmonostor (Mănăştur) on July 6, 1437, together with the representatives of the Magyar-speaking peasantry.[60] Mention must also be made of the problem of the religious cleavage between the Vlachs and the ecclesiastical authority of the Hungarian state. The Vlachs were Orthodox and resented any efforts, especially during the reign of Louis the Great, to force the Roman faith upon them. Attempts to impose the payment of ecclesiastical tithes upon the Rumanians met with widespread resistance.[61] In order to wean a *kenéz* away from his Orthodox religion, Hungarian nobility was bestowed on him if he would turn Catholic. A number of them did, and several *kenéz* families made the transition to Magyar nobility, showing little regard for their former people. They had become members of the ruling class.

By the end of the fourteenth and the beginning of the fifteenth centuries, there were major blocks of Rumanian inhabitants in the counties of Hunyad, Temes, Krassó, Fogaras, and Máramaros. Many of these regions had royal immunities and are known to have cooperated with each other on a regular basis. New waves of settlers continued to cross the Carpathians from Wallachia and added to the ever increasing number of Rumanian settlements in Transylvania and also along the lower Danube area of Hungary. The Turkish expansion in the fifteenth and sixteenth centuries only furthered this development. Although still excluded from the "Three Nations" that made up the political power in Transylvania, the Rumanians were becoming an increasingly significant force as a result of their numbers.

Slavic Settlements: Slovakian, Croatian, Slavonian, and Ruthenian

A wide variety of Slavic populations could be found within the borders of the Hungarian kingdom. Since much of the area of the Magyar state had been inhabited by diverse groups of Slavs even before the Hungarian conquest of the ninth century, there are only a few areas in the central plains where Slavic place names are missing. Slavic place names can also be found in scattered locations throughout the Transylvanian region.[62]

The largest group of Slavic inhabitants in Hungary proper were the Slovaks, who inhabited the northern tier of counties. If we superimposed the map of modern Slovakia upon this region, we would find that the sparsely populated northern area was inhabited predominantly by Slovaks, although the feudal nobility was Magyar. The lower counties of the modern Slovak state, however, were inhabited mainly by Hungarians, while in the middle band of counties there was a varied mix of populations between these two groups, with some Germans thrown in. While it is true that there was a slow northward expansion of the Magyar element in the fourteenth and fifteenth centuries, there was also a corresponding southward movement of the Slovaks.[63] The result was a thorough mix where so-called ethinic boundaries are impossible to establish. During the course of the fifteenth century, the Slovaks made some headway in establishing themselves in the formerly almost exclusively German-dominated cities.[64] As a result of the Hussite wars, there was also some movement of Czechs, or Bohemians, into the area of northern Hungary. This was especially true during the period when Jan Giskra was overlord of this area. Some of his Czech warriors settled down permanently in these territories.

Another area inhabited by a Slavic population was the region of Croatia and Slavonia, autonomous parts of the Hungarian kingdom. Slavonia was the western part of the land between the Dráva and Száva rivers. The area comprising Valkó, Szerém, and Pozsega counties was then still a part of Hungary. Valkó and Szerém were inhabited mainly by Magyars and Pozsega was already predominantly Slavonian, with only a few Hungarians.[65] Beyond the Száva River lay Croatia, and south of that, in the area increasingly threatened by the Turks, were Serbians.

The last group mentioned by Miklós Oláh in his "Hungaria" were the Ruthenians, who in the fourteenth and fifteenth centuries were still a very small ethnic group within the Hungarian state. They first settled in the area of Máramaros in eastern Hungary during the thirteenth century. Under the reign of Louis the Great, other Ruthenians were allowed to settle, here and in Bereg County.[66] Subsequently, the Ruthenians expanded mainly toward the north, into the areas of Ung, Zemplén, Sáros, and Szepes counties. Their social and economic conditions were unfortunately among the most miserable of any ethnic group. Unlike many of the Rumanians who were settled on royal estates and enjoyed some privileges, the majority of the Ruthenian population was located on private feudal domains.[67] Their leaders were at a disadvantage in securing privileges for themselves and for their people, nor did the Ruthenians enjoy royal protection as some Rumanians did. Almost invariably they sank to the level of serfdom.

Cumans, Jaziges, and Others

Finally, we come to a number of smaller groups who deserve mention but are not generally of great importance. First among these were the Cumans (Kunok), a people of Turkic origin who were first admitted into the kingdom by Béla IV prior to the Mongol invasion. Subsequently, other smaller groups joined them. In return for military service, they were given a large block of territory between the Danube and Tisza rivers. Their nomadic lifestyle and primitive ways caused friction with the native Magyars. Eventually, however, they settled down and were Christianized, and the process of assimilation began. Surrounded by almost purely Magyar-inhabited areas, it is not surprising that by the end of the fifteenth century the Cumans had become Hungarian in speech, although they clung to the privileges granted to them by the kings and still performed their military obligations as prescribed by the charters. The Jaziges (Jászok), probably of Alan descent, settled north of the Cumans in the thirteenth and fourteenth centuries and enjoyed some of the latter's privileges. They, too, were linguistically assimilated into their Magyar surroundings by the end of the medieval period.[68]

Jews lived in some of the Hungarian urban centers but were never as numerous as they were in Spain, Germany, or Poland. The major medieval Jewish centers were in Buda, Sopron, Székesfehérvár, and Kőszeg. Mention should also be made of Italian merchants found in a number of cities but especially numerous in Esztergom and Buda.

Conclusions and Observations

A synthesis such as this can do no more than give a broad outline of the multiethnic nature of the Hungarian kingdom in the fourteenth and fifteenth centuries. Two important questions have to be raised and answered in order to make our treatment complete and dispel any possible misunderstandings. First, was there such a thing as a "nationality policy" adopted by the kings or ruling elements of Hungarian society toward the non-Magyar population, and second, was there ever a conscious "Magyarization" of the ethnic minorities living within the borders of the kingdom? The answer to both of these questions is a resounding No. The presence of non-Magyar elements was used by the kings, the nobility, and the Church for their diverse and often selfish reasons. The goals could be political, economic, or military, and to achieve these aims the various ethnic groups could be used or even abused by the ruling classes. Nor was there a conscious policy of creating a multiethnic state in the Carpathian Basin. The fact that it did develop is the result of forces that were not willfully set into motion. Furthermore, there is no indication that there were efforts made by any segment of society to assimilate the non-Magyar elements by force. Fifteenth-century people just did not think in these terms. Depending on such factors as geography, social mobility, marriage, or even religious preference, certain non-Magyars became assimilated into the majority population, but at the same time some Hungarians became Slovaks or Germans in speech and customs.

In looking at late-medieval Hungary, do we detect the seeds of future ethnic conflict? Again, the answer is negative. Multiethnic states were common in the fifteenth century and they are common even today. That this particular state eventually broke up is due to many factors but was certainly not inevitable. If we look upon the multiplicity of causes that brought about the destruction of this multiethnic state, there can be no doubt that the curse of blind, excessive nationalism is among the most obvious, and unfortunately its bitter fruits are still with us today.

Notes

1. Jenő Szűcs, *Nemzet és történelem: tanulmányok* [Nation and History: Studies] (Budapest, 1974), pp. 28–29.

2. The division into four "nations" at Vienna occurred already with the first foundation under Archduke Rudolf IV in 1365. The reorganization of the university by Albert in 1389 resulted in the division described above. See Hastings Rashdall, *The Universities of Europe in the Middle Ages,* ed. F. M. Powicke and A. B. Emden, vol. 2 (London: Oxford University Press, 1958), pp. 241–42; Rudolf Kink, *Geschichte der kaiserlichen Universität zu Wien,* vol. 2 (Vienna, 1854), p. 51.

3. Károly Schrauf, *A bécsi egyetem magyar nemzetének anyakönyve, 1453-1630* [The Records of the Hungarian Nation at the University of Vienna, 1453-1630] (Budapest, 1902), p. 68.

4. The subsequent career of Altenberg is interesting, since he represents a new trend in fifteenth-century society. After completion of his studies at Vienna, where he received a bachelor's degree in 1454 and was *magister artium* in 1456, he returned to Transylvania and subsequently became mayor of Szeben, Schrauf, op. cit., pp. 39–68; Sándor Tonk, *Erdélyiek egyetemjárása a középkorban* [The University Attendance of Transylvanians in the Middle Ages] (Bucharest, 1979), pp. 335–36, no. 2310. In 1481 he prepared a law book of considerable importance. Gábor Balás, *Erdély jókora jogtörténete 1540-ig* [Transylvanian Legal History to 1540] (Budapest, 1977), p. 65.

5. Erik Molnár, *A magyar társadalom története az Árpádkortól Mohácsig* [Hungarian Society from the Period of the Árpáds to Mohács] (Budapest, 1949), p. 255.

6. István Szabó, "Magyarország népessége a 1330-as és az 1526-os évek között" [The Population of Hungary between 1330 and 1526], in *Magyarország történeti demo-*

gráfiája: Magyarország népessége a honfoglalástól 1949-ig [Historical Demography of Hungary: Hungary's Population from the Conquest to 1949], ed. József Kovacsics (Budapest, 1963), pp. 91–92.

7. György Acsádi, "Történeti statisztikai táblázatok" [Tables of Historical Statistics], *A történeti statisztika forrásai* [The Sources of Historical Statistics], ed. József Kovacsics (Budapest, 1957), p. 370.

8. First published at Pozsony (Pressburg, Bratislava) in 1735. Critical edition prepared by Kálmán Eperjessy and László Juhász, *Nicolaus Olahus: Hungaria-Athila* [Bibliotheca scriptorum medii recentisque aevorum] (Budapest, 1938), pp. 1–34.

9. "Totius huius Hungariae regnum continet in se nostro hoc tempore diversas nationes, Hungaros, Alemanos, Bohemos, Sclavos, Croatos, Saxones, Siculos, Valahos, Rascianos, Cumanos, Iaziges, Ruthenos et iam postremo Turcas. . . ." Ibid., pp. 33–34.

10. Elemér Mályusz, "A Magyarság és a nemzetiségek Mohács elött" [The Magyars and the nationalities before the Battle of Mohács] *Magyar müvelődéstörténet: Magyar Renaissance* [The Cultural History of Hungary: Hungarian Renaissance], ed. Sándor Domanovszky, vol. 2 (Budapest, 1940), p. 107.

11. The records cover only forty-three counties, with some lacunae. The areas of Transylvania and Croatia-Slavonia were not covered by the records, which have been edited by Johann Christian von Engel, *Geschichte des ungarischen Reichs und seiner Nebenländer,* vol. 1 (Halle, 1797), pp. 17–181. Original at National Széchenyi Library, Budapest, Cod. Lat. medii aevi no. 411.

12. Mályusz, op. cit.

13. The most detailed description of settlements in the fifteenth century are found in the work of Dezső Csánki, *Magyarország történelmi földrajza a Hunyadiak korában* [The Historical Geography of Hungary in the Age of the Hunyadis] (Budapest, 1890-1913), Szatmár and Szabolcs counties at the mouth of the Szamos, 1:463–502, 503–44; Bács, Baranya, and Bodrog counties, 2:131–83, 184–227, 451–566; Tolna county, 3:397–481.

14. Antal Fekete Nagy, "A település képe" [A View of the Settlements], *Magyar müvelődéstörténet,* vol. 2, pp. 129–31; also Ferenc Maksay, *A magyar falu középkori településrendje* [The Settlement Patterns of the Medieval Hungarian Village] (Budapest, 1971), pp. 23–24, 37–48.

15. Mályusz, op. cit., p. 118.

16. Ibid., p. 116.

17. *A történeti statisztika forrásai,* Table 8a, p. 389.

18. Mályusz, op. cit., p. 123; see also Benedek Jancsó, *Erdély története* [The History of Transylvania] (Kolozsvár, 1931), p. 177. According to the humanist Archbishop of Esztergom Antal Verancsics (1504-73), the population of Transylvania in the sixteenth century was one-fourth Rumanian. See *Verancsics Antal összes munkái* [The Complete Works of Antal Verancsics], ed. László Szalay and Gusztáv Wenzel, vol. 6 (Budapest, 1873), p. 109.

19. Erik Fügedi, *A 15. századi magyar arisztokrácia mobilitása* [The Social Mobility of Hungarian Aristocracy in the 15th Century] (Budapest, 1970), pp. 111–12, 134–35, 167.

20. The best summary of the whole question of the origins of the Hunyadi family is provided by Lajos Elekes, *Hunyadi* (Budapest, 1952), pp. 71–75. A charming but unsubstantiated tale, circulated since the sixteenth century, is that Hunyadi was the illegitimate son of King Sigismund of Luxembourg and thus not of Rumanian origin. See Gáspár Heltai, *Chronica az Magyarocnac dolgairol* [Chronicle Concerning the Deeds of the Hungarians] (Kolozsvár, 1575; facsimile ed., Budapest, 1973), pp. 80–82.

21. László Makkai, "Erdély népei a középkorban" [The Peoples of Transylvania

in the Middle Ages], *Magyarok és Románok* [Hungarians and Rumanians], ed. József Déer and László Gáldi (Budapest, 1943), 1:407–10.

22. Péter Ratkos "A szlovák nemzetiség fejlődése a 16. század végéig" [The Development of Slovak Nationality to the 16th Century], *Nemzetiség a feudalizmus korában* [Nationality in the Age of Feudalism] (Budapest, 1972), pp. 108–9.

23. See L. S. Domonkos, "János Vitéz: The Father of Hungarian Humanism (1408-72)" *The New Hungarian Quarterly,* 20 (1979): 142.

24. Jenő Szűcs, "Das Städtewesen in Ungarn im 15–17. Jahrhundert" *La renaissance et la reformation en Pologne et en Hongrie* [Studia Historica, 53], (Budapest, 1963), pp. 97–101.

25. *Corpus Juris Hungarici* (Budapest, 1899) Decretum VII, Articulus 3, p. 708.

26. Vera Bácskai, *Magyar mezővárosok a XV. században,* [Hungarian Market Towns in the Fifteenth Century] (Budapest, 1965), p. 14.

27. Jenő Szűcs, *Városok és kézművesség a XV. századi Magyarországon* [Cities and Craftmanship in 15th Century Hungary] (Budapest, 1955), p. 98.

28. Bácskai, op. cit., p. 61.

29. István Szabó, *A falurendszer kialakulása Magyarországon, X-XV. század* [The Development of the Village System in Hungary, 10th-15th Centuries] (Budapest, 1966), pp. 148–83.

30. András Kubinyi, "A főváros története a magyar és német elem egyenjogusításától a németek kiűzéséig" [The History of the Capital from the Time of Legal Equality Between Magyars and Germans to the Expulsion of the Germans], *Budapest Története* [The History of Budapest], vol. 2 (Budapest, 1973), p. 149.

31. Béla Iványi, "Das Deutschtum der Stadt Eperies im Mittelalter" *Südost-Forschungen* (1941), pp. 378–79.

32. András Kubinyi, "Buda és testvérvárosai az 1439-es tanácsválasztási reformig" [Buda and its Sister Cities until the Council Election Reform of 1439], *Budapest Története,* 2:71–72.

33. See Karl Mollay, *Das Ofner Stadtrecht. Eine deutschsprächige Rechtssammlung des 15. Jahrhundrets aus Ungarn* [Monumenta Historica Budapestinensia, I] (Budapest, 1959).

34. The Székelys were obligated by law to provide the king with roasted oxen at the time of coronation as a gift and not as a form of taxation. See Georgius Fejér, *Codex diplomaticus Hungariae ecclesiasticus et civilis,* vol. 10, part 2 (Buda, 1834), p. 510.

35. Károly Szabó, *A régi székelység* [The Ancient Székelys] (Budapest, 1890), pp. 131-32; Balás, op. cit., pp. 37-39.

36. Károly Szabó and Lajos Szadeczky, eds., *Székely oklevéltár* [Székely Chartulary], vol. 1 (Kolozsvár, 1872), p. 220.

37. For the text of the charter of privileges see Franz Zimmerman and Karl Werner, eds., *Urkundenbuch zur Geschichte der Deutschen in Siebenbürgen,* vol. 1 (Hermannstadt, 1892), pp. 32–34.

38. Balás, op. cit., p. 61.

39. Zimmerman and Werner, op. cit., vol. 4, p. 493.

40. This was called *census St. Martini.* See Ákos Timón, *Magyar alkotmány és jogtörténet* [Hungarian Constitutional and Legal History] (Budapest, 1906), p. 701.

41. Eudoxiu Hurmuzaki, ed., *Documente privitoare la istoria românilor* [Documents for the History of the Rumanians], vol. 2, part 2 (Bucharest, 1890), p. 154.

42. See G. Müller, *Die Graven des Siebenbürger Sachenlandes* (Hermannstadt, 1931), pp. 13–27.

43. This expression was increasingly used from the middle of the fifteenth century. See Timón, op. cit., p. 694, and n. 3.

44. Fejér, op. cit., vol. 5, part 1, p. 132.

45. Iványi, op. cit., pp. 365-66.

46. Béla Iványi, *Bártfa szabad királyi város levéltára, 1319-1526* [The Archives of the Free Royal City of Bártfa 1319-1526] (Budapest, 1910, no. 2397. See also Elemér Mályusz, "Geschichte des Bürgertums in Ungarn," *Vierteljahrschrift für Sozial und Wirtschaftsgeschichte,* 20 (1928): 384–85.

47. Branislav Varsik, "Sozial und Nationalitätenkampfe in den Städten der Slowakei im Mittelalter" *Zbornik filozofickej fakulty university Komenskeho* [Annals of the Philosophy Faculty of the Comnenian University] (Bratislava, 1965), p. 141; Ratkos, op. cit., pp. 109–11.

48. For fifteenth century letters and charters from the city Sopron see Jenő Házi, *Sopron szabad királyi város története; oklevelek és levelek* [The History of the Royal Free City of Sopron: Charters and Letters], vols. 2–6 (Sopron, 1923–28).

49. Fejér, op. cit., vol. 4, part 2, p. 132. See also A. Huscava, *Najstarsie vysady mesta Trnavy* [The Oldest Statutes of the City of Nagyszombat] (Trnava, 1933), p. 43.

50. Fritz Valjavec, *Geschichte der deutschen Kulturbeziehungen zu Südosteuropa: Mittelalter* [Südosteuropäische Arbeiten, 41] (München, 1953), pp. 246–47.

51. Grete Lang, "Die Nationalitätenkämpfe in Klausenburg im ausgehenden Mittelalter" (Diss., München, 1941).

52. See the study of Vera Zimányi, *A Rohonc-Szalonaki uradalom és jobbágysága a xvi-xvii. században* [The Estate of Rohonc-Szalonak (Gűssing) and its Serfs in the 16th and 17th Centuries] (Budapest, 1968), pp. 53–59. See also Mályusz, "Magyarság és a nemzetiségek," pp. 110–12.

53. *Documenta historiam Valachorum in Hungaria illustrantia,* ed. Imre Lukinich, Lászlo Gáldi, Antal Fekete Nagy and László Makkai (Budapest, 1941), pp. 20, 22.

54. István Kniezsa, "Keletmagyarország helynevei" [The Place Names of Eastern Hungary], *Magyarok és Románok,* pp. 116–65, gives a detailed analysis of this problem.

55. *Documenta historiam Valachorum,* pp. 38–41.

56. László Makkai, "Az erdélyi románok a középkori magyar oklevelekben" [Transylvanian Rumanians in Medieval Hungarian Charters], *Erdélyi Muzeum* (Kolozsvár, 1943), p. 36. Of the nine settlements where Rumanians are found only three were inhabited by them exclusively. In the other six they lived alongside Hungarians.

57. Kniezsa, op. cit., table, p. 158. Recent efforts to show the presence of Vlachs in Szatmár County as early as the eleventh century are unconvincing: Francisc Pall, "Românii din părţile Satmarene (Tinutul Mediaş) în lumina unor ducumente din 1377" [Rumanians in the region of Megyes (County of Szatmár) in the Light of some Documents from 1377], *Anuarul Institutului de Istorie din Cluj* [Yearbook of the Institute for History at Cluj], vol. 12 (Cluj, 1969), pp. 34–35.

58. For the institution of the *kenéz* see Ion Bogdan, "Despre cnejii Românii [Concerning the Rumanian kenéz], *Analele Academia Romîne,* Memoriile Sect. Istorie, ser. 2, vol. 26 (Bucharest, 1903), p. 47. See also the study of Maria Holban, "Marturii asupră rolului cnezilor de pe marile domenii din Banat in doua jumatate in secolului al XIV-lea" [Some Charters Touching on the Role of *Knez* in the Economy of Great Estates in the Banat During the Second Half of the 15th Century], *Studii şi materiale de istorie medie,* ed. Barbu T. Cîmpina, vol. 2 (Bucharest, 1957), pp. 407–20.

59. György Székely, "Az erdélyi románok feudalizálódása" [The Feudalization of the Rumanians in Transylvania], *Tanulmányok a parasztság történetéhez Magyarországon*

a 14. században [Studies Concerning the History of Peasantry in Hungary during the 14th Century] (Budapest, 1953), pp. 246–47.

60. Concerning the events of 1437 see the valuable article of Joseph Held, "The Peasant Revolt of Bábolna, 1437-1438," *Slavic Review* 36 (1977): 25–38.

61. See Stefan Lupsa, *Catolicismul şi românii din Ardeal şi Ungaria pîna la anul 1556* [Catholicism and the Rumanians in Transylvania and Hungary until 1556] (Bucharest, 1929). See also István Juhász, "A középkori nyugati misszió és a románság" [Medieval Westward Mission and the Rumanians], *Az Erdélyi Tudományos Intézet Évkönyve* [Yearbook of the Transylvanian Institute of Scholarship] (Kolozsvár, 1943), pp. 182–86.

62. The studies of György Győrffy throw some light upon the name and location of Slavic settlements from the tenth to the fourteenth century. Győrffy found indications of Slavic inhabitants almost everywhere. See *Az Árpád-kori Magyarország történeti földrajza* [Historical Geography of Hungary in the Age of the Árpád Dynasty], vol. 1 (Budapest, 1963), pp. 45, 165, 193, 208, 249–50, 423, 494, 527, 553, 571, 589, 606, 736, 835–36, 885.

63. A good example of this development can be seen in the county of Hont through which the river Ipoly flows. See István Bakács, *Hont vármegye Mohács előtt* [The County of Hont Before Mohács] (Budapest, 1971), pp. 31–34.

64. Branislav Varsik, "K socialnym a narodnostym bojom v mestach no Slavensku v stredoveku" [Concerning the Social and Nationality Conflict in the Middle Ages], *Slovaci a ich narodyn vyvin* [Slovaks and their National Development] (Bratislava, 1966), pp. 64–66.

65. Mályusz, "Magyarság és nemzetiségek," p. 117.

66. On the early society of Máramaros see Vilmos Bélay, *Máramaros vármegye társadalma és nemzetiségei* [The Social Structure and Nationalities of Máramaros County] (Budapest, 1943), p. 120ff.

67. Makkai, "Erdély népei a középkorban," pp. 394–98; Mályusz, "Középkori magyar nemzetiségi politika," p. 421.

68. Miklós Kring, "Kun és jász társadalomelemek a középkorban" [Cuman and Jazig Social Elements in the Middle Ages], *Századok* [Centuries] 66 (1932), p. 39ff.

Reformation Literature and the National Consciousness of Transylvanian Hungarians, Saxons, and Rumanians

LOUIS J. ELTETO

In 1519, Transylvanian merchants returning from the Leipzig Fair arrived in their native Hermannstadt (Nagyszeben, Sibiu) laden with printed Lutheran literature. With this they introduced the Reformation[1] into the kingdom of Hungary.[2]

That the ideas of Luther spread rapidly in Hungary before the Battle of Mohács (1526) is well-known. Less widely known is that they did so almost exclusively among Hungary's ethnic Germans. Two factors have caused this misunderstanding. First of all, most standard works on Hungarian history have been histories of Hungary, not of the Hungarians alone; secondly, the histories of the various denominations, such as the Lutherans, the Reformed, and the Unitarians, tended to pay little heed to the question of ethnicity during these preformative years. Yet both the geographic distribution and the list of names of the earliest reformers indicate clearly that the movement was, in the beginning, restricted to the Saxons in eastern Hungary (Transylvania) and to German settlements in the northern mining districts of the country. In addition, there was some early interest in the new teachings elsewhere in the towns of Hungary, as in Sopron (Ödenburg), Kassa (Kaschau, Košice), and Buda (Ofen), which were not strictly German but nonetheless possessed strong German congregations.[3]

The Hungarian Catholic church feared the spread of this "dangerous heresy." Along with the nobility, the church had been a unifying force in the Kingdom, perhaps the most important unifying force. Both hierarchies were, before Mohács, largely Hungarian, even though traditionally ethnic origin had not been a barrier to upward mobility within its ranks. Szalkai, Perényi, Szathmáry, Szegedi, and Bornemissza were the names one found among the Catholic eminent of the era. As for the nobility, they had sworn, as early as 1505 at the Congress of Rákos, to elect only a Hungarian for a king the next time they had a choice.

Before Mohács, the battle lines in the coming fight for the Reformation were clearly drawn between two ethnic groupings: the Hungarian establishment on the one hand, and the German on the other. One must not forget that the Germans also had a powerful establishment in Hungary, particularly the Saxons on their own territory. Provided from the time of their settlement with constitutional guarantees, they enjoyed broad political autonomy. In the ecclesiastic sphere, they were ultimately subjected to the Hungarian hierarchy, but even in this they had a high degree of local and regional freedom.

The battle was to be fought with laws and decrees on the one hand and propaganda on the other. The Parliamentary Acts of 1523, 1524, and 1525 were surprisingly harsh and made adherence to the new heresy a capital offense. In fact, the laws were never enforced. The government contented itself with staging book-burnings in the Saxon towns, with issuing warnings and appointing investigating committees.[4] The priesthood was ordered to preach against the new doctrines, and both sides resorted to pamphleteering.

In the latter, the Germans initially proved superior. Printing was a German craft, which was protected by the guilds, and there was at first not a single press operating in Hungary. (King Mátyás had had one established in Buda by a German named Andreas Hess, but the enterprise had proved short-lived.) The German reformers had Wittenberg to draw on for inspiration and for ammunition. But when Werbőczy, Hungary's leading politician, wanted to publish a pamphlet against the Lutherans, he had to go to Vienna to have it produced and could have it done only in Latin, at that. The first work printed in Hungarian came out after the Battle of Mohács, in Krakow, which was a nest of the Reformation. Only in 1536 was Hungarian typesetting established in Vienna. The first Catholic press in Hungary had to wait until 1577 for its founding, after the first phase of the spiritual war had been lost.[5]

It is difficult to understand why the Catholic side failed to grasp the importance of the printed word until the time of the Counter-Reformation. It is sufficient to say that the reason was complex and centered on the organization of the establishment, which was used to dealing with the people through a long and strict chain of command whose final link was the parish priest. Letters and hand copying were what the apparatus was set up to do, and to do well. The Roman church resisted innovation not only in the doctrinal sphere, but also in the technical.

Not that the Protestant side was engaging in mass propaganda. It is impossible even to estimate how many, or how few, of the public could read in sixteenth-century Hungary. There were church schools here and there, but it would be a mistake to think of a public accessible to print on either side around 1525. Yet the Lutheran propaganda was readily available to those who were important, which was primarily the clergy, and it was cheap, uniform, and rapidly distributable. Every parish priest who so desired could obtain his own booklets to read time and again in his native tongue, while the manuscripts, which his superiors may or may not have sent, were still in Latin. The psychological advantage was important for the Protestants, and the new teachings, often clothed in poetry, were more readily communicable by word of mouth than the old Latin texts. The vitality and the simple, classic elegance of many of the contemporary Lutheran works were outstanding, and half of Luther's battle was won by the warmth and the beauty of his language.

Had the political collapse of the Hungarian kingdom not come about in 1526, there would have been two likely outcomes to the ecclesiastic struggle: either the reestablishment of a unified Roman church in Hungary, which could have only been accomplished through force, perhaps with additional concessions to the German groupings, or the coexistence of a majority Hungarian Catholic church and a German Protestant church, with some geographic overlapping between them in certain areas. Evidence does not exist to suggest the viability of a third alternative: that of a purely Protestant Hungary split into two ethnic churches, much less unified into one organization.

But Mohács did come, and so did the Turks. The central authority of both the church and the state were weakened and almost destroyed. Within six months of the devastating fight, Hungary had been "blessed" with two kings and split into two factions: those of King János, the former viceroy of Transylvania, and of Ferdinand Habsburg. János ruled the East and Ferdinand the West, while the Sultan maintained a decisive presence in the central South. As to which side was right and which wrong, which loyal and which traitor, Hungarian historiography will perhaps never decide. The Ferdinand faction looked for a strong German alliance based on religious connections; János chose a modus vivendi with the Turk and counted on French support. The Hungarian division of the sixteenth century was a forerunner of the European split 100 years later, during the Thirty Years' War.

A frequently overlooked fact has been that while at first both Hungarian factions remained loyal to the Catholic faith, the church establishment itself stood overwhelmingly on the side of Ferdinand. Thus Eastern Hungary, out of which the Transylvanian Principality was to evolve, suddenly emerged as a Catholic country with a large German minority of Protestant sympathizers, and it was cut off from the central church organization. King János, although excommunicated, never became a Protestant; nevertheless, it was in his realm, and in the ranks of his followers, that Protestantism started to grow among Hungarians. It did not, however, develop along German lines.

The major appeal of the Protestant movement was its stress on the individual route to salvation and its emphasis on the use of the vernacular in teaching, preaching, and ceremonies. This was the first element that the Hungarians of the East learned from the German Protestants. And in doing so they also learned how to use the press for spreading their message.

At first they relied on the press abroad. The first religious work to be printed there in Hungarian was Benedek Komjáti's translation of the Epistles of Saint Paul (1533), followed rapidly by a Hungarian edition of the Lexicon of Murmellius. Imre Ozorai's *De Christo et eius Ecclesia,* a Hungarian work in spite of the title, was the first militantly Protestant argument (1535). István Gálszécsy published a hymnal and a catechism in Krakow in 1536. In that year, the aristocrat Tamás Nádasdy bought a press for János Sylvester, a very learned man and himself a printer, who translated and published the New Testament. Among other things, Sylvester also wrote and printed a famous grammar, his *Grammatica Hungaro-Latina,* the first contrastive work on Latin and Hungarian. Krakow and Wittenberg kept pouring forth new Hungarian works well into the middle of the century, when Hungarian presses finally became operational at Kolozsvár (Klausenburg, Cluj), between 1550 and 1600, and Debrecen, from 1561 in particular, with temporary establishments working elsewhere.

Aside from the works mentioned, there were also published other partial Bible translations, including Gábor Pesti's and Gáspár Heltai's; the first complete version to see print was Gáspár Károli's, in 1590. There were also produced psalters and hymnals (Gálszécsy, Bornemissza, Benczédi); religious lyrics and texts as parts of collections (Szkhárosi-Horváth, Batizi, Sztárai); epics and chronicles (Tinódi, Farkas, Benczédi); catechisms and apologetic works (Dévai, Batizi, Gálszécsy, Kálmáncsehi, Méliusz, Dávid); linguistic works (Dévai, Sylvester, Benczédi); and the first beginnings of the theological school drama (Sztárai). Bálint Balassi, one of Hungary's greatest poets ever, worked during this era. It was as if the floodgates had been opened suddenly. János Horváth, the great scholar of sixteenth-century Hungarian letters, has associated well over 100 writers of greater or lesser achievement with the Hungarian Reformation.[6] Works by writers of various religious conviction, from Erasmian Catholics and Lutherans to the strictest Calvinists and the most radical Anti-Trinitarians and Judaizers, appeared. In the early period, most writers were not Transylvanians, though loyal to King János and his cause. Later, the focus of literary activity shifted to Transylvania, where Protestantism, divided on both ethnic and denominational lines, evolved into powerful, new, established churches.

The Hungarian Reformation was not a progressive theological evolution from Catholicism through Lutheranism to Unitarianism and Calvinism, with the latter becoming dominant, but the result of a dynamic political dialectic process, to which ethnic divisions perhaps provide the ultimate key. Accordingly, the Lutheranism of Hungary's German minority became the antithesis of Hungarian Catholicism, while Hungarian Calvinism and Unitarianism formed the antithesis to both German Lutheranism and to the politically pro-German and German-dominated Catholicism of the West. Whatever the merits of this view, the literary evidence lends overwhelming support to the contention that it was the process of the Reformation that transformed the Hungarian-speaking population of the Hungarian kingdom, including that part that became the state of Transylvania, into a self-conscious nation. The very wealth of the literature printed in Hungarian in that era demonstrates, on the other hand, that this feverish activity in Hungarian letters was both a cause and an effect in the process.

The literature must have had an enormous effect. Almost all of it was meant to be ab ovo utilitarian, in the service of religion, to be sure, but of a religion that was now Hungarian in practice. There are strong indications, too, that the practical theology of the Hungarian churches of the time placed greater emphasis on Old Testamental parallels than on abstract debates regarding the meaning of the sacraments. The Psalms, for instance, sung in beautiful Hungarian renditions, became the main element of the Hungarian order of worship for obvious reasons, and the wrath of God, in the form of the Turk, was seen as divine punishment of the collective for which only the collective could atone. These symbols are very much present in the literature of the age, and they have remained important components of Hungarian religious and secular literature, indeed of the national psyche, to the present day.

Transylvania became politically separate from the Hungarian kingdom in the midst of the Reformation, around the middle of the sixteenth century. It became a state unto itself, with a particular political structure, its own legal system, its own history. But this separateness of history does not mean that Hungarian Transylvanians ever became Transylvanians in their national identity. The Hungarians and the Székelys, who were a Hungarian caste regardless of their origins, remained just as much Hungarians as if the kingdom had never collapsed, but were now more aware than ever of Hungarian nationhood. A similar statement, however, cannot be made about Transylvania's two other major ethnic groups, the Saxons and the Rumanians.

Until the Reformation, the Saxons were an autonomous body politic with their own language, which was a German dialect very different from any of the various standard German languages of the era, and were defined as a nation by the Hungarian Constitution. They possessed special privileges as a separate caste and class. In spite of occasional disagreement and strife, they were loyal subjects and supporters of the Hungarian crown, but not of the Hungarians per se. The distinction is important. As long as the Hungarian kingdom stood unified, they were members of it in their very Saxonhood. But the simultaneous collapse of Hungary and the coming of the Reformation awakened in them an awareness of also being Germans. In fact, this dual identity and loyalty has characterized Transylvania's Saxons until our own age, in which the backbone of their flourishing society became broken. Rightfully proud of their own achievements, history, and culture, they have remained nevertheless dependent upon the main German body politic since the Reformation, and their fortunes have risen and fallen along with those of Austria and Germany. Their importation of German culture from the West, in finished form, produced in them a paradox through the centuries: it elevated the Saxons in many ways above the Hungarians and the Rumanians, but on the other hand it stifled their own creativity. Saxon men of learning had abounded before the Reformation, but then they were also part of a universal European culture. Their numbers continued to be legion afterward, particularly in their clergy, but they became isolated. The tragedy of the Saxons was that they were collectively not strong enough to go it alone nor to become integrated into the broader German world, in which they remained but objects of curiosity. In literature, for example, they were never able to approach the Swiss, who could be considered a parallel in many ways. The Swiss were never really out of the German mainstream; the Saxons were.

During the Reformation, the Saxons took the initiative. Their crowning achievement became, however, not the establishment of an independent religion, nor even of a new literature. Instead, the Saxons built a magnificent church establishment, which was an organization of their own and served them well in protecting their separateness and preserving their identity until the coming of the current state religion, Rumanian Marxism-Leninism.

The names of many Saxon preachers from those early years could be listed, but to look for parallels among the 100 or so Hungarian writers would be fruitless for the *Sachsenland.* They are to be sought in Germany, not here. Yet there were exceptions: first and foremost that of the Saxon prophet, the "Luther of Transylvania," Johannes Honter or simply Honterus.

Honterus appeared in Kronstadt (Brassó, Braşov) in 1533, a man, in the words of G.D. Teutsch, the eminent historian of the Saxons, "who became the foundation and the rock of the new federation, the champion of God, through whom the Lord founded His Church here, a fountain from which flowed new moral and religious life for many generations."[7] His youth has been hidden in legend. Allegedly born in 1498, the son of a Saxon tanner named Georg Grass, it is believed that he studied extensively in Krakow, in Wittenberg, and in Basel. We know that he had indeed studied in Vienna, that he spent at least some time in Krakow, and that he was a very learned man by the time of his return. It is also a fact that he had learned a craft along the way that would now stand him in good stead: the craft of printing. Almost overnight he transformed Kronstadt into a religious and cultural center by establishing a press and a school there. A steady stream of Lutheran publications flowed from Kronstadt from then on, and soon Honterus also began to preach. The result of his efforts was the establishment of the Saxon Evangelical church, a church for which he provided both the theological and the organizational foundation in his most famous work, the *Kirchenordnung,* issued in 1542 for the Burzenland (Barcaság—a region around Kronstadt), then again for all Saxon churches in 1547, under the title *Kirchenordnung aller Deutschen in Siebenbuergen* (Order of Worship for all Germans in Transylvania). We duly note the words "aller Deutschen"—of all *Germans.* "But now the time is come," he states, "in which the Lord will awaken a new people unto himself; therefore let him who has ears to hear, hear."[8] And with this message the Saxons did become a new *Volk,* reborn as Germans in their native Transylvania and an example to others in thrift, diligence, learning, and virtue. A long succession of scholarly ecclesiastics in Kronstadt and Hermannstadt followed Honterus. They were outstanding citizens, judges, teachers, and preachers who formed a line uninterrupted until the chauvinism of our era, including the German chauvinism of the Saxons themselves, destroyed this gifted and honest people. In the sixteenth century, names of such brilliant men as Thomas Bomel, Matthias Fronius, Paul Kerzius, Simon Massa, and Michael Siegler can also be mentioned. All were intellectual leaders of their *Volk;* yet they do not belong, strictly speaking, in the field of letters. There were only three poets in this era: Hieronymus Ostermeyer of Grosscheuern (Nagycsűr, Şura Mare), and Andreas and Paul Scherer of Hermannstadt. Of them, even G.D. Teutsch, who writes only in superlatives of his Saxons, has simply said that Ostermeyer was known for his truth, simplicity, and sincerity, and that he wrote in German; and that the Scherers were not unworthy to stand at his side.[9] Germany had already stilled the muses in the *Sachsenland*.

The story of the Saxons cannot be, in this connection, complete without a footnote: Ferenc Dávid, the founder of the Unitarian church among the Hungarians of Transylvania, and Gáspár Heltai, Kolozsvár's outstanding printer, translator, and writer, who very nearly provided a complete Bible for the Hungarians, were both Saxons in origin. The former was that only on his paternal side, while the latter's mother and father were both Saxons. Heltai did not even start to learn Hungarian until his middle years but learned it so well that he set a standard for all to emulate. To his dying day, he called himself a Saxon, claiming that he had learned Hungarian and started to print Hungarian books only to prove he was not prejudiced against Hungarians. Nevertheless, his Saxon brethren considered him a traitor. Dávid, for his part, had been a Saxon priest and bishop before being expelled from Honter's church for his radical views and, no doubt, for his Hungarian and international sympathies. Let them be cases in point: not only did nationality usually define religion in Protestant Transylvania, but religion also came to define nationality.

But the best example of religion determining nationality is the case of the Rumanians of Transylvania.

Whether Rumanians were present in Transylvania in the year 500 or the year 1000 does not matter except in the context of political myth. They were certainly present by the year 1500. Though no one has accurate statistics, they seem to have accounted for between one-third and one-half of Transylvania's population, depending on how Transylvania is defined. Yet, politically as well as socially, they remained or were considered to be a foreign element by Hungarians and Saxons alike. The reason has far less to do with national or linguistic prejudices or even with the class struggle than Rumanian scholars of yesteryear or of the present attempt to portray. To refute these views, let it suffice for now to say that if it is true, as the Rumanians claim, that the Hunyadis were Rumanian, then even the highest office in the Kingdom of Hungary was open to them, provided they became Roman Catholics. For ethnicity meant very little or nothing before the Reformation. What did matter was religious affiliation.

The Rumanians were staunch adherents of the Byzantine or East Roman faith. The very name, Rumanian, is originally a religious appellation, not a national one. The Turks still call the Greeks and other members of the Byzantine church in the Balkans *rumlar,* or Romans. But so distant, so strange was this faith to the Western tradition that by the time of the Reformation its followers were often not even considered Christians by either the Catholics or the Protestants. It is striking that when Transylvanian references were made during this period to Rumanians as members of a religious group, they were likely to be called non-Christians, and efforts to missionize them were formulated in terms of making Christians of them.[10]

The attempt was made and overall it was a failure. Its story belongs chiefly to the seventeenth century, and to the annals of church history and religious legislation. The intent may have been in part to swell the ranks of the new denominations, but the aim was not to cause the Rumanians to give up their language and ethnicity. On the contrary, it was meant to bring the Word of God to these "heathen" in their own tongue and to create a printed medium for them, where none had been before.

The first step in this direction was undertaken in Hermannstadt, when a Rumanian catechism was printed, in 1544, at the expense of the city.[11] The next reference is also from a Saxon source. Simon Massa wrote of the year 1559: "In this year, on March 12, Johannes Benkner, Judge of Kronstadt, together with the other senators, reformed the church of the Rumanians, and obligated them to teach the doctrines of the catechism." The most famous work was done by a Rumanian convert named Coresi. In 1560 and 1561, he translated and printed the four Gospels, in Kronstadt, and the work was commissioned by the same Johannes Benkner. By about 1563, the rest of the New Testament had seen print, again through Coresi's effort, and probably with Saxon financing. Only second in importance to the Bible translations was a volume containing an exegesis and an order of worship. Nothing specific about its origins has been found, except that it was set in the same type used by Coresi around 1561. The work reveals some parallels with Heltai's first *Agenda;* it also displays some influence of Hungarian in its vocabulary, e.g., *taroasă* for *terhes, ocă* for *oka, otalmazui* for *oltalmazni, nebuntetuit* for *nem-büntetett (büntetlen).* The conclusion of Istvan Juhász, a historian of the Reformed church, was that the anonymous author of this in many ways original creation must have been a Rumanian priest well versed in the Gospels, with Protestant convictions and with enough knowledge of Hungarian to use Hungarian texts as a reference.[12]

That is the extent of the printed Protestant literature in Rumanian of which we know from the period in question. Did it have an effect, however? Did it have an impact on the development of Rumanian national consciousness? This question is difficult to answer. Judging from the very lukewarm reception and temporary spread of the Reformation among the Rumanian congregations, even in later years, when the Transylvanian state made the Rumanian mission its official objective and a complete Rumanian Bible was commissioned by Gábor Bethlen and finally issued under György Rákóczi I, in 1648, the answer seems to be no. In general, the Rumanian priesthood and their flock remained loyal to their Byzantine faith and rites, the language of which continued to be Old Slavic and Greek. Yet the rejection of the Reformation by Transylvania's Rumanians was just as decisive in shaping the destiny of their nation as its acceptance was fateful in molding the future of the Hungarians and of the Saxons.

Notes

1. Though definitions of the Reformation in Hungary vary, the author uses the term to mean only the period 1519–71, to the time the Roman Catholic István Báthori became the ruler of Transylvania.

2. G.D. Teutsch, *Geschichte der Siebenbürger Sachsen für das săchsische Volk* [History of the Transylvanian Saxons for the Saxon People], ed. Friedrich Teutsch, vol. 1, *Von den ăltesten Zeiten bis 1699* [From the Origins to 1699] (Hermannstadt: W. Krafft, 1925), p. 246.

3. For a further discussion of this question, see Louis J. Elteto, "The Reformation in Transylvania," *Itt-Ott*, 9, no. 2 (1977): 22–27.

4. Ibid.

5. János Horváth, *A reformáció jegyében* [Under the Sign of the Reformation], 2d ed. (Budapest: Gondolat, 1957), gives an excellent overview of Hungarian publishing in this early period.

6. Horváth, op. cit.

7. Teutsch, p. 253. All translations by author.

8. Quoted by Teutsch, p. 255.

9. Teutsch, p. 325.

10. See for example the resolution of the 1554 Diet of Marosvásárhely (Tîrgu-Mureş, Neumarkt), according to which a Christian serf could be condemned only on testimony of seven witnesses, whereas for a Rumanian three witnesses were enough. Cited in István Juhász, *A reformáció az erdélyi románok között* [The Reformation Among Transylvanian Rumanians] (Kolozsvár: Református Theologia, 1940), p. 24, from *Monumenta comitalia regni Transylvaniae* [County Documents of the Kingdom of Transylvania], vol. 1, 520, and Eudoxiu Hurmuzaki, *Documenta privitoare la istoria Românilor* [Documents Pertaining to the History of the Rumanians], vol. 2, part 5, p. 206, document no. 90, ed. Ovidiu Denuşianu (Bucharest: 1897). Juhász also refers (p. 80) to a letter of "Bishop György," placed in charge of the Rumanian mission by the Diet of 1566, in which the phrase "ide fele sok keresztyén oláh pap vagyon" (hereabouts there are many Christian Vlach priests) is used to contrast clergy under his jurisdiction, who were preaching in Rumanian, with the Orthodox priests who were not. Cited from Hurmuzaki, vol. 15, part 1, 627, document No. 1170, ed. Nicolae Iorga (Bucharest: 1902).

11. Juhász, p. 77.

12. Ibid., p. 75. For the history of Rumanian publishing in general during the time of the Reformation, see Juhász, chaps. 1–4.

The Transylvanian Concept of Liberty and Its Impact on the Kingdom of Hungary in the Seventeenth and Eighteenth Centuries

BÉLA K. KIRÁLY

The kingdom of Hungary under Matthias Corvinus (1458–90) was still a great power in East Central Europe, directly controlling provinces beyond its historical boundaries. By the coming of the Reformation, however, Hungary had come to mean only the traditional lands of Saint Stephen's Crown, including Transylvania, which had not yet become a separate political entity, and the associated triune kingdom of Croatia-Slavonia and Dalmatia. The medieval kings' traditional vassal territories, the banates (*bánságok*) that had served as Hungary's southern buffer, had already succumbed to the Turks.[1]

As Martin Luther was uttering his historic defiance in Worms in 1521, "I cannot and will not recant anything,"[2] Hungary's frontier troops were under Turkish siege in the fortress of Nándorfehérvár (Belgrade), which finally surrendered on August 29. The Turks thus broke through Hungary's southern line of defense. Luther's rupture with Rome and the simultaneous Ottoman penetration of Hungary's underbelly prefigured the most striking developments in early modern Hungarian history: the interdependent Ottoman conquest of central Hungary, the propagation of the new faith, the emergence of Transylvania as a separate political entity, and the complete enserfment of Hungary's peasantry, the process known to historians by Engels's term "second serfdom."[3]

Transylvania's Impact on Royal Hungary In the First Half of the Seventeenth Century

It was in the political and military interests of the Ottomans to secure the separation of Transylvania from Habsburg-controlled Hungary. In Habsburg hands, Transylvania would have served as a military base for offensives into the northern Balkans, where the main logistical and communications routes ran between Asia Minor and the Ottoman western Balkans. To deny the area to such military purposes, the Sublime Porte encouraged the creation of a separate Transylvanian state and took it under Ottoman protection once the principality had come into being. The crucial event was the fall of Buda (Ofen) to the Turks in 1541, which was followed by the gradual expansion of Ottoman control over all of central Hungary around Buda. The expansion of Ottoman control into northern Hungary (modern Slovakia) severed the regular year-round communications of Vienna and western Hungary (Transdanubia) with Transylvania. As Ottoman military power was consolidated in central Hungary, Habsburg military control over Transylvania came to an end. The military circumstances that made possible the Ottoman policy of separating Transylvania from Habsburg-ruled Hungary secured the principality's existence as an individual state for a century and a half.[4] Freed from the pressure of the Habsburg Counter-Reformation, Transylvania was now able to act on its own. A series of fundamental laws passed between 1550 and 1571 put Transylvania into the forefront of contemporary religious tolerance. In 1550, the diet of Torda (Turda, Thorenburg) granted freedom of worship to the Lutherans with the words: "Every man may hold to his God-given faith, and under no circumstances shall one religion interfere with another."[5] Another diet in 1556 secularized the incomes and property of all the Catholic dioceses. A year later, the diet of Torda declared the Lutheran church an "accepted religion" (*religio recepta*). According to this act, "Every man shall receive unmolested the religion of his choice; his church shall be free to choose its own preachers and to decide how the sacraments shall be taken; no party shall resort to vengeance or violence in competing with any other." This act enabled the Lutherans to set up their own senior church hierarchy and to hold synods. In 1564, the diet of Torda made Calvinism an "accepted religion." Finally, in 1568, the Transylvanian diet itself declared universal and complete freedom of worship, stating that, since faith was a divine gift born of hearing the Gospel, no obstacle could be put in the way of preaching it.[6] Transylvania, the united principality of three nations,[7] soon became also the land of four established churches—Catholic, Lutheran, Calvinist, and Unitarian, and thus the most tolerant state of its time in Europe. Such freedom was a beacon to the people of royal Hungary. Its borders open to refugees, Transylvania became a haven for Protestant preachers. To it they fled when persecuted by the agents of the Habsburg Counter-Reformation, and from it they returned to royal Hungary reinspired by the Transylvanian concept of freedom of conscience.

There was a profound difference between religious freedom in Transylvania and in western Europe. In the West, the idea of religious freedom was determined by the Treaty of Augsburg of 1555 and refined by the Treaty of Westphalia of 1648. Their provisions did not amount to much more than that a sovereign had the assured privilege of deciding his state's official religion (*cuius regio eius religio*), and that those who confessed religions other than their monarch's might emigrate elsewhere rather than risk being burned at the stake. The Anglo-French Treaty of Utrecht of 1713 went a step further by stipulating that France was to free Protestants imprisoned solely for religious reasons, but the treaty was rather exceptional. International treaties in western Europe usually specified the rights of religious minorities only when the confession of the inhabitants of ceded territories differed from that of the annexing power. The Treaty of Oliva between Sweden and Poland in 1660, for instance, guaranteed the religious freedom of the Catholic inhabitants of Livonia after its cession to Sweden by Poland and of those of Pomerania after its cession to Sweden by Brandenburg. The Treaty of Nijmegen of 1678, by which Louis XIV of France restored Maastricht to the Netherlands, preserved the religious freedom of the city's Catholics. Catholics' rights were one of the provisions of the Treaty of Ryswick of 1697. Catholic religious freedom was again guaranteed when Prussia annexed Silesia from Austria as a result of the Wars of Austrian Succession (1740–48) and in the Prussian acquisitions at the first partition of Poland in 1772. No international treaties in western Europe, however, guaranteed the religious freedom of individuals, and this was the essential point of distinction between Transylvania and western Europe. The Transylvanian concept and practice of freedom of conscience secured the rights of individuals both in Transylvania and, by international treaty, elsewhere in Hungary. This was far in advance of western European theory or reality.

Under Ottoman protection the Transylvanian state flourished. Besides the establishment of freedom of conscience and the constitutional freedoms of the estates, the economy grew and a fairly modern Transylvanian army was organized. The existence of the Transylvanian army also made a palpable contribution to the political development of royal Hungary. Its radius of military action extended beyond the river Leitha, the historic boundary between Hungary and Austria. The geopolitical significance of this to Transylvania was demonstrated during the reign of Prince Gábor Bethlen (1613–29). Bethlen intended to go to the aid of Bohemia in its struggle against Habsburg dominion. While his main army was too late to help the Czechs at the fateful Battle of White Mountain on November 8, 1620, his light horse skirmished with the flanks and rear of their victorious foes, the imperial army. Bethlen also twice invested Vienna, though neither siege was successful. Protected by distance, terrain, the reach of its army, and the interposition in central Hungary of its suzerain power, the Ottoman state, Transylvania functioned as a guarantor of constitutional and religious freedoms in Habsburg-ruled royal Hungary.

The first time Transylvania fulfilled this function was during the reign of Emperor Rudolf II (1552–1612) as King Rudolf I (1576–1608) of Hungary. Intent on reimposing Catholicism on the Hungarians, Rudolf in 1604 provoked their first popular insurrection against Habsburg rule. The insurrectionaries found a leader in István Bocskai (1557–1606), prince of Transylvania in 1605 and 1606, who fused the popular forces with his own army. Already at war with the Turks, the Habsburgs now faced an uncompromising civil war. A threefold settlement was finally forced on the dynasty: the Treaties of Vienna and Zsitvatorok of 1606 and the legislation of the Hungarian diet of 1608. Together these secured for Hungary religious freedom, constitutional autonomy, and the right of habeas corpus.

The Treaty of Vienna of 1606 extended complete freedom of worship to all barons, magnates, nobles, royal free towns, and Hungarian soldiers in fortified frontier areas.[8] It secured Hungarian autonomy by stipulating that the palatine[9] was to be elected by the Hungarian diet, and "with his Hungarian counsellors shall have plenary power and authority in all matters deemed necessary to preserve the kingdom of Hungary and the tranquillity and well-being of its inhabitants."[10] Not counting Hungary's brief periods of independence, under Ferenc Rákóczi II (1676–1735) from 1703 to 1711 and under Lajos Kossuth (1802–94) during the revolution of 1848–49,[11] this guarantee of the Hungarian government's administrative independence from all imperial institutions, won by the Hungarians with Transylvanian aid, was the greatest prize they extracted from the Habsburgs until the *Ausgleich* of 1867. The third accomplishment of this remarkable treaty was the right that "no one shall be punished who has not been indicted and convicted according to the law."[12]

The treaty provisions were ratified by the estates of the Habsburg hereditary provinces and underwritten by the Sublime Porte in the Treaty of Zsitvatorok. Hungary's religious, constitutional, and personal liberties thus became elements of the international relations in the Danube Basin.

The Hungarian Diet of 1608 codified these guarantees and extended them. It granted freedom of religion to all communities, not just the royal free towns. It freed Protestant churches from the tutelage of the Catholic bishops. It required the king to nominate two Protestant and two Catholic noblemen from among whom the diet would elect the palatine.[13]

Thanks to Transylvania's influence, Protestantism won an unconditional victory in Hungary. The solidity of this victory and the reality of Hungarian autonomy were dramatized on May 15, 1618, when Ferdinand, to assure his ascent to the Hungarian throne, signed a covenant containing sixteen conditions that he had to fulfill to be elected king. These conditions, which were in essence guarantees of the diet's laws of 1608, were embodied in the coronation oath he swore as King Ferdinand II in 1622.[14] The existence of the Transylvanian state was such a potent force in the affairs of the Habsburg rump kingdom that the same ruler who almost completely eradicated Protestantism from Bohemia and the Alpine provinces stood surely for it in Hungary.[15]

The Decline of Transylvanian Influence in Royal Hungary in the Second Half of the Seventeenth Century

The golden age of Transylvania as a state with its own Hungarian princes extended from the Bocskai insurrection (1604–06) to the death of Prince Gábor Bethlen in 1629. By his use of Transylvania's military and political potential, Bocskai made Hungarian constitutional and religious issues a factor in the East Central European balance of power. Bethlen raised them, for a while at least, into a general European question. During the second half of the seventeenth century, however, continual struggles for the princely throne among various pretenders who appealed for armed Ottoman assistance exhausted Transylvania's resources and diminished its sway over royal Hungary. The most serious harm done to Transylvanian power and influence was the result of the adventurous foreign policy of György Rákóczi II (1621–60), prince of Transylvania from 1648 until his deposition in 1657. In defiance of Habsburg hostility and Ottoman proscription, he concluded alliances with the Cossack hetman Bohdan Khmelnytzky (1595–1657) and with King Charles X (1622–60) of Sweden. In support of the Swedes, he led his troops into Poland in the winter of 1656–57 with an eye to gaining the Polish throne for himself.[16] After some initial successes, including the occupation of Warsaw and other Polish strongholds, Rákóczi was suddenly abandoned by his allies and forced to retreat in disarray, his army decimated by Polish and Crimean Tatar forces. Deposed on orders from the Sublime Porte, Rákóczi twice launched armed attempts to retake his throne, occasioning intervention and occupation by Ottoman and Crimean Tatar troops and the ruin of the principality's prosperity.

Transylvania's decline encouraged the Habsburgs to step up their absolutist efforts in royal Hungary. At first the Hungarian estates had to meet this new threat to the kingdom's religious and constitutional liberties on their own, but before long Transylvania was able to give them some aid and comfort, despite its weakened state. The absolutist inclinations of young King Leopold I (1657–1705) were enough to arouse the Hungarians' discontent, but the Treaty of Vasvár signed by the dynasty and the Sublime Porte on August 10, 1664, caused a political uproar all over Hungary. The Hungarians in general, and in particular the prominent military theoretician and patriot Count Miklós Zrínyi (1620–64), were convinced that the Ottoman army was on the point of collapse and the empire tottering. Had the Habsburgs continued the war, they believed, Hungary could have been liberated from the Turks.[17] The dynasty's readiness to make peace was seen as clear evidence of its lack of interest in the Hungarian cause. Nourished by Hungarian resentment of increasing Habsburg absolutism and dismay at the dynasty's uninterested foreign policy, a major *Fronde* took shape with the support of the highest dignitaries in the kingdom, including the palatine, Count Ferenc Wesselényi (1605–67), and the lord chief justice (*országbíró*), Ferenc Nádasdy. In 1671, Miklós Zrínyi's brother Péter (1621–71) organized an armed uprising. It was foiled, however, and its leaders were arrested and executed. Without Transylvanian help, this first round between dynastic absolutism and Hungarian constitutionalism ended in the defeat of Hungary's political elite.

The Habsburg response to the *Fronde* was to strengthen the German garrisons in Hungary, raise taxation, and intensify the Counter-Reformation. The dynasty's excesses finally drove the hard-pressed peasantry to rise up in a so-called *kuruc* rebellion. (*Kuruc* is derived from the Latin word *crux* [cross] from the symbol of György Dózsa's great peasant rebellion of 1514, originally planned as a crusade against the Turk.) After an amazing initial victory over the dynasty's professional troops, the *kuruc* insurgents were defeated in the fall of 1672 and put to flight. Scattered remnants of them escaped from Habsburg territory and regrouped either in Ottoman Hungary or Transylvania. If the principality was too weak to come to their military aid, it could still offer sanctuary to those fleeing Habsburg despotism.

Encouraged by its success against both the *Fronde* and the *kuruc* insurgency, the dynasty on February 27, 1673, flouted the Hungarian constitution by appointing Johann Ampringen, grand master of the Teutonic Order, to administer royal Hungary through an unconstitutional institution known as the *gubernium*. Further growth in taxes and the size of the German garrisons was accompanied by even more brutal measures against Protestants. The authorities arrested 730 Protestant ministers and gave them the choice of conversion to Catholicism or death. Those who refused conversion were finally spared the executioner and sentenced instead to be galley slaves. Their survivors were eventually freed by Dutch Admiral Michiel de Ruyter on February 12, 1676. The bloodiness of Habsburg administration took little time to alienate any remaining sympathy for the dynasty. This and an opportune international situation soon gave Transylvania, feeble though it was, a new chance to help in the defense of Hungarian liberties.

In the Transylvanian town of Fogaras (Făgăraş) representatives of King Louis XIV of France and the leaders of the Hungarian malcontents signed a treaty on April 28, 1675. Polish adherence to the compact raised the Hungarians' liberties, with Transylvania's help, into a European issue. The agreement was reaffirmed, this time without the Poles, by French and Hungarian plenipotentiaries in Warsaw on October 10, 1677. A 2,000-man Franco-Polish army in Louis XIV's pay was dispatched almost at once to Hungary to join the rebels. At the same time, a second army of French, Polish, and Hungarian *kuruc* volunteers was formed in Transylvania under French officers. One of the volunteers was young Count Imre Thököly (1657–1705), who was soon appointed to command the insurrectionary forces with the endorsement of Mihály Apafi I (1632–90), prince of Transylvania from 1661 till his death. The insurgents launched a remarkably successful campaign into northern Hungary.[18]

A French observer of their success, the Marquis de Feuquières, correctly saw that the driving force behind the Hungarians' protracted rebellion was the essential ingredient of any war of liberation: a high degree of motivation shared by a large number of fighters, motivation rooted in sociopolitical doctrines, interests, and goals. Feuquières noted that the Hungarians were fighting for their country's constitutional prerogatives, which their Habsburg rulers had tried to suppress by "Poison, Dagger, and Murder of the [Hungarian] Grandees." In his opinion, "the Hungarian cause was just" because the Habsburgs had violated their obligations as sovereigns, obligations that included prudent government. General sedition was the mark of a policy that inflamed large sectors of the population, and this was what had happened under the Habsburgs in Hungary. "If the Emperor had not distressed the Protestants and the Grandees of Hungary . . . , if he had not subverted the Privileges of the whole Nation . . . , this Commotion would not have been so general as it proved."[19]

The treaty signed by Leopold I and Louis XIV at Nijmegen on February 6, 1679, deprived the Hungarians of their valued French ally. The *kuruc* insurgents now found themselves between the Habsburg devil and the Ottoman deep blue sea, a choice between two evils, as has so often befallen East Central Europeans. Their forces marching from one victorious engagement to another, however, saved them the immediate necessity of making that choice. Intimidated by their success, the Habsburgs, who had always bowed more graciously to armed resistance from their subjects than to peaceful demands for their rights, now decided to offer concessions. The Hungarian diet was convened in Sopron on April 28, 1681. The result of this consultation between crown and estates was a compromise modeled on the Treaty of Vienna of 1606 and a precursor of the Habsburg-Hungarian compromises that were to culminate in the *Ausgleich* of 1867. The Sopron compromise did away with the *gubernium,* restored Hungary's administrative autonomy, put an end to the German garrisons' marauding, and curtailed the excesses of the Counter-Reformation by reaffirming freedom of religion, albeit on a lesser scale than that enacted by the Diet of 1608.

The compromise satisfied the estates, who now deserted the *kuruc* rebels. At the head of only disenfranchised elements of the population, with the limited support Transylvania could afford, and now perforce in alliance with the Sublime Porte, Thököly continued the struggle against the Habsburgs, remaining virtual ruler of northern Hungary.

When in 1683 Grand Vizier Kara Mustafa Köprülü led the last major Ottoman offensive in East Central Europe to the very gates of Vienna and laid siege to the city, Thököly, as a result of his tragic but indispensable alliance with the Turks, found himself among the auxiliaries of the Ottoman army. The relief of Vienna eight weeks later by the combined Polish army of King Jan Sobieski III (1624–96) and the imperial forces led by the duke of Lorraine (1643–90), set in motion the sixteen-year War of the Holy League. The main theater of operations was Hungary, which was left depopulated and devastated by the prolonged contest between its German liberators and Ottoman occupiers. With Ottoman blessing Thököly succeeded Mihály Apafi I as prince of Transylvania when the latter died in 1690, but it was but a shadow sovereignty. The invasion of Transylvania by Habsburg forces in the fall of the same year forced Thököly to flee, his ephemeral reign a mere footnote to Transylvanian history. The imperial forces soon occupied all Transylvania's fortresses and strongholds, and became the only effective power in the principality. Independent Transylvania, the guarantor of Hungary's liberties, ceased to be.

The Former Guarantor of Hungarian Liberties Becomes a Habsburg Military Base against Them

The imperial troops' occupation of Transylvania diametrically changed its role in Hungarian affairs. The Hungarian estates' hopes that, after the liberation of all the lands of Saint Stephen's Crown, Transylvania would be reincorporated into a unitary Hungarian state as it had been before the Ottoman conquest proved illusory. Rather than restore the entire Hungarian kingdom, the Habsburgs preferred to keep Transylvania separate. Leopold I had not recognized the election of five-year-old Mihály Apafi II (1676–1713) as prince of Transylvania during his father's lifetime in 1681, and in 1693 had him brought to Vienna. An absolute ruler over the rest of his realm, Leopold made a conciliatory exception of Transylvania. Barely had the imperial forces taken control there than he issued on October 16, 1690, the *Diploma Leopoldinum,* which affirmed the autonomy of the principality's administration, respect for its laws and institutions, and the freedom of its four accepted religions (Catholicism, Lutheranism, Calvinism, and Unitarianism). The Transylvanian diet was happy to accept such concessions to the principality, surrounded as it was by a sea of absolutism, and on February 7, 1691, took the oath of loyalty to Leopold. On May 14, 1693, Transylvanian representatives in Vienna subscribed to the *Resolutio Alvicziana,* which permanently separated the Transylvanian Chancellery from the Hungarian Royal Chancellery, severing Transylvania from the Hungarian body politic for almost two centuries to come.

The encirclement of royal Hungary by the establishment of imperial military bases in Transylvania was supplemented on September 8, 1698, by the creation of the Serbian Military Frontier in the south of the Banat. The Serbian Military Frontier together with the contiguous, already existing Croatian Military Frontier set up a military cordon loyal to the Habsburgs all along the southern border of the Hungarian kingdom. The dynasty had no intention of letting the Hungarians out from under Habsburg rule.

The last time Transylvania played any part in support of Hungary's religious and constitutional liberties was during the War of Independence of Ferenc Rákóczi II (1703–11).[20] This war fused two movements into a single struggle: the nobility's resistance against the unconstitutional tyranny of the Habsburgs and the popular *kuruc* insurrection. It was the first time in Hungarian history that the tradition and experience of opposition by the noble estate joined forces with a popular struggle for the social and economic betterment of the masses. The combination of the two gave the broadest possible social backing for action against Habsburg absolutism.[21]

The war demonstrated the Hungarians' considerable potential for resisting Habsburg might by force of arms. They were aided by the fact that large parts of the Habsburg armies were tied down in Italy,

Germany, and the Low Countries by the War of the Spanish Succession, which was raging at the same time. As the War of the Spanish Succession neared its end while the hostilities in Hungary were still dragging on, the major question came to be whether the Habsburg armies, through with action in the west and Italy, and concentrated in Hungary, would be able to bring Rákóczi's War of Independence to a speedy conclusion. Rákóczi was as alive to this question as anyone and moved to resolve it in his own favor. While he was negotiating for a new alliance with Czar Peter the Great (1672–1725), he laid plans for a strategic withdrawal and permanent defense in the northeast corner of Hungary based on fortresses and fortified towns. The first steps in this strategy and logistical preparations for a protracted area defense began in 1710. The most reliable commanders were placed over key defense establishments, the most important of which was the recently modernized fortress of Munkács.

Historians differ over the concluding phase of the war.[22] Some, such as Imre Lukinich, claim that the going was so hard for the imperial forces that a systematic offensive and sieges were beyond their capacity. Field Marshal Count János Pálffy (1663–1751), the imperial commander in chief, they argue, was simply in no position to launch the assault. Although it would have been only a matter of time before the Habsburgs would have brought the war to an end by force, it would have taken three or four more years of fighting, longer than the dynasty could have afforded.

Wise for once, the dynasty realized that most of the nobles in the *kuruc* camp were ready for a compromise. A speedy compromise seemed to offer greater advantages than a longer drawn-out war, which might well have alienated those nobles. The dynasty's smartest move, however, was to include in its compromise offer a key stipulation assuring the privileges of the "warrior estate" (*vitézlő rend*).[23] This won over these combatants, the backbone of Rákóczi's army, to a settlement, since it made continuing the war seem unnecessary. The Treaty of Szatmár (Satu Mare) was therefore signed on April 30, 1711, and endorsed by the regent, Empress Eleonora, on behalf of her son, King Charles III (Emperor Charles VI) (1685–1740). The treaty reestablished Hungary's autonomy and the privileges of the estates, assured the Protestants' freedom of conscience, and made free men of even the nonnoble warriors who had fought for Rákóczi's cause. In return, the Hungarian estates acknowledged the Habsburgs' hereditary right in the male line to the Hungarian crown. The treaty, in fact, reinforced the dualist system by which Hungary continued to be governed separately from the dynasty's hereditary provinces. Neither the famous compromise (*Ausgleich*) of 1867 nor the dual system it set up were new phenomena in Hungarian-Habsburg relations; rather they were the quintessence of that relationship—to no small degree because the Hungarians had time and again taken up arms in defense of their rights and autonomy.

While the Szatmár compromise secured much of what the estates had been fighting for, it also reaffirmed Transylvania's new status as a province ruled directly from Vienna and separate from the Hungarian realm. The dynasty was too fearful of the military potential of a united Hungary including Transylvania, which the Rákóczi War of Independence had so clearly demonstrated. As a preventive measure, the imperial garrisons in Transylvania were strengthened. The principality in Hungary's rear was no longer the guarantor of Hungary's liberties, but became instead a check on Hungarian political ambition and a guarantor of Habsburg power over royal Hungary. As an imperial base, it would place Hungary between two fires if the Hungarians were to rise up against the Habsburgs again. Hungarian insurgents would have had to face Habsburg forces from Transylvania to the east as well as those from the provinces to their west, no small reason for Hungarian docility during the eighteenth century. Only when Joseph II (1780–90) felt that his absolutism was so firmly entrenched in royal Hungary that he no longer needed military bases in Transylvania to secure Hungarian loyalty was the grand principality, as it had by then become, briefly reunited with the kingdom of Hungary. The ferment of the Hungarian feudal revolt of 1790–92[24] threatened Habsburg absolutist rule, however, and convinced the dynasty that Transylvania needed to be kept as a separately ruled brake on Hungary. After barely five years they were parted again.

This restored the Habsburg military cordon around Hungary, which had been completed by the first partition of Poland in 1772. Galicia and Bukovina in Habsburg hands with military bases at the dynasty's service reversed the role of the northern Carpathian Mountains. Even after Transylvania's loss to the Habsburgs, the passes through the Beskids and Tatras had served the Hungarians as a route to a friendly nation. Hungarian dissidents could find a haven in Poland as they once had in Transylvania. The first insurgent contingents of Ferenc Rákóczi II had entered Hungary from Galicia. The partition of Poland changed this frontier from a friendly one into a hostile one. Now Galicia and Bukovina were staging grounds for Habsburg aggression against Hungary. They served this function during the Revolution of 1848–49, when the Habsburg troops of General Count Frantz Schlick (1789–1862) and Colonel Christian Götz (1783–1849) invaded Hungary from Galicia in the fall of 1848. The major Russian offensive against Hungary in June, 1849, also came from there. The eighteenth century thus saw a fundamental transformation of royal Hungary's position within the Habsburg domains.

Conclusion

Transylvania had always been an integral part of Hungary ever since the Hungarians had settled in the Danube Basin within the great arc of the Carpathian Mountains.[25] A Transylvanian state separate from the Hungarian kingdom was created not in response to an inner, organic necessity but to satisfy outside, alien interests. The Ottoman conquest of central Hungary physically separated eastern Hungary—that is, Transylvania—from the western, Habsburg-ruled part of the kingdom. This physical reality was compounded by the Ottomans' policy of barring control of eastern Hungary to their mortal enemies, the Habsburgs. It was thus the Sublime Porte that promoted the creation of the principality of Transylvania and secured its autonomous existence. Statesmen of both royal Hungary and Transylvania considered the division of the kingdom and the principality to be only a temporary phenomenon. The intention remained through the centuries to reunite Transylvania with the rest of Hungary. Whatever the status of Transylvania, it continued to be regarded in principle as a part of the lands of Saint Stephen's Crown.

Geographically, Transylvania is an integral part of the Danube Basin, separated from the Balkans by the Carpathian Mountains, which in the seventeenth and eighteenth centuries were quite an effective barrier between the two areas. Trade between Transylvania and the Balkans was negligible. The lines of Transylvanian commerce followed the rivers that flowed into the river Tisza on the Great Hungarian Plain (*Nagy Alföld*) to the west.

Culturally, Transylvania was an integral part of western civilization, in the sense that western civilization has certain unique and peculiar characteristics that distinguish it from any other. These characteristics are the Hebrew heritage (the moral principles embodied in the Ten Commandments), the Roman heritage (the universality of man and the rule of law), and the Christian heritage (the fraternity of man). More specifically, western civilization originates in Rome and has evolved through medieval Catholic Christianity, the Renaissance, the Protestant Reformation, the scientific revolution, and the Enlightenment. This was the path of the cultural development of Hungary, including Transylvania. The Rumanian principalities (Moldavia and

Wallachia), on the other hand, developed according to the Byzantine tradition, which is built on the Hebrew heritage, the Roman heritage of the Eastern rather than the Latin empire, and the Christian heritage of the Orthodox churches rather than Catholicism. It is an evolution that excluded the Protestant Reformation and the scientific revolution. The Enlightenment penetrated the principalities only belatedly in the nineteenth century. Hence the vivid contrast that still exists between Transylvania, a part of western civilization, and the Danubian provinces with their Balkan heritage. No one with scholarly pretensions can or should claim that one is superior to the other. The only historical fact is that they are different. This distinction between civilizations is reflected in stone and brick along the line of the Carpathians. The easternmost examples of the Romanesque, Gothic, and Renaissance styles of the western heritage are to be found among the Hungarian and Saxon churches, houses, and monuments of Transylvania all the way to the western slopes of the Carpathians. Beyond the mountains to the east are the beautiful but strikingly different buildings of Byzantine civilization and style in Moldavia and Wallachia.

In human, physical, and economic terms, Transylvania has been an integral part of Hungary culturally, geographically, and, until the end of World War I, politically also. The accident of the great upheaval of 1914–18 rather than any objective factor bound it to an alien environment. Yet Transylvania should not be a source of friction between Rumanians and Hungarians. Rather, with its multiethnicity, it should serve as a bridge between the two nations. Lasting bridges are built on peace, however, not on conflict. Interethnic strife benefits neither Hungarians nor Rumanians; it can serve only foreign interests. Interethnic peace in turn requires certain preconditions, foremost among which is an ironclad guarantee of the right of each ethnic group to develop its language and culture freely. Transylvania could become a province in which the nations, as in the past, live together in peace and fraternity. Rivalry between them—and competition, after all, is a basic human urge—need not be wrong. Confined to cultural and scientific excellence and economic advance, competition could be a positive force. Only dominance is reprehensible. If we could but learn from history, this would be the lesson of the seventeenth and eighteenth centuries in Transylvania.

Notes

1. Ozorai and Sói banates (northern Bosnia), Macsói banate (northern Serbia), and Szörényi banate (northeastern Serbia and western Wallachia). See map in Bálint Hóman

and Gyula Szekfű, *Magyar történet* [Hungarian History] (Budapest, 1942), vol. 2, between pp. 152 and 153.

2. Harold J. Grimm, *The Reformation Era 1500–1650,* 2d ed. (New York, 1973), p. 114. The Hungarian delegation attended the Diet of Worms and appealed to the Holy Roman Empire for help, but they left the city empty-handed on April 20, just four days after Martin Luther's arrival. The delegation was headed by István Verbőczi (or Werbőczy), a leader of the gentry. Egyed Berzeviczy, "Magyarország az 1521-iki wormsi birodalmi gyűlésen" [Hungary at the Imperial Diet of 1521 in Worms], *Századok* [Centuries], 39 (1905): 452–56.

3. For a definition of "second serfdom" and an account of its evolution in Hungary and its neighbors, see Béla K. Király, "The Emancipation of the Serfs of East Central Europe," *Antemurale,* 15 (1971): 63–85.

4. Letter from Prince Zsigmond Báthory of Transylvania to György Király, commandant of Nagyvárad, dated June 2, 1597, from Gyulafehérvár (Alba Iulia). *Sárospataki Füzetek* [Sarospatak Notes], vol. 7 (1863), p. 760.

5. Imre Révész, Sr., *A magyarországi protestantizmus történelme* [The History of Protestantism in Hungary] (Budapest, 1925), pp. 49 ff; Lajos Rácz, "Vallási türelem Erdélyben és Magyarországon a XVI-VIII században" [Religious Tolerance in Transylvania and Hungary in the 16th and 17th Centuries], *Protestáns Szemle* [Protestant Review] 43 (1934): 198–204.

6. Sándor Bíró et al., *A magyar református egyház története* [History of the Hungarian Reformed Church] (Budapest, 1949), pp. 50–51; Révész, op. cit., p. 29; József S. Szabó et al., *A Protestantizmus Magyarországon* [Protestantism in Hungary] (Budapest, 1928), pp. 38–56; József S. Szabó, "Zwingli hatása Magyarországon" [Zwingli's Influence on Hungary], *Protestáns Szemle* [Protestant Review], 40 (1931): 689–94; Jenő Sólyom, *Luther és Magyarország: A reformátor kapcsolata hazánkkal haláláig* [Luther and Hungary: The Reformer's Contacts with Our Country to His Death] (Budapest, 1933).

7. The Hungarian estates, the Saxon burghers, and the Szeklers—the three "nations"—concluded their "union" in 1437; renewed in 1547, it endured until 1848. See Benedek Jancsó, *Erdély története* [History of Transylvania] (Cluj, 1931); László Makkai, *Erdély története* [History of Transylvania] (Budapest, 1944), pp. 221–71, 358–74; Karl Kurt Klein, *Saxonica Septemcastrensia* (Marburg, 1971), pp. 229–58; Elemér Mályusz et al., *Erdély és népei* [Transylvania and Its Peoples] (Budapest, 1941), pp. 164–70; Sándor Szilágyi, "Az Erdélyi alkotmany megalakulasa a szeparatio kezdetén" [The Establishment of the Constitution of Transylvania at the Outset of Separation], *Századok* [Centuries] 10 (1876): 36–48. The Sublime Porte watched zealously that the Habsburg government should not dominate Transylvania. In 1571 for instance, on the death of Prince János Zsigmond Zápolyai, Mustafa Pasha of Buda warned the Hungarian primate, Cardinal Antal Verancsics, against interference in Tranyslvanian affairs. László Szalay, *Erdély és a porta 1567–1578* [Transylvania and the Porte, 1567–1578] (Pest, 1862), pp. 6–7.

8. Act 22, 1606. *Corpus Juris hungarici, 1526–1608* (Budapest, 1899), pp. 992–93. For historical perspectives on the treaty, see Ferenc Márk, "Bocskay István és a bécsi beke" [István Bocskay and the Peace of Vienna], *Protestáns Szemle* [Protestant Review], 16 (1904): 217–25; Etele Thurzó, "A bécsi békekötés" [The Peace Treaty of Vienna], *Protestáns Szemle* [Protestant Review] 18 (1906): 357–75, 447–67; Géza Antal, "A magyar protestáns egyház külföldi érintkezései" [The Hungarian Protestant Church's Connections Abroad], *Protestáns Szemle* [Protestant Review] 20 (1908): 65–84.

9. A specifically Hungarian office comparable to that of a viceroy, who was head of the executive branch of Hungarian government, speaker of the House of Lords, commander in chief of the armed forces, and president of one of the chambers of the

Supreme Court—a very powerful office. See Béla K. Király, *Hungary in the Late Eighteenth Century: The Decline of Enlightened Despotism* (New York, 1969), pp. 83, 89, 93, 103, 181, 260, 265–66.

10. . . . *per Palatinum, et consiliaros hungaros . . . ad conservandum regnum Hungariae, eiusdemque regnicolarum quietum, et utilitatem videbuntur esse necessaria; plenariam potestatem, et facultatem habeat. . . . Corpus juris hungarici, 1526–1608,* p. 962.

11. The regime of Ferenc Rákóczi II declared the Habsburg dynasty dethroned in 1707, but the Treaty of Szatmár brought his own reign to an end in 1711. The Parliament of Debrecen proclaimed the Habsburgs deposed on April 14, 1849, but Lajos Kossuth resigned his presidential authority on August 11, 1849.

12. . . . *nemo nisi legitime citatus, jurisque ordine convictus puniatur. . . . Corpus juris hungarici, 1526–1608,* p. 966.

13. Ibid., pp. 10–11. This requirement was reaffirmed by the Treaty of Nickolsburg (Mikulov, in modern Czechoslovakia) of 1621, the Second Treaty of Vienna of 1624, and the Treaty of Linz of 1645. This last secured freedom of religion even for individual serfs. The first Lutheran palatine (*nádor*) was Baron Tamás Nádasdy (1498–1562), elected in 1554. Mihály Horváth, *Nádasdy Tamás élete* [Life of Tamás Nádasdy] (Buda, 1838).

14. The following conditions were incorporated into Ferdinand II's coronation oath. They represented the maximum freedoms gained by the Hungarians thanks to the power of the Principality of Transylvania:

The Pacta Conventa of Ferdinand II: The Sixteen Conditions Guaranteeing to Hungary Freedom of Conscience and Constitutional Liberties.

1. The constitutional freedoms and liberties guaranteed to Hungary by the Treaty of Vienna and subsequent legislation will be honored.

2. All gravamina will be settled by future diets to be held not less often than every three years.

3. Hungary and its annexed territories will be governed by their own citizens, and no Hungarian troops will fight on foreign soil.

4. The fortified frontier zone of Hungary will be put under Hungarian command.

5. The right of habeas corpus will be respected; only Hungarian judiciary will have the right to practice in Hungary, and they will be permitted to do so without administrative interference.

6. Neither the crown nor the nobility will infringe freedom of conscience.

7. The palatine will be elected.

8. The crown will maintain the defenses of the fortified frontier zone.

9. The privileges of the royal free towns and the mining cities will be safeguarded.

10. The Holy Crown [of Saint Stephen] will be kept in Hungary under guard by Hungarian laymen of any accepted religion.

11. No part of the territory of Hungary will be ceded away.

12. Peace with Bohemia and Transylvania and other adjacent provinces will be maintained in accordance with the Treaty of Vienna.

13. Domestic tranquillity will be assured, and no foreign troops will be deployed [in Hungary].

14. Territories, towns, and strongholds under Austrian occupation will be restored to Hungary.

15. The privileges of the *hajdu* soldiery will be preserved.

16. Ferdinand shall not intervene in the governance of Hungary so long as his father Matthias II [1608–19] lives.

Corpus juris hungarici, 1608–1657 (Budapest, 1899), pp. 175–83.

15. Protestantism indeed survived. In Hungary and Transylvania in the early nineteenth century, there were 1,971 Calvinist parishes, 737 Lutheran parishes, and 110 Unitarian parishes and 54 Unitarian affiliates (congregations without the status of parishes). István Lassu, *Az ausztriai birodalomnak statisztikai, geográphiai és historiai leírása* [Statistical, Geographical, and Historical Description of the Austrian Empire] (Buda, 1829), pp. 108–11. In the late nineteenth century, the religious affiliations of Hungary's various nationalities were as follows (given in percentages):

	Roman Catholic	*Uniate*	*Orthodox*	*Lutheran*	*Calvinist*	*Unitarian*	*Jewish*
Hungarians	56.0	2.1	0.2	4.0	30.8	0.8	5.6
Germans	66.5		0.3	20.2	1.3		11.4
Slovaks	68.8	5.4		23.7	0.5		1.1
Rumanians	0.3	36.7	63.3				
Ruthenes	0.5	96.1	0.2				0.1
Serbs & Croats	62.2	0.4	37.0				0.1

Béla Bartha, "Statisztikai tanulmányok a magyar protestantizmusról" [Statistical Studies on Hungarian Protestantism], *Protestáns Szemle* [Protestant Review] 2 (1890): 39.

16. W. E. D. Allen, *The Ukraine: A History* (New York, 1963), pp. 111, 131, 143.

17. Count Zrínyi was a vigorous advocate of a native standing army as the one sure way to rid Hungary of Ottoman rule. To no avail, for the Habsburgs were opposed to setting up any such autonomous Hungarian army, lest it turn against them instead of the Turks. *Ne bántsd a magyart: Az török áfium ellen való orvosság avagy az töröknek magyarral való békessége ellen való antidótum* [Do Not Harm the Hungarians: A True Remedy for the Turkish Opiate or a True Antidote to a True Peace between the Turks and Hungarians], written in 1660 or 1661, first published in 1705, and reprinted several times thereafter; László Négyesy, ed., *Gróf Zrínyi Miklós válogatott munkái* [Selected Works of Count Miklós Zrínyi] (Budapest, n.d.), pp. 293–320.

18. For Habsburg efforts to mobilize European public opinion against Hungary, see Béla Köpeczi, *Magyarország a kereszténység ellensége: A Thököly-felkelés az európai közvéleményben* [Hungary, the Enemy of Christendom: The Thököly Insurrection in European Public Opinion] (Budapest, 1976).

19. Lt. Gen. [of the French Army] Antoine Manassés Pas, Marquis de Feuquières [the "Wizard"], *Memoirs Historical and Military* (London, 1736), 1:224–25.

20. Ferenc Rákóczi II of Borsi (1676–1735) was prince of Transylvania (1704–11), ruling prince of Hungary (*vezérlő fejedelem*) (1705–11), and prince of the Holy Roman Empire. When his mother Ilona Zrínyi was taken captive after successfully defending the fortress of Munkács against its Habsburg besiegers for three years, Rákóczi was taken to Austria and raised there by his appointed guardian Cardinal Leopold Kollonich. The owner of 1.9 million yokes of land, Rákóczi became perpetual high sheriff of Sáros County in 1694. In 1697, he refused an offer to lead a peasant uprising, but in the face of increasing Habsburg tyranny he turned to Louis XIV in 1700 to try to enlist his support for a *Fronde* rather than a general insurrection in Hungary. Betrayed and arrested, Rákóczi escaped and took refuge in Poland. At the renewed invitation of insurgent leaders, he accepted what he had rejected in 1697 and on June 6, 1703, entered Hungary at the head of a small band of peasant rebels. Béla Köpeczi and Ágnes R.

Várkonyi, *II. Rákóczi Ferenc,* 2d ed. (Budapest, 1976), pp. 113–14. For a wealth of contemporary sources, see Köpeczi and Várkonyi, eds., *Rákóczi tükör: Naplók, jelentések, emlékiratok a szabadságharcról* [A Rákóczi Survey: Diaries, Reports, Memoirs from the War of Liberation] (Budapest, 1973); and Köpeczi, *A Rákóczi-szabadságharc és Franciaország* [The Rákóczi War of Liberation and France] (Budapest, 1966).

21. See Béla K. Király, "War and Society in Western and East Central Europe during the Eighteenth and Nineteenth Centuries: Similarities and Contrasts," idem and Gunther E. Rothenberg, eds., *War and Society in East Central Europe,* vol. 1 (New York, 1979), pp. 1–33.

22. Mátyás Molnár, ed., *A Rákóczi-szabadságharc vitás kérdései: Tudományos emlékülés 1976 januar 29–30* [Unsettled Questions of the Rákóczi War of Independence: A Scholarly Memorial Conference, January 29, 30, 1976] (Vaja-Nyíregyháza, 1976).

23. Rákóczi had granted his most outstanding fighters these privileges, which were those of the *hajduk.* This kind of freedom had first been accorded by Prince István Bocskai of Transylvania after his insurrection of 1604–06 against the Habsburgs, which, like Rákóczi's war, had ended in compromise, the Peace of Vienna of 1606. The main strength of his insurgent army had been the *hajduk,* fiercely independent cattlemen-cum-bandits, who fought gallantly for his cause. See Béla K. Király, ed., *Tolerance and Movements of Religious Dissent in Eastern Europe* (Boulder, Colo., 1975), pp. 208, 210–12. In reward Bocskai emancipated them from the jurisdiction of their lords, settled them in land-grant communities (the *hajdu* towns), and guaranteed them their rights to own property and to personal freedom. These privileges he conferred on all his meritorious soldiers who were not already members of the estates. The emancipated *hajduk* constituted the "warrior estate," a new stratum in Hungarian feudal society. The creation of the warrior estate was a subterfuge to avoid mass emancipation and to establish a kind of citizen soldiery, a well-spring of revolutionary warfare. See Ferenc Julier, *Magyar hadvezérek* [Hungarian Military Leaders] (Budapest, n.d.), pp. 283–316.

24. See Béla K. Király, "Prussian Diplomatic Adventure with Poland and the Feudal Revolt in Hungary, 1790," *The Polish Review* 12, no. 1 (Winter 1967): 3–11.

25. Paul Teleki, *The Evolution of Hungary and Its Place in European History* (New York, 1923), pp. 150–51. See the recent related debate "On Transylvanian Ethnicity," *Current Anthropology* 20, no. 1 (March 1979): 135–48. See also Gyula Kristó, "Romaiak és vlachok Nyesztornál és Anonymusnál" [Romans and Vlachs in Nestor and Anonymus], *Századok* [Centuries] 112, no. 4 (1978): 623–61; Lajos Tamás, *Rómaiak, románok és oláhok Dácia Trajánában* [Romans, Rumanians and Vlachs in Trajan's Dacia] (Budapest, 1935).

The author wishes to express his thanks to Professor Stephen Fischer-Galaţi, editor of "East European Monographs," for permission to condense part of the author's study, "The Sublime Porte, Vienna, Transylvania and the Dissemination of the Protestant Reformation in Royal Hungary," in Béla K. Király, ed., *Tolerance and Movements of Religious Dissent in Eastern Europe* (Boulder, Colo.: East European Monographs, 1975), pp. 199–221.

III. TRANSYLVANIA IN THE HABSBURG EMPIRE AFTER 1790

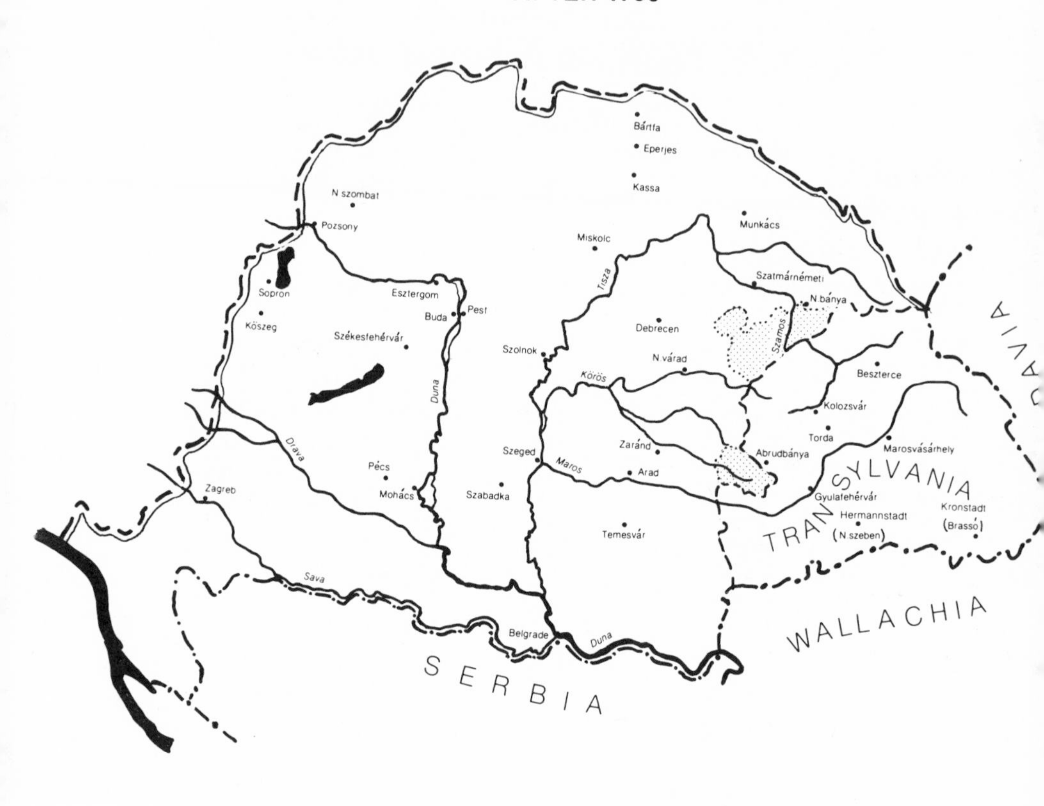

Bártfa
Eperjes
Kassa
N.szombat
Pozsony
Munkács
Miskolc
Tisza
Szatmárnémeti
Sopron
Esztergom
N.bánya
Pest
Buda
Kőszeg
Székesfehérvár
Debrecen
Szamos
Szolnok
N.várad
Beszterce
Körös
Duna
Kolozsvár
Torda
Zaránd
Marosvásárhely
Szeged
Abrudbánya
Dráva
Maros
Pécs
Arad
TRANSYLVANIA
Zagreb
Mohács
Szabadka
Gyulafehérvár
Hermannstadt
(N.szeben)
Kronstadt
(Brassó)
Temesvár
Sava
WALLACHIA
Belgrade
Duna
SERBIA

LEGEND:

International Borders
Border of Hungary
Border of Transylvania
Kingdom of Hungary
Habsburg Empire
Ottoman Empire
The Partium
Other States

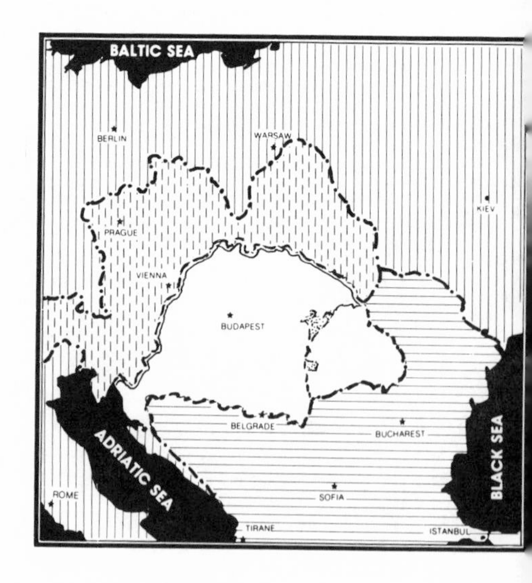

BALTIC SEA
BERLIN
WARSAW
KIEV
PRAGUE
VIENNA
BUDAPEST
BELGRADE
BUCHAREST
ADRIATIC SEA
BLACK SEA
ROME
SOFIA
TIRANE
ISTANBUL

Nationalism and the Polarization of National Destinies 2

The last 200 years have witnessed the emergence of modern nationalism and certain exclusivist demands on the loyalties of the inhabitants of most states of the world. The peoples of Transylvania are no exception. The linkage that was created between the conception of nationality and the conception of state was henceforth an important guidepost in the thinking of Rumanians, Hungarians, and Germans, as well as of the smaller nationality groups who inhabit Transylvania. The nineteenth century, in particular, saw the beginning of the assertion of differing, and even conflicting, interpretations of national destiny. Although the previous centuries had already established the basic patterns of the respective national cultures and their coexistence in Transylvania, the reigns of Joseph II (1780–90) and Leopold II (1790–92) accentuated the differences on a political level: Joseph II by trying to impose German as the official language of the empire, his brother by actively playing off the nationalities against one another to consolidate Habsburg centralization. International events, particularly the revolution in France, also added to the tensions between the nationalities by popularizing both the concept of popular sovereignty and the rightness of nationalistic sentiments.

In Transylvania, the Rumanian peasant rising of 1784 is perhaps the first hint of things to come. It is followed shortly, on a much higher plane, by the submission of the two *Supplexes* to the Habsburg rulers (1790, 1792) and by the ever increasing Hungarian demand that Transylvania and royal Hungary be reunited.

Joseph Held's study on the Horea-Cloşca-Crişan rising reflects the changing mood in the relations of the Transylvanian nations. Although this was a classic peasant revolt, with mainly socioeconomic causes, its timing and its combination with discontent in the Orthodox Christian fold (composed overwhelmingly of Rumanians) makes it a manifestation of early ethnic Rumanian "nationalism." The Held analysis provides a balanced description of the causes for unrest, a profile of the traits and motives of the leaders, and finally a succinct summary of the consequences.

Sixty-five years of development in "national consciousness" took place between 1784 and 1848. This continued to increase the emotional and psychological distance among Rumanians, Hungarians, and Germans. Consequently, when the Revolution of 1848–49 swept through the Habsburg empire, the inhabitants of Transylvania found themselves on opposite sides in the struggle. Istvan Deak's study focuses on this struggle. He does not trace the process of polarization, but seeks instead to answer some basic questions about this event and the long-term effect it had on interethnic relations. In its sweep, the essay links the past to present realities. At the same time, it points out that the real winners and losers of the struggle were not determined on the battlefield.

Paul Bődy's essay attempts to bridge a larger slice of time in the evolution of Rumanian-Hungarian relations. Its focus is not on one traumatic event, but on the intellectual developments that provided the framework for Rumanian-Hungarian contacts between 1840 and 1870. Bődy's concern is to present the efforts of reconciliation in spite of 1784 and 1848–49.

The reflections of Edsel Walter Stroup and S. B. Vardy address the same historical events and questions as Held, Deak, and Bődy. However, they take issue with some of the preceding interpretations and draw different conclusions about some of the points raised.

Together, these essays portray the political confrontations of the peoples of Transylvania. They also reveal that nationalist orientations were reaffirmed rather than restrained by the experiences of the late eighteenth and the nineteenth centuries. Thus, when the next opportunity for confrontation occurs in 1918–20, the results are again characterized by nationalist exclusivism.

IV. AUSTRO-HUNGARIAN EMPIRE, 1867

Bártfa
Eperjes
Kassa
N.szombat
Pozsony
Munkács
Miskolc
Tisza
Szatmárnémeti
N.bánya
Sopron
Esztergom
Budapest
Kőszeg
Székesfehérvár
Debrecen
Szamos
Szolnok
N.várad
Beszterce
Körös
Duna
Kolozsvár
Torda
Zaránd
Abrudbánya
Marosvásárhely
Drava
Szeged
Maros
Arad
Pécs
Mohács
Szabadka
Gyulafehérvár
Zagreb
Brassó
Temesvár
N.szeben
RUMANIA
Sava
Belgrade
Duna
SERBIA

GEND:

International Borders
Border of Hungary
Habsburg Empire
Hungary
Ottoman Empire
Rumania
Serbia
Other States

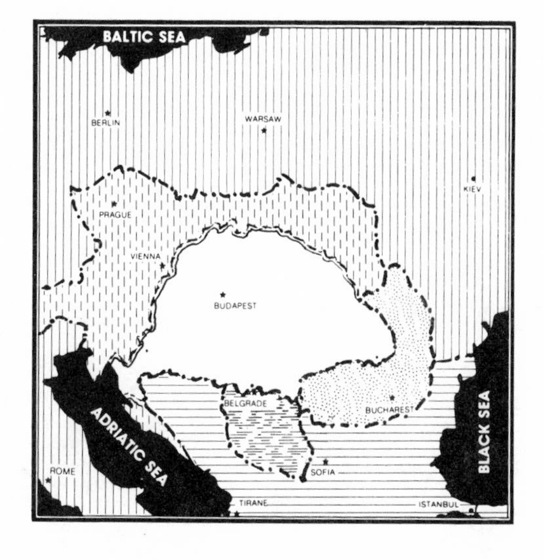
BALTIC SEA
BERLIN
WARSAW
KIEV
PRAGUE
VIENNA
BUDAPEST
BELGRADE
BUCHAREST
ADRIATIC SEA
BLACK SEA
ROME
SOFIA
TIRANE
ISTANBUL

The Horea-Cloşca Revolt of 1784–85: Some Observations

JOSEPH HELD

Introduction

The outlines of the peasant revolt of 1784–85 in Transylvania are not very difficult to establish. Unrest was endemic in the southern portions of the province, where the mountains harbored fugitives and various highwaymen who periodically raided the traveling merchants. On January 3, 1784, Emperor Joseph II ordered a trial census of the peasantry for the purpose of signing them up for the border forces as auxiliary militiamen. This created a great deal of hope, especially among the Rumanian peasants of the Abrudbánya (Abrud, Gross-Schlatten) region, that they would be freed of their feudal obligations once they had joined the army. During the summer, however, royal agents were sent to calm the unrest among the peasants by assuring them that they would have to continue serving their lords and fulfilling their obligations to them. Obviously these agents were not believed; in late October or early November, open revolt began at the Zalátna (Zlatna) estate of the treasury, spreading to the adjoining mining districts, then into Hunyad and Krassó-Szörény counties. By the end of the month, peasants armed themselves against the lords in some villages of the Maros River valley. The unrest spread throughout the province. After some initial hesitation, the imperial authorities decided to intervene and sent regular troops against the rebellious people. They successfully suppressed the revolt by early December. The leaders were betrayed to the authorities by some Rumanian peasants and were caught later in the month; they were interrogated in January, 1785, and with one exception (who either committed suicide or died of some unknown cause) were executed in February in the presence of representatives of a large number of villages. Their bodies (including that of the one who died in jail) were quartered and put on exhibit in various regions of the province in order to provide an example for future rebels. The causes of the unrest were then explored by the royal commission, who placed the blame partly on inept royal officials but mainly upon the shoulders of a recalcitrant Hungarian nobility for their alleged sabotage of imperial reforms intended for the rationalization of the administration of Transylvania. The revolt did for the Rumanians of Transylvania what the massacre of Mádéfalva had done for the Székelys in 1764,[1] namely, it brought home to them the realization that their conationals across the Transylvanian borders probably constituted a better guarantee of their well-being than did the existing institutions of the Habsburg state. In this way the unsuccessful revolt became a powerful catalyst of early Rumanian nationalism.

Peasant revolts in Europe's feudal age followed a recognizable pattern.[2] Part of this pattern concerned peasant beliefs that too many innovations—usually in the form of new tax regulations—were destroying a formerly "better" or even "freer" way of life. Revolts of this nature usually began when improvements in peasant life were promised but not delivered by the authorities, creating expectations that the authorities never really intended to fulfill. It usually seemed to the peasantry that royal intentions to improve their lot were being sabotaged by "bad advisors" at court or by the local nobility; they perceived that their foe was not the royal authority but rather its underlings.

The leadership of peasant uprisings usually came from various social strata, and only a few of the leaders were peasants themselves. Most often the leaders were disgruntled petty noblemen or priests, or even craftsmen from nearby cities or towns, and sometimes discharged soldiers. The often indiscriminate looting and burning that accompanied peasant disturbances as well as the attacks on villages and individual peasants who refused to join the rebellion resulted in the gradual loss of support for the peasant warriors among their own social class and the isolation of the rebels from the most satisfied elements in peasant society. The demands of the rebellious peasants were usually too particularistic—centering mainly on the solution to some local problem—to attract universal societal support.[3]

Many such peasant revolts occurred from the fourteenth through the eighteenth centuries, most notable among them the English rising of 1381, the movement of the French Touchin in the late fourteenth century, the peasant rising of Bábolna in 1437–38 in Transylvania, the Hungarian rebellion of György Dózsa in 1514, the Karinthian peasant revolt of 1515, the great German peasant war of 1525–26, and the French, Russian, and Chinese risings of the seventeenth century.[4] The Horea-Cloşca revolt of 1784–85 represented a late wave of these classic peasant movements.

This last uprising displayed many elements of classic peasant revolts. These included unfulfilled expectations for the abolition of feudal obligations, for a possibly freer life for the peasants as militiamen in the border regiments, and for the general betterment of life for the entire peasantry. An added feature that made the short-lived uprising so significant, foreshadowing later popular movements in Eastern Europe, was the issue of an early Rumanian nationalism. There was also the problem of religious discrimination against Orthodox Christians in Transylvania, the majority of whom belonged to the ethnically Rumanian population.[5]

To be sure, we cannot as yet speak in terms of a modern-day national consciousness dominating the thinking and aspirations of the Transylvanian Rumanian peasants who made up the bulk of the warriors in 1784; but the fact was that they regarded the nobility, whose majority happened to be Hungarian, as the chief agents of their oppression.[6] At the same time, since the geographic boundaries of the Rumanian language roughly corresponded to the boundaries of the Orthodox faith in Transylvania, the common opponents of the faith and of nationality appeared to be the non-Orthodox, Roman Catholic, or Protestant Hungarians as a whole.[7]

When exploring the issues in Transylvania in 1784, we will want to know more, first of all, about the social conditions of the population as a whole; this will help us understand the bases of peasant grievances. We will also want to explore the leadership of the revolt, to find out who the peasant leaders really were, what goals were set by them, and what the short-term and long-range consequences of their movement were. In a short essay such as this, the author does not intend to provide a more detailed description of the actual course of events than the short account above but will concentrate on these questions, being fully aware of the tentative nature of the answers provided by the available sources.

The Social Issues

By the late eighteenth century, the population of Transylvania, now part of the Habsburg Empire but administered separately from Hungary, was 1.45 million inhabitants.[8] In comparison with the situation a century before, this figure represented the doubling of the population. However, the increase was only partly the result of natural growth; most of it came from immigration, largely from the Danubian Principalities, consisting mainly of Rumanian peasants.[9] There was also a reverse movement of Hungarians, especially Székelys, leaving Transylvania for the Moldavian lands. Consequently, by the mid-eighteenth century, over half, or fifty-five percent, of the population were ethnically Rumanian; about thirty percent were Hungarian, another ten percent were Saxons, while the rest were South Slavs. One peculiarity of the social composition of the population was the fact that only about 52,000 people lived in the cities and towns, while the rest resided in villages. This pointed to an important social characteristic that was to plague the entire region for the next two centuries, namely, the fact that it lacked an urban middle class.

Accordingly, the two economically, politically, and socially important branches of society consisted of the nobility and the peasantry. The nobility made up an unusually large segment of the population—close to ten percent—including women and children. The majority of the nobles were ethnically Hungarian, although there were many Rumanian noblemen, and a narrow stratum of Saxon patricians may also be considered in this category. But the nobility as such was not a homogeneous stratum. About 260 of the richest, most powerful families were the so-called magnates, possessing the largest estates in the province, dominating practically every facet of social life in Transylvania. The rest of the nobility lived under more modest conditions, sometimes not very different from those of the peasantry.[10]

The policies of the Habsburg administration in Translyvania were openly exploitative, representing an early colonial regime, throughout the entire eighteenth century. These policies were devised to syphon off the wealth of the province through a system of tariffs and taxes, regardless of the consequences of such policies on the economic base that was already strained by the population increase. In order to be able to derive the maximum income from Transylvania for the royal treasury, the administration's first task appeared to be to free the peasants from landlord control—and from the accompanying feudal obligations paid to the nobility. It was at this point that the interests of the peasantry and the royal representatives seemed to coincide. But this was only apparent. In fact, the Habsburg rulers were not that much interested in easing the burdens of the peasants; they simply wanted to free them from landlord control in order to have them exploited by the state.[11] These policies, of course, ran directly counter to the very survival of the nobility as a social group.

In comparison with the life style of similar social groups in Hungary proper and in the Austrian crownlands, the Transylvanian nobles were poor indeed. With the exception of the magnates, their sole means of survival as nobles depended upon the services and obligations rendered by the serfs. In order to increase their income and "catch up" with the nobility of the rest of the Habsburg Empire, many Transylvanian nobles (following the example of their fellow nobles elsewhere in the Habsburg lands) gradually altered peasant obligations until, during the second half of the eighteenth century, the peasants' burdens were considerably increased.[12] What was especially injurious was the steep increase in the number of days required of the peasants to work on their lord's land; by the second half of the century, most of the workweek of peasants was spent on the *robot,* leaving them little time to work their own plots.[13] While the Habsburg administration tried by various means to lower the peasants' obligations to the nobility, the nobles naturally resisted these efforts as a direct attack upon their lifestyle and social status, and tried to achieve just the opposite.

However, the situation was not the same on all noble estates. On the lands of the magnates, for instance, there was enough ploughland available for the use of the peasants, and they were permitted to till these lands for their own benefit after the fulfillment of their obligations. But the lesser nobles felt forced to exclude many peasants from lands that the latter had used for generations, as these nobles saw greater profits if they used these lands themselves. At the same time, they demanded more days of labor from the serfs. Furthermore, while the magnates were generally away from their estates most of the year, the lesser nobles were in daily contact with the serfs, who saw in them the personification of their exploitation. It must be emphasized once again that most lesser nobles were Hungarians, while a large number of serfs were ethnically Rumanian. Not only did they belong to different language groups, but to different religious denominations as well. No wonder that the fury of the revolt of 1784–85 was to be directed against the lesser nobility, i.e., the Hungarians.

There also existed a great deal of arbitrariness in peasant-landlord relations, and not only in Transylvania, but throughout the entire Habsburg Empire. The demands of the lords varied not only from province to province, but sometimes even within individual estates. This was the case not only in privately held estates, but also on lands controlled by the royal treasury, such as, for instance, the estate of Zalatna, where the spark of the revolt was eventually struck. Arbitrariness not only fostered dissatisfaction and tension in the countryside, but it seriously interfered with the orderly administration of the province, especially the collection of taxes.[14]

Vienna realized early in the eighteenth century that no systematic taxation could be devised without the uniform regulation of landlord-peasant relations. In the views of Maria Theresa and her son, Joseph II, "enlightened rule" in the empire required the reduction or even elimination of peasant obligations to the landlords, in order to free peasant resources for the purposes of the state.[15] Nor could the empire create a strong military organization, one that it increasingly needed in the face of challenges from France, Prussia, and Russia, without drawing upon the masses of the peasantry for soldiers, if not for the regular army, at least for the border guards. Since the peasants were, for the most part, under the jurisdiction of the nobles, the evident aim of the enlightened absolutist Habsburg state was to transform and restrict the system of serfdom that, in these instances, seemed to have outlived its usefulness.[16] But the stiff opposition of the nobility, centering on the county administrations that they controlled, slowed down or even sabotaged all royal attempts at reform.[17]

The peasantry itself was divided into several social strata ethnically as well as economically. There were Rumanian peasants following the Orthodox faith, or of the Uniate church; there were also Hungarian, Saxon, and South Slav peasants living in the province, belonging to other religious denominations. They were either *dominicales* (tenant farmers), having a contractual relationship with their landlords, or were ordinary *iobagiones* (serfs), settled on and tied to the land. Although a tenant was theoretically free to move and did not need his lord's permission to get married, and his sons were free to chose a craft if they so pleased (all these restrictions were applied to the serfs), the tenant was subject to the lord's juridical and administrative authority.[18] The Habsburg emperors tried, first of all, to set limits on the amount of peasant obligations due the landlords. Thus, Maria Theresa attempted to equalize peasant status by declaring all peasants to be free tenants.[19] When Joseph II came to rule alone, he was determined to further reduce the weight of feudalism in his realms. Between 1783 and 1785, he not only declared all serf obligations to be abolished in Transylvania and Hungary proper (also in Bohemia and the crownlands), but also ended the age-old restrictions on marriage, on the freedom to move, and of occupation. At the same time, he issued a decree imposing a thirty percent tax on peasant incomes in lieu of the former feudal obligations.[20] Although this was a severe demand, since the peasants possessed little cash money, the overall intentions of the emperor were interpreted by the people, especially the Rumanian peasants, as proof of his good will towards them. In turn, the nobility's opposition to the royal decrees (never cleared by the duly constituted legal authorities) was regarded by the peasants as an openly hostile act not only against the emperor but also against themselves.

The military situation in the Balkan peninsula after the expulsion of the Turks from Hungary at the end of the seventeenth century demanded that the empire build up its border forces. In turn, the state needed more soldiers to man the outposts of the realm. More soldiers naturally meant the need for more money for their maintenance; this could only be achieved through the reorganization of the empire's taxation policies and through the partial elimination of special privileges that exempted the largest group of the wealthiest inhabitants, the nobility, from the tax rolls.

As early as 1762, Maria Theresa had tried to establish a new system of border defenses in Transylvania (similar to the military border created in the Croatian lands of the empire), which led to the resistance and massacre of the free Székelys by the regular Habsburg army at Mádéfalva.[21] On the other hand, large numbers of Rumanian serfs welcomed the establishment of border regiments, since by joining these forces they expected to gain freedom from their serf obligations. When Joseph II opened recruitment on a trial basis in 1784, the Rumanian peasants of the Beszterce (Bistritz, Bistriţa) region signed up en masse, as did the male population from numerous villages near Gyulafehérvár, the capital of Transylvania, and from some villages in the Maros River valley. This only strengthened the nobles' resolve to oppose the establishment of the border regiments, since they regarded the recruitment of peasants without their permission as evidence of the high-handedness of the Habsburg state. Accordingly, they did everything in their power to stop the peasants from joining the army. At the same time, the imperial authorities became alarmed by the apparent success of their own initiative; they were surprised at the intensity of peasant reponse to their call and began cancelling the recruitment drive.[22]

By then, the emperor's reforms included decrees for religious toleration in Hungary and Transylvania, orders for the unification of the chancelleries of the two political entities, and the creation of new administrative districts, replacing the age-old system of county government. Joseph II also declared that ability, not birth, was to be the basis of future appointments to government offices and that German would replace Latin as the language of the administration in his domains, including Transylvania, within three years.

Many of the Rumanian peasants greeted these reforms with jubilation. At a stroke of the emperor's pen, their religion gained equal status with the other religions of Transylvania,[23] their status as serfs had been greatly eased, and once again they were called to sign up for the border forces. They cared little about changes in the official language, which was alien to them in any case. When the administrators tried to intervene with their signing up for the army, they regarded this as a conspiracy against the emperor's orders. But long-simmering discontent did not break out into open rebellion on the lands controlled by the nobility. Actual trouble started on the estate of the treasury at Zalatna.

Peasant unrest was, of course, not a new phenomenon in Transylvania. Peasants-turned-highwaymen periodically raided villages and small towns. After each raid they withdrew into the mountains or, if the pursuit were too vigorous, they moved into Moldavia or Wallachia through the mountain passes. Entire counties were made unsafe by these highwaymen during the eighteenth century. In Arad and Zaránd counties, few merchants ventured on the open road without strong escort, and the villages paid regular tribute to the highwaymen.[24] Nor were the robbers lacking in local sympathy. They were often considered the successors to the legendary fighters against the Turks who had freed captive peasants and took vengance on the Muslim enemy. For many peasants, the highwaymen were now simply fighting another oppressor who happened to be either an Austrian official or a Hungarian nobleman.[25]

Many of the bands were made up of former soldiers who had found army life too demanding and thus deserted. They were resourceful men who were thoroughly familiar with the locality in which they operated and often knew the administrators on a personal basis. In Arad County, they even captured the head of the county administration, Count András Forray, and held him for ransom and for a pledge of amnesty.[26] Most highwaymen were ethnically Rumanian; according to some reports, entire districts were involved in their affairs, the peasants accepting and selling their loot and providing safe havens for them between raids.[27] Some of the highwaymen were to play an important role in the revolt of 1784–85.

The problems of the estate of Zalatna were not new either, and they reflected peasant discontent in a microcosm. The administrators of the estate pressed the peasants for more and more days of labor. At the same time, they were involved in a scheme to deprive the treasury of some of its income from the estate, a scheme discovered during 1784. After the scandal, the administrators were replaced by new ones, who tried to press the peasants to fulfill their obligations to the estate in order to erase the memory of the past. Another problem was that the peasants were forbidden to clear forest lands for cultivation, since the trees were needed for the mines administered by the estate. Given contemporary agrarian techniques and an expanding population, the peasants did need more land; their interests, thus, clashed sharply with those of the estate. The estate also demanded higher taxes from its serfs for the support of the ever-expanding population of officials and of the village judges who served both the estate and the county authorities. A long-standing peasant grievance came to the fore in early 1784, when the peasants protested the authorities' discriminatory practices against the Orthodox faith. This had already caused a minor disturbance at the estate in the 1740s.[28]

Yet, the immediate cause of the outbreak was a seemingly insignificant dispute over peasant innkeeping rights. Such disputes were, naturally, inherent in the system of serfdom. These rights were included in patents originally issued by the Princes Báthory of Transylvania in the sixteenth century, but were gradually forgotten and disregarded. In 1784, the estate leased innkeeping rights to certain merchants. When copies of the original patents were found and submitted by the peasants to the governor of the estate, they were told that their rights were no longer valid and that the estate was entitled to lease the innkeeping privileges to whomever it chose. This argument was accepted by the county administration.

The Leaders

Nicola-Vasilii Urs, nicknamed Hora (Horea) for his strong voice,[29] was born around 1730 in Zaránd County. He is called a serf by all sources, but he certainly was not an ordinary peasant. He was actually a carpenter by trade; according to the customs of the time, he travelled a great deal, seeking work and becoming well-acquainted with conditions of life among the simple people. By the time he appeared on the scene, he was regarded as spokesman for the Rumanian peasants at the Zalatna estate and was considered a troublemaker by the officials.[30] It seems that he remained a great traveler; sources maintain that he visited Vienna four times,[31] each time seeking and gaining an audience with the emperor—an unlikely possibility—requesting imperial help against the exploitation of the peasants by the estate officials and the Hungarian nobles.[32]

It would be well to reiterate that Horea was not a peasant in the ordinary sense of the term; he did not make his living by tilling the soil or raising animals. Despite the undoubtedly broader perspective that he gained during his travels, he failed to grasp the full meaning of imperial policies in Transylvania. He was absolutely, if naively, convinced that the running conflict of the emperor with the nobility placed the ruler in the same camp with the peasants. He expected imperial approval—if not outright, direct support—in the coming peasant uprising against the "common enemy." He believed that the emperor's sympathies were strong enough to stay the hands of local military commanders at least until the peasants succeeded in eliminating the influence of the Hungarian nobles from the Transylvanian province once and for all.

Ion Oarga, or Cloşca, was a serf from the village of Carpinis, located near Abrudbánya. He was seventeen years Horea's junior when the uprising began. He was loyal to Horea to the very end; their friendship may have begun (and became cemented) during Horea's journeys to Vienna, on which Cloşca probably accompanied him. He was the most likely author of the document presenting peasant demands during the uprising. Although we know very little of Cloşca's life, he certainly did not appear to have been just another ordinary peasant of the eighteenth century either.[33]

Giurgu Marcu, called Crişan, the third leader of the peasant uprising, was a former professional soldier. We do not know if he was discharged from the army or if he simply deserted; we only know that he was about Horea's age. He was the military organizer of the uprising, an excellent tactician, and a sharp-eyed strategist. It was probably Crişan who organized the distribution and movement of the peasant forces during the uprising; he foresaw that only through simultaneous attacks in various regions could the uprising gain enough momentum for success. We know that he, too, was originally from Zaránd County, but there is little else in the documents about his earlier life.[34]

The nineteen-year-old son of Nicola-Vasilii Urs, Ion Horea, was the fourth major leader of the revolt. He worked closely with Cloşca at the outbreak of the uprising, but he gained an independent command as the fighting progressed. However, he was nicknamed after his father; this shows that he did not have enough time to assume a separate identity and, thus, remained the least important of the four leaders of the uprising.

There was a sizeable contingent of soldiers and highwaymen—about 150 or so out of 4,000–5,000 fighters—who made up the second echelon of the leadership of the peasant troops. They provided the tactical know-how for the insurgent army, teaching the peasants the swift, organized movements that characterized their type of warfare. Their major problem was the poor armament of their troops. As long as they faced only the frightened and disorganized nobility, they had an easy and victorious campaign; however, as soon as they had to contend with the troops of the regular army, their fighting spirit quickly disappeared.

The demands of the insurgents were formulated as the revolt progressed. At first, in the white heat of hatreds that accumulated over the years, the only desire of the peasants was to kill the nobles, burn their castles or houses together with the documents of peasant servitude, and carry away as much of the nobles' property as could be found. However, after the initial fury of the revolt was spent, Horea and

Cloşca proceeded to formulate more precise—if simplistic—aims that, they seemed to believe, corresponded to the ideas of the reform-minded emperor.

The demands were few and to the point. First of all, the peasants asked for the abolition of the privileges of the nobility. This meant that the peasants were no longer to be required to provide a living for the noblemen. However, mindful that the nobles would need a way to make a living, they suggested, perhaps somewhat naively, that the nobles be given positions in the imperial bureaucracy as suited their individual abilities. This way the emperor's declaration about ability as the basis for office would have been fulfilled. The next demand was the confiscation of all noble estates and their distribution among the peasantry. Finally, the last demand argued that the nobility, no longer being in a privileged position, should be required to pay state taxes, as were the rest of the population. By this, the public burdens would be distributed more evenly among the population.[35] In plain language, the Rumanian peasants wanted political equality and land reform; if fulfilled, these demands would have automatically taken care of local grievances and ended serfdom in Transylvania in fact as well as in theory.

These demands also reflected the influence of the European Enlightenment as it filtered down from the royal court through the provincial administrators to the peasantry. If Joseph II really wanted to rationalize his administration, so the peasants seemed to reason, and if the major obstacle in his way was the resistance of the nobility, the peasants would not only eliminate this obstacle by force, but would make sure that the emperor would have enough men to choose from to upgrade his bureaucracy. If he were anxious to establish an equitable system of taxation, the peasants would help him in this endeavor by making all people equal. The demand for land reform reflected the conviction that land, the basis of all wealth and security in that age, should be shared among those who could derive the greatest benefits from it.

The Consequences

The immediate consequences of the revolt were not as severe as could be expected or as the nobility wanted them to be. Despite the hundreds of noble families indiscriminately massacred by the insurgents, the retributions were comparatively mild. It was true that about thirty-seven men were executed in a most barbaric manner (though not at all unusual in that "enlightened" age) by the authorities to instill in future would-be revolutionaries fear of the power of the state.[36] But the commission set up by Joseph II to examine the causes of the revolt suggested leniency towards ordinary participants, freeing many of them and commuting the sentences of others. Joseph II believed that the royal administration of Transylvania was at least partly to be blamed for the uprising, and he also maintained that, had his reforms been executed without obstruction by the nobility, the revolt could have been avoided. Accordingly, the emperor urged the Transylvanian administrators to proceed with the execution of royal decrees without further delay as the best guarantee of the social peace of the province.[37]

But the long-range consequences of the uprising were more serious. They included the intangible but certainly greater consciousness of national hatreds and suspicion between Rumanians and Hungarians in general. Just as the Rumanian peasants and their spokesmen after the uprising, the Orthodox priests, and the emerging Rumanian intellectual class transferred their hatred of the Hungarian nobility to all Hungarians regardless of class, so the Hungarians reciprocated. Both peoples were to enter an age of strident, jingoistic nationalism. The ideologues of each nation were eventually to deny the other nation's right to existence. The struggle for national supremacy in Transylvania was to be buttressed by all sorts of myths and outright lies, usually based on the primitive argument of "who was there first," as if ethnic groups who have lived on a territory for nearly a millenium could ever be regarded by anyone as "newcomers."

NOTES

1. The massacre of Székelys at the village of Mádéfalva on January 7, 1764, has not yet been fully explored by historians. It is a dark chapter in the history of the "enlightened" ruler, Maria Theresa. Some important sources of this event include the following: Bálint Hóman and Gyula Szekfű, *Magyar történet* [Hungarian History] (Budapest, 1936), 5: 124–26; László Makkai, *Erdély története* [History of Transylvania] (Budapest, 1943), pp. 484–93; Lajos Szádeczky, *A székely határőrség megszervezése, 1762–1764* [The Establishment of the Székely Border Guards, 1762–1764] (Budapest, 1908); István Balló, *A mádéfalvi veszedelem* [The Calamity of Madefalva] (Budapest, 1906); Henrik Marczali, *Erdély története* [History of Transylvania] (Budapest, 1935), pp. 220–25; Domonkos Teleki, *A székely határőrség története* [The History of the Székely Border Guards] (Budapest, 1877).

2. The literature of this subject is as large as it is controversial, colored no doubt by the ideological biases of the disputants. See, for instance, Rodney H. Hilton, *Bond Men Made Free. Peasant Movements and the English Rising of 1381* (London, 1973); Roland Mousnier, *Fureurs Paysannes: Les paysannes dans les Révoltes du XVIIe Siécle* (Paris, 1967); Barrington Moore, Jr., *Social Origins of Dictatorship and Democracy, Lord and Peasant in the Making of the Modern World* (Boston, 1966).

3. See, for instance, my earlier study, "The Peasant Revolt of Bábolna, 1437–1438," *Slavic Review* 36, no. 1 (1977): 25–38. See also Boris Porchnev, *Les soulèvements*

populaires en France de 1623 (Paris, 1963); Leon Bernard, "French Society and Popular Uprisings under Louis XIV," *French Historical Studies* 3, no. 4 (1964): 454–74.

4. For the English and French *jacqueries* see Hilton, op. cit.; for the Dózsa rebellion, see László Geréb and György Székely, *A magyar parasztháboruk irodalma* [The Written Record of the Hungarian Peasant Wars] (Budapest, 1950); for the Austrian revolt see Martin Mayer, "Die inner-österreichiesche Bauernkrieg des Jahres 1515, nach alteren und nemen Quellen," *Archiv für Österreichische Geschichte* 65 (1884): 17–43; the literature of the German peasant uprising is so large and well-known that it is not necessary to list it here.

5. The religious policies of the Habsburg monarchs in the eighteenth century are discussed in Alfred R. von Arneth, *Maria Theresia* (Wien, 1879), 10:131–57. Joseph II's decrees of toleration are published in *Collectio benignorum normalium Resolutionum caes. reg. materia commissionis ecclesiasticae,* 2 vols. (Pest, 1785–96). See also Georg Holzknecht, "Ursprung und Herkunft der Reformideen Kaiser Josefs II auf kirchlichem Gebiete," *Forschungen zur inneren Geschichte Österreichs* 11 (1914); Karl Ritter, *Kaiser Joseph II und seine kirchlichen Reformen* 2 vols. (Regensburg, 1867). Antal Meszlényi, *A jozefinizmus kora Magyarországon 1780–1846* [The Age of Joseph's Reforms in Hungary, 1780–1846] (Budapest, 1934); for Habsburg policies concerning the Uniate church and Orthodoxy, see Herbert Klima, "Die Union der Siebenbürger Rumänen und der Wiener Staatrat im theresianischen Zeitalter," *Südost Forschungen* 6 (1941): 249–60.

6. See, for instance, Benedek Jancsó, "Az erdélyi románság legrégibb hiteles statisztikája," [The Oldest Dependable Statistics Concerning the Transylvanian Rumanians] *Századok* [Centuries] 34 (1900): 41–42; see also Marczali, op. cit., pp. 226–28. In fact, there were some Hungarian and Saxon peasants who joined the rebellion; see Zsigmond Jakó, *Adatok a torockói jobbágylázadások történetéhez* [Data Concerning the History of the Peasant Revolts in Torockó] (Kolozsvár, 1945).

7. See Paul von Mitrofanov, *Joseph II*, 2 vols. (Vienna, 1910); Wilhelm Lustkandl, *Die josephinischen Ideen und ihr Erfolg* (Wien, 1881); W. Bruckner, *Die Reformen Kaiser Josefs II* (Jena, 1867); Tibor Baráth, *L'Absolutisme éclaire en Hongrie* (Paris, 1936); Mihály Horváth, *Magyarország történelme* [History of Hungary] (Budapest, 1873), 7:465–99; Henrik Marczali, *Magyarország II József korában* [Hungary in the Age of Joseph II] 3 vols. (Budapest, 1882–1888); for the suppression of the revolt, see Ödön Olchváry, "A hóra-lázadás leverésére kivezényelt katonaság magatartása," [The Role of the Military Units Sent to Quell the Horea Rebellion] *Hadtörténelmi Közlemények* [Annals of Military History] 17 (1916):107–42.

8. For population statistics in Transylvania, see Gusztáv Thirring, "II József magyarországi népszámlálásai," [The Population Censuses in Hungary During the Reign of Joseph II] *Magyar Statisztikai Szemle* [Hungarian Statistical Review] 9 (1931):112–34; Károly Tagányi, "Az 1787. évi első népszámlálás eredményei," [The Results of the First Population Census of 1787] *Magyar Gazdaságtörténeti Szemle* [Review of Hungarian Economic History] 3 (1896):281–82; and Gusztáv Thirring, *Magyarország népessége II. József korában* [The Population of Hungary in the Age of Joseph II] (Budapest, 1938).

9. Josef März, *Josef II Kaiser und Siedlungspolitiker* (Berlin, 1938), pp. 316–18. See also Nicolae M. Pop, *Populaţia Banatului in timpul lui Iosif II* [The Population of the Banat During the Age of Joseph II] (Timişoara, 1943); Makkai, op. cit.; Jancsó, op. cit.

10. Makkai, op. cit.

11. See Henrik Marczali, "Magyarország adórendszere 1780-ban," [Hungary's Tax System in 1780] *Budapesti Szemle* [Budapest Review] 26(1881):370–87. See also Robert Braun, *II József közigazgatási reformeszméi* [The Administrative Reform Ideals of Joseph II] (Arad, 1900), p. 106.

12. See Gábor Salacz, "Tessedik Sámuel javaslatai a parasztság helyzetének javítására," [The Proposals of Samuel Tessedik Concerning the Improvement of Peasant Conditions] *Debreceni Szemle* [Debrecen Review] (1928) pp. 418–24; see also the contemporary report, by Pál Spielenburg, *Szabad elmélkedések a földeknek kimérése szerént felállitandó adózás systémájának tökéletlenségéről.* [Unrestricted Reflections on the Imperfections of the Proposed System of Measuring Landed Property Taxation] (Kassa, 1790); and Marczali, op. cit., 1:202–13.

13. Makkai, op. cit.; see also Zoltán I. Tóth, *Parasztmozgalmak az Erdélyi Érchegységben 1848-ig* [Peasant Movements in the Transylvanian Ore Mountains to 1848] (Budapest, 1951).

14. See Friedrich Walter, *Die österreichische Zentralverwaltung. Die Zeit Josephs II und Leopold II, 1780–1792* 2 vols. (Wien, 1950), 1:1, part 1. See also Marczali, op. cit., 2:30–37.

15. See Johann Zinner, *Animadversiones in jus publicum Hungariae,* ed., F. R. Grossing (Kassa, 1786). See also László Fürdős, *A II. József-féle kataszteri felmérés Magyarországon* [The Cadaster Land Survey of Hungary Under Joseph II] (Szeged, 1931).

16. For the politics of serfdom and Joseph II's attitudes towards it see Horváth, op. cit., 7:578–79. See also Zsigmond Pál Pach, *Az eredeti tőkefelhalmozódás Magyarországon* [The Earliest Capital Accumulation in Hungary] (Budapest, 1952); Jenő Berlász, "Az 1784-i erdélyi parasztfelklés és II. József jobbágypolitikája," [The Transylvanian Peasant Rising of 1784 and the Policies of Joseph II Regarding the Serfs] in *Tanulmányok a parasztság történetéhez Magyarországon, 1711–1790* [Studies Concerning the Peasantry in the History of Hungary 1711–1790] (Budapest, 1952).

17. Of contemporary observations of this resistance see *Collectio ordinationum imperatoris Josephi II et repraesentatiorum diversorum Hungariae comitatum* (Diószeg, 1790); *Collectio repraesentatiorum et protocollorum incl. atatuum et ordinum regni Hungariae* (Pest, Buda, Kassa, 1790), pp. 252–69. See also Otto Meltzl, "Die Gravaminalvorstellung des Siebenbürgischen Adels an Kaiser Josef II," *Archiv des Vereins Siebenbürgische Landeskunde* (1887), pp. 177–202; Miklós Forgách, *Patriotische Vorstellung an den Monarchen in Betreff der Wiederherstellung der vormaligen Regierungsform in Ungarn* (Pozsony, 1788). See also Friedrich Zieglauer, *Die politische Reformbewegung in Siebenbürgen zur Zeit Josefs II und Leopold II* (Wien, 1881).

18. Robert A. Kann, *A History of the Habsburg Empire. 1526–1918* (Berkeley, Los Angeles, London, 1975), pp. 195–99. See also Horváth, op. cit.; Marczali, op. cit., 1:22, 265–66.

19. See the urbarial decree of Maria Theresa in *Mi, Mária Theresia . . . Urbáriumokat vagy-is Földes Uraság Robottinak és adózásinak rendét Vármegyékben igazságossan el-intéztetni akarjuk . . .* [We, Maria Theresia . . . wish to Justly Regulate the System of Taxation in the Counties and the Performance of Socage-Service to the Landlord] (Wien, 1767). See also Ignácz Acsády, *A magyar jobbágyság története* [The History of Hungarian Serfdom] (Budapest, 1906), pp. 340-52.

20. See note 11 above.

21. See note 2 above.

22. For the literature on this and other issues pertinent to an understanding of peasant grievances, see O. Beu, *Bibliografia răscoli lui Horia* [Bibliography of the Horea Rising] (Sibiu, 1944).

23. The privileged religions of Transylvania that enjoyed toleration before the stabilization of Habsburg rule in the province were Roman Catholicism, Calvinism, Lutheranism, and Unitarianism. Orthodoxy was not included among these religions, but it was "tolerated." See István Miskolczy, "Az erdélyi felekezeti viszonyok Bajtai püs-

pöksége alatt, 1760–1772," [Religious denominational relations during Bishop Bajtai's tenure] *Békefi Emlékkönyv* [Békefy Album] (Budapest, 1912), pp. 328–39. See also S. Dragomir, *Istoria Desrobirei Religioase a Românilor olim Ardeal in secolul XVIII* [The History of the Religious Liberation of Rumanians During the Eighteenth Century] 2 vols. (Sibiu, 1920–30); Benedek Jancsó, "A hazai görög-keleti román metropolia története," [The History of the Rumanian Orthodox Metropolitanate in Our Homeland] *Századok* [Centuries] 35(1901):609–14.

24. See Marczali, op. cit., 2:1–35.

25. Ibid.

26. See Sándor Márki, "Forray András esete. Adat a Hóra-lázadás történetéhez," [The Case of András Forray. A Datum Concerning the History of the Horea-Rebellion] *Hazánk* [Homeland] 1(1884): 23–24.

27. Benedek Jancsó, "A Hóra-világ," [The World of Horea] *A román nemzetiségi törekvések története* [The History of Rumanian National Aspirations] (Budapest, 1899), 1:1–32.

28. Zoltán I. Tóth, op. cit.

29. See Lajos Siess, "Relationem de Tumultu et Insurrectione Gentis Vallachiae in Transylvania contra Nobilitatum et Nationem Hungarum, 1784–1785," in Lajos Merényi, "A Hóra-világ kismártoni krónikája," [The Chronicle of the World of Horea in Kismárton] *Történelmi Tár* [Historical Depository] (1901), pp. 1–40; Endre Veress, "A Hóra-világ Hunyad megyében," [The World of Horea in Hunyad County] *A Hunyad Megyei Történelmi és Régészeti Társaság Évkönyve* [The Historical and Archealogical Association's Yearbook of Hunyad County] 13(1903): 210–30; it is interesting to note that Keith Hitchins committed a rather elementary error in his *The Rumanian National Movement in Transylvania, 1780–1849* (Cambridge, Mass., 1969), pp. 37–38, when he described this nickname as a result of Urs's skill in dancing the *hora,* a folk dance. See also Nicolae Densuşianu, *Revoluţiunea lui Horea in Transylvania şi Ungaria 1784–1785* [Horea's Revolution in Transylvania and Hungary 1784–1785] (Bucharest, 1884), pp. 5–7.

30. See I. Lupaş, "Kaiser Josef II und der Bauernaufstand in Siebenbürgen," *Südostdeutsche Forschungen* 3(1938):674–79. See also Tóth, op. cit.

31. This has been mentioned by most sources, but is a highly questionable point. Even if Horea did go to Vienna four times, it seems difficult to imagine that he was received four times by the emperor. But contemporary sources seem to agree that Horea was a special person favored by Joseph II. See *Horja und Kloska Oberhaupt und Rathgeber der Aufrührer in Siebenbürgen* (Nagyszeben, 1785) and *Kurze Geschichte der Rebellion in Siebenbürgen* (Strassburg, 1785).

32. Tóth, op. cit.

33. He was, according to contemporary sources, a man of deep conviction, a good speaker and a charismatic leader. See M. Popescu, "Spicuiri noi despre Horia, Cloşca şi Crişan," [Reflections About Horea, Cloşca and Crişan] *Revista Archivelor* [Archival Review] (1926), pp. 411–15. See also Densuşianu, op. cit.

34. See Nicolae Edroiu, *Horea's Uprising. The 1784 Romanian Peasants' Revolt of Transylvania* (Bucharest, 1978), pp. 23–25.

35. See Ferenc Szilágyi, *A Hóra-világ Erdélyben* [The World of Horea in Transylvania] (Pest, 1871); C. Stoianescu, *Revoluţia lui Horia* [Horea's Revolution] (Timişoara, 1937); Dan Prodan, *Răscoala lui Horia în Comitatele Cluj şi Turda* [The Horea Rebellion in Cluj and Turda] (Bucharest, 1938).

36. See Victor Cucuiu, *Moartea eroilor Horia, Cloşca şi Crişan* [The Heroic Death of Horea, Cloşca and Crişan] (Cluj, 1937). See also Nicolae Iorga, "Horia, Cloşca şi Crişan," *Revista Istorică* [Historical Review] 33(1937):337–59.

37. Tóth, op.cit.

The Rumanian-Hungarian Confrontation, 1840–70

PAUL BŐDY

Early in the nineteenth century, movements of literary, political, and national revival emerged among the peoples who inhabited the multinational Habsburg Empire. One of the consequences of these movements was the awakening of a keen sense of national consciousness. Intense national rivalries developed in the course of the assertions of national pride among Hungarians, Rumanians, Slovaks, Croatians, Serbs, and others. An acute Rumanian-Hungarian confrontation emerged in the period after 1840 and reached its climax in political and military conflict in the Revolution of 1848.

Although these movements of national revival frequently encouraged national militancy, they should not be seen exclusively in that light. Essentially these movements represented highly diversified social, cultural, and political aspirations, of which national consciousness was one aspect among several. Furthermore, national feeling was not necessarily an element of discord. In fact, both before and after the Revolution of 1848, prominent Hungarian and Rumanian leaders sought to resolve national animosities and create the basis for durable cooperation. These initiatives proved to be partially successful in moderating national conflicts in the course of the nineteenth century.

As we survey the contemporary Rumanian-Hungarian controversy and its historical origins, it is instructive to reconstruct not only the divisive but also the conciliatory aspects of the Rumanian and Hungarian movements of reform in the nineteenth century. By doing so, the author of this essay seeks to contribute to a better understanding of a very crucial phase of Rumanian-Hungarian relationships and of the history of both peoples' national revival.

The Hungarian revival, developing from 1790 to 1848, consisted of a great variety of literary, intellectual, political, and public-policy aspirations. Their common focus was the recognition that Hungarian society and culture were in some manner underdeveloped and that it was therefore necessary to reform contemporary Hungarian society. The Hungarian revival not only proposed the ways of transformation, but sought to make specific contributions to an improved society.

One of the key tendencies of the Hungarian revival was the movement to develop a literate Hungarian language as the medium of cultural, social, and political life. Two distinct consequences of this movement can be observed. It resulted, first, in a nationwide opposition to the policies of Emperor Joseph II to introduce German as the language of Hungarian public life. Second, it encouraged other nationalities, such as the Rumanians, to assert their own language and to promote its development. The second impact proved to be of lasting importance, particularly because leaders of the Hungarian national movement went so far as to seek to establish through legislation and political action the dominant position of the Hungarian language in public life.[1]

Another major concern of the Hungarian revival was the enactment of social and political reforms that would transform traditional Hungarian society into a modernized nation. At least three major public policies were involved in this aspiration. First, there was the intent to reform the social and political organization of Hungary in accordance with the equality of all persons before the law, individual and civil liberties, and a representative system of government. Another set of proposals concerned the political, constitutional, and economic relationships between Hungary and the Habsburg Empire. Third, Hungarian reform leaders increasingly recognized the need to consider the aspirations of non-Hungarian nationalities.

The Hungarian and Rumanian revivals had certain common elements, but also a number of contrasting features. One common element was that both movements derived their inspiration from the eighteenth-century European Enlightenment. For example, the Hungarian Ferenc Kazinczy, modernizer of the Hungarian language, was a faithful student of the French Enlightenment and of German classicism. Samuil Micu, the founder of modern Rumanian, was deeply influenced by the contemporary Austrian Enlightenment as a student at the University of Vienna. Other examples abound. It is conclusive that the common heritage of both movements included a keen assimilation of the Enlightenment and a strong desire to improve Hungarian and Rumanian society.

But equally significant are the differences. One of these was the dominant tendency of the Rumanian movement to concentrate on the development of the Rumanian language, the expansion of Rumanian education, and the social improvement of the Rumanian people. In contrast, the Hungarian movement had a much more complex and a much broader scope. It was strongly committed, as was the Rumanian movement, to national advancement and improvement, but in addition it advocated programs of social and political reform, reorganization of the Habsburg Empire according to constitutional principles, and integration of emerging nationality movements into a modernized Hungarian society.

Another highly significant difference was the divergent social status of those who advocated the Hungarian and Rumanian movements. The Rumanian movement was led by members of the Uniate clergy who had studied in Rome, Vienna, and Transylvania. As a result, the leadership of the Rumanians had very limited opportunities for political action. In contrast, leaders of the Hungarian movement were predominantly noblemen involved in political activities, local governmental administration, and public discussions. The Hungarian leadership was very much an active political elite, strongly influenced by public-policy, economic, and political issues. These divergencies between the Hungarian and Rumanian national movements suggest an additional factor for the emergence of potential animosities between the leadership of the two national groups.[2]

The Rumanian-Hungarian controversy emerged at a time when the Hungarian revival advocated programs to reconstruct traditional Hungarian social and political institutions. An important element of these programs was the proposal to make the Hungarian language dominant in all aspects of public life. Unfortunately, influential leaders of the Hungarian revival sought to implement that proposal in such a way that it provoked the justified concerns of non-Hungarian national groups. An example of the national discord aroused by this issue was the enactment of legislation by the Hungarian Parliament in 1844 declaring Hungarian the official language of the kingdom of Hungary, extending to all aspects of public life.[3] Another matter of great anxiety was the frequently expressed intent of prominent Hungarian reformers to restrict the role of minority languages in Hungary through legislation and educational assimilation.[4]

While influential Hungarian leaders held these views, it is equally important to note that several prominent representatives of the Hungarian revival rejected them. Ferenc Kazinczy and Ferenc Kölcsey, two pioneers of the Hungarian literary revival, believed in the inherent value of each national language as a source of culture and enlightenment. Count Stephen Széchenyi, the father of Hungarian reformers, criticized these views in his public addresses of 1841 and 1842. In addition, the Hungarian revival advocated the introduction of reforms that sought to attain the advancement of all social and ethnic groups in Hungary. All these examples illustrate that the Hungarian revival comprised significant elements of a social and political modernization program that was potentially acceptable to Hungarians as well as to non-Hungarian nationality groups.[5]

The Revolution of 1848 witnessed the first important clash between the Hungarian and Rumanian national movements. But this clash was not at all predetermined. In fact, at several points during the revolution, initiatives were undertaken by both sides seeking a political compromise. At the beginning of the revolution, the Rumanian leadership of Hungary expressed its support for the Hungarian cause. Rumanian leaders endorsed the union of Transylvania with Hungary, which was an important objective of the Hungarian national movement.[6] In Transylvania, the question of union with Hungary became the subject of extended discussions among Rumanians. While it is true that the Rumanian national assembly of Balázsfalva (Blaj, Blasendorf) expressed its opposition to union, it is also important to note that influential elements of the Rumanian population in Transylvania were prepared to accept union and would have done so if other social and national demands had been seriously considered by the Hungarian leadership.[7]

Among the several complex problems that surfaced in the Revolution of 1848, one of the principal causes of the conflicts between Rumanians and the Hungarian leadership was unquestionably the inadequacy of the reform measures incorporated into the Hungarian April Laws of 1848. This legislation established the constitutional basis for social and political reforms in Hungary. Although these laws expressed the principles of a representative political process, a modernized social system, and the constitutional protection of civil, political, and personal liberties, they failed to meet the expectations of the Rumanians in Transylvania in several important respects. The April Laws failed to secure peasant ownership of land, they preserved the position and influence of the Hungarian nobility both at the local and national levels of government and they designated the Hungarian language as the mandatory language of public life. Nor did they make provisions for the protection of minority nationality rights.[8]

The history of the Hungarian Revolution of 1848, and especially its failure, illustrates well that the inadequacies of the April Laws played a significant role in the Rumanian-Hungarian confrontation. Two problems were particularly crucial. First, peasant uprisings throughout the revolutionary period showed that the reforms of 1848 failed to satisfy the needs of the peasants. Although members of the Hungarian Parliament pressed for a modest program of peasant land allotment, the revolutionary leadership opposed its enactment. Second, the Rumanian military opposition to the Hungarian revolutionary cause demonstrated that nationality rights had not been addressed in a satisfactory manner.

On the positive side, however, one should note that there was a recognition on the part of Hungarians and Rumanians of the importance of reaching a political understanding. Based on that recognition, the Rumanian-Hungarian controversy in 1848 could possibly have been resolved. This potential is particularly evident from the negotiations toward an understanding between Hungarian and Rumanian leaders. In response to Rumanian demands, the Hungarian government drafted a bill on nationality rights just prior to the defeat of the revolution. Nicolae Bălcescu, a prominent leader of the Rumanian revolutionary movement, encouraged this initiative and was prepared to establish political cooperation with the Hungarian government. These efforts came too late to have any impact in 1848–49. Yet it is worthwhile, in the context of this discussion, to recall the Hungarian-Rumanian negotiations and particularly to consider the analysis of the Transylvanian problem as stated by Bălcescu in 1849.

> It is not legitimate, useful, or possible to suppress the non-Rumanian population of Transylvania, which constitutes almost a third of its population. Extended settlement has established definite and undeniable rights even for very small nationalities. The rights of any nationality are sacred and should be respected. The way of nature supersedes historical rights, since man possesses the earth and not the earth man. The solution to the problem of Transylvania should not be sought by the domination of any one of the people that live there, but by establishing equal rights for each individual and each nationality, in order to establish harmonious cooperation.[9]

Following the failure of the Hungarian Revolution of 1848, an important phase of the Rumanian-Hungarian relationship began. In the period from 1860 to 1870, a series of political initiatives were undertaken, designed to reexamine the nationality conflicts of 1848 and to develop effective approaches to their resolution in a spirit of mutual understanding. To a large extent, the initiators of these approaches had been prominently involved in the revolutionary events of 1848. Painfully aware of the failure of their efforts, they attempted to address the question of nationality rights from a new perspective. For these reasons, the postrevolutionary period provides one of the most significant historical experiences for understanding not only the nineteenth century, but also the contemporary Hungarian-Rumanian controversies relating to Transylvania.

One should note, by way of historical background, that the Rumanians of Transylvania made significant social, cultural, and political progress as a result of the Hungarian revolutionary legislation of 1848.

As provisions of the emancipation of serfs were implemented in the 1850s, a total of 173,781 Rumanian peasant families, constituting approximately fifty percent of the Rumanian population of Transylvania, acquired land amounting to an average of ten acres and became independent landholders. This development made possible the establishment of a Rumanian landholding class in Transylvania. The city of Brassó (Braşov Kronstadt) in southern Transylvania became a thriving center of commerce, benefiting primarily Rumanian commercial establishments. Over 100 Rumanian commercial firms operated in the city in the 1850s. But the most important Rumanian attainment was in the field of cultural and educational development. Both the Rumanian Orthodox church and the Rumanian Uniate church attained autonomous status and the right to establish their corporate organizations, including educational institutions. As a result, over 300 new Rumanian Orthodox schools were established in the period after 1848.[10]

Starting in 1861, serious discussions of the nationality question surfaced again. The occasion for these discussions was the convocation of the Hungarian Parliament in 1861 to draft a response to imperial governmental initiatives for restoring Hungarian constitutional self-government. One element of the Hungarian response was to recognize, during the session of the Hungarian Parliament in 1861, the importance of protecting the rights of national minorities in Hungary.

The principal spokesman for such a Hungarian position was the prominent Hungarian reform leader, József Eötvös. Eötvös proposed to the Hungarian Parliament of 1861 the selection of a parliamentary committee to prepare a report on the protection of nationality rights. Eötvös was delegated chairman of this committee and was responsible for the majority report, submitted to the Hungarian Parliament in June, 1861. This report is one of the most important documents in the evolution of the postrevolutionary initiatives to define and protect the rights of national minorities in Hungary. Therefore, a review of its recommendations is crucial to an understanding of the Rumanian-Hungarian confrontation in the nineteenth century.[11]

Eötvös's report outlined a solution for the protection of nationality rights that was based on the free exercise of personal and political rights within a decentralized constitutional state. Since the 1840s, Eötvös had advocated reforms of Hungarian political and social institutions, based on the protection of civil and political liberties within a representative constitutional order. To a large extent, the April Laws reflected the program developed by Eötvös and his associates on the question of constitutional procedures. Eötvös approached the protection of national minority rights in 1861 on the basis of the same principles, arguing that the assurance of civil liberties was the cornerstone of any lasting program to safeguard national minority rights. His position is stated in an earlier essay on nationality rights:

"If we seek the guarantee for the exercise of nationality rights in the freedom of the individual, then the existence of the diverse nationalities in the state will become the guarantee of individual and simultaneously of political freedom."[12]

In the report of 1861, Eötvös specified several types of guarantees to protect nationality rights. First, all citizens would have the right to address municipal, county, and state officials in their native language. They would also be entitled to receive communications from these authorities in their native language. Second, all municipalities and counties would be assured the right to determine their official languages of communication to be used in public deliberations and official communications. At the same time, they would be obligated to use second and third languages if requested by minority populations. The only restriction on the choice of languages by these jurisdictions was the rule proposed in the report that all counties should communicate with the central Hungarian government in the Hungarian language. Third, the report outlined the rights of associations, schools, churches, and nationality organizations. Each church parish would be free to determine its official language of communication and the language used in school instruction. Each church would be entitled to establish primary and secondary schools and to determine for those schools the language of instruction. Each association and organization would be free to establish educational, cultural, and social institutions and to promote their development according to their charters of organization.[13]

Several characteristics of Eötvös's proposals should be noted. First, their underlying principle was that individual and minority rights should be safeguarded by the guarantees of the rights of citizenship, which were exercised by all citizens regardless of their ethnic identification. As a result of these guarantees, civil, political, and minority rights would be protected by a commonly accepted constitutional process. Further, Eötvös provided for an uncommonly free choice of language usage by individuals, municipalities, counties, educational institutions, and private organizations. His most farreaching proposal was the controversial provision to allow counties the choice of their official languages. In addition, the report reflected Eötvös's conception of a pluralistic and autonomously organized political structure, in which a variety of ethnic, religious, political, and cultural loyalties could be sustained without fear of repression or persecution. Given the complexity of ethnic relationships in Hungary and Translyvania, this conception represented possibly the most realistic approach to a political system capable of protecting minority nationalities in a constitutional and representative governmental process.

In sharp contrast to Eötvös's program on nationality rights stood the approach advocated by national congresses of Serbian and Slovak intellectuals in 1861. The aim of their proposals was to organize autonomous national territories, separated from each other by linguistic boundaries, in which one nationality exercised supreme political control. The Serbian congress proposed the creation of a Serbian territory, to be governed by a Serbian national assembly and a Serbian national executive. Within that territory all political affairs would be conducted in the national language, but each township would have the right to determine its language.[14] The Slovak congress proposed a similar approach, with the added requirement that only the Slovak language would be used in school, church, and political affairs.[15]

Of great interest is an intermediate proposal, prepared by two Rumanian members of the Hungarian Parliament of 1861, Louis Wlad and Sigmund Popovics. They were the authors of a minority report on nationality rights submitted to the Hungarian Parliament in 1861. Their recommendations agreed substantially with Eötvös's definition of linguistic rights for individuals, governmental jurisdictions, and organizations, while extending the right of counties to use minority languages in communications with the central Hungarian government. The Rumanian report also accepted Eötvös's recommendations on the cultural and educational autonomy of churches, associations, and educational organizations. The principal difference from Eötvös's draft was the declaration that all peoples inhabiting Hungary and Transylvania should be recognized as nations with equal rights, particularly in regard to their use of languages.[16]

Two significantly divergent approaches to the protection of nationality rights can be distinguished as they evolved in the 1860s. One based nationality rights on the coercive power of one linguistic majority, dominant within a specific territory. This conception sought to establish the equivalent of a unitary national state and intended to suppress or assimilate national minorities. Within such a system of government, national minorities were not permitted to exist. The approach developed by Eötvös was designed to safeguard, within a decentralized and representative political process, the rights of minority and majority nationalities at all levels of governmental jurisdiction. Such an approach was anchored on the protection provided by a common constitutional system and common rights of citizenship.[17]

Eötvös's approach is particularly significant as a response to the

Rumanian-Hungarian confrontation in the 1860s. Prominent Rumanian spokesmen supported Eötvös's position, as developed in his parliamentary statements and the Report of 1861. Ioan Faur, a Rumanian member of the Hungarian Parliament of 1861, stated the position of Rumanian moderates in his parliamentary address of June 10, 1861, approving the proposal of Eötvös that Hungary could best fulfil the needs of national minorities by recognizing and implementing minority rights through extended rights of citizenship.[18] A comparable position was developed in the minority report of 1861, prepared by Wlad and Popovics. Unfortunately, Eötvös's recommendations never became law. In 1867–68, when his proposals were seriously considered by the Hungarian Parliament, a storm of nationalist opposition blocked their enactment. At that time, Eötvös's approach was again supported by moderate Rumanian groups, particularly the Rumanian political journal *Concordia*.[19] During the final discussions in the Hungarian Parliament on the nationality bill, Eötvös's position was strangely vindicated by Louis Wlad, when he proposed in his parliamentary address of November 26, 1868, that Eötvös's report of 1861 be used as the basis of a Nationality Act that would guarantee the rights of all national minorities. Significantly, Wlad accepted the provisions of Eötvös's original recommendations of 1861 as a fully satisfactory solution for the protection of the Rumanian minority. He made the following comment in the course of his address:

> I wish to observe . . . that the majority bill dispenses privileges because it determines that the official language of counties will be the Magyar and permits exceptions only in so far as officials are ignorant of Magyar. This provision clearly contradicts the bill of 1861 prepared under the direction of the minister of public instruction, which permitted the free use of languages by townships and counties.[20]

Though Eötvös's recommendations on the protection of minority rights were not accepted by the Hungarian Parliament in 1868, he did exert considerable influence on Hungarian policies of education that substantially contributed to the extraordinary educational and cultural development of Rumanians in Hungary and Transylvania in the four decades after 1868. As Minister of Public Instruction from 1867 to 1871, Eötvös's major achievement was the preparation, enactment, and substantial implementation of the Elementary Education Act of 1868. This law assured organizational autonomy and self-government to all churches, associations, and school systems, with particular guarantees of freedom of choice in the language of instruction and religious education. The law also authorized townships to establish tax-supported public schools, where all children would receive instruction in their native language.[21] Eötvös was also instrumental in the enactment of legislation guaranteeing the corporate self-government of the Rumanian Orthodox church, a policy that he believed essential to the cultural and educational growth of the Rumanian nationality.[22]

These policies enabled the Rumanians of Translyvania to establish and conduct their own system of education in private, religious, and tax-supported public schools. They were guaranteed the free use of Rumanian as the primary language of instruction and the free exercise of their religion. The progress of Rumanian education can be evaluated by a brief survey of the educational development of the Rumanian Orthodox schools in the period after 1870. There were 1,294 Rumanian Orthodox schools in Hungary and Transylvania in 1870. Forty years later, in 1919, their number was 1,238. In the intervening period, Hungarian governments sought to weaken Rumanian schools, but largely as a result of the charter of autonomy secured by Eötvös for Rumanian education these policies proved ineffective. By comparison, Slovak Catholic schools declined from 1,236 in 1870 to 253 in 1910.[23]

Joseph Eötvös prepared the way for a judicious approach to the protection of national minorities that has application even in our own day. He demonstrated that the protection of national minority rights is possible only in a political system based on self-government and the free exercise of rights of citizenship. Even though his approach to nationality rights was not implemented in pre-World-War-I Hungary or in contemporary Rumania, his recommendations for resolving conflicts of nationality suggest a sane and humane policy for twentieth-century political practice. The basic premise of his approach can be summarized on the basis of his major political treatise, *The Influence of the Ruling Ideas of the 19th Century on the State,* published in 1851:

> If the absolute sovereignty of the majority is recognized, then every majority—especially in the age of national aspirations—will employ its power for the suppression of minority nationalities, so as to make the state identical with the concept of nationality. If the absolute sovereignty of the majority is not recognized, then each nationality will be guaranteed certain inalienable rights which are independent of the sphere of state sovereignty.[24]

NOTES

1. There are several excellent summaries of the Hungarian revival and of the Hungarian language reform movement in English: C. A. Macartney, *The Habsburg Empire, 1790–1918* (New York: Macmillan, 1969), pp. 284–97 presents a balanced assessment. Ervin Pamlényi, ed., *A History of Hungary* (London and Wellingborough: Collet's, 1975), pp. 209–54 summarizes the Hungarian viewpoint. An excellent scholarly analysis of the Hungarian language policies in the 1840s can be found in Gyula Miskolczy, *A horvát kérdés története és irományai a rendi állam korában* [The history and sources of the

Croatian issue in the feudal period] (Budapest: Magyar Történelmi Társulat, 1927), 1:296–322.

2. The best English-language study of the Rumanian revival is unquestionably Keith Hitchins, *The Rumanian National Movement in Transylvania, 1780–1849* (Cambridge: Harvard University Press, 1969). Another indispensable guide is the series of studies on Rumanian-Hungarian relations by the Hungarian historian Zoltán I. Toth. Some of his essays have been published in Dániel Csatári, ed., *Magyarok és Románok* [Hungarians and Rumanians] (Budapest: Akadémiai Kiadó, 1966).

3. C. A. Macartney, op. cit., pp. 292–97.

4. Ibid. A more detailed discussion can be found in Domokos Kosáry, *Kossuth Lajos a reformkorban* [Louis Kossuth in the Era of Reform] (Budapest: Antiqua, 1946), pp. 206–31.

5. Paul Bődy, *Joseph Eötvös and the Modernization of Hungary, 1840–70,* Transactions of the American Philosophical Society, vol. 62, 2 (1972), pp. 14–16.

6. Zoltán I. Toth, "Kossuth, Dragos és Papfalvi," [Kossuth, Dragos and Papfalvi], *Magyarok es Románok,* pp. 330–39.

7. Keith Hitchins, op. cit., pp. 181–218; Zoltán I. Toth, "A nemzetiségi kérdés Magyarországon 1848–49-ben," [The Nationality Question in Hungary in 1848–49] *Magyarok és Románok,* pp. 208–19.

8. My analysis of this issue is presented in Paul Bődy, op. cit., pp. 48–54. See also Ervin Szabó, *Társadalmi és pártharcok a 48–49-es magyar forradalomban* [Social and factional struggles in the Hungarian Revolution of 1848–49] (Budapest: Szikra, 1949), pp. 167–316.

9. Zoltán I. Toth, "A magyar-román szövetség kérdése 1848–49-ben." [The Question of the Hungarian-Rumanian Alliance in 1848–49] *Magyarok és Románok,* pp. 249–87, reviews Hungarian-Rumanian relations. The quotation is from Nicolae Bălcescu, *Istoria Romînilor sub Mihai-Voda Viteazul* [History of the Rumanians under Voivod Michael] (Bucharest, 1937), pp. 297–98.

10. Zoltán I. Toth, "Az erdélyi és magyarországi románok abszolutizmus korabeli történetéhez," [On the History of the Rumanians of Hungary and Transylvania in the Age of Absolutism], *Magyarok és Románok,* pp. 376–92.

11. This report can be consulted in *Az 1861. évi április 2-án Pesten egybegyült országgyűlés képviselőházának irományai* [Papers of the House of Representatives of the Hungarian Parliament Assembled on April 2, 1861] (Pest, 1861) 2:129–31.

12. "Nemzetiség," Fol. Hung. 2999, 7, Manuscript Collection, Széchenyi National Library (Budapest, n.d.).

13. My analysis of these recommendations can be found in Bődy, op. cit., pp. 83–84.

14. Published in G. Gábor Kemény, *Iratok a nemzetiségi kérdés történetéhez Magyarországon a dualizmus korában* [Documents relating to the History of the Nationality Question in Hungary in the Age of Dualism] (Budapest: Tankönyvkiadó, 1952), 1:36–39.

15. Ibid., 1:28–35.

16. The minority report is published in ibid., 1:45–48.

17. The full discussion of this interpretation is developed in Bődy, op. cit., pp. 81–84.

18. *Az 1861. évi április 2-án Pesten egybegyült országgyűlés képviselőházának naplója* [Records of the House of Representatives of the Hungarian Parliament Assembled on April 2, 1861], Pest, 1861, 2:102–4.

19. *Concordia,* July 10, 1867.

20. Address of Louis Wlad, November 26, 1868, *Az 1865-dik évi december 10-dikére hirdetett országgyűlés képviselőházának naplója* [Records of the House of Representatives of the Hungarian Parliament Convoked on December 10, 1865] (Pest, 1868) 11:93.

21. Bődy, op. cit., pp. 101–8.

22. Ibid., pp. 115–18.

23. Ibid., p. 118.

24. József Eötvös, *A XIX. század uralkodó eszméinek befolyása az álladalomra* [The Influence of the Ruling Ideas of the Nineteenth Century on the State] (Pest, 1851), 1:74–5.

The Revolution of 1848–49 in Transylvania and the Polarization of National Destinies

ISTVAN DEAK

The Revolution of 1848–49 was the most complex and tragic episode in Transylvania's recent history. It was also the most exhilarating. It was a time when romantic poets and bombastic politicians heralded the coming of equality and fraternity; a time when priests of various denominations beseeched the God of their nationality for special consideration; a time when national flags fluttered over the heads of teeming, exultant mobs; a time when thousands were killed in the name of equality, fraternity, and nationality. Not since the Turkish and Tartar invasions of the seventeenth century had Transylvania known so much suffering; nor would it suffer worse agony until the end of the Second World War.

The historic outlines of this extraordinary year have been treated extensively in other studies; therefore, this author will not try to narrate the actual course of events but will attempt to ask and to answer a number of questions that are on the minds of all those interested in the fate of this fascinating province.

With the possible exception of the Horea-Cloşca revolt in the late eighteenth century, Transylvania had known no ethnic conflict before 1848; in other words, people were not attacked and harmed because of their nationality. Why then did such a terrible development take place during the Springtime of the Peoples? Could the nationality conflict have been avoided? What were the major forces operating during the civil war, and to what ends was the war fought? Who profited from the struggle, and who were its true losers? How did the revolutionary year affect later Transylvanian developments? These are the questions that the author will try to answer here, but first it may be worthwhile to enumerate a few facts.

Not to be confused with that much larger area that is today commonly referred to as Transylvania, the historic Transylvanian province had been for many centuries one of the most important possessions of the Hungarian crown. Over these centuries, Transylvania had known long periods of political greatness and virtual independence, as well as long periods of abject subservience to a foreign power, yet her constitutional affiliation with the Holy Crown of Saint Stephen remained uncontested. But, and this is an important "but," ever since the end of the seventeenth century the Habsburg monarchs had treated Transylvania as an administrative entity completely separate from the kingdom of Hungary, also known as Inner Hungary. The Habsburg emperor-king was also grand duke of Transylvania and, as such, he was served by a Transylvanian Chancellery in Vienna and a Vice-Royal Council, or *Gubernium,* in Transylvania. Compare this with the status of Croatia-Slavonia, which, although legally a sovereign kingdom, was in reality governed by the Hungarian Chancellery in Vienna and the Hungarian Vice-Regal Council in Budapest. Croatian and Slavonian deputies attended the Hungarian Diet at Pozsony (Pressburg, Bratislava); Transylvanian deputies sat in their own diet at Kolozsvár (Cluj, Klausenburg). Unlike Croatia, Transylvania had its own administration, its own legal and judicial systems, and its own very peculiar society and economy. This separateness, under the constitutional umbrella of oneness with Inner Hungary, constituted a fundamental contradiction in the status of Transylvania before 1848—a contradiction that the reforming leaders of Hungary and Transylvania attempted but failed to resolve either before or during the revolutionary year.[1]

Territorial unification was, of course, not only a Hungarian goal; it was also the goal of Germans, Italians, Poles, Ukrainians, Romanians, Serbs and Croats, Czechs and Slovaks, Greeks, and others in nineteenth-century Europe. Still, a sharp distinction must be made here between those peoples, such as the Italians, who aimed at unification on the basis of nationality, and those peoples, such as the Germans, the Poles, or the Hungarians, who combined their claim for national self-determination with their insistence on constitutional-historical rights. What complicated matters enormously was that the liberal reformers, those contemporary champions of national unification, saw nothing incompatible in the two different claims. They viewed territorial unification as a God-given right, as the sine qua non of national survival, and as the starting point for modernization and prosperity. They conceived of territorial disunity as inherently harmful and reactionary and of territorial unity as universally beneficial and progressive.

The Hungarian claim for national self-determination was clearly inadequate in reference to Transylvania. No one on the Hungarian side denied that Transylvania was a multinational province with an absolute majority of Romanians. Juggling statistical data was to be a privilege of later generations. Contemporary Hungarian statistics showed that in Transylvania 830,000 Hungarians (more than half of whom belonged to the Székely nation) shared the province with 1,200,000 Romanians, 200,000 Saxons, and some 70,000 Gypsies, Armenians, Serbs, and Greeks.[2] Yet these demographic data in no way disturbed the Hungarian liberals in their drive for Hungary's unification with Transylvania. They believed, as did liberals all over Europe, that an enlightened nation had the right—nay, it had the obligation—to lead other, less enlightened nationalities on the path of reform and prosperity. In turn, the liberals asserted, the less enlightened nationalities had the duty to recognize the dominant political position of their guide and savior. This was the view that the German liberals held toward the Poles, the Polish liberals toward the Ukrainians, the Czech liberals toward the Slovaks, and the Hungarian liberals toward their own Slavs and Romanians. In all of Louis Kossuth's pre-1848 writing and speeches on Transylvania, there is no mention of the problem of nationalities, only of the problem of Transylvania being a backward province. Kossuth worried about the possible harmful effect that unification with politically, socially, and economically undeveloped Transylvania would have on the more progressive institutions of Hungary; he did not fear the possible opposition of Romanians and Saxons to the union.[3] As for the radicals to the left of Kossuth, they were even more firmly convinced that the Magyar nation was entitled to guide other nations on the path to democracy. This was the position of Petőfi, Táncsics, and Vasvári toward the Slavs and Romanians in Hungary and Transylvania, as it was, incidentally, of Marx and Engels toward the Czechs and Poles in Germany.

The universal rise of liberal nationalism did not alone insure the coming of a civil war in Transylvania; other factors worked toward that end also. As it is well known, only the Hungarian nobility in that province, plus the Székely and the Saxon nations, enjoyed full political rights; ennobled Romanians simply assumed membership in the Hungarian nobility. Moreover, severe legal distinctions separated the religious denominations of the above-named three political nations from the religious denominations of the other nationalities. The new Romanian middle class of priests, merchants, and intellectuals possessed the money and the know-how, but not the legal authorization, to exercise full political rights. Székelys in Saxon territory or Saxons in Hungarian Transylvanian territory remained second-class citizens, because Transylvanian law distinguished not only between estates, denominations, and nations, but also between national territories; the law offered each political nation considerable privileges within, but not outside, its own territory. Finally, Transylvania was one of the poorest provinces in the Habsburg Monarchy, where industrial development had barely begun before 1848, where landowners lacked capital for investment, and where Maria Theresa's urbarial ordinances had never been fully implemented. The distinction between the lord's *demesne* and the peasant's own allotment remained obscure; the serfs' labor obligation increased significantly before 1848, and seizure of servile lands by the landowning nobility was a far more common occurrence than in the Hungarian kingdom. All this led to a series of peasant disturbances that had to be forcibly suppressed. It is a historical truism that before 1848 Transylvania was a gravely troubled province with unsettled political, social, and economic conditions.

Small wonder, therefore, that when the news of the European Spring revolutions arrived in Transylvania it created both enthusiasm and consternation. At first, all seemed to go well as youthful Hungarian and Romanian demonstrators marched arm in arm in the streets of Transylvanian cities, hailing fraternity and reform. But then all the old problems came to the fore, together with a host of new problems. It soon occurred that the landowners of the province were as reluctant to emancipate the peasants, whose robot labor they could not possibly spare, as the peasants were anxious to end forced labor, to recuperate their lost allotment, and to stop paying taxes and dues. The idea of union with Hungary, so strongly demanded by the radicals in Budapest on March 15 and more cautiously pursued by the Diet at Pozsony, was accepted by most of the educated Transylvanians; but while the Magyar nobles wanted union first and domestic reform later—under the tutelage of the Hungarian state—the Romanian political leaders wanted domestic reform first and union only at an unspecified later date. The Saxons wanted no union at all, because it would have inevitably put an end to their extensive privileges. Here, then, were the seeds of civil war, and civil war came all too soon.[4]

Would it have been possible to avoid the bloody conflict? Yes, if moderation had been exercised by all. But moderation was not a respected virtue in 1848, and the few moderates were soon shunted aside. Within a short time, there arose in Transylvania a number of power centers, each very active and each expressing the interests and desires of a particular group. Let us now attempt to categorize these power centers according to their beliefs and the methods they employed.

From right to left on the political spectrum, the first category was made up of remnants of the Ancien Régime: conservative landowning magnates, high functionaries of the *Gubernium,* and commanders of the Imperial-Royal Army stationed in the province. These men, best represented by the head of the Transylvanian Army General-Commando, General Baron Anton Puchner, were opposed to all the national and social movements then agitating Transylvania and, as a consequence, were soon reduced to almost total political impotence. But these conservatives were made of resilient stock. They did not give up; rather, they slowly came to understand the need to go to the masses in revolutionary times. In order to save the old social order and the Habsburg Monarchy, they concluded the most unlikely alliances with, among others, such people as the Saxon burghers and the Romanian revolutionary peasants. As a result, the conservatives emerged victorious at the end of the war.

A second category was made up of such moderate nationalists as Hungarian Royal Commissioner Baron Miklós Vay and the Romanian bishop Andreiu Şaguna, who, although they pursued opposite political goals, were united in their hostility to radicalism and their loyalty to the throne. It was such moderates who could have done the most to prevent a civil war, but, as they lacked the strength and the courage to prevail over the militants of their own nationality, they failed completely.

A third category was formed of such true liberal nationalists as the Kossuthist government commissioner László Csányi and the Romanian newspaper editor Simion Bărnuţiu, who feared social unrest no less than the conservatives but whose national enthusiasm caused them to mobilize the very peasants they feared. These politicians bore a main responsibility for the bitterness of the civil war.

In a fourth category could be classed such democratic popular leaders as the Romanian guerrilla chief Avram Iancu[5] and the Hungarian free-corps commander Imre Hatvani, who knew little restraint in the pursuance of their radical political and social goals and who, although ideologically almost identical, ended up as bitter enemies of one another. When, in the spring of 1849, Avram Iancu finally consented to negotiate with the Hungarians, it was his fellow democrat Imre Hatvani who launched a sudden attack on Iancu's forces, thereby causing the end of the negotiations and the Romanian murder of Kossuth's Romanian delegate to Iancu.

Aside from these easily identifiable groups of people, we find many other groups or important individuals who pursued particular interests during the conflict. There was the Polish General Józef Bem, who led the Hungarian army in many victorious campaigns, but who willingly offered amnesty to his Saxon and Romanian opponents in the hope of mobilizing all the Transylvanians for the liberation of his Polish fatherland. Or there was Ioan Dragoş, the Romanian political leader from Inner Hungary, who tried conciliation between Iancu and Kossuth in order to ameliorate the lot of Inner Hungary's 900,000 Romanians and who was murdered by Iancu's partisans for his pains. Or we can turn to Nicolae Bălcescu, the revolutionary liberal from Wallachia, who attempted to arrange a truce in Transylvania so that Romanians and Hungarians together would fight his enemies, the Russians. Finally, we must mention the peasants, who, whether Magyars, Székelys, or Romanians, had almost identical economic interests, but who nevertheless ended up fighting and dying for national goals they barely perceived themselves.[6]

In the final analysis, there were only two camps: the camp of Kossuth and that of Kossuth's enemies. In the first camp were Hungarian noblemen, burghers, and peasants, almost the entire Székely nation, Polish legionnaires, a remarkable number of Romanians, and such soldiers of the Habsburg army who had chosen or had been compelled to fight on the Hungarian side. The other camp was made up of Romanian border guards, burghers, and peasants, Saxon merchants and artisans, as well as imperial-royal soldiers of every conceivable nationality, including many Hungarians. It would be useless to ask which camp had justice on its side, or which was more progressive. Such a question might make sense in the context of Inner Hungary's struggle against the Austrians; in the context of Transylvania, both sides were right and wrong at the same time. The Kossuth camp upheld the great liberal reform ideas of the period; it also upheld the interests of the Hungarian noble landowners. The other camp upheld the right of oppressed nationalities to a free development; it also upheld the right of the Habsburg Monarchy to dominate all the nationalities. On the Austrian side, conservative generals and old-world aristocrats incited illiterate Romanian peasants to rape and murder Hungarian families. On the Hungarian side, liberals and democrats incited Székely soldiers to burn down prosperous Saxon towns and to hang Romanian peasants. In the course of this mad war, the original noble goals of the Springtime of the Peoples were gradually forgotten. National unification, civil and political rights, emancipation, and national autonomy became empty slogans. Instead, Habsburg officers fought for a Great Austria, Hungarian politicians for a Great Hungary, and Romanian leaders for a Great Romania.

The imperialist struggle came to an end when the Russian army intervened and restored order in the province. Now, finally, began the work of painful restoration.

If one asks who were the real winners in the conflict, one could hardly point to the militarily victorious Russians or Austrians. The Russians went home immediately after the war, having gained nothing for their effort but international hostility and Austrian ingratitude. The Austrian empire was allowed to continue, but with somewhat impaired prestige and without the ability either to restore the Ancien Régime or to create a lasting new construct. The Saxons had fought a war of self-defense in 1848; they remained on the defensive until 1867, when they lost the last remnants of their historical autonomy. Paradoxically, it was the Transylvanian Hungarians who had won the war. Militarily they had been defeated in 1849; but, as the victorious Russians and Austrians had failed to make a revolution from above, the Hungarian nobles were able to keep their extensive possessions and, hence, in the long run, also their political influence. It would not be wrong to say that the Russian and Austrian armies had saved the Hungarian nobility. Within a few years, the Transylvanian administration fell back into Hungarian hands and, in 1867, Transylvania was reunited with then triumphant Hungary. The real losers of the civil war were the Romanians. They had suffered enormously in 1848–49, and politically they had gained nothing from the conflict. Under Francis Joseph there was to be neither a Great Romanian Empire, nor a sovereign Romanian Duchy under the Habsburg crown as the Romanian National Committee had planned. There was not even to be a Romanian autonomous territory in Transylvania.

Yet, ultimately, even the Romanians profited from the revolutionary upheaval, if not politically, then socially and economically. Without the great Hungarian reforms of March, 1848, without civil rights, extended suffrage, religious equality, and peasant emancipation, modernization would have come even later to the province. Transylvanian progress and prosperity in the second half of the nineteenth century and the rise of the organized Romanian political movement were the direct consequences of the laws that the Hungarian Diet had adopted at Pozsony. Thus, even though ethnic antagonisms and mutual fear continued, the Transylvanian balance sheet was not entirely bleak.

Notes

1. There are only a few books, in a Western language, on the pre-1848 history of Transylvania. Romanian views are militantly presented in Cornelia Bodea, *The Romanians' Struggle for Unification, 1834–1849* (Bucharest: Academy of the Socialist Republic of Romania, 1970), and Constantin Daicoviciu and Miron Constantinescu, eds., *Breve historie de la Transylvanie* (Bucharest: Editions de l'Académie de la République Socialiste de Roumanie, 1965). The best interpretation by a Hungarian historian, in a Western language, is László Makkai, *Histoire de Transylvanie* (Paris: Presses Universitaires de France, 1946). Keith Hitchins, *The Romanian National Movement in Transylvania, 1780–1849* (Cambridge, Mass.: Harvard University Press, 1969) deals sympathetically with the Romanian struggle for cultural and political identity.

2. László Kőváry, *Erdélyország statistikája* [The Statistics of Transylvania] (Kolozsvár, 1847), p. 197.

3. Istvan Deak, *The Lawful Revolution: Louis Kossuth and the Hungarians, 1848–1849* (New York and London: Columbia University Press, 1979), p. 127 et passim. Also, by the same author, "István Széchenyi, Miklós Wesselényi, Lajos Kossuth and the Problem of Romanian Nationalism," *Austrian History Yearbook*, vols. 12-13, pt. 1 (1976–77), pp. 69–77.

4. There are a number of substantial printed documentary collections on the Transylvanian events of 1848–49, from which most of the information for this paper has been drawn. They are: Silviu Dragomir, *Studii şi documente privitoare la revoluţia Românilor din Transilvania în anii 1848–49,* [Studies and Documents Concerning the Rumanian Revolution in Transylvania in 1848–49] 4 vols. (Sibiu-Cluj: Cartea Românească din Cluj, 1944–46); Elek Jakab, *Szabadságharczunk történetéhez: Visszaemlékezések 1848–1849-re* [Concerning the History of Our War of Independence: Recollections 1848–1849] (Budapest: Rautmann Frigyes, 1880); László Kőváry, ed., *Okmánytár az 1848–49-ki erdélyi eseményekhez* [Archival Collection Concerning the Transylvania Events of 1848–49] (Kolozsvár: Demjén László, 1861); and *Kossuth Lajos összes munkái,* [The Complete Works of Louis Kossuth] 11 vols. (Budapest, 1948–66), vols. 12–15.

5. See Silviu Dragomir, *Avram Iancu* (Bucharest: Editura Ştiinţifică, 1965).

6. The best source on the Transylvanian peasants is Zsolt Trócsányi, *Az erdélyi parasztság története, 1790–1849* [The History of the Peasantry in Transylvania, 1790–1849] (Budapest: Akadémiai Kiadó, 1956).

From Horea-Cloşca to 1867: Some Observations

EDSEL WALTER STROUP

A great deal of gratitude is due to the authors of the foregoing essays for their clear, concise, and thought-provoking presentations dealing with a topic that is generally acknowledged to be extremely difficult and complex. Indeed, the objectives of each essay are carried out so well within the brief formats established by their authors that the bulk of the following remarks are of a supplementary or alternative nature enlivened only occasionally by differences and reservations.

The most pronounced reservations and suggested modifications center on Professor Held's article on the 1784 Rumanian peasant revolt in Transylvania, which consequently receives the lion's share of the attention in the ensuing pages. Professor Held rightly notes the "tentative nature" of his conclusions, for he has necessarily touched on some of the most difficult problems in modern Hungarian history. Moreover, he has done so in a straightforward, admirable, and even courageous fashion. However, although his statements provide truth and insight, the reader is left with two general impressions that are too extreme. First, there is the impression of Joseph II working to liberate the serfs and being opposed by the Hungarian nobles who "sabotaged every and all attempts at reform," and who were presumably motivated solely by a reactionary desire to preserve their privileged position. Second, there is the impression that the Rumanian peasant revolt was a rather reasonable affair whose participants eventually demanded well-thought-out objectives compatible with Joseph's Enlightenment rationalism—"political equality," "land reform," and "equitable taxation." In order to present some very necessary modifications of these impressions via additional information and views, it is perhaps logical to deal at some length, first, with Joseph's "peasant policy" in Hungary in general and, second, with the unique, even bizarre, nature of the 1784 Transylvanian rebellion.

When Professor Held states that Joseph II "was determined to end serfdom as an institution altogether," he joins some eighteenth-century contemporaries and a subsequent line of historiography that very likely far overestimated what Joseph did and what he intended to do for the peasant.[1] In his famous Serfdom and Buying-In Patents of November 1, 1781, which were applied to Transylvania in 1783 and to Inner Hungary, in unified form, in 1785, Joseph did prohibit the use of the term "serf." But since serfdom in its extreme form of being bound *ad personam* to a lord generally existed neither in Hungary nor elsewhere in the monarchy, and since contemporaries were objecting to the term "serfdom" as too onerous, Joseph's prohibition was more psychological and symbolic than substantive. Actually, "subject" rather than "serf" more accurately reflected contemporary conditions, and the Patents were largely an updating of his mother's urbarial regulations of 1767. Moreover, the contents of the Patents and of his preparatory edict to the central administrative authorities in Buda in August, 1783, were for Inner Hungary mostly rights that were well-grounded in earlier and constitutionally formulated Hungarian laws,[2] viz., the facilitation of the subject peasant's free migration, marriage, apprenticeship, and, above all, land tenure, together with the ability to defend it at law. The factor that Joseph had hit upon as constituting his abolition of serfdom, namely, his striking down of the necessity of the lord's permission for a subject to migrate, could in practice only be exercised by subject peasants who were solvent and had fulfilled all their obligations. Indeed, those who have been so struck by Joseph's abolition of serfdom as to assume he intended to turn the subjects into free men have overlooked paragraph five of his Serfdom Patent, which restated the subject's obligation to perform *robot,* to make payments in cash and produce in return for the use of his holding, along with the concluding phrase: "subjects are bound to render obedience to their lords in virtue of the existing laws."[3]

As some of Joseph's later actions in Hungary show, he was hardly a social revolutionary. Rather, his object was, as he himself wrote, to establish throughout the monarchy a uniform and efficient system of hereditary subjection.[4] His desire for increased revenues led him to advocate reenforcing the subject peasant's legal land tenure and to support the prosperous peasant's legal status vis-à-vis his lord. Yet, though it was unknown among the peasantry who helped historians create the legend of "the Good Emperor," Joseph's Enlightened Absolutism had greater interest in the prosperity of the well-to-do peasant than in promoting the landless or poor peasant who cultivated only a few *hold* (1 *hold*=1.43 acres). It is often overlooked that most of Joseph's Patents restate the rights of the lord as well as those of the subject. Paragraph 47 of a 1786 edict provided heavy penalties for subjects who migrated illegally to escape the traditional urbarial obligations or more modern contracts.[5] In October, 1786, Joseph wrote that the well-to-do peasant was the most useful to the state, and he differentiated between the good, landholding peasant and the poorer cotter. In 1788, he issued a proclamation that made the granting of credit to a subject dependent upon the landlord's permission and prohibited the easy exchange of holdings among subjects from one village or county to another, and he expressed notable concern that harvest, wine, and livestock records be secured in the interest of tax collection. In a decision of 1786, which was of lasting importance to a healthy agrarian economy but did little for the poorer peasantry, he opted for the "inalienable and indivisible" inheritance of peasant holdings by one heir.[6]

To support our case further—without subscribing to the overdone hostility of much of recent Hungarian Marxist historiography toward the Habsburgs—let us point to an excellent study by É.H. Balázs, upon which we have relied for the above information and which reveals in some detail a whole series of petitions by poor Hungarian peasants in 1782. It records the negative responses by Joseph and his bureaucracy in favor of the revenue-generating holdings of the richer peasants. Given this knowledge of the forward-looking but essentially conservative nature of Joseph II's peasant policy, it will subsequently be seen that it was far less likely to be compatible with the demands of the Rumanian peasants in the 1784 Transylvanian rebellion than Professor Held's study indicates.

The only really revolutionary innovation of Joseph's peasant policy was a tax plan and Hungarian land survey announced on February 10, 1789, subsequently postponed, and finally dropped entirely.[7] This tax, mentioned by Professor Held as "an imposed tax of thirty percent on peasant incomes in lieu of former feudal obligations," proposed raising the entire *contributio,* or war tax, on the basis of a uniform levy on all land. The rate was to be fifteen percent of the gross yield with no deduction for seed or expenses, plus an additional eighteen percent from the urbarial peasant to the lord for church, school, and community maintenance. Joseph claimed that it would help the peasant, but an increased revenue was surely his major objective. Moreover, there is some question if it would have lightened the peasant's burdens; in some areas it may have meant his retrogression.[8]

Joseph's plan to impose unilaterally such an important tax on Hungary actually threatened the country's independence. It attacked the constitutional principle that fundamental change—in effect the exercise of sovereignty—in Hungary could only be introduced by agreement between the monarch and the noble political nation in a legally convoked diet.[9] The nobility had protested heartily enough at the issuance of the earlier peasant Patents but had perforce accepted them. However, presented with the tax plan, the county assemblies redoubled their demands for a Diet to negotiate the matter. Joseph replied that as absolute ruler he had no desire to discuss a tax at any diet. Instead, he pushed the land survey and tightened the screws of the imperial tariff system that kept Hungary an economic colony. The nobility argued that even if they acquiesced and their cooperation brought an end to discriminatory tariffs the nation would still have no control over the assessment and expenditure of taxation controlled by an absolute monarch.[10]

One may be inclined to condemn the Hungarian nobility's opposition to Joseph's efforts to modify and perhaps improve the subject peasant's condition. But it would be both inaccurate and unjust to overlook his coeval attempts to seize, on the back of the peasant, so to speak, unrestricted power in Hungary. The Hungarian noble nation was aroused at least as much by his unconstitutional methods as by the substance of his reforms. In opposing him, the nobles preserved not only their own privileges but also the nation's rights, constitutional structure, and separate existence.

As is well known, Joseph's policies brought the nation to the edge of a "feudal revolt," and he was stopped on all fronts prior to his death at 5:30 A.M. on February 2, 1790. The nobility could barely refrain from rejoicing, but in the compromise with his successor, reestablishing the status quo, the Hungarian Diet did legalize his Serfdom Patent in the form of Laws XXXV and XXXVI of 1791, though pointedly basing them on earlier Hungarian laws.[11]

In retrospect, one is inclined to agree with Friedrich Walter's negative view of Joseph's "all or nothing" tactics,[12] and with the judgment that Joseph's peasant policy was "a mere gesture and not very promising in its realization."[13] In Hungary as well as Transylvania, where paradoxically the influence of the Habsburg bureaucracy was the strongest, his policy failed most miserably. Whether under the Serfdom Patent of 1781 or the laws of 1791, it was rare in that age to find a subject peasant who was both solvent and motivated to exercise the right of migration. This right had little meaning or appeal as long as economic diversification and opportunities were limited by Vienna's discriminatory tariff toward Hungary. The great majority of subject peasants stuck tenaciously to their holdings even when their lord tried to move them. Similarly, the authorization of free apprenticeship and marriage had little effect in Hungary, where the lords' intervention in such matters was never a major issue. In all probability, Joseph II's Enlightened Absolutism never intended to raise the subject peasant to complete equality before the law or to give him legal title to his former urbarial holding as true landowner. In contrast to impressions that might be derived from Professor Held's essay, these were to be the accomplishments of the Reform Era and the Hungarian April Laws of 1848—both in Inner Hungary and in Transylvania.

In searching for the origins of the 1784 Rumanian peasant revolt in Transylvania, Professor Held is correct in pointing to the arbitrary nature of lord-subject relations and to the increasing demands on the subjects by the petty nobility. This phenomenon occured in Inner Hungary as well during the eighteenth century, but it was more intense in Transylvania, whose socioeconomic condition was habitually fifty years behind that of central Hungary. But there were additional causes for the revolt, perhaps equally significant, which Professor Held left undeveloped or omitted altogether.

The actual source of the revolt was on the Habsburg Imperial Treasury estates of Zalatna (Zlatna) and Felsőbánya (Baia Sprie) in Zaránd County in the southwestern corner of Transylvania. On these estates nearly 10,000 Rumanian serf families held only 10,500 *hold* (15,000 acres) of very poor hillside ploughland that was subject to erosion and early frosts that devastated their corn crops. In addition, the eighteenth-century interest in the improvement of agricultural methods, then affecting Inner Hungary, was as yet unknown on these estates, and the subjects' holdings produced barely enough to feed a third of the total of about 45,000 individuals. They supplemented their income with wood handicrafts and, especially, by working in the Imperial Mines. Yet frequently they had only scraps to eat.[14]

As state serfs, they were very much under the thumb of the imperial bureaucracy, which extended from estate and mine officials through the central Transylvanian governmental institutions to Vienna itself. Their direct petitions for relief to Vienna date from 1778 in accordance with a practice authorized by Maria Theresa, much to the annoyance of landowners in general and of the Imperial Chancellery itself. Horea's name first appears among these Zalatna petitioners in 1780, and again in 1783, and then in the spring of 1784 when he apparently spoke before Joseph. At least Joseph mentioned him by name in a subsequent letter, though Henrik Marczali states that the future leader of the rebellion made no greater impression on the emperor than numerous other petitioners.[15]

The imperial bureaucracy was notoriously slow to act on anything, but it excelled in the languor with which it treated peasant petitions. On October 6, 1784, the Imperial Treasury referred what was apparently the original 1780 petition back to the central administrative institutions in Transylvania. In his correspondence with his brother, Leopold, Joseph himself blamed the Imperial Treasury for delay in the Zalatna case. He complained that even after his personal intervention and appointment of a special committee, a report arriving in March did not come before the Treasury until November, and that "the Zalatna Treasury Lands, which are under the Mines' Treasury, have officials who especially excel in all sorts of abuses and oppression."[16] Here, in Joseph's own words, is a significant underlying cause of the revolt. In the same vein, historian László Makkai laconically observed that the Imperial Treasury "had never been a kinder lord to the serfs than the Hungarian or Saxon landlords."[17] He further observed that the restriction of liquor licensing, referred to by Professor Held as innkeeping rights, raised the cost of a drink. This resulted in a mob attack on two Armenian licensees at the Topánfalva (Cîmpeni) market fair on May 24, 1782. Apparently Horea was one of the leaders of the rioters. But he escaped arrest, and his 1783 trip to Vienna was prompted on behalf of those who were still incarcerated. The disposition of this case also was still hanging fire within the Viennese bureaucracy as of 1784.

Hence, just as Transylvanian conditions were generally somewhat worse for the subject peasant than those existing in Inner Hungary, so it seems that the condition of the state serfs in Zaránd County may have been worse than that of the subjects of Hungarian and Saxon lords in Transylvania at large. Henrik Marczali even stated that blaming the Hungarian nobility in Transylvania for the Rumanian eruption "would not be just" since "the greatest abuses which directly caused the outbreak were not carried out under the power of the Hungarian lords, but on the lands of the Imperial Royal Mines," the German officialdom of which lacked the patriarchal nature of the private estates, and made the system "unbearable."[18]

László Makkai, rather than finding the chief cause of the revolt in lord-subject relations of any type, saw the causes in the more general context of "injuries to the Orthodox religion, social misery, and a primitive race hatred."[19] And perhaps modern historians do overlook the strong religious feelings in this revolt too easily. Transylvania led all Europe in 1571 by establishing legal equality among Catholics, Calvinists, Lutherans, and Unitarians within a single political structure. However, the Greek Orthodox faith continued to be a "tolerated" rather than a "received" religion, albeit with a bishopric at Gyulafehérvár (Karlsburg, Alba-Iulia). Under Habsburg pressure, this see accepted the essentials of Catholicism in 1698, thus creating the Uniate, or Greek Catholic, church, but it failed to attract the majority of Rumanians, who remained Orthodox. Maria Theresa relented in 1761, and, although retaining the Uniate bishopric, which continued to be favored by the state, she appointed an autonomous Rumanian Orthodox bishop for Transylvania only. Not only did the state continue to discriminate officially against the Orthodox church, but members of this faith by definition did not have legal access to offices or certain trades. Religion was habitually regarded as a virtually interchangeable badge of nationality, and the other peoples of Transylvania regarded the Orthodox Rumanians as alien and suspect, a reaction reinforced by the uneducated lower Orthodox clergy who lived on the level of the lowest ranks of the peasantry.[20] In sum, religious feeling explains part of the fury of the revolt, especially if one considers that the application of Joseph's 1781 Toleration Patent to Transylvania was more or less sabotaged by his own appointees. This situation was actually worsened by the tone of his imperial orders.[21]

In another view, the eminent historian Gyula Szekfű saw "the most important explanation" for the revolt in the successive waves of "half-nomadic" Rumanians who immigrated into Transylvania from the Danubian Provinces, especially during the 1770s and 1780s. Most of them used the territories where the revolt was to erupt as a sort of geographic staging area, viz., Hunyad (Hunedoara), Zaránd, Alsó-Fehér (Alba de Jos), and the eastern edges of Krassó-Szörény (Caraş-Severin) and Arad counties. Szekfű observed that the heavily wooded mountains between Transylvania and Inner Hungary, particularly, had been a reservoir for these wandering Rumanian herdsmen for decades. However, their nomad instincts "could no longer be exercised in the civilization of the county, city, landlord, and state organization which surrounded them."[22] This view agrees with Charles d'Eszlary's emphasis of the cultural conflict between this type of Rumanian and the more settled peoples of Transylvania.[23] These unassimilated Rumanians remained completely outside the normal contemporary lord-subject relationship and shunned agriculture. When they did reluctantly turn to it, according to a 1791 observor, few troubled to cultivate beyond a meager subsistence level. They often extracted an "annual tribute" from the owners of horses and cattle as insurance against theft or to save barns from "being burnt to the ground after harvest."[24] Many of them mixed with deserters from the imperial forces and turned to outright banditry, which was so endemic in the 1770s and 1780s that the counties of southwestern Transylvania devised serious proposals for the consolidation of peasant villages in the interest of protection.[25] This situation was so similar to the Indian frontier in America that Henrik Marczali drew the analogy in the context of the 1784 revolt.[26] Prior to the revolt in 1783, conditions were so hazardous that Joseph ordered the reannexation of fourteen insecure communities in Szörény County to the Military Border, but the situation still remained unstable.[27]

Thus, in addition to the more general problems of lord-subject relations and religious differences, the existence of robber bands, the large wandering population, and the desperate condition of the state serfs on the imperial estates all combined to make this corner of Transylvania rather unique. In Marczali's words, the area was "selected" for a rebellion."[28] Due to these special circumstances, Gyula Szekfű even argued that "the Horea uprising was not a typical nationality movement, nor a typical agrarian rebellion, but something beneath these—the blind surge of unfortunate masses who had not yet risen to the agricultural level of a village economy." He substantiated this by noting that the rebellion did not spread among the 65,000 Rumanians living in the Saxons' territories, nor in the Szamos (Someş) River valley, nor even in the more densely populated northern counties whose Rumanians had long since been successfully integrated into the agricultural economy.[29]

There appears to be validity in this view, since in the spring of 1783 when Joseph saw the deplorable condition of the Transylvanian peasants with his own eyes he issued his Patent from Nagyszeben (Hermannstadt, Sibiu) abolishing their "servile and menial humiliation."[30] The measure applied to the entire province, and it raised overwrought expectations everywhere. Yet it was only in the southwestern corner that the revolt erupted. It should be noted that there the lower Orthodox clergy were telling the believers that the emperor and the Hungarians were locked in a mortal struggle and, should the Rumanians take up arms against the landlords, the ruler would stand on their side. Accordingly, Joseph's announcement of both a general census and the opening of enlistments in the Rumanian Border Guards in the summer of 1784 proved to be a hapless combination. Almost immediately on August 18 and 25, the Transylvanian central government informed the Viennese Chancellery of trouble in Hunyad County. In defiance of all estate and county authority, entire villages left their lands to enlist, not only to be free of urbarial dues, but under the specious reasoning that the emperor had chosen them to receive arms as a nationality to enforce his imperial will over the lords and the other nationalities. The Imperial Army officers did nothing to discourage this belief, though they did refuse to enroll the peasants en masse and tried to send them back to their villages. However, Count András Hadik, president of the War Council in Vienna, did respond to official appeals.

He canceled the recruitment and authorized the jailing of those who defied authority.[31]

By the end of summer Vienna believed that the crisis was over, and Joseph, who never had taken it seriously, ignored all warnings. János Zeyk, Hunyad County *alispán*, reported that the good-will of the Rumanian serfs "toward even the best landlords"[32] was very doubtful, and he expected a great upheaval. A second official urged recognition that the conscription had brought the county to the brink of anarchy. Yet, even contrary to the advice of the Transylvanian government, Joseph ordered a resumption of enlistments for October 28. He was busy at the time punishing a rebellious Transylvanian magnate, Miklós Wesselényi of Szolnok County, and was delighted at the opportunity of taunting the Hungarian nobility with one of his customary lectures. Joseph, in fact, misapprehended the situation. In his view the peasant was at most overzealous, but it was the nobles' unforgivable disobedience to his will that was the major source of the Transylvanian problems.[33] On October 31, the very day the Transylvanian revolt of 1784 erupted in Zaránd County,[34] Joseph ordered the Transylvanian military to use armed force against the nobles who resisted the conscription, and he confided with acerbity to his brother that he would punish their "arrogance."[35]

Even after the news of the revolt reached Vienna, Joseph did nothing for two weeks. According to the Venetian ambassador's report, he believed the "unpleasant news," as he termed it on November 12, to be exaggerated by the Hungarian nobility in order to block his salutary reforms.[36] Hence, he issued no orders for the military in Transylvania to suppress the rebellion. This suited the inclination of the military commander in Transylvania, General Baron Preiss, as he had bad relations with Governor Bruckenthal, whose frantic pleas for help he gleefully ignored.[37] The military's inaction raised the insurrectionists' prestige beyond all hopes and encouraged an increasing belief that their actions were approved by the emperor.[38] Within a week the rebels burned twenty-seven communities to the ground, and on November 7 they even laid waste to the lands of the Habsburg Military Border and Imperial Mines Treasury.[39] This was in the vicinity of Abrudbánya (Abrud) and Verespatak (Roşia Montana), just across the border from Zaránd County into Alsó-Fehér County. But on the same day, to the south, just across the Maros (Mureş) River into Hunyad County at Déva, a hastily assembled *bandérium* (military muster) of Hungarian nobles broke the rebels' siege of the town and threw them back, inflicting heavy losses.[40] The next day the nobles summarily executed forty-four of their prisoners, and this affair seemed to disturb

Joseph as much as the rebellion itself. He forbade the noble military musters and at last ordered the military to take limited action with small detachments. "Due to advanced age,"[41] Preiss was put on the retired list and replaced on November 20 by General Fabris, a Venetian. On November 21, a Lieutenant Colonel Schultz of the Imperial Army was offering the rebels, excepting their leaders, amnesty and rectification of urbarial abuses in return for surrender. The rebels, their ranks swelled with an undetermined number of bandits and deserters, did not accept the proffered amnesty and refused to surrender. Throughout November, Joseph regarded the rebels with a certain sympathy, and on November 27 he issued orders not to treat them too harshly. But on November 29, Horea occupied Illy on the Maros River and openly defied the imperial troops while his followers proclaimed him "King of Dacia." This act and an eloquent appeal from the energetic Hadik on December 2 finally awoke Joseph to the fact that the rebels not only wanted to do away with Hungarian landlords, but with all governmental and social structure. Once the military received firm orders, the revolt was suppressed with relative ease by eighteen companies of Székely Border Guards under Lieutenant Colonel Kray. After their defeat on December 7, the Rumanians themselves turned Horea and the other leaders over to the authorities on December 27.[42] On February 28, 1785, Horea and Cloşca were broken on the wheel at Gyulafehérvár before a large crowd, and parts of their quartered bodies with those of Crişan, who had committed suicide earlier, were displayed affixed to the gates of four Transylvanian towns.[43]

This was the miserable end to an affair caused in part by Joseph II's rigid faith in his own judgement and uncompromising pursuit of Enlightenment concepts. But with all its fortuitous antecedents and elements, the revolt might still have been avoided, or might not have developed as it did, without the elusive and troublesome Horea. Whether or not he was a carpenter, he came from the lower ranks of society and possessed an active imagination plus a conspiratorial temperament. He was semieducated, according to László Makkai, who added the interesting information that the future leader was "intoxicated with oaths and secret ceremonies" administered by Masonic lodges in Vienna. In Makkai's view, the "King of Dacia" never really knew what he wanted. Marczali and Szekfű believed Horea was simply a Zalátna Treasury estate peasant without any education whatsoever.[44]

Whatever the case, it appears that Horea exhorted the Zaránd County peasants to rebellion in clandestine meetings, so the revolt cannot be called entirely spontaneous. According to General Count Ferenc Gyulay's report, written to Hadik from Nagyszeben on November 12, Horea met with the peasants under a certain bridge as well as in a church on a mountain near the village of Meszták (Mesteacan) not far from Brád. It was there just prior to the revolt that Horea, who had just emerged from jail, showed his followers a gold cross and a Patent from the emperor, written in gold letters, supposedly authorizing them to kill the entire nobility. General Gyulay was at a loss to know where "that rotten guy" obtained such items, and neither has anyone else ever discovered their origin; but according to Gyula Szekfű, it was later discovered that the cross was ecclesiastical, and the Patent was an authorization for Turks to hold religious services in Vienna. In any case, these items had the desired effect, and Horea administered a semireligious oath to his followers to kill all the nobles.[45]

The influence of this incitement, followed so closely by the revolt, appears obvious. In the early days of the revolt, as far north as Torda (Turda) County, a Rumanian was overheard expounding the view that "the Rumanians' star has risen, and the Hungarians should go back to Scythia because they [i.e., the Rumanians] were the oldest inhabitants of Transylvania."[46] And in the initial days of November, the insurrectionists themselves proclaimed that in accordance with the commands of God and the emperor, anyone not of the Orthodox faith and in Rumanian dress was to be impaled on a stake or beheaded.[47]

Given the extreme nature of such emotions, the bloody course, the excessive demands, and the ultimate failure of the revolt were all foreshadowed. The first recorded victims were two Zaránd County magistrates who called upon the rebels to disperse,[48] and by the end of the relatively short uprising, 133 villages were burnt to the ground and 4,000 persons had been killed.[49] General Gyulay's report lists a whole series of Zaránd and Hunyad towns in which many nobles lived. These towns were totally destroyed and a mere three people escaped. The report characterizes the rebels as "howling lions committing unspeakable raving acts of murder."[50] Protestant and Catholic churches were defiled and burnt;[51] in Dühük, the Catholic priests were tortured to death.[52] Literally hundreds of Hungarian noble families were murdered without regard for age or sex, and pregnant women were special objects for dismemberment.[53] Occasionally one of the lower Orthodox clergy spared a young woman and forced her into a marriage ceremony with one of the rebels with the object of making the "Rumanian religion" supreme in Transylvania.[54] Obviously, such crude travesties had no shadow of sanction from the higher Orthodox clergy, who cooperated with the authorities to the utmost to end the rebellion. The Uniate clergy also participated in this effort, and it is of interest that one who did so was Samuil Micu, a coauthor of the well-known 1791 *Supplex libellus valachorum.*[55]

In the initial days of the revolt, as noted, the rebels killed those with noble status. County officials, judges, prosperous town dwellers, estate administrators and overseers, and even some Orthodox clergy who urged the insurrectionists to desist were among the first to be slaughtered. However, shortly after November 12, reports from three of the affected counties noted that the rebels had turned on the Hungarian peasantry as well. Thus, the widespread apprehension among the nobility of a general peasant jacquerie proved exaggerated. Contrary to repeated directives from Joseph, the nobles held hasty military musters in the counties adjacent to the rebellion and even beyond. But in spite of the great alarm, the rebels' increasing attacks on Hungarian peasants made it very unlikely that the rebellion, as large as it was, would include all Transylvania, let alone great areas of Inner Hungary. Even when the revolt did touch Torda (Turda) and Kolozs (Cojocna) counties to the north, it was in diminished form, and "the Székely people rose to protect the Hungarian propertied classes."[56] Despite such early setbacks, the high water mark of the rebellion was around November 19–21, when Imperial Army officers attempted to negotiate a settlement with the rebel leaders. Actually believing they had won, the rebels issued the demands analyzed by Professor Held, which, in essence, called for the abolition of the socioeconomic order and the division of properties among themselves. Moreover, unmentioned by Professor Held, the rebels demanded that everyone in Transylvania adhere to the Orthodox creed. Unknown to them, in a letter of November 20, Joseph had decided they were "people running amok," though he still hoped to return them to "dutiful tranquillity" with negotiation. As noted, when the emperor at last understood the excessive nature of the rebels' acts and demands, Horea's followers were easily beaten by regular imperial forces at Topánfalva (Cîmpeni) on December 7, after which, for all purposes, the bloody revolt was ended.[57]

The nature of the whole rebellion from beginning to end inclines one toward Gyula Szekfű's flat statement that not a single intelligent, educated man took part in it. Beyond Horea, Cloşca, and Crişan, it appears that the only other leadership came from Imperial Army deserters and the lowest stratum of the Orthodox clergy. There were rumors of a foreign officer who led the peasants, but this was never proven.[58]

The rebels may have received some arms from Mihai Popescu, a Russian agent of Rumanian origin,[59] but according to the November 7 account of András Forray, Arad County *alispán,* very few had firearms, and most carried pitchforks and the habitual Rumanian cudgel. In contrast to Professor Held's terminology of "warriors," "independent command," and "tactical know-how," Henrik Marczali concluded that the rebels never were in a condition for warfare, and their successes were due to their great numbers and surprise.[60] To this should be added Joseph's delay in using force against them.

The objectives of the revolt according to Professor Held were the rather moderate demands of political equality, land reform, and equitable taxation, which "reflect the atmosphere of the European Enlightenment." Yet Henrik Marczali concluded that the movement's leaders showed no higher insight than the outlandish hope that the emperor would support them.[61] Gyula Szekfű stated that Horea and the masses behind him were groping for a primitive freedom that would have been independent of all state and social order. He concluded, "genuine national aspirations, or an institutional state structure, or even Horea's phantom of a 'Dacian Kingdom,' far surpassed the intellectual abilities of these rebels."[62] One is inclined to agree with his assessment, knowing the gruesome nature of the rebellion and the hopelessly inflated demands issued by its leaders. If the rebellion's demands somehow reflected the rational atmosphere of the Enlightenment, its fanatical objectives of social, racial, and religious exclusiveness did not. In addition, the Enlightenment's panacea of pure and dispassionate reason was likely inadequate when faced with the singular history of Transylvania. In a similar vein, many historians have wrongly assumed that the problems of Hungary or of the total monarchy at any given point in time simply involved the adjustment of relations among peoples all more or less at the same level of historical development.

One thing is certain about the 1784 Rumanian peasant revolt in Transylvania: both the contemporary press and many historians since have saddled the Hungarian nobility and, to a lesser extent, the Hungarian state with the entire responsibility for it. Articles in 1784 and 1785 in the *Hamburg Politisches Journal* held up the "hated feudal regime of the Catholic and foreign Hungarian tyrants"[63] as the sole cause of the eruption. The *Journal* did not mention the impossible Habsburg bureaucracy, the miserable conditions on the Imperial Treasury estates, the well-meant but precipitant reforms of Joseph II, the emperor's misapprehension of classes and events, Rumanian immigration from beyond the Carpathians, the endemic robber bands, or even the poor agricultural land in southwestern Transylvania. The *Journal,* which appealed to the German bourgeoisie of the Enlightenment, did mention, however, that the only difference between Horea and the "demagogue" George Washington was that the former had not been blessed with the success of the latter.

In conclusion, the tragic events of 1784 were recorded in numerous Transylvanian family chronicles and long remembered in an area where long memories abound. A generation later the surprise was not that the long-suffering Rumanians and Hungarians fought one another, but that the Rumanians and Hungarians of the Liberal age so nearly cooperated in 1848.

Professor Deak is, of course, correct to emphasize the diversity bordering on confusion that existed in Transylvania in 1848 and 1849, a subject too often characterized in Western text references as a racial war of aggressive Hungarians oppressing unfortunate Rumanians. Yet it is known, for example, that the Fifty-fifth Battalion of the forces fighting for Hungary was composed largely of Rumanians.[64] Moreover, the Transylvanian events of 1848, especially in Rumanian historiography[65] since at least World War II, are seen as an important manifestation along a continuum leading inevitably to irredentist goals. Yet, in reality, virtually all of the Rumanian leaders in 1848–49 sought the solution to their people's problems within the context of the Habsburg Monarchy.[66] Bishop Andreiu Şaguna, rather ignored by recent Rumanian historiography,[67] even hesitated to apply to the Habsburgs for a national territory.[68] In this respect Professor Deak's references to a "Great Romania" and a "Great Romanian Empire" must be taken advisedly. It is true that the erudite Gyula Szekfű, for example, was convinced that the Rumanian intellectual classes for decades before 1848 had been encouraging the growth of a "Dacian dream,"[69] and it is also true that there were many references in contemporary speeches to the "descendants of Dacians and Trajan's Legions."[70] Yet Stephen Fischer-Galaţi, for one, has had the fortitude to suggest that irredentism had little concrete appeal for the majority of Transylvanian Rumanians until they were confronted with the reality in 1918.[71] This also applies to the Saxons, who, though they lost their power in 1868, as Professor Deak indicates, continued their opposition to the Hungarian state until 1890, at which point they made their peace with the Hungarian government and reversed themselves only in 1918 when news of the Paris peace decisions reached them.[72]

If not primarily for irredentist goals, why then did the Rumanians of Transylvania oppose the union of this historic principality to Inner Hungary in 1848? Professor Deak states that the Rumanians wanted domestic reform first and the union only at an unspecified date, and he saddles the liberal nationalists with "a main responsibility for the bitterness of the civil war." But he also makes a most significant statement, since he is an internationally recognized authority on Kossuth, that in all of Kossuth's pre-1848 writings there is no anticipation of nationality problems in Transylvania.[73] Elsewhere he has maintained on many occasions that Kossuth had no intention of oppressing Hungary's minorities but intended to liberate them,[74] a point entertained with doubt by modern Rumanian historians.[75] Finally, Keith Hitchins has remarked that all the Rumanians wanted was social justice and recognition of their nationality. If all this is true, then just what was the cause (or causes) of the rupture between the Transylvanian Rumanians and the Hungarian state in 1848?

It would appear from all these elements that the Rumanians and Hungarians were not terribly far apart in 1848, a fact noted by both Zoltán I. Tóth and Professor Bődy in his paper. Certainly, it could only have been to the advantage of the Rumanians to see serfdom abolished and to receive equal civil rights in a union of Transylvania with Hungary. This union would do away with the old estates system of three privileged nations, which was a medieval constitutional structure formed when the Rumanians were either numerically insignificant or without political organization, and which was, as C. A. Macartney termed it, suspended in time "like a fly in amber."[76]

With these considerations in mind, it is possible to suggest a different emphasis to explain the 1848–49 Rumanian-Hungarian conflict in Transylvania than that in Professor Deak's able overview. Whereas Professor Deak states, with some reason, that it would be useless to determine which camp was more progressive or had justice on its side, the problem might also be approached more in the view of Zoltán I. Tóth and others: namely, that it was in the best interests of the Rumanians to come to terms with the Hungarians, providing their nationality received reasonable recognition; that in the context of the situation the liberal nationalist Hungarian reformers were the more original and perhaps also the more sincere progressives; and that the dissident Rumanians, while subscribing to the same social ideals, were prisoners of their habit of looking to Vienna and were duped into fighting to uphold a reactionary absolutism. Moreover, the responsibility for this development may weigh a bit more heavily on the Viennese and Transylvanian absolutists of the Ancien Régime than Professor Deak indicates.

Gyula Szekfű stated that the responsibility for instigating a bloody racial war lay with Vienna and that as early as March, 1848, Kollowrat ordered the strengthening of the anti-union forces in Transylvania.[77] Fearful of a stronger Hungary, Vienna deliberately delayed its approval of the Transylvanian Governor József Teleki's urgent request to convoke the Transylvanian Diet.[78] Long accustomed to dominating the lifeless constitutional structure of Transylvania, Vienna then attempted to forestall the Diet's vote in favor of union by the sequence of its instructions of subjects for debate.[79] In addition, tacit encouragement was given to the nationalities. In contrast to the enthusiasm for the Hungarian reforms exhibited in March and April by Rumanian gatherings in the Transylvanian towns of Marosvasárhély (Tîrgu Mureş), Abrudbánya (Abrud), Balázsfalva (Blaj), Topánfalva (Cîmpeni), and Zalatna (Zlatna), and in contrast to the early articles written in favor of the union in the Rumanian paper *Gazeta de Transylvania*[80] one finds the Rumanians turning against the union by mid-May. The contemporary Hungarian historian Mihály Horváth ascribed this remarkable about-face to a coalition of reactionary Transylvanian office holders, large land holders, and Saxon patricians who took their cue from Vienna; agitators successfully fostered the idea among the Rumanians that the union constituted a threat to their nationality and accused Hungary of traitorous separation from the monarchy.[81]

These fears were reflected in the sixteenth point of the May 15 Rumanian meeting at Balázsfalva, a rather backward-looking demand that the Rumanians should constitute a fourth privileged nation in a presumably separate Transylvania. The other points were, as King Ferdinand told a Rumanian delegation to Innsbruck on June 11, already guaranteed by the Hungarian April Laws. With the Rumanian demands for social justice thereby assured, Rumanian-Hungarian negotiations revolved foremost around nationality guarantees. Although these negotiations promised some success in September of 1848, the Rumanians still cast their lot with the absolutists of the court. Even when the Austrian Constitution of March 4, 1849, brought little satisfaction to Rumanian aspirations, renewed Rumanian-Hungarian contacts in May, July, and August of 1849 failed to bring a settlement.

If it is true, as Professor Deak states, that the real winners of 1848 were the great Hungarian landowners of Transylvania, saved by the repressive Austrian-Russian intervention, this had hardly been the intention of the reforming nobles of Inner Hungary who had brought forth the progressive April Laws for the benefit of everyone—including the Rumanians who fought against them.

In reading Professor Bődy's excellent essay, one is struck by how much flowed from the Hungarian legislation of 1848 and 1849. The post-1867 Hungarian legislation guaranteeing the Rumanian Orthodox church and its educational system was really born in Laws XIII and XX of 1848. Eötvös's famous Nationalities Law of 1868 was foreshadowed in Szemere's Project of Pacification for the Transylvanian Rumanians and in the Szeged Nationalities Law of July 2, 1849, which, according to Gyula Szekfű, was one of the first such laws in all of Europe.[82]

Certainly, as Professor Bődy notes, it is undeniable that the Hungarian April Laws of 1848 had "serious limitations." But this was to be expected in a body of legislation that—though the changes had been debated for sixteen years—was passed in the space of about two weeks. Still, one wonders just how the April Laws assured the continued domination of the Hungarian nobility in the Parliament and governmental process, since the franchise for Inner Hungary at least was one of the most liberal in its property qualifications for the Europe of that day; if the July Parliament of 1848 consisted of seventy-two percent noble landowners, this was due to social and economic patterns rather than legal stipulations. Further, one wonders if the real weaknesses in the April Laws were, in fact, responsible for the defeat of the revolution. The peasant uprisings throughout the period reflected very complex and maddening problems of land tenure hardly solved in some instances by 1918. It is certain that the contemporary historian Mihály Horváth discounted these peasant disturbances,[83] while subsequent historians have attributed considerable significance to them.[84] Concerning the failure of the April Laws to satisfy the nationalities, Gyula Szekfű stated that many of the extremist leaders of the nationalities wanted only the unrealistic and unattainable goal of territorial separation and they would have rejected minority guarantees, which until then were unknown in their modern form.[85] In any event, neither the dissident nationalities nor the Austrians caused the failure of the Hungarian Revolution, but rather the Russian intervention. Whether the adherence of the nationalities to the Hungarian side would have reversed the outcome is problematical.

Finally, as Professor Bődy ably indicates, Eötvös's 1868 Nationalities Law could well serve as a model for the present day. But it should be noted, as he intimates, that once Eötvös (and Deák) passed from the scene, it was largely ignored in favor of Magyarization in Transylvania. The Springtime of the Peoples occurred in 1848 and, sadly enough, not in the 1867–1918 period.

NOTES

1. For information on the Patents, see C. A. Macartney, *The Habsburg Empire 1790–1918* (New York: Macmillan, 1969), pp. 127–28, and n. 1; C. A. Macartney, ed., *The Habsburg and Hohenzollern Dynasties in the Seventeenth and Eighteenth Centuries* (New York: Walker, 1970), p. 176.

2. For example, the first Hungarian law to grant serfs the right of free migration was Law LXX of 1298. See, for a discussion, Charles d'Eszlary, *Histoire des Institions publiques hongroises,* 3 vols. (Paris: Librairie Marcel Riviere et Cie, 1959–65), 2:345 and n. 175, 3:313.

3. Macartney, *Habsburg and Hohenzollern Dynasties,* p. 177.

4. Macartney, *Habsburg Empire,* p. 127.

5. É. H. Balázs, "Die Lage der Bauernschaft und die Bauernbewegungen 1780–87; zur Bauernpolitik des Aufgeklärten Absolutismus," *Acta Historica* 3, no. 3 (1956): 324. Information in the remainder of this paragraph, unless indicated otherwise, is drawn from Balázs, ibid., pp. 299–300, 314–18, 320, 325.

6. His decision in this matter generally stood until 1868. For a commentary and the text of his decision forwarded to the State Council on October 15, see Macartney, *Habsburg and Hohenzollern Dynasties,* pp. 179–80.

7. Joseph had toyed with this plan as early as 1783. Balázs, op. cit., p. 321. It was held for November 1, 1790, but Joseph died in February.

8. This was a complex matter, and opinions vary. See for a sample, Macartney, *Habsburg Empire,* pp. 129–30; Victor L. Tapié, *The Rise and Fall of the Habsburg Monarchy,* trans. Stephan Hardman (New York: Praeger, 1971), p. 215; Ernst Wangermann, *From Joseph II to the Jacobin Trials: Government Policy and Public Opinion in the Habsburg Dominions in the Period of the French Revolution* (Oxford: Oxford University Press, 1959), pp. 31–5. Joseph ardently wished to tax the produce from the allodial, i.e., the immediate estates of the nobles, and he made a good argument to Chancellor Pálffy that the peasants would benefit; see Balázs, op. cit., pp. 321–22.

9. For an erudite explanation of this constitutional principle with examples, see d'Eszlary, op. cit., 3:38–51.

10. Balázs, op. cit., p. 48.

11. Béla K. Király, *Hungary in the Late Eighteenth Century: The Decline of Enlightened Despotism* (New York: Columbia University Press, 1969), p. 173; Macartney, *Habsburg Empire,* p. 141 and n. 1; Macartney, *Habsburg and Hohenzollern Dynasties,* p. 177; C. M. Knatchbull-Hugesson, *The Political Evolution of the Hungarian Nation,* 2 vols. (London: Nation Review Office, 1908), 1:228 and ns. 2, 3.

12. Friedrich Walter, "Aufklärung und Politik am Beispele österreiches" *Österreich in Geschichte und Literatur* 9, no. 7 (September, 1965): 352.

13. Balázs, op. cit., p. 300. Information in the remainder of the paragraph, ibid., pp. 299–300.

14. Henrik Marczali, *Magyarország története II. József korában,* [The History of Hungary during the Reign of Joseph II] 3 vols. (Budapest: A. M. Tud. Akadémia Könyvkiadó-Hivatala, 1885–88), 3:27; Bálint Hóman and Gyula Szekfű, *Magyar történet,* [Hungarian History] 5 vols., 7th ed. (Budapest: Magyar Királyi Egyetemi Nyomda, 1941–43), 5:137.

15. Marczali, op. cit., 3:27–28; László Makkai, *Erdély története* [The History of Transylvania] (Budapest: Renaissance könyvkiadóvállalat, 1944), p. 494.

16. Marczali, op. cit., p. 28.

17. Makkai, op. cit., p. 494.

18. Marczali, op. cit., 3:31.

19. Makkai, op. cit., p. 495.

20. Macartney, *Habsburg and Hohenzollern Dynasties,* p. 201.

21. Marczali, op. cit.

22. Hóman and Szekfű, op. cit., vol. 5, quote 136, 137; see also 138, 139.

23. d'Eszlary, op. cit., 3:408.

24. Macartney, *Habsburg and Hohenzollern Dynasties,* p. 199.

25. Hóman and Szekfű, op. cit., 5:137. Ignácz Acsády mentions Temes as well as Hunyad and Zaránd counties as being greatly troubled by this problem of banditry. *A magyar jobbágyság története,* [The History of Serfdom in Hungary], 2d ed. (Budapest: Imre Faust, 1944), p. 412.

26. Marczali, op. cit., 3:31.

27. Ibid., p. 22; For the problem of the robber bands with a Marxist slant, see Balázs, op. cit., pp. 303–04.

28. Marczali, op. cit., 3:37.

29. Hóman and Szekfű, op. cit., 5:136, quote 139.

30. Acsády, op. cit., p. 412; Marczali, op. cit., 3:21.

31. Acsády, op. cit., pp. 412–13; Marczali, op. cit., 3:22–23.

32. Marczali, op. cit., 3:23.

33. Ibid., p. 24.

34. Acsády, op. cit., p. 413.

35. Marczali, op. cit., 3:25.

36. Ibid., p. 30.

37. Hóman and Szekfű, op. cit., 5:138.

38. Marczali, op. cit., 3:33.

39. Ibid., Acsády, op. cit.

40. Makkai, op. cit.; Hóman and Szekfű, op. cit.; Balázs, op. cit., p. 307. Balázs records that the nobility also "grabbed up arms and inflicted serious losses" on the rebels at Torockó (Rimetea) as well as at Déva.

41. Marczali, op. cit., 3:32. The information on the course of the rebellion through Horea's capture is found in this source, pp. 31–35.

42. Hóman and Szekfű, op. cit.; Makkai, op. cit.

43. Makkai, op. cit., Balázs, op. cit., p. 311.

44. Marczali, op. cit., 3:33; Hóman and Szekfű, op. cit., 5:137, Makkai, op. cit.

45. Marczali, op. cit., 3:29–30; Hóman and Szekfű, op. cit., p. 138; Acsády, op. cit.

46. Marczali, op. cit., 3:33.

47. Ibid., p. 31.

48. Hóman and Szekfű, op. cit., 5:137.

49. Acsády, op. cit.

50. Marczali, op. cit., 3:29.

51. Acsády, op. cit.

52. Makkai, op. cit.

53. Marczali, op. cit.; Hóman and Szekfű, op. cit.

54. Hóman and Szekfű, op. cit., 5:138; Balázs, op. cit.

55. Hóman and Szekfű, op. cit.; Balázs, op. cit., p. 309. The *Supplex Libellus Valachorum* was a request for the recognition of the Rumanians as a "fourth" nation coequal with the predominately Hungarian nobility, the Saxon patricians, and the once-powerful Székelys in Transylvania. Joseph's successor, Leopold II, rejected it, in part, due to the excesses of the 1784 rebellion.

56. Balázs, op. cit., p. 308.

57. Information in this paragraph, ibid., pp. 307–11.

58. Hóman and Szekfű, op. cit.; Marczali, op. cit., 3:33.

59. Makkai, op. cit.

60. Marczali, op. cit., 3:34.

61. Ibid., p. 33.

62. Hóman and Szekfű, op. cit.

63. Ibid., p. 139.

64. Ibid., pp. 426–27; Zoltán I. Tóth, *Kossuth és a nemzetiségi kérdés 1848–1849-ben* [Kossuth and the Nationalities Question in 1848–1849], in *Emlékkönyv Kossuth Lajos születésének 150. évfordulójára* [Commemorative Book on the 150th Anniversary of the Birth of Louis Kossuth], 2 vols. (Budapest: 1952), 2:320.

65. As an example, see Andrei Oţetea, "The Rumanians and the Disintegration of the Habsburg Monarchy," *Austrian History Yearbook* 3, pt. 2 (1967): 450–76.

66. Keith Hitchins, *Orthodoxy and Nationality: Andreiu Saguna and the Rumanians of Transylvania, 1846–1873* (Cambridge, Mass., and London, England: Harvard University Press, 1977), pp. 55–60, 65, 70–71.

67. Ibid., p. 315.

68. Ibid., pp. 70–71.

69. Hóman and Szekfű, op. cit., 5:404.

70. Ibid., p. 405.

71. Stephen Fischer-Galaţi, "The Rumanians and the Habsburg Monarchy" *Austrian History Yearbook* 3, pt. 2 (1967): 430–49.

72. Macartney, *Habsburg Empire,* pp. 727–28.

73. An interesting example of Kossuth's pre-1848 thought as well as his historicism is available in English. See the account of Kossuth's legal arguments for the reincorporation of the "Partium," those areas of Inner Hungary adjacent to Transylvania and illegally attached to Transylvania by the Habsburgs (namely, Zaránd, Kraszna, Middle-Szolnok, and Kövár) in Great Britain, Parliament, House of Commons *Sessional Papers,* vol. 58 (1851), "Correspondence Relative to the Affairs of Hungary, 1847–1849, Presented to both Houses of Parliament by Command of Her Majesty, August 15, 1850," pp. 22–29.

74. See, for example, Istvan Deak, "Comments," *Austrian History Yearbook,* 3, pt. 1 (1967): 308.

75. Cornelia Bodea, "Comments," *Austrian History Yearbook* 12–13, pt. 1 (1976–1977): 55; Radu R. Florescu, "Debunking a Myth: The Magyar-Romanian National Struggle of 1848–1849," *Austrian History Yearbook* 3, pt. 1 (1967): 83.

76. C. A. Macartney, *Hungary and Her Successors: The Treaty of Trianon and its Consequences 1919–1937* (London: Oxford University Press, 1937, reprint ed., 1965), p. 257.

77. Hóman and Szekfű, op. cit., 5:398.

78. Mihály Horváth, *Magyarország függetlenségi harczának története 1848 és 1849-ben* [The History of the 1848–1849 Hungarian War of Independence], 3 vols. (Geneva: Miklós Puky, 1865), 1:43.

79. Ibid., pp. 40, 62.

80. György Spira, *A magyar forradalom 1848–49-ben* [The Hungarian Revolution of 1848–1849], (Budapest: Gondolat, 1959), p. 148.

81. Horváth, op. cit., 1:44–46.

82. Hóman and Szekfű, op. cit., 5:407.

83. Horváth, op. cit., 1:30–31.

84. Spira, op. cit., pp. 136–41.

85. Hóman and Szekfű, op. cit., 5:406–07.

National Oppression or Social Oppression? The Nature of Hungarian-Rumanian Relations in Transylvania

S. B. VARDY

Although this may sound somewhat pretentious to some, and although the kingdom of Hungary also had its share of political misfortunes, I am convinced that in the course of the many centuries of Magyar pre-eminence in the Carpathian Basin there was something that we can call *Pax Hungarica*. It was this *Pax Hungarica* that guarded the unity, social order, and nationality peace in the area from the ninth to the nineteenth century. True, there were many problems during those centuries. But most of these problems, which today are often characterized as manifestations of "Magyar oppression" of the national minorities, stemmed not so much from the dominance of the largely Magyar Hungarian nobility over the various nationalities of the Carpathian Basin, but rather from the nature of the prevailing social and economic conditions. The feudalistic and highly stratified social system made the peasant masses—irrespective of their nationality—economically and personally dependent upon the nobility. This phenomenon, however, was not limited to the lands of the Hungarian crown; it was characteristic of the social development throughout much of Central and Eastern Europe. Within this area that encompassed the lands of the so-called second serfdom, the peasants of medieval and early modern Hungary were undoubtedly better off than those of Russia or of the Danubian Principalities of Moldavia and Wallachia. And this holds true even though the exploitation in those lands was the result of the rule of a native boyar class and not of an alien or nationally distinct nobility. In the case of the Danubian Principalities, between 1711 and 1714 the native princes were replaced by the Greek Phanariots. But even some of these were really Hellenized Rumanians. Moreover, whatever this change may have brought in the ethnic composition of the ruling element of the eighteenth and the early nineteenth century, the latter could hardly be held responsible for the social oppression and exploitation of the earlier centuries under native princes and under a native boyar class. Similarly, the exploitation of the Moldavian and the

Wallachian peasants cannot be blamed upon the Turks alone—as has become the custom among some historians. Contrary to most other parts of southeastern Europe that fell under Ottoman rule, the Rumanian Principalities were never fully integrated into the Turkish administrative system. Thus, during much of the Ottoman domination the Rumanian peasants were ruled and exploited by their own native princes and by their own native nobility. In other words—and this is the main point to be kept in mind—the exploitation of the peasant masses by the nobility—whether in Moldavia, Wallachia, or in Hungarian or Habsburg-ruled Transylvania—was basically always a social phenomenon, at least up to the nineteenth century. If the sources are credible, then in this area of social exploitation the Wallachian and the Moldavian (Rumanian) boyars out-performed their counterparts, i.e., they were always more oppressive than the Hungarian nobility in Transylvania. If this were not true, history would not have witnessed the continued and unceasing flight of the Wallachian and the Moldavian peasants into Transylvania throughout most of the medieval and modern periods. Apparently these Rumanian peasants felt that to exchange the rule and exploitation of their own native boyars for the rule and exploitation of the Hungarian nobility was not such a bad deal after all.

In light of these well-known historical facts and developments, it is really a mistake to try to make some of the fifteenth- and sixteenth-century peasant rebellions of Hungary and of Transylvania into some sort of "national uprisings" against the allegedly oppressive rule of certain alien landowning classes—which is a distinct tendency in the historiography of some Eastern European nations. To do so is not only anachronistic and tendentious, but also contrary to the basic facts of the region's history.

The protective mantle of *Pax Hungarica,* of course, was not completely free from various early forms of national antagonism. But these antagonisms were largely limited to the occasionally tense relationships between various privileged groups within the Crownlands of Saint Stephen. A good example of this phenomenon is the fluctuating relationship among what were called the Three Nations of Transylvania (i.e., the Magyars, the Székelys, and the Saxons), each of which was resentful toward the others for their real or alleged encroachments on its long-standing privileges. As such, even this so-called national antagonism was not much more than the manifestation of attempts to preserve certain group rights derived from medieval royal grants by the kings of Hungary, and from long-standing historical traditions.

In light of the above, therefore, one can conclude that up to the early nineteenth century, the lands of the Hungarian crown were basically free from national antagonisms. Moreover, insofar as the lands of *Pax Hungarica* were not really "milk and honey" and also experienced social exploitation, this exploitation fell equally heavily on all lower social classes, irrespective of their nationality.

National antagonisms arose largely as a result of the triumph of the ideology of nationalism at the end of the eighteenth and the beginning of the nineteenth century. The first to fall under its influence in the Danube Valley—discounting the Germans—was the educated segment of the Hungarian nobility ("Natio Hungarica"). The nationalism of the non-Magyar nationalities came after, and largely in consequence of, the Hungarian national revival. Of course, this does not mean that there were no scattered manifestations of national consciousness before this period. But these were limited to a very few educated intellectuals and writers. As an example, there is the case of Bishop Inocenţiu Micu-Klein and his disciples of the Transylvanian Latinist School of the eighteenth century. But such early manifestations among the non-Magyars in the lands of the Hungarian crown were preceded by numerous and much earlier similar manifestations among Magyar intellectuals (e.g., the poetry and other writings of such sixteenth- and seventeenth-century authors as Bálint Balassi, Miklós Zrínyi, and Miklós Bethlen).

The following comments deal specifically with the studies of Paul Bődy and Istvan Deak. Both authors concern themselves basically with mid-nineteenth-century developments, and both of them attempt to examine some of the roots of the Hungarian-Rumanian national antagonism that has plagued the relations of these two nations for the past century and a half, and which—in light of recent developments in Rumanian-controlled Transylvania—does not seem to be subsiding.

Paul Bődy's paper focuses on József Eötvös's efforts to find a solution to the growing national antagonisms in the kingdom of Hungary. It examines the role of this great Hungarian reformer and statesman in the period between the 1840s and the 1860s. But Bődy also presents a brief summary of what preceded these efforts, including references to both the Hungarian and the Rumanian linguistic, literary, and cultural revivals, as well as to the major Hungarian push for social and political reform during the so-called Hungarian Reform Period of the second quarter of the nineteenth century. He also points out that the majority of the Hungarian national leaders of those days regarded the nation-state as their ideal and simply assumed that social and political reforms would take care of everyone's problems. For this reason, they failed to listen to those among them, including Ferenc Kazinczy, Ferenc Kölcsey, István Széchenyi, and József Eötvös, who recognized that unless accompanied by special provisions for their national aspirations, social and economic reforms alone would hardly satisfy Hungary's non-Magyar citizens.

In failing to recognize the significance of these factors, the spokesmen of Magyar liberalism erred seriously. Their errors and shortcomings, however, should not be interpreted as errors that were peculiar to them or errors that the leaders of the non-Magyars would not have committed had they been in a position to do so. Today's events, i.e., the violation of the national rights of the Magyars in some of the succession states, provide ample proofs for this assertion.[1] But even in those days, not even the liberal Nicolae Bălcescu was willing to exchange his goals in the area of nationalism for gains in the field of liberalism. For as he said: "For my part, the question of nationality is more important than liberty."[2]

Two points of minor disagreements with Bődy's otherwise worthy essay are his remarks about the Rumanian national revival and his belief about the workability of Eötvös's views on the national minority question.

In his efforts to be absolutely fair and objective, Bődy has placed an equation mark between the Hungarian and the Rumanian national and linguistic revivals. Thus, he discussed the "movement to develop a literary Hungarian language" at the end of the eighteenth and early nineteenth century as if this development were identical with a comparable development among the Rumanians. Nothing could be further from the truth. The fact is that, in spite of the long dominance of Latin as Hungary's administrative and literary language, the Magyar literary language has a long tradition reaching back at least to the thirteenth century, and by the sixteenth century it had already produced a significant literature both in a prose and in a poetic form.[3] All that had to be done in the late eighteenth and early nineteenth century was to take this already existing literary language, update it, and expand its vocabulary—an undertaking that even the Germans had to do. Moreover, the administrative language and the language of the Diet of Transylvania had always remained Magyar, even during the centuries when this was not true for Hungary proper.[4] Furthermore, while the administration of Royal Hungary switched over to Latin, the Turkish pashas of Hungary continued to correspond with Vienna in the Magyar language.[5]

The situation, of course, was totally different with the Rumanians, whose literary language was Old Church Slavonic, written in the Cyrillic alphabet, right into the nineteenth century. As opposed to the Hungarians, therefore, the Rumanians had to start virtually from scratch in their attempt to create a literary language out of the spoken vernacular. This difference between the Hungarian and the Rumanian linguistic revivals also applies to the level of their respective national consciousness at the time of the initiation of this movement, as well as to the recognition rendered to them by others, including the fathers of Marxist socialism (Marx and Engels)—a point that was also mentioned by Professor Deak in a different connection. During the Middle Ages only the Magyars, the Czechs, and the Poles were able to establish significant and truly lasting states in East Central Europe. Moreover, notwithstanding their misfortunes in and after the sixteenth century, the Magyars still managed to retain an important position of power within the Habsburg Empire—a significance that was underlined many a time during these centuries, right to and including their partnership with Austria after 1867. None of the other nationalities of the Danubian Basin, including the Rumanians, was able to match these achievements.

Although a few years ago I too held similar views,[6] today I find unacceptable Dr. Bődy's claim that József Eötvös's proposals on the nationality question could have solved the minority problems of nineteenth-century Hungary. Eötvös's proposals constituted perhaps the most liberal and conciliatory views in contemporary Hungary. But the failure of the largely Eötvös-inspired Hungarian Nationalities Law of 1868 was due not only to the nonimplementation of its spirit and even some of its paragraphs by members of the post-Eötvös generations, but also to the fact that the only feasible solution at that rather late date would have been some sort of federalization. And such a federalization of the kingdom of Hungary, including Transylvania, should have been carried out even at the expense of creating additional minorities in each of the newly formed nationality areas.

While Bődy concentrated on Eötvös's views concerning the desired restructuring of Hungary to fit the needs of the nineteenth century, Professor Deak dealt specifically with some of the problems created by the revolutionary upheavals of 1848–49 in Transylvania. His study represents one of the most balanced treatments of this question. His conclusions that everyone was good and bad at the same time, that everyone suffered and made others suffer, that for these sufferings everyone has to take a share of the blame, and that in the final analysis everyone lost and won at the same time may be viewed by some as an overly balanced presentation. But his assessment to the effect that although "the real losers of the civil war were the Rumanians . . . , [yet] ultimately even . . . [they] profited . . . , if not politically then socially and economically'' deserves our attention. This is a particularly significant point, for it also underlines some of the earlier assertions of this essay concerning the relative social oppression in Hungarian Transylvania versus Rumanian Wallachia and Moldavia during the Middle Ages and the early modern period. Nor should one forget that the serfs of Greater Hungary—including the Transylvanian Rumanians—were emancipated nearly two decades earlier than their counterparts in united Rumania. Moreover, even after emancipation, there remained a distinct qualitative difference between the way of life of these two groups of Rumanian peasants—to the distinct advantage of those under Hungarian rule. Therefore, one can only agree with Professor Deak's claim to the effect that ''the Transylvanian balance sheet was not entirely bleak.''

Much more could and should have been done to ease the differences and to lessen the burden on the Magyar and non-Magyar peasantry of Hungary. But it is rather easy to judge one's predecessors with the hindsight of a century or more. Instead of simply judging the past, however, one should also ask the question: Have those who are in charge of the destinies of various national minorities today learned from the mistakes of the past? Or are they simply repeating those mistakes and then intensifying their impact through means that only a modern totalitarian state has at its disposal? These are questions that are certainly worth pondering.

Notes

1. On these developments see especially Bulcsu Veress's study in the present volume on the international legal order and Rumanian minority policies.

2. Quoted in Hans Kohn, *The Habsburg Empire, 1804–1918* (Princeton: D. Van Nostrand Company, 1961), p. 110.

3. The reference here is to the works of such poets as Bálint Balassi (1554–94) and Sebestyén Tinódi-Lantos (c. 1505/10–1586), such Magyar-language historians as István Benczédi-Székely (c. 1510–c.1563) and Gáspár Heltai (c. 1490/1510–1574), and such noted Protestant preachers as Mátyás Dévai-Bíró (c. ?–1545), Imre Ozorai (16th century), Gál Huszár (?–1575), Péter Méliusz-Juhász (c. 1536–1572), and Ferenc Dávid (?–1579). Cf. Tibor Klaniczay, József Szauder, and Miklós Szabolcsi, *History of Hungarian Literature* (Budapest: Corvina Press, 1964), pp. 34–53; S. B. Vardy, *Modern Hungarian Historiography* (Boulder and New York: Columbia University Press, 1976), pp. 13–14.

4. See the papers of the Transylvanian Diet between 1540 and 1690 in *Monumenta comitialia regni Transsylvaniae—Erdélyi országgyülési emlékek* [Notes and Documents of the Transylvanian Diet] 21 vols., ed. Sándor Szilágyi (Budapest: Magyar Tudományos Akadémia, 1875–98).

5. See *A budai basák magyarnyelvű levelezése, 1553–1589* [The Magyar Language

Correspondence of the Pashas of Buda, 1553–1589], ed. Sándor Takáts, Ferenc Eckhart, and Gyula Szekfű (Budapest: Magyar Tudományos Akadémia, 1915); and its continuation by Gustav Bayerle, *Ottoman Diplomacy in Hungary: Letters from the Pashas of Buda, 1590–93* (Bloomington: Indiana University Press, 1972).

6. On my earlier views regarding the workability of Eötvös's proposals on the national minority question see S. B. Vardy, "Baron Joseph Eötvös: The Political Profile of a Liberal Hungarian Thinker and Statesman." (Ph.D. diss., Indiana University, Bloomington, Indiana, 1967); idem, "Baron Joseph Eötvös on Liberalism and Nationalism," *Studies for a New Central Europe,* ser. 2, no. 1 (New York: 1967–68), pp. 65–73; idem, "Baron Joseph Eötvös: Statesman, Thinker, Reformer," *Duquesne Review* 13, no. 2 (Fall 1968): 107–19; and idem, "The Origins of Jewish Emancipation in Hungary: The Role of Baron Joseph Eötvös," Ungarn-Jahrbuch, vol. 7 (Munich, 1976), pp. 137–66, also reprinted in *Duquesne University Studies in History* (Pittsburgh, 1978).

Transylvania in International Relations 3

The polarization of national destinies, which was traced in the studies of the previous section, culminated in the political and military showdowns of the twentieth century. World War I, French support, Béla Kun's Commune, and the Treaty of Trianon enabled Rumania to gain possession of Transylvania. The interwar confrontation of status quo and irredentist forces and the efforts of great powers to control, neutralize, or realign Eastern Europe set the stage in turn for the showdown of World War II. This struggle saw the Vienna Award of August, 1940, return Northern Transylvania to Hungary and the Paris Treaty of 1947 cede it again to Rumania. The political and diplomatic history of the Rumanian-Hungarian confrontation is the concern of the following studies by Peter Pastor, Stephen Fischer-Galaţi, and Stephen D. Kertesz.

Peter Pastor's study outlines the diplomatic and political events that shifted control over Transylvania from Hungary to Rumania. Pastor traces the World War I developments and examines Rumania's shifting diplomatic maneuvers as well as the internal political developments within Hungary to the collapse of the Károlyi government in March, 1919.

Stephen Fischer-Galaţi approaches the Transylvanian developments mainly from the perspective of the political interests and concerns of the neighboring great powers. His study examines the Transylvanian-Rumanian-Hungarian confrontation in terms of the interwar perceptions of France, the Soviet Union, Italy, and Germany. He traces these relations from the end of World War I to the beginning of World War II.

Finally, Stephen D. Kertesz provides a meticulous, step-by-step summary of Rumanian-Hungarian relations from the period immediately preceding the Second Vienna Award to the post-war disposition of the Transylvanian question at Paris and New York in 1946–47. His analysis combines the insights of the diplomatic participant with those of the international political specialist and scholar. The Kertesz study traces the fate of Transylvania mainly in relation to Soviet objectives and policies at that time. It shows that even minor rectifications of the Trianon-established frontiers, initially supported by the American secretary of state, James Byrnes, received no serious consideration at the

Paris Peace Conference. The Trianon frontiers were reestablished. However, unlike the treaty following World War I, the Paris compact failed to guarantee the rights of minorities. The minorities of Transylvania were to be "protected" by the human rights provisions of the United Nations Charter. This consideration relegated the fate of minorities mainly to the realm of Rumanian domestic politics.

V. TRANSYLVANIA AND THE MILITARY LINES OF DEMARCATION FROM NOVEMBER 1918 TO MARCH 1919

Bártfa
Eperjes
Kassa
N.szombat
(Pozsony)
Bratislava
Munkács
Miskolc
Szatmárnémeti
N.bánya
Sopron
Esztergom
Budapest
Kőszeg
Székesfehérvár
Szolnok
Debrecen
N.várad
Tisza
Szamos
Beszterce
Körös
Cluj
(Kolozsvár)
Duna
Torda
Zaránd
Abrudbánya
Marosvásárhely
Szeged
Maros
Arad
Drava
Pécs
Mohács
Szabadka
Zagreb
Alba Iulia
(Gyulafehérvár)
Brașov
(Brassó)
Temesvár
Sava
RUMANIA
Belgrade
Duna
SERBIA

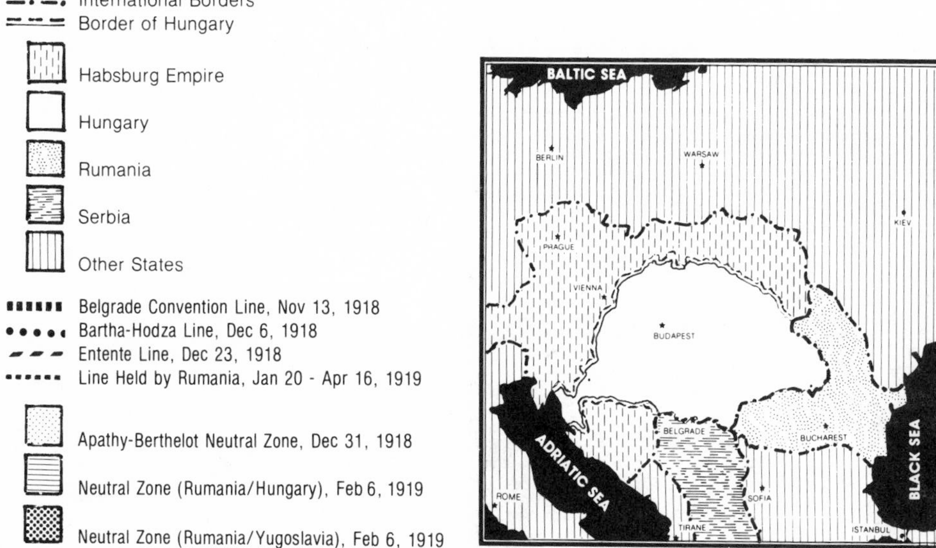
LEGEND:
International Borders
Border of Hungary
Habsburg Empire
Hungary
Rumania
Serbia
Other States
Belgrade Convention Line, Nov 13, 1918
Bartha-Hodza Line, Dec 6, 1918
Entente Line, Dec 23, 1918
Line Held by Rumania, Jan 20 - Apr 16, 1919
Apathy-Berthelot Neutral Zone, Dec 31, 1918
Neutral Zone (Rumania/Hungary), Feb 6, 1919
Neutral Zone (Rumania/Yugoslavia), Feb 6, 1919
BALTIC SEA
BERLIN
WARSAW
KIEV
PRAGUE
VIENNA
BUDAPEST
BELGRADE
BUCHAREST
ADRIATIC SEA
BLACK SEA
ROME
SOFIA
TIRANE
ISTANBUL

VI. EAST CENTRAL EUROPE AND TRANSYLVANIA AFTER WORLD WAR I

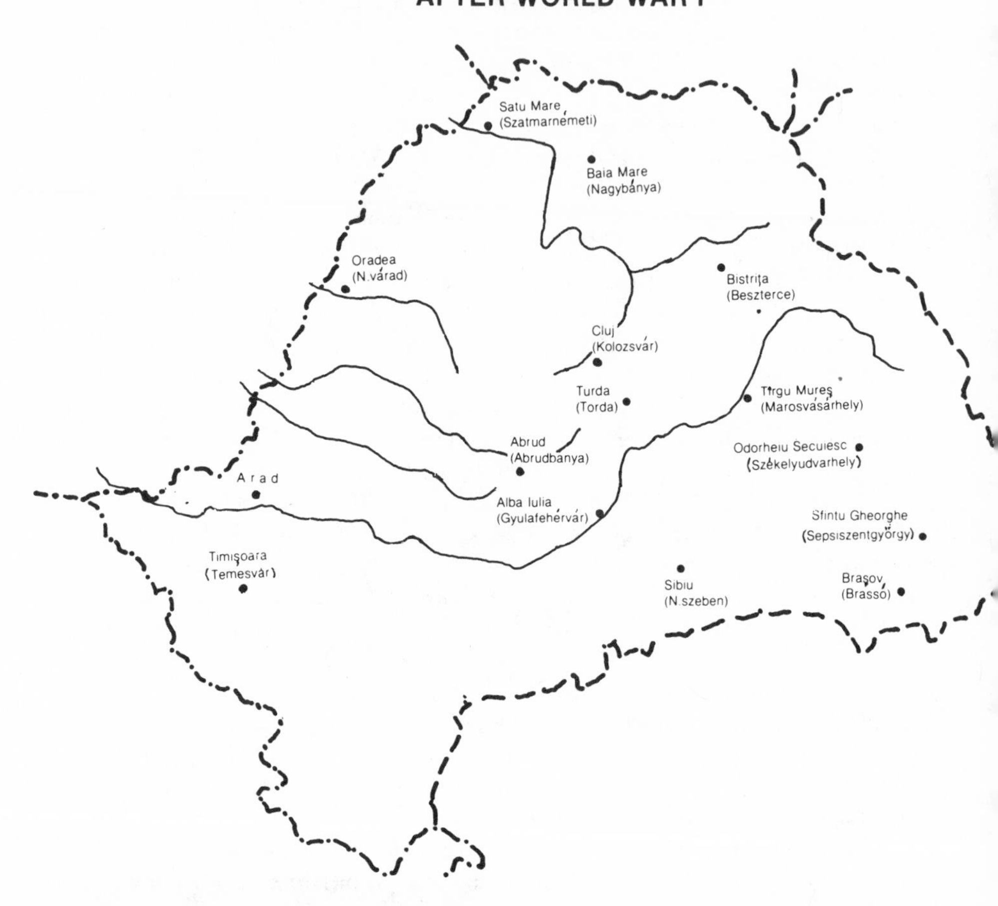

LEGEND:

- International Borders
- Border of Transylvania
- Austria
- Czechoslovakia
- Hungary
- Rumania
- Transylvania
- Yugoslavia
- Other States

VII. THE SECOND VIENNA AWARD AND THE PARTITION OF TRANSYLVANIA, 1940

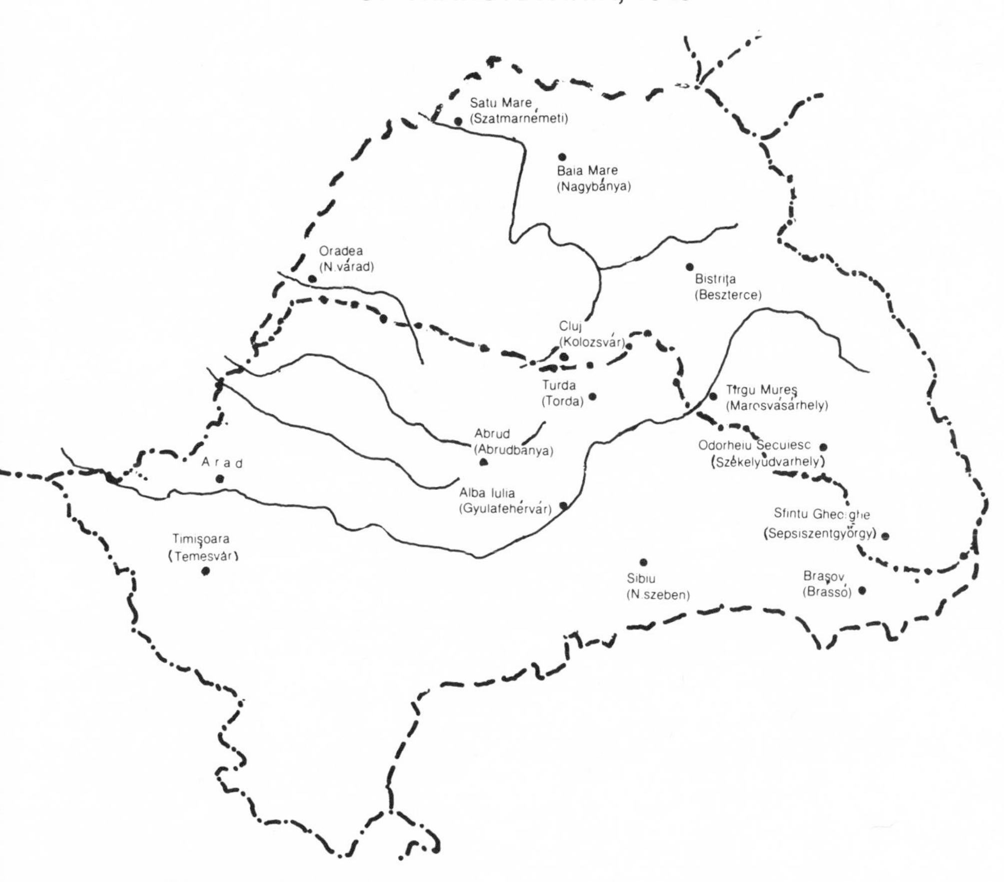

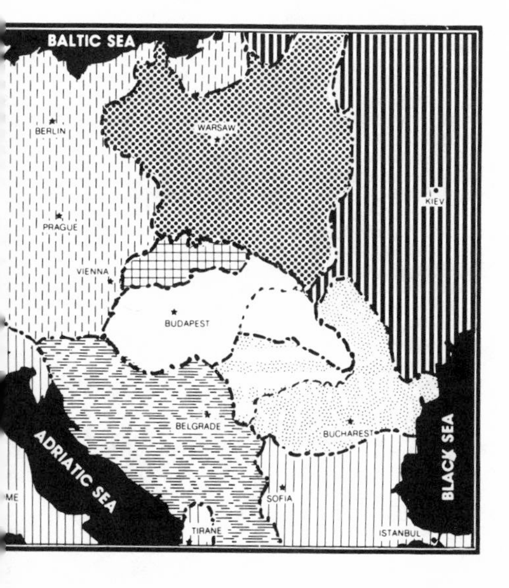

LEGEND:

- International Borders
- Border of Transylvania
- Germany
- Hungary
- Poland
- Rumania
- Slovakia
- USSR
- Yugoslavia
- Other States

The Transylvanian Question in War and Revolution

PETER PASTOR

In 1856, the Congress of Paris sanctioned the union of the Rumanian Principalities, and on this occasion the Austrian diplomat Baron Prokesch-Osten observed that the "Rumanians aspire to create an independent state which is to include Bukovina, the Rumanian portion of Transylvania and the Banat, with the Balkans as frontiers."[1] Twenty-two years later, in 1878, an independent Rumanian state was formed with objectives much like the ones predicted earlier. It aimed to expand its borders in order to include all Rumanians living in neighboring lands. The Hungarian province of Transylvania, whose population was fifty-five percent Rumanian, could not escape the attention of those who favored a greater Rumania.[2] This implied potential confrontation as Hungarian policy at the turn of the century was based on the integrity of the imperium. Neither Hungary nor Rumania was willing to search for a mutually acceptable solution that could have led to bilateral agreements.

The Transylvanian question, a by-product of conflicting goals, awaited another solution, which would involve the great powers and be shaped by the needs of power politics. It did not lead to a mutually acceptable resolution of the problem. Increased great power involvement with this issue during the Great War and during the Hungarian revolution of 1918–19 led to instability and tension and to a solution that formed a new phase of the Transylvanian question.

In 1913, Rumania entered into the Second Balkan War against Bulgaria and with the subsequent Treaty of Bucharest of August 10, 1913, forced a defeated Bulgaria to cede southern Dobruja to Rumania.[3] A similar war for Transylvania thus seemed very inviting and military confrontation with Hungary became a strong possibility.

Such a resolution of the Transylvanian question, however, was complicated since Rumania and Hungary were allies in the Triple Alliance. Moreover, an attack on Hungary represented an attack on the Dual Monarchy, and a war of such magnitude could only have been carried out with great power support. This would have required Rumania to switch its loyalty to the Entente camp, which was possible. Concerning the situation, Russian Foreign Minister Sergei Sazanov noted in December 1913, that

> Rumania's position among the Balkan countries recalls in many respects that of Italy in Europe. Both powers suffer from megalomania, and as they are not strong enough to realize their plans openly, they have to content themselves with an opportunist policy, constantly watching to see on which side the power lies, and going over to that side.[4]

The German leaders, representing the dominant power in the Triple Alliance, were also aware that Rumania could leave the alliance and thus contribute to the strength of the Entente.[5] Germany, therefore, sought to urge a compromise solution upon Hungary.[6] This was the first indication that a great power might resolve the Transylvanian question. On October 27 and 28, 1913, seemingly as a result of German pressure, the prime minister of Hungary, István Tisza, reentered into negotiations with leaders of the Rumanian National party in Hungary. Tisza had initiated similar talks in 1910 and believed that an agreement on educational reforms, concessions on the Rumanian language usage, and the formation of new election districts favoring the Rumanians would put an end to the appeal of irredentism.[7]

The leaders of the Rumanian minority in Hungary did not consider Tisza's offer substantial enough. Although Emperor-King Francis Joseph did his best to convince Tisza to continue negotiations for the sake of the Dual Monarchy's foreign policy, on February 20, 1914, the prime minister reported to Parliament that his offers had been rejected.[8] The opposition Independence party, which objected to any concession, welcomed the news.

The Independents, whose basic aim was to loosen Hungary's ties with Vienna, accused Tisza of succumbing to German and Austrian pressures.[9] The paper *Magyarország* [Hungary], closely identified with the Independents' policy, declared that the "two Istváns represent the beginning and the end of the unitary state." This was the reference to King Saint István (Stephen), the eleventh-century founder of the Hungarian state, and to István Tisza, who, because of his attempted deals, was seen as its destroyer. As a final line of defense, the paper demanded quid pro quo: high offices for some Magyars living in Rumania in return for Tisza's offers.[10]

The Magyar politicians in Transylvania were also moved by Tisza to change the status quo. They believed that any change from within would embolden Rumania. For this reason, on December 7, 1913, the Transylvanian Alliance, *Erdélyi Szővetség,* was established under the leadership of István Apáthy, a leader of the Independents in Transylvania. The new organization was to prepare the Transylvanians for self-defense and alert all the Hungarians of the fact that the province was virtually defenseless against an attack by Rumania. In the interest of Transylvania, Apáthy also called for universal suffrage. This policy would have increased the political power of the Rumanian minority in Hungary. However, since the Hungarians had a plurality in Hungary as a whole, their universal enfranchisement also would have increased their strength. It was felt that this, in turn, would facilitate protection of Hungarian interests in those Hungarian districts where they were in a minority.[11]

The Independent party leaders were increasingly convinced that Rumanian aspirations over Transylvania were encouraged by Germany. For this reason, Count Mihály Károlyi, who considered the shaping of the party's foreign policy platform as his bailiwick, called for changes in the Dual Monarchy's foreign policy. He saw a need for an Austro-Hungarian rapprochement with the Entente, and this prompted his trip in the spring of 1914 to Paris, where he had an interview with French Prime Minister Raymond Poincaré. Károlyi had also intended to visit Russia, another member of the Entente, because Rumania had claims on Russian-held Bessarabia, and he viewed Russia as a potential ally.[12] Károlyi believed an Entente alliance would bring about a solution to the Transylvanian question that would be favorable to Hungary. Yet such a one-sided solution would not have contributed to the area's tranquility. This was the first time that French input to the Transylvanian question was considered, and, ironically, five years later it was the French who were instrumental in bringing about a one-sided resolution that favored Rumania rather than Hungary.

The opposition's views were not able to alter the Dual Monarchy's foreign policy in the months preceding the war. Their vociferous protests, based on Magyar nationalism, reinforced the resolve of the champions of the Habsburg cause who sought to minimize Hungarian influence in the empire. The heir to the throne, Francis Ferdinand, was receptive to German exhortations and Rumanian pressures that reinforced his desire to reorganize the empire.[13]

In November, 1913, Nicolae Filipescu, the war minister and leader of the conservative faction in Rumania that considered Russia as the everlasting enemy, revived a favorite solution to the Transylvanian problem. It was proposed that with the transfer of Transylvania to

Rumania, the Rumanian kingdom could join a federated *Grossösterеich,* enjoying rights similar to those accorded to Bavaria by the German Empire.[14] These proposals were received with enthusiasm by the new Austro-Hungarian ambassador in Bucharest, Ottokar Czernin, who was Francis Ferdinand's most trusted advisor on foreign affairs.[15] The assassination of Francis Ferdinand in Sarajevo ended prospects for such a solution, much to the relief of the Hungarians, who disliked him. Because of the heir's well-known unpopularity in Hungary, the assassination was at first attributed to the Hungarians.[16]

World War I, which was triggered by the assassination, pitted the Triple Alliance against the Entente, but Rumania, though a member of the Triple Alliance, abstained from action. As Sazanov predicted, it awaited the most opportune moment and the most favorable offer of compensation before choosing sides.

On July 30, even before the empire declared war on Russia, which was then mobilizing, Sazanov offered Transylvania to Rumania in return for its support of the Entente, and the next day Russia proffered Rumania the same prize for neutrality. The latter proposal, which could not have been matched by the Central Powers, was accepted by Rumania in a secret treaty signed in Saint Petersburg on October 1.[17] This treaty was the first diplomatic recognition of Rumania's claim to Transylvania by a great power.

Russia's commitment was made in the name of the Entente, although the treaty was drawn up unilaterally. It was not, however, challenged by her Western allies.[18] At the outbreak of the war, Russia thus became the primary power proposing to decide the fate of Transylvania, and although this role was lost to Russia in 1917, it was recovered by the Soviet Union at the end of World War II.

On April 25, 1915, the Rumanian government presented the Entente with demands which, if fulfilled, would put the country in the ranks of the Entente. The territories for which Rumania asked would stretch its borders from the river Prut to the river Tisza; they included Bukovina, Transylvania, and the Banat. Early in July, the Russians accepted the Rumanian terms, and later the Western allies also gave their approval. These demands were essentially the same as those included in the Secret Treaty of Bucharest the following year.[19]

In the light of Russia's generous offers, Germany's counteroffer of Russian-held Bessarabia in exchange for Rumania's neutrality had little weight. The Rumanian government seemed bent on gaining Transylvania. Mindful of the fortunes of war, it was swayed by its prime minister, Ion Brătianu, who as early as August 3, 1914, had declared that "the question of the Rumanians in Transylvania dominates the whole situation."[20]

Even though Russia agreed to the transfer of Transylvania, Rumania continued to seek concessions from the Central Powers that would bring about the same results. Thus on September 7, 1914, Czernin transmitted a Rumanian offer to Vienna. It requested the transfer of Bukovina to Rumania and Transylvania's political autonomy in return for Rumania's neutrality and possible future alliance. The proposal, had it been accepted, would have assured territorial gains without Rumania having to fire a shot.

The offer was dismissed by Tisza, who believed Hungary could hold out until the arrival of German troops if hostilities developed with Rumania. Although Germany did its best to force Tisza to initiate further concessions, his counteroffer to Rumania was limited to the transfer of the Austrian Bukovina province. Responding to German pressure, Tisza angrily noted that "the tragic role played by poor Francis Ferdinand in the fool's game with the Rumanians" has been adopted by the Germans.[21]

The German desire to keep Rumania out of the war forced Tisza to revive the proposals that had been made earlier that year. This time however, he approached the religious leaders of the Rumanian communities in Hungary and Transylvania, and he even offered the Rumanians of Hungary the right to display the Rumanian colors and amnesty for political prisoners.[22] The clergy was favorable to these offers, but the official circles in Rumania were not.[23] The Hungarian Independence party also opposed the concessions. On November 9, the day after Tisza publicized his proposal, *Magyarország* accused the prime minister of trying to change the unitary state into a tribal federation. In a facetious tone, the paper called on Metropolitan Metianu, the negotiator for the Rumanian minority, also to represent the Magyar tribe, whose colors and language were not recognized in the Imperial Army. To end the Habsburg domination, the paper demanded universal suffrage, which was felt would free the "Magyar tribe" from the repression.[24]

It was evident that Tisza's offer was insufficient to satisfy the Rumanians, yet too generous to please his opponents in the Hungarian Parliament at a moment when he wished to shape an "union sacré" in Budapest. Therefore, Tisza abandoned his proposals when it became evident that, for the present, Rumania would not join the Entente on the shaky Eastern Front.

The Entente's push for Rumania's entry into the war came in June, 1916, in the wake of the Russian offensive, which was then weakening.

Perceiving Rumania's role as pivotal, Entente envoys in Bucharest signed a secret treaty with the Rumanians on August 17, which gave Rumania practically all of the Magyar lands on the left bank of the Tisza River.[25] The Entente accorded Rumania a territory where Magyars outnumbered the Rumanians and where the borders far surpassed the historical frontiers of Transylvania; but unknown to Rumania, a secret Franco-Russian accord was also drawn up that called for the review of wartime promises to Rumania at the conclusion of the hostilities. Territorial changes were to be shaped by post-war conditions.[26] Yet, despite the shaky legitimacy of Rumanian demands, Brătianu correctly pointed out that "whatever the outcome of the war, the claims established will remain."[27]

Great power interest determined the solution of the Transylvanian question rather than the needs of Hungary or Rumania. Rumanian Marxist historians now claim that Rumania's entry into the war was motivated by a desire to liberate the Rumanians in Hungary. No criticism is voiced about the true nature of the Secret Treaty of Bucharest,[28] which merely corrected one injustice with another. Instead of a Rumanian irredenta in Hungary, a Hungarian irredenta was to be created in Rumania.

On the evening of August 27, a half hour after its invasion of Transylvania, the Rumanian government declared war on the Dual Monarchy. Since the Hungarian-Rumanian frontiers were not fortified, initial advances proceeded smoothly. The frontier villages and the old Saxon town of Brassó (Kronstadt, Braşov) were occupied. Logistic problems and poor leadership, however, limited the invading force of 400,000 to the occupation of southern Transylvania.

In the third week of September, the Central Powers began a counteroffensive with 200,000 troops, and by the end of November their armies were threatening Bucharest. Early in December, the arrival of a French military mission, headed by General Henri Berthelot, was expected to fill the leadership gap in the Rumanian army. Berthelot, who was Joffre's chief of staff during the Battle of the Marne, hoped to repeat the feat along the Argeş River and to execute a "Rumanian Marne." His efforts consumed the remaining Rumanian reserve divisions without halting German advances.[29]

The Rumanian capital fell that same month, forcing the Rumanian government to retreat to Jassy. Two-thirds of Royal Rumania (the Regat) was now occupied by the Central Powers, but as long as the Russian allies provided support for the Rumanian government, the Rumanian army managed to hold the line. The Bolshevik revolution and Russia's subsequent withdrawal from the war, however, forced the Rumanians to seek an armistice. This was signed on December 9, 1917, against treaty obligations and the wishes of the Allies, who favored the withdrawal of the Rumanian army into southern Russia.[30] Following the armistice, it was left to the Central Powers to divide the spoils. It was now Hungary's turn to demand Rumanian territories. Although the examined Rumanian Marxist literature claims that Hungarian "imperialist" territorial interests spread well south of the Danube,[31] evidence contradicts this view.

The Hungarian nationalists of the Transylvanian Alliance declared as early as September, 1917, that there should be no intervention in the sovereign affairs of Rumania. This odd declaration was based on the fears that if this policy were not followed, the projects of Francis Ferdinand could be revived and a personal union between Austria-Hungary and Rumania could develop. This was perceived as being against Hungarian interest and a way through which Rumania could gain Transylvania "through the back door."

Instead, the Alliance went on record as favoring only slight frontier adjustments, which would push the Hungarian frontier to the Rumanian side of the Carpathians. The new strip or border defense zone (*határőrvidék*) was to be settled with "dependable" populations so as to prevent the recurrence of another swift Rumanian invasion.[32] The position was embraced by Prime Minister Sándor Wekerle, who replaced Tisza, and on December 4 Apáthy was notified that the Hungarian government favored frontier adjustments for which Rumania could be compensated.[33]

Minutes of the Council of Ministers indicate support of the moderate stand by the Wekerle cabinet, but the Hungarians' major fear was that imperialistic German demands would interfere with Rumania's traditional role as Hungary's trading partner, which would result in the loss of all Hungarian political leverage in Rumania. Moreover, they suspected that a conquered Rumania, stripped of the chance for independent economic development, would present a constant revisionist threat to Hungary. In light of the German position, moderation was favored, which would facilitate negotiations and lead to a speedy peace.[34]

Following negotiations, the Peace Treaty of Bucharest was signed on May 7, 1918, which assured Hungary of new frontiers along a 500-kilometer stretch, 2 to 5 kilometers from the original line. This took away about 5,000 square kilometers from Rumania.[35] However small these changes, they indicated that Hungary had embarked upon territorial aggrandizement into lands which historically had not belonged to her. In June, 1918, the ministerial council called for absorption by the neighboring districts and counties of these new strips, which were added to the imperium.[36] This edict indicated the territorial enlargement of Transylvania within the Magyar state. The solution, which was achieved by Germany's dominance over Rumania, indicated a one-sided arrangement. A search for a just compromise was again evaded due to great-power involvement in the Transylvanian question, and Hungarian territorial gains proved to be short-lived. By October, 1918, it became evident to the Central Powers that the war was lost. To save the floundering Habsburg realm, Emperor Charles issued his Manifesto of October 16. It proclaimed the federalization of the Austrian half of the Dual Monarchy, but stressed that the change "did not touch the integrity of the lands of the sacred Hungarian crown."[37] The call came too late to save the empire; in the Hungarian kingdom the nationalities demanded the right of self-determination.

On October 12, Rumanian minority representative Alexandru Vaida-Voevod read the declaration of the Rumanian National party in the Parliament, which called for the right of self-determination for Rumanians in Hungary and Transylvania. The Hungarian government, however, failed to respond to these demands, and Mihály Károlyi offered an alternative compromise, the federalization of the Hungarian realm. He had quit the Independents in 1916 because of their continued pro-war policy, and with a small group of followers he espoused democratic changes in Hungary and an ethnic federation within Hungary's historic frontiers. He also believed that radical reforms would convince the nationalities to remain in Hungary.

On October 25, Károlyi became the president of the newly formed counter-government, the Hungarian National Council, which was supported by the Károlyi party, as well as by Oszkár Jászi's Radical party and the Social Democrats, both of which had no representation in Parliament. The Council espoused Western-style democratic reforms, and recognized the secession only of Croatia. The intention to maintain Transylvania as an integral part of Hungary was indicated by the affiliation of the Transylvanian Committee with the National Council. The former represented the Magyars of Transylvania and was presided over by István Apáthy;[38] and, on the night of October 31, a bloodless revolution brought the Hungarian National Council to power. King Charles recognized the demands set forth by the group and appointed Károlyi to head the new government. Following the king's abdication in early November, Hungary was declared a republic.

On the day of the revolution, Rumanian politicians in Budapest formed their own national council. It was made up of six National party representatives and six Socialists. Their aims were to take over the administration of those parts of Hungary and Transylvania that were inhabited by Rumanians and to represent them in negotiations with the Hungarian authorities.[39] The Rumanian position, while not synonymous with Hungarian hopes, did not stipulate secession. Contrary to past practices, the Hungarian government was willing to negotiate and offer compromises but was still reticent to change the frontiers.

The frontier question was now up to the victorious Allies and to the upcoming Peace Conference, and the Hungarian government assumed it was in a good position to negotiate. In accordance with Wilsonian principles, it was a democratic state and Károlyi, who headed the government, had a pro-Entente reputation. Confusion about Allied intentions with respect to Rumania also seemed to them to create an atmosphere amenable to an understanding between Hungary and Rumania.

The Hungarian government sought to resolve several problems during the first few days of November. Germany, which was technically at war even after the Austro-Hungarian armistice of Padua, had its troops in Transylvania under General Mackensen. The Hungarians feared that any attempt to disarm them would lead to a German refusal to deliver coal. This alarmed the Hungarians, since on November 5 the Ministerial Council learned that Hungary only had one and a half days' supply of coal. To save the country from economic paralysis, the ministers decided to empower Prime Minister Károlyi to seek a meeting with General Franchet d'Esperey, the Allied commander of the Balkan armies, which were still moving against the German armies.[40] It was hoped that a military convention would be signed in which the terms of the occupation and the demarcation lines would be defined. Agreement, it was felt, would represent a de facto recognition of the Károlyi government and, as a consequence, Allied aid.

The Hungarian delegation's conference with Franchet d'Esperey led to the signing of the Belgrade Military Convention of November 13, 1918, and an Allied demarcation line in Transylvania was drawn along a line extending from the city of Beszterce (Bistriţa) to the Maros (Mureş) River and the town of Szabadka (Subotica). This meant a partition of Transylvania with the southern part under Allied occupation. According to the terms of the treaty, the present Hungarian administration would remain in place until the Peace Conference decided otherwise, but it remained unclear as to whether the Allies would allow the Rumanian occupation of Transylvania and recognize it as an Allied power.[41] While these issues still had to be resolved, Allied attitudes favoring the Rumanian cause became clearer and the demands of the enlarged Rumanian National Council became bolder. On November 3–4, the Council shifted its seat from Budapest to Arad, and its initial interest in cooperation changed to rigidity.[42]

On November 6, the Council reiterated its right to "represent the whole Rumanian nation in Hungary and in Transylvania."[43] Three days later, it sent an ultimatum to Budapest in which it demanded the transfer of complete authority over twenty-three counties and partial authority over three others.[44] This included Transylvania as well as areas outside the province, including some purely Magyar-inhabited counties.[45] The Hungarians responded by offering to hold negotiations, which took place in Arad on November 13–14. The Hungarian delegation, led by Oszkár Jászi, offered the abolition of the counties, which were the administrative units of old Hungary. Instead, he proposed the creation of national areas that were similar to the "Swiss cantons" and would have administrative and cultural autonomy. These cantons were to send representatives to the central government in Budapest. As a temporary measure, he proposed the transfer of administrative power to the Rumanian council, where a Rumanian majority existed. A representative of the Rumanian administration could thus find a place in the Hungarian government.

Jászi's offer put an end to the geographical conception of Transylvania. It indicated that the new Hungarian policy favored the reorganization of the state into an "Eastern Switzerland." This plan offered the nationalities full autonomy, thus seemingly fulfilling Wilsonian demands. It was expected that this policy would bring about Allied recognition of Hungary as an independent state,[46] but the Rumanian National Council, led by Iuliu Maniu, Alexandru Vaida-Voevod, Vasile Goldis, and Ion Erdelyi, rejected the Hungarian offer and demanded full sovereignty for the Council. The Hungarian delegation returned to Budapest emptyhanded.[47] However, Maniu's subsequent visit to Budapest at the end of November and his conciliatory attitude there revived hopes for a negotiated settlement.[48]

In response to his favorable stance and expecting moderation, the Hungarian government agreed to provide transportation for Rumanians in Transylvania to attend a Popular Assembly sponsored by the Rumanian National Council in Alba Iulia (Gyulafehérvár). On December 1, the Alba Iulia meeting overwhelmingly decided to unite the twenty-six counties with the kingdom of Rumania. Interwar Hungarian historiography, misjudging the reasons behind the Hungarian government's action, branded it as treachery,[49] which was a baseless charge. The Rumanian Marxist claim that Jászi was informed by Maniu about the Assembly's intention to unite Transylvania with the Regat was also incorrect. Equally untrue and tortuous has been the Rumanian argument that the Hungarian government, whose actions had been prompted solely by its desire for reconciliation, had symbolically recognized Rumanian sovereignty over Transylvania by providing the transport.[50]

According to the Hungarian minister of welfare, the socialist Zsigmond Kunfi, the Hungarian ministers recognized that "Magyar hegemony was lost." The moral was that only "radical democracy and autonomy to the nationalities" could lead to the survival of the state.[51] On November 29, Minister of Nationalities Jászi reiterated his belief that the nationalities in Hungary would use self-determination for the sake of a confederation. He admitted, however, that if they decided otherwise, the Hungarian government could do nothing to stop them.[52]

The Alba Iulia decision forced the Hungarian government to consider alternatives to confederation. One course of action was outlined by Jászi in a message to the worried Hungarian National Council of the Erdőd (Ardud) District. The council leaders reacted negatively to the Alba Iulia declaration, which had also called for Rumanian sovereignty over their county, Szatmár. They sent objections to Budapest, wondering why their district, with a slight Magyar majority and with many purely Magyar villages, should belong to Rumania.

To allay the council's fear, Jászi replied that the plan of a Rumanian imperium over Szatmár was not accomplished yet, but in such an eventuality, the Hungarian government would see to it that the national rights of the Magyar minorities would be protected.[53] This message indicated that government officials considered overlapping sovereignty as an alternative solution to the Transylvanian question. Put into practice, the concept might have reconciled the self-determination of the Rumanian majority with the needs and expectations of the large Magyar minority in Transylvania. Jászi's plan could also be considered as the minimum program, in contrast to the maximum, represented by the project for a confederated Hungary within the confines of the former Hungarian kingdom. Although the Hungarian government continued to press for the maximum, fully expecting this position to be challenged at the Paris Peace Conference, the existence of Jászi's minimum program was evidence that a compromise solution would have been considered.[54]

The legitimacy of the Alba Iulia decision was rejected. According to Jászi, the Rumanians could not speak in the name of the majority since the combined Magyar and Saxon population of the contested counties represented fifty-seven percent of the total inhabitants. It was significant that the Allies also questioned the legitimacy of the Rumanian claim on the same basis.[55]

The Rumanian government's initial response to Alba Iulia was guarded, as it seemed to offer a lesser prize than the one Bucharest wanted. In fact, the advancing Rumanian troops in Transylvania were told that the government's aim was to establish a greater Rumania, stretching to the Tisza River.[56] If this could be considered as Rumania's maximum aim, no minimum plan similar to Jászi's overlapping sovereignty for Transylvania seemed to be entertained by the Rumanian government. Its objection to the minority treaties a year later indicated that the royal government sought no compromise and wanted absolute control over its new subjects.[57]

Responding to the developments in Alba Iulia, the new Hungarian tactic emphasized fostering the non-Rumanian national councils in Transylvania. These had not been consulted nor were they represented at Alba Iulia. The National Council of the Hungarians in Transylvania was encouraged to organize a counterassembly and to call for a Hungarian Transylvania. The Hungarian government also favored the organization of a separate Székely national council and approved plans for the creation of a Székely republic.[58] The major purpose of these activities was to show the West that the Rumanians were not the sole inhabitants of the contested territories.

On December 4, the Ministerial Council decided to appoint István Apáthy as commissioner of the twenty-six counties demanded by the Rumanians. His role was to prevent the transfer of these counties to Rumania.[59]

Apáthy, who was the president of the Magyar National Council in Transylvania, was reputed to be a Magyar chauvinist, and his appointment, therefore, represented a hardening of attitudes in Budapest. This was prompted by the realization that the Belgrade treaty had been flaunted by the Czechs, with French acquiescence. The Yugoslavs had occupied Baranya County and now it was feared that Rumania would detach more than just Transylvania from Hungary. When Jászi was questioned about the advisability of Apáthy's appointment, he brushed the objection aside by noting that he was trusted by the Magyars in Transylvania.[60]

Preparations for military resistance were also undertaken. Early in December, a staff for the Székely division was organized.[61] Its members were soldiers of the former Székely battalions and some Transylvanian infantry divisions.[62] According to Apáthy, the strength of these troops reached 3,000 by the end of the month.[63] These preparations for defense were necessitated less by the declaration of Alba Iulia than as a consequence of the announced intention of Rumania to gather for the kingdom those territories that had been promised it by the Entente in 1916.

Although the Rumanian army did not reenter the war against Hungary, it did march into southern Transylvania. The first troops crossed the Carpathians on November 13. Marosvásárhely (Tîrgu Mureş) was occupied on December 2, Beszterce (Bistriţa) on December 4, and Brassó (Braşov) on December 7. By mid-December, the royal troops reached the Allied-Hungarian demarcation lines set by the Belgrade Convention. On December 24, the Rumanian troops entered Kolozsvár (Cluj).[64] General Presnan, the commander in chief of the Rumanian Army, reiterated the Rumanian desire to continue its advances to the Nagykároly (Carei)-Nagyvárad (Oradea)-Békéscsaba line.[65] In contradiction to the Belgrade Convention, the Rumanians took over the administration in the occupied areas.[66]

In northern Hungary, the French government approved the territorial changes in the name of the Allies, while in Transylvania territorial changes were made without Allied sanction but with the approval of General Henri Berthelot. Berthelot, as commander of the Allied forces in Rumania and in southern Russia, disregarded his commander Franchet d'Esperey and seemed to give a carte blanche to Rumania. Possibly, his actions were partially prompted by a desire to atone for his failures in 1917. More importantly, he expected that the fulfillment of Rumania's demands would buy Rumanian support for France's anti-Bolshevik intervention in southern Russia.[67] General Franchet d'Esperey disapproved of Berthelot's pro-Rumanian stance and protested his insubordination.

In response to further Rumanian advances, apparently supported by the French, the Hungarian Council of Ministers were forced to decide on appropriate governmental measures. Consideration was given to the resignation of the government and a call for the Entente to govern Hungary, which was on the brink of chaos. Passive or active resistance to the piecemeal absorption of Hungarian lands by Rumania was also discussed. Oszkár Jászi proposed that the ministers should take direct leadership over the counties, which meant ten ministers governing ten defined areas. Kunfi suggested that, instead of decentralizing, the government ought to map out its imperium along a solidly Magyar ethnic frontier. He concluded that this was the price Hungary would have to pay for a lost war.

The cabinet finally decided to issue instructions to Apáthy to agree to the occupation of Transylvania by Rumanian troops, but only as representatives of the Allies. Apáthy was to insist on Rumanian acquiescence to the retention of Hungarian police forces in the occupied areas. These were to be representatives of the Hungarian administration, as sanctioned in the Belgrade Convention.[68]

Instead, on January 3, at the Rumanian-occupied city of Kolozsvár (Cluj), Apáthy was pressured by Berthelot into accepting a new demarcation line. The new agreement allowed the Rumanians to hold the Nagybánya (Baia Mare)-Kolozsvár-Dés (Dej) line, which separated them from Hungarian troops by a fifteen-kilometer-wide neutral zone.

The new line pleased neither the Hungarians nor the Rumanians. Budapest objected because it appeared that the Hungarian government had accepted a revision of the Belgrade demarcation lines without an overall settlement. For this reason the cabinet disavowed the agreement, claiming that Apáthy was not empowered to agree to changes in the terms of the Belgrade Convention. The Rumanians also disregarded the Apáthy-Berthelot agreement because it curtailed the further expansion of their imperium.[69] Under the circumstances, the hapless Apáthy could do nothing but resign his post soon thereafter. This did not prevent the angered Rumanian authorities from arresting him, and with the intention of putting him on trial they took him to Nagyszeben (Sibiu, Hermannstadt). An indemnity was put on Kolozsvár (Cluj).[70]

Berthelot's superiors, General Franchet d'Esperey and even the prime minister and minister of war, Clemenceau, were displeased with Berthelot, who had entered into the agreement without consulting his superiors.[71] They, however, were forced to accept the agreement as a fait accompli. In his report, Franchet d'Esperey expressed his hope that the new agreement would finally satisfy Rumanian aspirations.[72]

The Hungarian government, powerless to change the situation, recognized the futility of insisting on the integrity of Transylvania and accepted Apáthy's resignation. His position was left vacant, which meant that the Commissariat for Transylvania was eliminated,[73] and on January 23, 1919, the Council of Ministers decided for the first time that no other option was left to the government but military resistance. To stop further Rumanian advances, it decided to order a holding action along the county line of Bihar (Bihor). An all-out war against Rumania was still rejected, since the Council had neither the manpower nor energy supplies available with which to fight.[74]

The Peace Conference, which opened in Paris in mid-January, did not include representatives from the defeated countries, and although the Hungarians were not present, the conferees disapproved of Rumanian expansion. The Peace Conference also refused to accept the Entente commitments made to Rumania in 1916, and on January 25, the day after Alba Iulia was acclaimed in the Rumanian Parliament, the peacemakers accepted President Wilson's resolution against the use of force for territorial gain. They set up a "Commission for the Study of Territorial Questions Relating to Rumania" in order to examine its claims to parts of Russia, Serbia, Bulgaria, and Hungary.[75]

Ignoring Allied wishes, the Rumanian troops continued to advance. By the end of January, they held a line running from Máramarossziget (Sighetul Marmaţiei) to Zilah (Zalău), Csucsa (Ciucea), Nagysebes (Valea Drăganului), and the Szamos (Someş) River and occupied most of Transylvania. By then, the Székely division had amassed some 7,000–8,000 men and almost reached divisional strength,[76] while according to Hungarian estimates, the Rumanians had three divisions, with a total of 10,000 poorly equipped men.[77] Military clashes between the Hungarians and the Rumanians already had taken place and further conflict was imminent.[78] Franchet d'Esperey, therefore, requested that the peacemakers in Paris establish a neutral zone between the Rumanians and Hungarians. He expected that the Rumanians would be ordered to withdraw to the Apáthy-Berthelot line. Instead, on February 26, the Peace Conference, on the recommendation of the French General Staff, accepted a demarcation line allowing Rumania to occupy a line outside historical Transylvania. This established a neutral zone, with the Hungarian line being reminiscent of that accorded to Rumania in 1916. The French General Staff favored this arrangement so as to assure a united front against the Bolsheviks in Russia. They depended on Rumania to be a natural ally in the anti-Bolshevik crusade, and Hungary's territory served as the price for Bucharest's loyalty. The Allied representatives, who were not informed of the French military's true intentions, acquiesced. Satisfying Rumanian demands at the expense of defeated Hungary seemed to be the easiest way to bring about peace in that "remote" area.[79]

The Transylvanian question was thus resolved by the great powers, who were responding to their own interests, and Hungary and Rumania were not permitted to work out a bilateral agreement, which would take into consideration the national interests of the Hungarians, Rumanians, and Saxons. On March 20, the terms for the new demarcation line were transmitted to the Hungarian government in the form of an ultimatum. They were rejected, and the Hungarian government resigned. The fall of the Károlyi regime spelled the end of the democratic Republic of Hungary.

The new government, made up of a communist-socialist fusion, ushered in a second revolution. The Socialist Federated Soviet Republic in Hungary (Magyarországi Szocialista Szövetséges Tanácsköztársaság) aimed to fight an all-out war against the Rumanians. This policy went further than was favored by the Károlyi government. Led by Béla

Kun, the regime embraced a maximum policy of a federation, but now it was to be within a Soviet system. At a time when a Europe-wide proletarian revolution was expected, this program, tainted with a new ideology, foreclosed any compromise with "boyar" Rumania. The Hungarian Soviet Republic hoped to achieve its aim by making an alliance with the Red Army and fighting against the common enemy: "Entente Imperialism."

The Kun regime, therefore, depended on the "new Russia" to help preserve a Hungarian Transylvania, which was first promised to Rumania by "old Russia." These hopes, like the Károlyi government's expectations of Allied fairness, remained unfulfilled. The Bolsheviks were too busy defending their own perimeters and did not, or could not, come to Soviet Hungary's aid. This led to the demise of the commune after 133 days. The Rumanian demarcation line set down on February 26 soon became the political boundary between Hungary and Rumania. It left a Magyar irredenta in Rumania and a revisionist state in Hungary, and both have kept the Transylvanian question alive.

Notes

1. Sherman D. Spector, *Rumania at the Paris Peace Conference: A Study of the Diplomacy of Ioan I. C. Brătianu* (New York, 1962), p. 15.

2. Charles and Barbara Jelavich, *The Establishment of the Balkan National States, 1804–1920* (Seattle, 1977), p. 246.

3. Jalavich and Jelavich, op. cit., p. 221.

4. Friedrich Stieve, *Isvolsky and the World War* (New York, 1926), p. 190.

5. Fritz Fischer, *Germany's Aims in the First World War* (New York, 1967), pp. 42–45; Arthur J. May, *The Passing of the Habsburg Monarchy 1914–1918* (New York, 1966), 1:208.

6. Jenő László, *Erdély sorsa az uniótól Trianonig* [The Fate of Transylvania from the Union to Trianon] (Budapest, 1940), p. 75.

7. Ferenc Pölöskei, "Tisza István nemzetiségi politikája az elsö világháború elöestéjén" [The nationality policy of István Tisza on the Eve of World War I], *Századok* [Centuries] 104, no. 1 (1970): 14–15.

8. Ibid., pp. 19–20; Péter Hanák, ed., *Magyarország Története 1890–1918* [The History of Hungary 1890–1918] (Budapest, 1978), 2:853–54; Vasile Netea, *The Union of Transylvania with Rumania* (Bucharest, 1968), p. 32.

9. "Károlyi Riadója" [The Alarm of Károlyi], *Magyarország* [Hungary], Jan. 2, 1914.

10. *Magyarország*, Jan. 4, 1914.

11. *The Apáthy Papers*; Quart. Hung. 2456, Dec. 7, 1913, Széchenyi Library Archives, Hungary.

12. I. Diószegi, "The Independence Opposition and the Monarchy's Foreign Policy (1900–1914)," in D. Nemes et al., *Etudes Hongroises 1975* (Budapest, 1975), 2:228–32.

13. Arthur J. May, *The Habsburg Monarchy 1867–1914,* (New York, 1968), p. 443.

14. Benedek Jancsó, *A román irredentista mozgalmak története* [The History of Rumanian Irredentist Movements] (Budapest, 1920), p. 303.

15. May, *The Habsburg Monarchy,* p. 470.

16. Joachim Remak, *Sarajevo* (New York, 1959), pp. 33–35.

17. Spector, op. cit., 26; Jenő Horváth, *Felelősség a világháborúért és a békeszerződésért* [Responsibility for the War and the Peace Treaty] (Budapest, 1939), pp. 370–71.

18. Kenneth J. Calder, *Britain and the Origins of the New Europe, 1914–1918* (Cambridge, 1976), p. 39; Spector, op. cit., p. 34.

19. Calder, op. cit., p. 40; Spector, op. cit., p. 28.

20. Z. A. B. Zeman, *The Gentlemen Negotiators* (New York, 1971), p. 80.

21. Peter Pastor, *Hungary between Wilson and Lenin: The Hungarian Revolution of 1918–1919 and the Big Three* (New York, 1976), p. 15.

22. Hanák, op. cit., p. 1116; Jancsó, op. cit., p. 414.

23. Jancsó, op. cit., p. 415.

24. *Magyarország,* Nov. 9, 1914.

25. Norman Stone, *The Eastern Front* (New York, 1975), p. 273.

26. Spector, op. cit., pp. 35–37.

27. Glenn E. Torrey, "Rumania and the Belligerents 1914–1916," in Walter Laquaur and George L. Mosse, eds., *1914 The Coming of the First World War* (New York, 1966), p. 184.

28. Miron Constantinescu, *Etude d'Histoire Transylvain* (Bucharest, 1970), p. 92; Vasile Netea, op. cit., p. 38.

29. Stone, op. cit., pp. 274–280.

30. Jelavich and Jelavich, op. cit., p. 293.

31. Constantinescu, op. cit., p. 62.

32. *The Apáthy Papers* Quart. Hung. 2459, Sept. 30, 1917.

33. Sándor Wekerle to István Apáthy, Dec. 4, 1917, Papers of the Prime Minister, K26, M.E. 1918, 8242 Res. XVI, National Archives, Hungary.

34. Papers of the Prime Minister, K 26, M.E. 1918, XVI 3949, 9/MT, March 7, 1918; copy in: Emma Ivanyi, ed., *Magyar minisztertanácsi jegyzőkönyvek az első világháboru korából 1914–1918* [Minutes of the Hungarian Council of Ministers during World War I, 1914–1918] (Budapest, 1960), pp. 415–17; for German aims in Rumania see Fischer, op. cit., 515–23.

35. László, op. cit., p. 95; Jancsó, op. cit., 450; the Austro-Hungarian military staff wanted a strip seventy percent larger than favored by the ministerial council, see Vilmos Nagybaczoni Nagy, *A Románia elleni hadjárat, 1916–1917* [The Campaign against Rumania, 1916–1917] (Budapest, 1922), p. 120; a Hungarian work published in the early 1960s claims that the Hungarians intended to annex considerably large territories. This claim does not appear in a recent publication by the same author, see József Galántai, *Magyarország az első világháboruban* [Hungary in World War I] (Budapest, 1964), p. 304; Hanák, op. cit., p. 1186.

36. Minutes of the Council of Ministers, June 15, 1918, Papers of the Prime Minister, K 26, M.E. 1918, 9249 Res. XVI, National Archives, Hungary.

37. United States, Department of State, *Papers Relating to the Foreign Relations of the United States, 1918 Supplement I, The World War* (Washington, 1933), vol. 1, p. 307.

38. *The Apáthy Papers,* Quart. Hung 2455, manuscript of "Erdély az összeomlás után" [Transylvania after the collapse].

39. Keith Hitchins, "Romanian Socialists and the Nationality Problem in Hungary, 1903–1918," *Slavic Review* 35, no. 1 (March 1976): 87.

40. Minutes of the Council of Ministers, Nov. 5, 1918, K 27, Mt. jk., National Archives, Hungary.

41. György Ránki, ed., *Magyarország Története 1918–1919, 1919–1945* [The History of Hungary, 1918–1919, 1919–1945] (Budapest, 1976), p. 93; Pastor, op. cit., pp. 61–65.

42. Zoltán Szász, "Az erdélyi román polgárság szerepéröl 1918 őszén" [The Activities of the Rumanian Bourgeoisie in Transylvania during the Fall of 1918], *Századok* [Centuries] (1972): 321; for similar facts but different interpretation, see Constantinescu, op. cit., p. 108.

43. Constantinescu, op. cit., p. 103; Netea, op. cit., p. 46.

44. Constantinescu, op. cit., p. 111.

45. The Rumanian National Council to the Hungarian National Council, Nov. 9, 1918, Papers of the Minister without portfolio, in Charge of the Preparation for Self-determination of the Nationalities Living in Hungary, K 40, M.E., National Archives, Hungary.

46. Minutes of the Council of Ministers, K 27, Mt. jk., Nov. 28, 1918, National Archives, Hungary.

47. Gábor Vermes, "The Agony of Federalism in Hungary under the Károlyi Regime, 1918–1919," *East European Quarterly* 6, no. 4 (1972): 496.

48. Minutes of the Council of Ministers, Nov. 28, 1918.

49. For an example, see László, op. cit., p. 117; for a criticism of interwar historiography on this topic, see György Litván, "Magyar gondolat—szabad gondolat" [Hungarian Thought-Free Thought] (Budapest, 1978), p. 114.

50. For the Rumanian interpretation see Miron Constantinescu, "The Act of Union, 1st December 1918," in Office of Information and Documentation in Social and Political Sciences, *Highlights of Rumanian History* (Bucharest, 1975), 1:77.

51. Minutes of the Council of Ministers, Nov. 28, 1918.

52. Minutes of the Council of Ministers, K 27, Mt. jk., Nov. 29, 1918.

53. Erdődi Nemzeti Tanács to Jászi, and reply, Dec. 3, 1918, Papers of the Minister without Portfolio, K 40, M.E., National Archives, Hungary.

54. Minutes of the Council of Ministers, K 27, Mt. jk., Dec. 28, 1918.

55. Spector, op. cit., p. 93.

56. Maria Ormos, "Az ukrajnai francia intervencióról és hatásairól Közép-Európában, 1918 oktober-1919 április" [The Impact of the French Intervention in the Ukraine on Central Europe, October 1918–April 1919], *Történelmi Szemle* [Historical Review] 1977, nos. 3–4, p. 423, n. 56.

57. Zsuzsa L. Nagy, "Magyar határviták a békekonferencián 1919-ben" [Debates Over Hungary's Borders at the Peace Conference in 1919], *Történelmi Szemle,* 1978, nos. 3–4, p. 452.

58. Böhm to Jászi, Dec. 5, 1918, Papers of the Minister without Portfolio, K 40, M.E., and Minutes of the Council of Ministers, K 27, Mt. jk., Dec. 17, 1918.

59. Minutes of the Council of Ministers, K 27, Mt. jk., Dec. 4, 1918; Batthyány to Apáthy, Dec. 7, 1918, *The Apáthy Papers,* Quart. Hung. 2455.

60. Minutes of the Council of Ministers, K 27, Mt. jk., Dec. 8, 1918.

61. Endre Koréh, "Erdélyért" [For Transylvania] *A székely hadosztály és dandár története, 1918–1919* [The History of the Transylvanian Division and Brigade, 1918–1919] (Budapest, 1929), p. 35.

62. László, op. cit., p. 120.

63. *The Apáthy Papers,* "Erdély az összeomlás után."

64. Ránki, op. cit., p. 113–17.

65. Ibid., p. 96.

66. Böhm to Jászi, Jan. 29, 1919, Papers of the Minister without Portfolio, K 40, M.E.

67. Peter Pastor, "Franco-Russian Intervention in Russia and the *Vix Ultimatum*: Background to Hungary's Loss of Transylvania," *The Canadian-American Review of Hungarian Studies*, vol. 1, nos. 1–2, 1974, p. 14. This essay is based on unpublished archival sources from the French Military Archives and the Archives of the Ministry of Foreign Affairs, Paris.

68. Minutes of the Council of Ministers, K 27, Mt. jk., Dec. 18 and Dec. 19, 1919; *The Apáthy Papers* "Erdély az összeomlás után."

69. Minutes of the Council of Ministers, K 27, Mt. jk., Jan. 27, 1919.

70. Minutes of the Council of Ministers, K 27, Mt. jk., Jan. 13, 1919.

71. Pastor, *Hungary between Wilson and Lenin*, pp. 88–90; Ormos, op. cit., p. 422 and 424, fn. 57.

72. Jean Bernachot, ed., *Les armées alliées en Orient après l'Armistice de 1918-Comptes-rendus mensuels adressés par le commandant en chef des armées alliées en Orient, á l'etatmajor de l'armée á Paris, de decembre 1918 á Octobre 1920* (Paris, 1972), p. 164.

73. Minutes of the Council of Ministers, K 27, Mt. jk., Jan. 23, 1919.

74. Minutes of the Council of Ministers, K 27, Mt. jk., Jan. 21, 1919.

75. Spector, op. cit., p. 80.

76. Jancsó, op. cit., p. 489.

77. Papers of the Minister without Portfolio, Jan. 29, 1919.

78. Koréh, op. cit., p. 198.

79. Pastor, *Hungary between Wilson and Lenin*, pp. 122–23; Ormos, op. cit., p. 431.

Primary sources from the Hungarian archives were collected during my stay in Hungary on an International Research and Exchanges Board (IREX) grant, January–July, 1978. I am grateful for the Board's material support. For their comments on drafts of this essay I wish to thank Professors Joseph Held and Gábor Vermes.

The Great Powers and the Fate of Transylvania Between the Two World Wars

STEPHEN FISCHER-GALAȚI

The continuing controversies, agitation, and expressions of anger and dissatisfaction by one or another ethnic group inhabiting Transylvania and the corollary attention paid to Transylvanian problems by the countries most involved, Romania and Hungary, and by Great Powers concerned with stability and instability in Eastern Europe would tend to indicate that the "Transylvanian Question" was anything but resolved at the end of World War II.

It is generally agreed that the resolution of the Transylvanian problems recorded at the end of World War I were deficient in most respects. The causes for continuing tensions some sixty years later are, however, less evident even though they have been identified and exploited by interested parties in terms of cynical denial of the root causes of the Transylvanian Question. In the simplest possible terms—and indeed the terms of identification of the problem have been and continue to be simplistic—it has been assumed that the irreconcilable historical differences between Romanian and Hungarian national (and nationalist) interests have created conditions that have made peaceful coexistence between Romanians and Hungarians and, by extension, between Romania and Hungary, impossible both before and particularly after World War I. This paramount emphasis on nationality and nationalism, however, ignores the ultimate determining factors for instability in Transylvania, to wit, the concern and actions of the Great Powers in general and of Nazi Germany and the Soviet Union in particular. Indeed, it seems fair to say that the Transylvanian Question since World War I has been primarily a direct or indirect function of the actual, potential, or perceived dangers posed by the Soviet Union and Soviet communism in Eastern Europe.

Mistreatment and other forms of discrimination against national and religious minorities are a rule of modern history in Eastern Europe. The Hungarian rulers of Transylvania were as intolerant of the Romanians before World War I as the Romanian rulers of Transylvania were of the Hungarians after the war. And neither Hungarians or Romanians displayed fondness of Jews, Saxons, Szeklers, or Gypsies living in Transylvania. Yet it would be difficult to argue that these conditions, reflective mostly of the political interests of the ruling circles of Budapest and Bucharest, endangered the political stability or precluded coexistence among the various ethnic groups inhabiting Transylvania. What mattered ultimately was the rulers' rationale for holding Transylvania in the Hungarian or Romanian body territorial and politic and the external powers' rationale for exploiting Romanian-Hungarian rivalries for their own benefit.

The Hungarian arguments, which are presented and analyzed in detail in other papers comprising this volume, are self evident. Since Transylvania had been an integral part of the Hungarian body politic for "1,000 years", the loss of the province and its incorporation into Greater Romania was an affront to the Hungarian nation, a symbol of military defeat in World War I and, as such, an intolerable and unacceptable occurrence. Whatever reasons might have been advanced in support of territorial revisionism aimed at reincorporation of Transylvania into Hungary in the interwar years—such as illegitimacy of possession by the Romanians, abuse of minority rights by Romanian authorities, and other rationalizing arguments—the fact remains that the ultimate motivation was simply territorial revisionism. The Romanian arguments in favor of acquisition and retention of Transylvania in the twentieth century are hardly more complex. In short, they are based on the assumption that Transylvania has been historically a Romanian province whose inhabitants, even during the long years of foreign rule, were primarily Romanians and that, therefore, on the basis of the eternally valid principle of self-determination of nationalities, Transylvania belongs to Romania. These two adverse and essentially irreconcilable positions of the Hungarian and Romanian rulers of the twentieth century have greatly facilitated the task of the European powers concerned with the advancement of their own political interests through the standard practice of encouraging, fomenting, and exploiting discord among rival nationalities and nations. This, in the last analysis, determined the fate of Transylvania after World War I, and in this determination, at least for Romania, the key factors were those related to Romania's relations with and attitude toward the Soviet Union and Russian communism.

To consolidate claims to Transylvania and, for that matter, also to Bessarabia, the political leaders in Bucharest posed, from at least as early as 1918, as defenders of Eastern Europe (by extension of the Allied Powers' interests in that part of the continent) against communism. There can be little doubt that the Romanian position, so eloquently stated by Ion I. C. Brătianu, was largely based on genuine concern over the Bolshevik threat to Romanian interests in general and to specific Romanian plans for the incorporation and retention of Bessarabia in a greater Romania.[1] It is also true that the Bolshevik menace was at all times considered a valuable trump card in Brătianu's games with the leaders of the Great Powers in Paris, who, in the Romanians' view, were indecisive in dealing with the Bolshevik threat and in ratifying Romanian plans for permanent incorporation of Transylvania and Bessarabia into the Romanian body politic.

It is unnecessary to recapitulate here the complex, well-known negotiations involving these questions at the Paris Peace Conference. It should, however, be emphasized that the action of the Romanian armies directed against Béla Kun were in no small measure undertaken by genuine Romanian fears of Communist imperialism. Moreover, the discrediting of Kun and, by extension, of the "Judeo-Communist" character of Hungarian and Russian Bolshevism was considered imperative for unequivocal and unrestricted Romanian rule in both Transylvania and Bessarabia without any obligatory acceptance of participation in governance by minority groups, by political organizations representative of minority group interests, or, for that matter, by circumscription of Bucharest's total power through imposition of minority-rights guarantees in the peace treaties affecting Romania. In sum, to Brătianu and the Romanian leaders who regarded Greater Romania as a country to be ruled by Romanians alone for the benefit of the ultimate exponents of Romanian nationalism—the Bucharest "mafia"—the Bolshevik menace was an essential and invaluable asset.[2]

Whether the ratification at Trianon of Brătianu's demands would have occurred even without Romania's military intervention against Kun is a matter of speculation; but there is no speculation about the ratification of Romania's incorporation of Bessarabia and the recognition by the Powers concerned with Russian imperialism and revisionism after 1920 of Romania's paramount role in the "struggle against Bolshevism."

It is also clear that in the 1920s the Romanian rulers were relatively unconcerned over Hungarian revisionism with respect to Transylvania and with the possibility of Budapest's receiving support for its demands from Mussolini's Italy. Nor was Bucharest concerned about criticism of its minority policies in Transylvania emanating from abroad since it regarded any intervention seeking observance of minority treaties as interference in Romanian internal affairs and, in any case, as unenforceable as long as Romania stood in the forefront of the opposition to Bolshevism and Soviet territorial revisionism. On the other hand, Bucharest remained preoccupied by Moscow's determination to deny the legitimacy of the incorporation of Bessarabia into Greater Romania and by specific Russian actions designed to undermine Romanian rule in Bessarabia and, by extension, to place in jeopardy the validity of Romanian claims to and rule in Transylvania as well.[3]

The evidence of direct anti-Romanian actions undertaken by the USSR in the 1920s is abundant. The convention of October 28, 1920, whereby the British Empire, France, Italy, and Japan recognized Romanian sovereignty in Bessarabia, was rejected as invalid by the USSR. Moscow even denied the validity of that part of the convention that stipulated that, upon Russian request, the Council of the League of Nations could be empowered to arbitrate the Russo-Romanian dispute over Bessarabia. In short, the Kremlin insisted that Romania was illegally occupying Bessarabia. And it was because of this intransigent attitude that the Soviet Union refused to make any concessions. Romania's attempts, in the early 1920s, to seek accommodation with the USSR on all issues except the Bessarabian fell on deaf ears as the Kremlin encouraged revolutionary activities by Bolshevik elements in Bessarabia.[4] The establishment in October, 1924, of the Autonomous Moldavian Soviet Socialist Republic as a focal point for eventual reincorporation of Bessarabia into the USSR indeed eliminated the possibility of peaceful resolution of Russo-Romanian differences.[5]

Whether there was a direct linkage between Soviet and Hungarian revisionism in these years is not known.[6] However, such a danger was perceived by Bucharest, which evidently realized that its actions against Béla Kun's Hungary, its anti-communist positions in Bessarabia, and the official banning of the Romanian Communist party after the crushing of the Russian-inspired revolt of Tatar Bunar, in Bessarabia, in 1924 augured badly for the future.[7] In fact, the protracted negotiations with the USSR, which continued on an intermittent basis during the 1920s and 1930s and which failed to resolve the Bessarabian question to the satisfaction of Moscow, were assuming increasingly greater importance in Romania's foreign policy in the 1930s as the Transylvanian question reared its potentially ugly head in the wake of the renascence of German power.

Romania's desire to secure a resolution of the Bessarabian question was prompted by pressure from France as Paris became increasingly more apprehensive over the rise of Hitler and the activities of Mussolini in areas of vital French interest. Yet no amount of pressure could persuade Bucharest to abandon possession of Bessarabia.[8] By the same token, no matter how desirous of promoting its relations with

France the Soviet Union might have been it was never sufficiently anxious to renounce its territorial claims to Bessarabia. It is noteworthy that France never tried to persuade Bucharest to make any compromises in matters territorial except in the case of Bessarabia; in other words, the Transylvanian question was not considered to be one that could jeopardize the interests of France in Eastern Europe.[9] It is also noteworthy that Germany was for a long time uninterested in exploiting the potentially advantageous opportunities provided by Hungarian revisionism in Transylvania and that until 1938 the only power that encouraged and supported Hungarian revisionism in that province was Italy.[10] This is not to say, however, that Germany, the USSR, and to a lesser degree France and Great Britain were indifferent to actual and potential advantages or disadvantages that could ensue from the escalation of Hungarian revisionist clamor, which began to assume increased stridency by 1938. It is also essential to note that until 1938 not even Romania displayed undue concern over Hungarian revisionist agitation. In 1938, however, following the extraordinary and unanticipated showing of strength by the extreme right in the Romanian elections of December, 1937, and the parallel acceleration of Hitler's *Drang nach Osten,* the Transylvanian question assumed, at least for the Romanians, potentially dangerous proportions.[11]

The essential elements of the Transylvanian problems and of the evolution of European diplomacy until the Vienna Diktat of August, 1940, have been familiar to students of European diplomacy and of Eastern European problems for some time now.[12] One key aspect, that of the connection between Soviet and Hungarian revisionism per se and in the general context of Russo-German and Russo-French and British relations, however, has been largely neglected. It is true that the data are scanty, but such information as exists tends to assign primary significance to direct or indirect Russian actions in the resolution of the Transylvanian question in the manner determined by Hitler in 1940.

The posing of Hungarian demands to Germany and Italy is now traced back to 1936. The German response, prior to 1938, was discouraging to the extent to which Berlin repeatedly stated its lack of readiness to support Hungarian territorial claims to Transylvania. However, on the eve of 1938, Germany sought to direct such claims toward Czechoslovakia, clearly Germany's primary priority at that time. By contrast, Mussolini was basically supportive of Hungary's aspirations in Transylvania, but verbal support mattered little to either Budapest or Bucharest, given the reserved attitude of the Germans.[13]

It has been suggested that Hitler's reluctance to encourage the

Hungarian aspirations was due, in part, to his desire to use the extreme right-wing political organizations in Romania, particularly the Iron Guard, as instruments for Berlin's policies of penetration into Romania. Such an assumption is at least partly correct inasmuch as the Romanian right, despite its opposition to King Carol's rule and to his pro-French orientation, was united in the general Romanian opposition to any alteration of the status quo in Transylvania.[14] It has also been suggested that the German policy of moderation reflected concern over the anti-Hungarian attitudes of the Saxons of Transylvania, who clearly preferred Romanian to Hungarian rule. However, these considerations were essentially minor in 1938 when Hitler's primary thrust was in the direction of Czechoslovakia and when German policies were designed to minimize any risks from premature encouragement of revisionist moves against Romania. Hitler realized that it would serve no purpose to consolidate the weak French system of alliances in Eastern Europe at a time when the resoluteness of France and Great Britain in opposing German territorial demands appeared to be faltering, by injecting the issue of Hungarian territorial claims. Moreover, Hitler was anxious to prevent any possible action directed against Romania by other revisionists, most notably the USSR but also Bulgaria. Thus, despite the lack of overt support, the Hungarians were satisfied that the Transylvanian question had at least been posed and, as 1938 progressed, the Romanians became concerned over the posing of that question.

The exact position of the USSR on these issues is unknown except for Moscow's unwillingness to make any concessions to Bucharest on Bessarabian issues. Recent tracts by Romanian historians have emphasized the support given by Romanian Communists to the "democratic forces" opposed to alteration of the status quo in Transylvania in 1938 and subsequent years.[15] True as this may be, there has been no evidence presented in support of any fundamental change in Moscow's traditional anti-Romanian positions with respect to Bessarabia in 1938 and subsequent years. Thus, the attitude of the Romanian Communists in the late 1930s must be related merely to the "popular front" policies perpetrated by the Kremlin and was evidently not reflective of actual Russian territorial aims. In fact, from such evidence as has become available, Moscow was singularly unconcerned about the possibility of alienating the anti-Hungarian members of the Romanian movement by any action it may have decided to take and was supporting pro-Romanian manifestations purely for tactical purposes.[16]

It is also evident that after Munich and particularly after the First Vienna Diktat, which, on November 2, 1938, awarded southern Slovakia and southern Ruthenia to Hungary, neither Hitler nor Mussolini were in any way anxious to allow Hungarian revisionism to upset their ever more ambitious plans for hegemony in Eastern Europe. The better orchestrated Hungarian demands for restitution of substantial parts of Transylvania to Hungary elicited only prudently negative responses from Berlin and Rome as Hitler was mapping a total strategy for Hungary, Romania, and the USSR.[17] The Romanians, by early 1939, were fully aware of the game plan of the Axis powers and were paying much closer attention to those than to the guarantees issued belatedly by France and Great Britain with respect to the territorial integrity of Greater Romania. Nor was Bucharest reassured by the continuing professions of support for the Romanian cause in Transylvania emanating from the pro-Axis right and from the pro-Soviet left. For Rumania realized that Hitler and Mussolini were obviously using the Transylvanian question as an instrument for dividing and conquering the rest of Eastern Europe at a time when King Carol and his advisers were growing increasingly more leery of Russia's intentions toward Romania and more apprehensive over the willingness and ability of the guaranteeing powers to abide by their commitments.

Little is known about the role played by Transylvania and Bessarabia in the negotiations between Moscow and the Western Allies and/or Nazi Germany in the spring and summer of 1939.[18] But it stands to reason to assume that the two questions were discussed and that acceptance by Germany of the validity of Moscow's claims to Bessarabia and Northern Bukovina, as incorporated in the secret clauses of the Hitler-Stalin pact of August, 1939, had to be related to Moscow's acceptance of the proposed revision of the territorial status of Transylvania in Hungary's favor. Actual evidence in support of such a hypothesis is, however, available for the period immediately antedating the prolonged negotiations that led to the Vienna Diktat of August, 1940.

It is noteworthy that the Hungarian demands for restitution of Transylvanian territory assumed a peremptory character at the very moment of the issuance of the Soviet ultimatum of June 26, 1940, for the restitution of Bessarabia and Northern Bukovina. Although the possibility of advance German and Hungarian knowledge of the date of the Soviet ultimatum cannot be excluded, there is no doubt that a linkage between Moscow and Budapest was firmly established by July 1, when the Soviet minister to Budapest and the Hungarian minister to Moscow were advised of the Kremlin's endorsement of the legitimacy of Hungary's claims to Transylvania. Other supportive evidence is available for the same period from Hungarian and Romanian sources that reinforces the view that the dismemberment of Romania was indeed envisaged and desired by Moscow at that time. Whether, however, Russia's encouragement of Hungarian, as well as of Bulgarian, revisionism was motivated by a desire to insure the neutrality of these countries in the event of a foreseeable German-Russian war or whether it was part of a master plan for the attainment of all Russian revisionist desiderata in Eastern Europe at a time of Nazi commitment to the attainment of more immediate goals in Europe is unclear. What is known, however, is that Molotov's support of Hungary's demands precipitated Romania's decision to negotiate with Hungary for the best terms available. Budapest's demands were, however, unacceptable to Bucharest, and the result was the Romanians' quest for arbitration by Germany.[19]

It is noteworthy that even as late as August, 1940, Hitler was apparently unprepared to grant the optimum Hungarian demands, since the Germans were convinced that Romania was of greater military value to the Axis than Hungary both because of the former's fears of Russia and because of its natural resources, which, in Hitler's view, were not to be controlled by the Hungarians in any manner. It is in this context that the intervention of Russia, which took place during the five days preceding the Vienna Diktat, assume great significance. The Russians staged a series of border incidents on the Prut River between August 23 and August 25 while actively and concurrently encouraging the Bulgarian demands for the restitution of southern Dobrudja and at least tacitly encouraging the "minimum" Hungarian demands, which were regarded as outrageous by Bucharest. It has been suggested that the Russian actions were deliberately exaggerated by the German negotiators in Vienna to appease the Romanians and justify the magnitude of the award made to Hungary on August 29. This hypothesis, however, is questionable (since Ribbentrop was free to make any decision) unless one were to assume that Germany was afraid of a possible arrangement between Hungary and/or Romania and the USSR designed to frustrate Germany's plans for both countries. Such an assumption, however, cannot be made in good conscience. A more likely explanation for the Russian actions toward Romania, Bulgaria, and Hungary is to be found in Stalin's determination to support all revisionist causes, to have a voice in the determination of the frontiers of Romania, and by extension to weaken Romania's allegiance to Germany following the dismemberment of Transylvania by a German Diktat. In fact, as soon as the award that favored Hungary's claims was announced in Vienna, the Romanian Communists joined in the violent mass protests staged against the Axis powers and Hungary throughout Transylvania and other parts of Romania.[20]

Although the Russian policies did not prevent the advent to power of General Ion Antonescu and the eventual Romanian joining of the Germans in the war against Russian communism and for the recouping of the Romanian territories lost to Russia in 1940, the Kremlin was able to exploit the resentment against the Vienna Diktat, which remained alive in Romania during World War II. Stalin's sanctioning of the return of Transylvania to Romania in 1945 was indicative of the significance attached to Transylvania by both Moscow and Bucharest and of the role assumed by the Kremlin in the determination of the Transylvanian question.[21]

Whether the Kremlin envisaged this entire scenario in August, 1940, is uncertain. But that this possible scenario was within the realm of Russia's long-range plans for Romania and Eastern Europe cannot be doubted. The Romanians were aware of Russian intentions throughout the interwar period, and the Hungarians were also conscious of the potential advantages to be derived from Russia's anti-Romanian attitudes in an eventual resolution of the Transylvanian question. And it is undeniable that the Romanians and the Hungarians remain aware of Russia's interests in Transylvania forty years after the Vienna Diktat.

NOTES

1. The most comprehensive treatment is contained in Sherman David Spector, *Rumania at the Paris Peace Conference* (New York: Bookman Associates, 1962), p. 67 ff.

2. Eva S. Balogh, "Romanian and Allied Involvement in the Hungarian *Coup d'Etat* of 1919," *East European Quarterly* 9, no. 3 (1975): 297–314; Spector, op. cit., pp. 222–25; Rudolf L. Tőkés, *Béla Kun and the Hungarian Soviet Republic* (New York: Frederick A. Praeger, 1967), p. 199 ff.

3. A comprehensive discussion containing ample bibliographic references will be found in Walter M. Bacon, Jr., *Behind Closed Doors: Secret Papers on the Failure of Romanian-Soviet Negotiations, 1931–1932* (Stanford: Hoover Institution Press, 1979), p. 3 ff.

4. See in particular Stephen Fischer-Galaţi, "The Moldavian Soviet Republic in Soviet Domestic and Foreign Policy," in Roman Szporluk, ed., *The Influence of East Europe and the Soviet West on the USSR* (New York: Praeger Publishers, 1975), p. 231 ff.

5. Bacon, op. cit., p. 7; Stephen Fischer-Galaţi, "Moldavia and the Moldavians," in Zev Katz, ed., *Handbook of Major Soviet Nationalities* (New York: The Free Press, 1975), p. 417.

6. The likelihood of such relationships has been suggested by students of Soviet foreign relations. However, until the appearance of Béla Vágo's forthcoming book on Transylvania no hard evidence has been made available to researchers.

7. See the perceptive analysis contained in Ghita Ionescu, *Communism in Rumania, 1944–1962* (London: Oxford University Press, 1964), p. 1 ff.

8. Bacon, op. cit., p. 7 ff.

9. Ibid.; Anthony Tihamér Komjáthy, *The Crises of France's East Central European Diplomacy, 1933–1938* (Boulder and New York: East European Quarterly and Columbia University Press, 1976), p. 143 ff.

10. Béla Vágo, "Le Second Diktat de Vienne: Les Preliminaires," *East European Quarterly* 2, no. 4 (1969): 415–37; Robert M. Bigler, "Heil Hitler and Heil Horthy!" *East European Quarterly* 8, no. 3 (1974): 251–72.

11. Nicholas M. Nagy-Talavera, *The Green Shirts & the Others* (Stanford: Hoover Institution Press, 1970), pp. 274–308; Al. Gh. Savu, *Dictatura regală, 1938–1940* [Royal Dictatorship, 1938–1940] (Bucharest: Editura Politică, 1970), pp. 99–120.

12. Vágo, op. cit., p. 415 ff. and Béla Vágo, "Le Second Diktat de Vienne: Le Partage de la Transylvanie," *East European Quarterly* 5, no. 1 (1971): 47–73.

13. Vágo, "Le Preliminaires," p. 415 ff. with ample references.

14. Savu, op. cit., p. 99 ff.; Nagy-Talavera, op. cit., p. 296 ff.

15. Typical of such statements are those contained in Ştefan Pascu, ed., *The Independence of Romania* (Bucharest: Editura Academiei R.S.R., 1977), p. 209 ff.

16. Ionescu, op. cit., p. 54 ff.; Savu, op. cit., p. 361 ff.; Jack Gold, "Bessarabia: The Thorny 'Non-Existent' Problem," *East European Quarterly* 13, no. 1 (1979): 47–74.

17. An interesting study related to these issues is by William O. Oldson, "Romania and the Munich Crisis: August–September 1938," *East European Quarterly* 11, no. 2 (1977): 177–90. See also Eric Roman, "Munich and Hungary: An Overview of Hungarian Diplomacy during the Sudeten Crisis," *East European Quarterly* 8, no. 1 (1974): 71–97.

18. An exhaustive study of these problems is by Marilynn J. G. Hitchens, *Germany, Russia and the Balkans: Prelude to the Nazi-Soviet Non-Aggression Pact, April–August 1939* (Boulder, Colo.: East European Monographs; New York: Columbia University Press, 1983).

19. Vágo, "Le Partage de la Transylvanie," p. 47 ff.

20. Savu, op. cit., p. 407 ff.

21. Ionescu, op. cit., p. 110 ff.; Stephen Fischer-Galaţi, *Twentieth Century Rumania* (New York: Columbia University Press, 1970), p. 70 ff.

From the Second Vienna Award to Paris: Transylvania and Hungarian-Rumanian Relations During World War II

STEPHEN D. KERTESZ

It is a curious fact that the Soviet Union was the first great power during the Second World War that showed a willingness to support revisions of the frontier between Hungary and Rumania. When Soviet troops occupied Bessarabia and part of Bukovina at the end of June, 1940, and during the following days and weeks, Foreign Minister Vyacheslav Molotov made several friendly statements and promises to the Hungarian envoy in Moscow, József Kristóffy, who reported them in telegrams to Budapest and later summed up Molotov's statements in a report as follows:

> 1. the Soviet Union has no claims whatever against Hungary; 2. the Soviet Government is striving to establish good neighborly relations with Hungary; 3. the Soviet Government considers Hungary's territorial demands against Rumania well-founded and will support them at the peace conference; 4. the Soviet Union's attitude will remain as explained above, in case of a conflict between Hungary and Rumania; 5. the Soviet government is ready to begin negotiations for a trade treaty with Hungary.[1]

Yet at the peace negotiations in 1945–46, Molotov objected even to consideration of an American initiative that proposed to examine the possibility of improving relations between Hungary and Rumania through a modest boundary revision on ethnic grounds. This essay will examine how events developed between these two different Soviet positions.

The Road to Vienna

The Soviet Union renewed diplomatic relations with Hungary in September, 1939,[2] and the extreme right in Hungary did not cease to praise the wise cooperative policy of the two greatest powers in Europe, Germany and Soviet Russia. Telegraphic communications and railway connections were established between Hungary and the Soviet Union. Following a Soviet initiative, the Hungarian government in October, 1940, exchanged the Hungarian Communist leader, Mátyás Rákosi (in an Hungarian jail), for banners taken by the Russian army in

1849, when it intervened on behalf of Austria in crushing the war of independence in Hungary. However, the anti-Soviet attitude of the Hungarian public was obvious, especially in connection with the Russo-Finnish war. Public demonstrations and collections were organized for Finland, and Hungarian volunteers left the country, with the help of the authorities, to fight in Finland against the Soviet army.

During this period, Rumania began to worry about the possibilities of a Soviet attack, and a special emissary of the Rumanian king asked the Italians to "work on the Hungarians," because any Hungarian threat on the Rumanian rear would "oblige the Rumanians to come to an agreement with the Russians."[3] Hungarian Foreign Minister István Csáky assured the Italian foreign minister, Galeazzo Ciano, that "Hungary will not take the initiative in the Balkans and thus spread the fire,"[4] but he emphasized Hungary's demand for equality of treatment for the Hungarian minorities in case Rumania should cede territory to Russia or Bulgaria without fighting.[5] The Hungarian policy was expressed even more clearly by Prime Minister Paul Teleki on a visit to Rome in March, 1940. Ciano noted that "he [Teleki] will not do anything against Rumania, because he does not want to make himself responsible, even indirectly, for having opened the doors of Europe to Russia. . . . Teleki has avoided taking any open position one way or the other but has not hidden his sympathy for the Western Powers and fears an integral German victory like the plague."[6] Later Teleki frankly told Ciano that he hoped "for the defeat of Germany, not a complete defeat—that might provoke violent shocks—but a kind of defeat that would blunt her teeth and claws for a long time."[7]

Shortly thereafter, Hungarian hopes for possible Italian help against the Germans were diminished. On the pretext that Russia would soon move into Bessarabia, Germany intended to occupy the Rumanian oil fields. The German General Staff approached the Hungarian General Staff and requested free passage through Hungary and possibly Hungarian military participation. The reward for Hungary's cooperation allegedly would have been Transylvania. The Hungarian government sent a special messenger to Rome who explained that "For the Hungarians there arises the problem either of letting the Germans pass, or opposing them with force. In either case the Hungarian liberty would come to an end."[8]

During these Hungaro-Italian negotiations the Germans began the occupation of Denmark and Norway, and the Italian ambassador to Germany, Bernardo Attolico, denied the rumor of a German attack on Rumania. The Duce advised the Hungarians to "keep calm and moderate, and . . . accede to the German requests." Ciano commented:

"This was not the answer the Hungarians expected and hoped for. They went so far as to ask whether, in case of military resistance, they could count on Italian help. Mussolini smiled; "How could this ever be," he said, "since I am Hitler's ally and intend to remain so?"[9]

The spectacular occupation of the smaller Western European states by Germany and the unexpected collapse of France deeply impressed the Hungarian public. In fact, these events caused general consternation. The government press manifested a dignified reserve and, when Italy declared war on France and Great Britain, Csáky stated that Hungary would continue her nonbelligerent status.

Soviet Russia reacted to the German victories in the West by the incorporation of the Baltic states and Rumanian territories. Following a Russian ultimatum, Rumania evacuated Bessarabia and northern Bukovina and ceded these territories to the Soviet Union. Simultaneously with these events, Hungary made military preparations along the Rumanian frontier and decided to solve the Transylvanian question by force, if necessary. Hitler vetoed Hungarian military actions and invited Teleki and Csáky to a conference in Munich. They met on July 10 in the presence of the German and Italian foreign ministers, Joachim Ribbentrop and Ciano. Hitler warned the Hungarians against unilateral action, advised them to initiate bilateral negotiations with Rumania and promised to support their initiative in Bucharest. The Rumanians procrastinated and would have preferred Hitler's arbitration instead of bilateral negotiations with Hungary. King Carol informed the Germans of Rumanian willingness to return to Hungary 14,000 square kilometers of the territory the Trianon Treaty had transferred to Rumania.

In August, the Rumanian government agreed in principle with Bulgaria concerning retrocession of South-Dobrudja, but declined to entertain the Hungarian claims. The Hungarian government could not accept the negative Rumanian attitude because the Peace Treaty of Trianon transferred to Rumania a larger territory than that retained by Hungary, and according to the Rumanian census 1.5 million Magyars remained in Transylvania. Budapest could not disregard the fate of this large Hungarian population. Eventually, the Rumanians reluctantly agreed to bilateral negotiations. The Hungarian and Rumanian delegations met in Turnu-Severin (August 16–24), but they could not find a common basis for agreement.[10]

Meanwhile Rumania renounced the Anglo-French guarantee of Rumania's political independence (July, 1940). Some great powers expressed approval or understanding of the Hungarian thesis. As mentioned, Molotov declared to the Hungarian envoy, Kristóffy, on July 7, 1940, that the Soviet government considered the Hungarian claims well-founded and would support them at the peace table. At the time of the negotiations in Turnu-Severin, Molotov again stated to Kristóffy that the Hungarian claims were justified.[11] According to the reports of the Hungarian envoys in London and Washington, George Barcza and John Pelényi, respectively, high officials in the British Foreign Office and in the Department of State showed an understanding toward Hungary's policy in the Transylvanian question.

After the failure of the bilateral negotiations, both Hungary and Rumania mobilized, and a conflict seemed imminent. Under these circumstances Hitler resolved to take a direct hand in the affair since a conflict in southeastern Europe would have resulted in serious complications for Germany and could have hindered the flow of Rumanian oil. In addition, the possibility of Russian intervention in a Hungarian-Rumanian conflict also existed. Later the German leaders repeatedly pointed out to the Hungarians that Germany had to decide the Hungaro-Rumanian conflict in order to save Rumania from collapse and from Russian intervention.[12] The German and Italian governments invited the representatives of the Hungarian and Rumanian governments to Vienna. The day before the meeting Hitler told Ciano that he was leaving the decision up to him and Joachim Ribbentrop. The only thing he had at heart was that "peace be preserved there, and that Rumanian oil continue to flow into his reservoirs."[13]

The Vienna Award and German Domination

The Hungarians thought that the Axis Powers would mediate, but were not prepared to submit the issue for arbitration. Ribbentrop assailed the recalcitrant Teleki in Vienna. He accused Hungary of having adopted anti-German policies on more than one occasion. His words were "rather threatening."[14] Finally the Hungarian delegation asked Budapest for full power to submit the issue to Italo-German arbitration. This document was deposited at the German legation in Budapest only half an hour before the second Vienna Award was delivered on August 30, 1940. A Crown Council in Bucharest authorized the Rumanian delegation to accept the arbitration. Based mainly on ethnographical considerations, the Award restored the northern part of Transylvania to Hungary. At the same time, Germany and Italy guaranteed the territorial integrity of Rumania, which still retained the major and economically more important part of Transylvania with a minority of more than a half million Hungarians.[15] There was a general outcry in Rumania against the Vienna Award, and at the same time disappointment in Hungary was great. The new frontier created difficulties for Hungary from the point of view of communications, and it left under Rumanian control the most important mineral assets and resources of Transylvania, such as the district of Meggyes-Kissármás (Mediaş-Sărmaşel) with mineral, oil, and natural gas deposits. King Carol resigned in favor of his son Michael and left the country. Thereafter, Prime Minister Ion Antonescu became the dictator of Rumania.

The Award caused serious friction between Moscow and Berlin. Germany informed the Soviet Union only after the Vienna decision had been delivered, and Molotov claimed that Germany violated the Nonagression Pact, which provided for consultation in questions of common interest to both countries. Molotov declared that the German government "could not have been in doubt that the Soviet government was interested in Rumania and Hungary."[16]

Hungary's position nonetheless was made more difficult by the pro-Nazi reorientation of Rumania's foreign policy, which was achieved with amazing speed. Rumania resigned from the League of Nations and from the Balkan Entente and began to transform the internal structure of the country according to National-Socialist principles. The most dangerous step, however, was the invitation extended by Rumania in early October, 1940, to the German "instructor corps." General Friedrich Paulus stated, in his deposition at Nuremberg, that an entire panzer division was transferred to Rumania, manifestly as a training unit but actually for the purpose of preparing the Rumanian army for war. These troops had to cross Hungary, and some military personnel were also stationed in Hungarian railroad stations "to maintain the lines of communication between Rumania and Germany."[17] Although Teleki restricted the Germans to a few important railroad stations, this was the beginning of the German military penetration into Hungarian territory. Shortly after these events, Hungary adhered to the Tripartite Pact (November 20, 1940) concluded on September 27, 1940, in Berlin between Germany, Italy, and Japan. This was considered one of the means for maintaining the relative independence of Hungary in Axis Europe.[18] But the Hungarian government refused to accept a secret additional protocol that aimed at the implementation of the Pact in the field of newspapers and propaganda. Such a cooperation naturally would have led to the liquidation of all anti-Nazi opposition newspapers in Hungary.[19]

Hungary's adherence to the Tripartite Pact was followed by catastrophic events. Prime Minister Teleki committed suicide on April 3, 1941, the eve of the crossing of Hungary's boundary by German troops marching to attack Yugoslavia. On the evening of April 2, he had received a telegram from the Hungarian envoy in London that the British

Foreign Office informed him that if Hungary took part in any German action against Yugoslavia, it must expect a declaration of war upon it by Great Britain. Winston Churchill noted in his memoirs "His suicide was a sacrifice to absolve himself and his people from guilt in the German attack upon Yugoslavia. It clears his name in history. It could not stop the march of the German armies nor the consequences."[20]

Teleki's successor was his foreign minister, László Bárdossy, a professional diplomat, but a man of scant political experience. Although a patriot and originally an anti-Nazi, he followed a pro-German policy. He had been Hungarian minister to Rumania at the time of the second Vienna Award. Impressed by the energetic pro-Nazi policy of the Rumanian dictator, Marshal Ion Antonescu, he believed that limited cooperation with Germany was the only means for maintaining some independence for Hungary in German-dominated Europe. When the independence of Croatia was proclaimed in Zagreb on April 10, Regent Horthy declared that, since Yugoslavia had ceased to exist, the Hungarian Army would protect the Magyar population living in territories taken from Hungary by Yugoslavia in 1918. Between April 11 and April 14, and without serious fighting, the Hungarian Army occupied part of the former Hungarian territory transferred to Yugoslavia by the Trianon Treaty.

Under Bárdossy, Hungary's international position rapidly grew worse. On April 8, 1941, Great Britain severed diplomatic relations with Hungary, since it had become a base of military operations against the Allies. Following the outbreak of the German-Russian war, Bárdossy was induced by the General Staff to declare war on Russia, on June 27, without consulting Parliament. The city of Kassa (Košice) was bombed allegedly by Soviet planes on the preceding day, and Bárdossy considered this action a casus belli.[21] The declaration of war caused violent protests from the opposition parties. At the time, the chief of staff of the Hungarian Army, General Henry Werth, suggested that the war against Russia would be just a matter of weeks and Hungary must not be late this time. He had announced the forthcoming attack on the Soviet Union at a secret meeting of Hungarian Army corps commanders in May, 1941, and stated that Rumania and Hungary would take an active part on the side of Germany.[22]

The British declaration of war against Hungary (December 6, 1941)[23] and the severance of diplomatic relations with the United States (December 12, 1941), followed by an Axis-enforced declaration of war (not recognized by the United States), were the other important international events during Bárdossy's premiership.

Hungary's entry into war with the English-speaking powers was not without dramatic incidents. When the American minister to Hungary, Herbert Pell, representing British interests in Hungary, handed over on November 29, 1941, the above-cited British ultimatum, Bárdossy according to his own record of the conversation replied as follows: "Your information comes as a surprise. I never believed it would go that far, nor that England could help the Soviets only by declaring war on us . . . There are no Hungarian forces fighting in Russia now. We have withdrawn our forces from the front. The Hungarian Government is not participating in any direct military action . . . Most of the Hungarians placed their faith in English fairness to judge the present situation. They will feel hurt by such a decision of the British government."

In the course of the ensuing conversation, Pell showed a most understanding attitude toward Hungary. Counselor Howard K. Travers stated that the American Legation tried every means to prevent a declaration of war by England on Hungary after the first rumors of such a decision. Minister Pell said that he considered the decision of the English government as his own defeat.[24]

After Pearl Harbor, Hitler declared in the Reichstag that a state of war existed between Germany and the United States. As a subterfuge, the Hungarian government simply stated its solidarity with the Axis and severed diplomatic relations with the United States. According to the files of the Hungarian Foreign Ministry, in answer to the question of Minister Pell "Does it mean war?" Bárdossy replied with a categorical "No."

The Italian minister and the German chargé d'affaires at Budapest called the next day on Bárdossy, urging the Hungarian government to declare war on the United States.[25] The Hungarian declaration of war was duly dispatched. This declaration, together with those of the other satellites, was rightly characterized later in a note of the American government delivered in Budapest by the legation of Switzerland on April 7, 1942. This note considered the satellite declarations of war as made "under duress, and . . . contrary to the will of the majority of the peoples of the countries in question." Similarly, President Roosevelt stated in a message to Congress on June 2, 1942, that although the governments of Bulgaria, Hungary, and Rumania had declared war against the United States, "I realize that the three governments took this action not upon their own initiative or in response to the wishes of their own peoples but as the instruments of Hitler." However, on the recommendation of President Roosevelt, Congress declared war on Bulgaria, Hungary, and Rumania on June 4, 1942. The next day President Roosevelt signed the declarations of war.[26]

The state of war with the United States and Britain was considered a great misfortune in Hungary. Yet it proved to be a blessing in disguise at the armistice and peace negotiations. Without a state of war with the English-speaking powers, the affairs of the Danubian countries would have been settled exclusively by the Soviet Union, and the Hungarians would have been expelled from Czechoslovakia.

The reluctance of Hungary and the other Danubian satellites to declare war on the United States reflects the fact that the free will of small nations is very limited in a world conflagration. Bárdossy well described the tragic dilemma of Hungarian statesmen when he told Mussolini's representative in Budapest, Filippo Anfuso, that: "God confronted us with Hitler. If the Germans demand something, I always give a quarter of it. If I refused categorically, they would take everything, which would be worse."[27]

From the autumn of 1941 onward the German attitude toward Hungary stiffened. Up to that time Hungarian military help in Soviet Russia had been of token value. Time and again the Nazis pointed out to the Hungarians that the Rumanians, Slovaks, Czechs, and Croats were more cooperative toward Germany and that Hungarian unfriendliness might have unpleasant consequences. In January, 1942, Ribbentrop himself came to Hungary to convey Hitler's insistence upon a 100 percent mobilization of all Hungarian resources needed for a speedy termination of the war. He dangled the idea of territorial concessions to Hungary in Transylvania with their magnitude depending on the amount of Hungarian support. This, combined with threats, was the usual German device. Ribbentrop extolled the merits of Antonescu, the Rumanian dictator. He pointed to Rumania's complete participation in the war as a shining example for Hungary to follow.

Bárdossy, seeking to reduce to a minimum Hungarian participation in the war, refused to yield to German pressure for total mobilization. He argued with Ribbentrop that Hungary could not be expected to send all her military forces abroad, leaving her own frontiers undefended. This had been the main cause of Hungary's First World War catastrophe. Germany's interests, he said, could not be served by an unruly Hungary, in which all production would be seriously curtailed. Ribbentrop expressed regrets about this unexpected reply, intimating that it was likely to lessen Hitler's good will toward Hungary. Eventually Bárdossy agreed to Hungary's increasing participation in the war, and Hitler's next move was the dispatching of General Keitel to Budapest with a large military suite to discuss details. Even so, for the spring offensive in Russia, he could bring about the mobilization of but one-third of Hungary's military forces.[28]

Since Regent Horthy was dissatisfied with Bárdossy's policy, he had to resign in March, 1942. His successor, Miklós Kállay, sought to extricate Hungary from the German grasp. This was no easy undertaking, for the country was completely encircled by German satellites and German-occupied territory. Changes were made only gradually and with great discretion.

In the face of the growing assertiveness of Hungarian independence, the Germans stirred up interest in the formation of a Rumanian-Croat-Slovak bloc against Hungary. Hungary's relations with the two German-protected puppet states, Tiso's Slovakia and Pavelić's Croatia, were unfriendly, and relations with Rumania were even worse, having several times approached the point of a severance of diplomatic relations. Both Hungary and Rumania were manifestly preparing for a private showdown at the end of the general war, if not sooner.

As first secretary of the Hungarian Bucharest legation, in 1942 I had a special assignment regarding the affairs of the Hungarian minority in southern Transylvania.[29] Thus I witnessed the Antonescu regime apply ruthless discriminatory measures against members of the Hungarian minority group. Thousands of tragic cases accumulated in the files of our legation and consulates. Dozens of desperate people came daily to the legation. The Rumanian authorities confiscated all foodstuffs from them and they could not feed hungry children. Diplomatic protests had no results whatever. The Rumanian government on their part complained about the persecution of the Rumanians in northern Transylvania. The whole situation seemed utterly confused and hopeless.

Hitler himself envisaged a war between Hungary and Rumania but desired to postpone it. He explained his views on the matter to Mussolini, recalling how he had stated to the Rumanians and Hungarians that

> if, at all cost, they wanted to wage war between themselves, he would not hinder them, but they would both lose by it. However, it would be a problem if both countries now withheld petroleum for the war which they wanted to fight between themselves later. It would be the duty of the Foreign Ministers of the Axis to deal with both countries persuasively and calmly so as to prevent an open break.[30]

In order to avoid an open conflict in the Axis camp, Berlin and Rome decided, in the summer of 1942, to appoint an Italo-German commission headed by a German and an Italian plenipotentiary minister (Hencke and Roggeri) to study the complaints of the Hungarian minority in southern Transylvania and those of the Rumanian minority in northern Transylvania. The commission spent almost two months in Transylvania, investigated hundreds of individual cases, and prepared a long report that recommended several measures to the Hungarian and Rumanian governments aimed at ameliorating the situations of their respective minorities.[31] Italo-German military commissions were established in northern and southern Transylvania. These watchdog commissions informed the German and Italian governments of the troubles in Transylvania and tried to improve the situation of the minorities by means of direct intervention with the local authorities.

By the end of 1942, Mihai Antonescu, deputy prime minister and foreign minister, under the impulse of a strange misunderstanding, initiated a conciliatory policy toward Hungary, and the Hungarian government readily reciprocated. Both governments made some small conciliatory gestures and prepared a list of questions to be settled through bilateral negotiations. Kállay appointed Miklós Bánffy, a Transylvanian and former foreign minister, to begin informal negotiations with a Rumanian personage to be appointed by Ion Antonescu. Bánffy's official mission was intertwined with another Rumanian initiative. Iuliu Maniu, the Transylvanian leader of democratic opposition in Rumania, believed in early 1943 that British and American paratroops would be sent to Danubian Europe and wanted to meet secretly with István Bethlen, a former prime minister of Transylvanian origin, to discuss Hungaro-Rumanian cooperation against Germany. Bethlen received Maniu's confidential message and wanted to establish contact with him but had apprehensions that the Germans would be informed of their meeting and, therefore, asked Bánffy to get in touch with Maniu. As mentioned, Bánffy travelled legally to Bucharest and his mission was to discuss specific problems of the Hungarian minority in Rumania and those of the Rumanian minority in Hungary. He arrived in Bucharest on June 18, 1943, and met a few days later the Rumanian negotiator, Mironescu, a former prime minister and foreign minister. Bánffy was unable to discuss the problems designated in the memoranda of the two governments because Mihai Antonescu instructed Mironescu to discuss only territorial questions, while Bánffy was authorized to negotiate solely measures to be taken for the improvement of the situation of minorities in the two countries. Mironescu informed Bánffy that the Rumanian government had denounced in Berlin and Rome the Vienna Award[32] and was unwilling to negotiate on the basis of the existing status quo. The Hungarian and Rumanian positions were irreconcilable and there was no reason to continue the meetings.

Thereafter, the indomitable Bánffy got in touch with opponents of the Antonescu regime. The most important was his conversation with

Maniu, who came to Bucharest to meet him. Since a police car watched Maniu's residence until 11:00 P.M., Bánffy visited him during the darkness of night. The two Transylvanians agreed that military cooperation between Hungary and Rumania would be desirable against the Germans, but Maniu wanted to include the Yugoslavs as well and emphasized that Rumania would never recognize the Vienna Award. While Bánffy proposed the maintenance of the status quo until the peace conference, Maniu demanded the immediate recognition of the Rumanian territorial claims and suggested that with the expected coming into being of large economic units the frontiers should lose their importance. The failure of Bánffy's mission on both official and opposition levels demonstrated the inexorable nature of the conflict between the two countries. The policy of rapprochement came to an inglorious end.[33] Mihai Antonescu changed his mind, and the Germans continued their squeeze play, using the conflicting territorial aspirations of Hungary and Rumania to their advantage.

In Transylvania, the Italo-German conciliatory efforts proved to be superficial palliatives, and the Germans supported the Rumanians almost openly. This policy was strengthened by the fact that Rumania had a strategic key position in the war against Soviet Russia, had carried out a full mobilization, and in general had contributed to the German war effort incomparably more than Hungary. Hitler's dislike of Hungary was well known and has been proven by many documents.[34] But he had a great liking for the Rumanian dictator, Ion Antonescu. As Hitler's interpreter, Paul Schmidt, later was to put it, Antonescu was "one of Hitler's closest intimates and was even kept more closely in the picture than Mussolini. He was the only foreigner from whom Hitler ever asked for military advice when he was in difficulties. . . . He made long speeches just like Hitler, usually starting off at the creation of Rumania, and somehow relating everything he said to the hated Hungarians, and the recovery of Transylvania. This hatred of Hungary, too, made him congenial to Hitler, for the Führer despised the Magyars."[35] Antonescu indicated to the Führer his determination to recover northern Transylvania by force of arms and "Hitler took a secret pleasure in Antonescu's outbursts against the Hungarians, and even went so far as to hint that he might perhaps give him a free hand later in his plans of conquest."[36]

Surrounded again by a sort of revived Little Entente, which was protected this time by Germany, the Hungarian government, on its part, tried to rely on Italy. This policy was bound to fail because Italy gradually declined to the status of Hitler's vassal, and Mussolini decided to fight along with Hitler until the very last. Despite several disappointments, the Hungarians tried to win Italy's support because they saw no other alternative.

For these reasons, the Hungarian government sought to explore tentatively the possibilities of electing an Italian king. The advanced age of the regent was another reason for such soundings. The Duke of Aosta, cousin of Victor Emmanuel III, and a possible candidate of the Hungarian government for the throne of Saint Stephen, became seriously ill and died in March, 1942. Then the Hungarians sought to strengthen Hungary's independence with the establishment of a personal union with Italy under King Victor Emmanuel. But the Duce reacted adversely to this plan, saying that he had entertained a similar proposition in regard to the Duke of Aosta, "but with him dead, nothing else will be done."[37]

Prime Minister Kállay was anxious to clarify personally the delicate political problems in Rome and arranged for a trip to Italy in November of 1942. This was postponed by Mussolini because of the collapse of the Libyan front. "In fact, this is not the time to welcome any guests," remarked Ciano.[38] Eventually Kállay visited Rome in early April, 1943. The main object of his visit was to gain Italian support for the policy of resistance to Germany. When Kállay referred to the fact that the Axis was retreating on every front, Mussolini interrupted him, saying that "Hitler assured him that in the summer he would settle with the Russians once and for all." Kállay replied that he could only discuss the presently existing situation and pointed out that "Hungary could not give a single soldier for this offensive."[39] He avoided mentioning the question of separate peace, but brought up the possibility of a separate common policy within the Axis of Italy, Hungary, and possibly Finland and extolled the benefits of a desirable common Italo-Hungarian policy on the Balkans. Then he explained to the Duce that he wanted gradually to extricate Hungary from the war and lead it back into a state of nonbelligerency. Mussolini assured Kállay of his friendship, tried to justify Italy's foreign policy in a historical context, and warned Kállay that "We cannot even think of a separate peace."[40]

During this period, there was some similarity between the foreign policies of Hungary and Rumania. Both countries overestimated Italy's capability to resist Germany and Mussolini's willingness to change the course of his pro-Axis policy. Rumania's deputy prime minister and foreign minister, Mihai Antonescu, followed a strong pro-Italian policy. He had hoped that Italy would be able to establish contacts and conclude an armistice with the Western Powers. He established close personal relations with Bova Scoppa, the Italian minister to Rumania since

July, 1941. M. Antonescu had hoped that under Italy's leadership Rumania and possibly Hungary, Finland, and other small states could cooperate and conclude an armistice and change sides during the war. Bova Scoppa described in his memoirs[41] M. Antonescu's ideas and endeavors in this respect. While visiting Rome in early June, 1943, Scoppa submitted a "*Promemoria*" to Giuseppe Bastianini, Ciano's successor as foreign minister since February, 1943. This memorandum reflected the Rumanian evaluation of the military and political situation and M. Antonescu's ideas as to the steps to be taken.[42] Scoppa also met Ciano, who told him frankly: "Con Mussolini non c'e niente da fare. E'un muro chiuso."[43]

Finally Bastianini informed Scoppa on June 15 that the Duce agreed with Mihai Antonescu on many points but would like to wait two more months with the suggested diplomatic initiative when the military situation would be good. In any case, he invited Antonescu for an exchange of views. This visit took place at the end of June. Antonescu was warmly received and Mussolini emphasized again that negotiations should start in two months. Then the belligerent and neutral states would be convoked by Hitler or without Hitler to a conference to decide Europe's future. Antonescu finally realized that Mussolini had replaced policy by pipe dreams.[44] Events in Italy soon took a different turn. The English and Americans landed in Sicily in July, 1943, Mussolini was forced to resign, and Marshal Badoglio's government signed an armistice treaty on September 3, which was made public five days later.

Another common error was the belief in Budapest and Bucharest that British and American troops would occupy the Danubian countries. Hungarian and Rumanian politicians assumed that the United States at the peak of its power would not tolerate the establishment of Soviet hegemony in Danubian Europe. Hungary established some contacts in 1942 with British and United States representatives, and both Hungarian and Rumanian diplomats and special emissaries in neutral countries put forth a series of peace feelers in 1943 and 1944. Appraisal of these manifold and complicated diplomatic moves are outside the scope of this paper. One should note, however, that the British and Americans faithfully informed the Soviet government of the Hungarian and Rumanian approaches.[45]

Armistice in Russia's Europe

The parallelism between Hungarian and Rumanian politics changed drastically in 1944. Hungary was occupied by German troops on

March 19, 1944, according to a carefully prepared plan, Marghareta I. The looming shadow of the Nazi dictator became a cruel reality. Hitler's promise to Horthy concerning the exclusively military character of the occupation proved worthless. The Gestapo started its usual work. Prominent Hungarian patriots were jailed, deported, or forced underground. Persecution and mass deportation of Jews began. Prime Minister Kállay never resigned formally and he found asylum in the Turkish legation. The new head of the government, Döme Sztójay, a former general and Hungarian minister to Germany, had always advocated a policy of submission to Nazi Germany. His government dissolved the trade unions and the opposition parties, such as the Smallholders, the Democrats, and the Social Democrats, and, in close collaboration with the Germans, carried out the Nazification of Hungary. Horthy assumed an ostensibly passive attitude in the first months, later resisting more or less openly the occupying Nazi forces and their Hungarian accomplices. The fact that the Germans did not directly take over the major government agencies left open some possibilities for the future.

Although events in subjugated Hungary strengthened Marshal Antonescu's position in Hitler's camp, Rumanian politics took suddenly an unexpected turn. On August 23, King Michael dismissed and arrested Marshal Antonescu and Mihai Antonescu, proclaimed surrender, and appointed a new government of national unity with the nonpolitical General Constantin Sanatescu as premier. Rumania declared war on Germany and the Rumanian army changed sides with lightening speed and fought against the Germans. The quick and effective action of the Rumanian army was an immense benefit to the Russians. Marghareta II, the German plan for the occupation of Rumania, could not be carried out and the German army, in disorderly retreat, did not even defend the passes in the Carpathian Mountains. The Soviet army and the regular Rumanian divisions were followed by the "Voluntary Guards" of Maniu, and they introduced a regime of terror in the regions inhabited by Hungarians. In view of the large-scale atrocities and robberies, the Soviet High Command intervened in some instances to protect the defenseless Hungarian population, and the Allied Control Commission in Bucharest ordered on November 14 that the returned Rumanian functionaries and the "Maniu Guards" evacuate Northern Transylvania. From this time on, the autochthon population, Hungarians and Rumanians together, organized an autonomous administration, and Northern Transylvania enjoyed for months an exemplary public order with constructive cooperation of the native population.

The Italian and Rumanian examples were warnings to Hitler. He decided to prevent similar events in Hungary and concentrated German armored divisions in the outskirts of Budapest. When Regent Horthy's armistice proclamation was read on Budapest radio on October 15, the German armored divisions moved into the capital, pro-Horthy military commanders were arrested, the Lakatos government was deposed, and the Germans installed an Arrow Cross government under Ferenc Szálasi. Horthy was taken prisoner and deported with his family to Germany. A chapter of Hungarian history came to an end.

A new life began in Russia's Europe with the armistice period. The rules of international and domestic politics have fundamentally changed in countries occupied by the Soviet army. The armistice agreement was signed with Rumania on September 12, 1944, and its article 18 explicitly stated:

> An Allied Control Commission will be established which will undertake until the conclusion of peace the regulation of and control over the execution of the present terms under the general direction and orders of the Allied/Soviet/High Command, acting on behalf of the Allied Powers.

The Hungarian Armistice Agreement was concluded on January 20, 1945; its article 18 is identical with Article 18 of the Bulgarian Armistice of October 28, 1944, which set forth:

> For the whole period of the armistice there will be established in Bulgaria an Allied Control Commission which will regulate and supervise the execution of the armistice terms under the chairmanship of the representative of the Allied/Soviet/High Command, and with the participation of representatives of the U.S. and U.K.
>
> During the period between coming into force of the armistice and the conclusion of hostilities against Germany, the ACC will be under the general direction of the Allied/Soviet/High Command.

There are two major differences between the two texts. The Rumanian armistice simply stated that the ACC would be under the direction and control of the Soviet Command, acting on behalf of the Allied Powers during the whole armistice period. The Bulgarian and Hungarian texts provided that the ACC would regulate and supervise the execution of the armistice terms under the chairmanship of the representative of the Soviet High Command, *and with the participation of representatives of the U.S. and U.K.*. A second paragraph of Article 18 in these two armistice agreements restricted the general direction of the Soviet High Command to the period between coming into force of the armistice and the conclusion of hostilities against Germany. The United States proposed that in the post-hostilities period tripartite control should replace Soviet dominance, but this proposal was not accepted by the European Advisory Commission in London because of Soviet opposition.

These changes were supposed to secure greater British and United States influence in the Bulgarian and Hungarian ACC. This formula was worked out by Foreign Secretary Anthony Eden and Molotov on October 11, 1944, when the definitive percentage figures for influence in the Balkan countries were established as follows:

Rumania	
Russia	90%
The Others	10%
Greece	
Great Britain (in accord with United States)	90%
Russia	10%
Yugoslavia	50-50%
Hungary	
Russia	80%
The Others	20%
Bulgaria	
Russia	80%
The Others	20%

The percentage figures, which in a mystical way symbolized the influence of the outside powers, differed in the case of Hungary and Bulgaria from those published in Churchill's memoirs[46] where the influence in Hungary was given as a fifty-fifty balance and in Bulgaria seventy-five percent for Russia and twenty-five percent for the others.

The Churchill-Stalin meeting on October 9 was followed by long argumentative sessions between Eden and Molotov, who advocated higher percentages for Russia in Bulgaria, Yugoslavia, and Hungary. Concessions were combined with power in the ACC. Eden yielded in the case of Hungary and Bulgaria, and the results were the above mentioned percentage figures and the seemingly more flexible text of Article 18 of the Bulgarian Armistice.

Since plans for an Anglo-American landing in the Balkans were abandoned, Churchill wanted to secure British predominance in Greece in exchange for Soviet predominance in Rumania. In the subsequent Eden-Molotov negotiations, Soviet supremacy was recognized in Hungary and Bulgaria as well.[47]

When these negotiations were concluded, Eden noted in his diary

"We obtained what we wanted on almost all points. I should say 90 per cent overall. In particular, they will summon Bulgars out of Greece and Yugoslavia tonight."[48]

In the weeks preceding these negotiations, the British were afraid that Soviet troops invading Bulgaria might occupy western Thrace and possibly march in the direction of Athens. Another possibility could have been Soviet recognition of Bulgarian claims to Thrace. Either action could have led to far-reaching political developments detrimental to British interests in the Mediterranean.

The Anglo-Russian percentage agreement in October, 1944, was a bilateral deal about which Churchill did not inform Roosevelt, although the Department of State received more or less accurate information of the percentages from several United States embassies. Stalin admitted from the outset that Greece was primarily a British concern. When subsequently Molotov haggled over the percentages in the other countries, Eden finally told him that he was not interested in figures. "All I wanted was to be sure that we had more voice in Bulgaria and Hungary than we had accepted in Rumania, and that there should be a joint policy in Yugoslavia."[49] How Eden hoped to obtain fifty percent British influence in Communist Yugoslavia and twenty percent in Soviet-occupied Bulgaria and Hungary never was made clear.

The Anglo-Russian bilateral sphere of influence agreement of October, 1944, was not the continuation of a provisional arrangement between the British and Russians that was approved by President Roosevelt in June, 1944, for a three-months' trial period. That time Churchill argued that someone must "play the hand" in the Balkans. It seemed reasonable to him that the Russians should deal with the Rumanians and Bulgarians, and Britain should deal with the Greeks and Yugoslavs.[50]

These were some of the diplomatic and military developments and agreements that determined Hungary's and Rumania's international situation at the close of hostilities.

In the course of preparations for peace, it soon became clear in the Hungarian Foreign Ministry that Moscow wanted nothing but a recasting of the armistice agreements into peace treaties. The Western powers did not or could not influence the basic Soviet objectives. Hungary was essentially governed by the Soviet-dominated ACC during the armistice period. Despite this almost hopeless situation, we tried in Budapest to break through our isolation with peace preparatory notes, addressed to the three major victorious powers. These "peace aim" notes posed the general problems of Danubian Europe in constructive terms, advocating regional economic solutions, freedom of navigation on the Danube, deemphasis of nationalism, close cultural cooperation with neighboring states, "spiritualization" of frontiers and, above all, self-determination of peoples and an effective international protection of national minorities.

The Soviet-enforced consolidation of Communist-dominated puppet governments in Rumania and Bulgaria, in violation of the Yalta Declaration on Liberated Europe, as well as various manifestations of the same policy in Hungary, had forecast a gloomy future. The ink had hardly dried on the Yalta Agreement when Soviet Deputy Commissar of Foreign Affairs Vyshinsky went to Bucharest and pressured King Michael to dismiss General Nicolae Radescu's coalition government and appoint Petru Groza premier. Since Groza presented a solid National Democratic Front (FND) government—the FND was a Communist-sponsored organization—the king refused to appoint Groza's candidates. Vyshinsky retorted that this was an unfriendly act to the USSR and that Rumania might cease to exist as a sovereign state. Thus, the king had no choice and the FND came to power. Within three days, the Russians restored Northern Transylvania to Rumanian administration to demonstrate Soviet support of Groza's government. Although Groza tried to introduce a conciliatory policy toward the Hungarian minority, his success was limited, and all benefits of the autonomous position of Northern Transylvania came to an end.

Rumania and Bulgaria had been on the highway of Russian expansion toward Constantinople for centuries, and installation of reliable Communist-dominated governments in Bucharest and Sofia was an urgent matter for the Kremlin. Hungary's situation seemed more favorable. During the London Conference of Foreign Ministers, in September, 1945, both the United States and the Soviet Union recognized the coalition government of Hungary and established diplomatic relations with it. At the same time, Washington refused to recognize the unrepresentative governments of Rumania and Bulgaria. The defeat of the Communists and the victory of the Smallholders party in Budapest municipal elections in October and at the general elections in November, 1945, caused a short-lived optimism in the country and abroad. Western newspapers saw an indication "that even in areas beyond Anglo-American control . . . the peoples of Europe can be given a chance to choose their own officials honestly and openly" (*The Christian Science Monitor,* October 9, 1945). Despite, or rather because of such favorable Western reactions, the turn of domestic politics in Hungary strengthened Soviet support for Bucharest. But this was not evident in Budapest. Soviet envoy Georgij M. Pushkin urged the Hungarian government to accept the Czechoslovak proposals concerning an exchange of population and transfer of Hungarians from Czechoslovakia. He even suggested to Foreign Minister János Gyöngyösi that Hungary should rather raise territorial claims against Rumania, another former German satellite. Marshal Klementy Voroshilov further intimated to Prime Minister Zoltán Tildy that Hungary might obtain some territorial compensation from Rumania if it behaved well and accepted the Czechoslovak proposals concerning the settlement of the Hungarian question in Czechoslovakia, which meant the transfer of Hungarians from Czechoslovakia to Hungary through exchange and expulsion.

The Role of Transylvania in Soviet Policy

As the armistice agreement declared the Vienna Award of August 30, 1940, to be null and void, the Hungarian government was looking for a solution of the Transylvanian problem along new lines. The revival of the ethnographic arguments, which were the basis of the Vienna Award, was considered unwise and was rejected at the outset. Although a variety of projects were prepared for solution, I would have preferred a general rather than specific demand until we ascertained what support we could get from the great powers. I was overruled, and the foreign minister decided to accept a plan worked out by a member of the Paul Teleki Institute for Political Science, Imre Jakabffy. This proposal envisaged the return of 22,000 square kilometers to Hungary with roughly 1,600,000 inhabitants. According to the 1930 Rumanian census, this territory was inhabited by 865,620 Rumanians and 495,106 Hungarians. In the 1941 census, the proportion of the Hungarians was somewhat higher, but this difference did not change the basic disproportion. Meanwhile, over one million Hungarians would have remained under Rumanian sovereignty. The idea was to counter-balance the number of the Hungarian and Rumanian minorities in Hungary and Rumania. It was assumed that these conditions would have resulted in better treatment for minorities in both countries.

In early April, the Soviet government invited leading members of the Hungarian government to Moscow, and this was considered a good occasion to raise the question of Transylvania. A meeting held under the chairmanship of the president of the republic on the eve of the departure for Moscow endorsed the Jakabffy plan, but decided that the delegation should have in reserve an alternate solution aiming at only the border districts with a clear Hungarian majority. Following the meeting, I was ordered to prepare the alternate plan that night. In a few hours, experts in the Teleki Institute worked out another plan, which proposed the return to Hungary of 11,800 square kilometers and 967,000 people. According to the Rumanian figures of 1930 the Hungarians had a slight majority (442,000 as compared to 421,000 Rumanians) in this territory. Ethnographically, the second plan looked better, but it would have caused economic difficulties to the local inhabitants both in Rumania and in Hungary.

The delegation returned from Moscow full of optimism.[51] They had been extremely well received. Soviet hospitality knew no bounds. They were lavishly entertained. On April 11, 1946, Molotov and Stalin devoted several hours to discussions with the members of the Hungarian delegation. The atmosphere seemed most friendly. In addition, there were some positive results. The period for the fulfillment of the reparation liabilities was extended from six to eight years. Stalin promised an early return of the Hungarian prisoners of war and recognized the validity of the Hungarian claim for equal rights of Hungarians in Czechoslovakia. The Soviet demand for $15,000,000 for the restoration of Hungarian railroads was cancelled,[52] and the delegation believed that they had received a Soviet pledge for the support of Hungarian territorial claims against Rumania.

Gyöngyösi explained to the leading officials of the Foreign Ministry how the discussion concerning Transylvania developed. According to him, Stalin, after listening to the Hungarian arguments and requests, turned to Molotov and asked him if there was a basis for such aspirations. Molotov correctly replied that Article 19 of the Rumanian armistice agreement left the way open for Hungary's territorial claims regarding Transylvania.[53] Stalin nodded and said that the Hungarians thus seemed to be really entitled to raise claims. The next day, V. Dekanozov, in charge of Southeastern European affairs in the Soviet Foreign Ministry, strongly advised the Hungarian foreign minister that, before raising territorial claims, direct negotiations should be attempted with the Rumanian government. Later Molotov repeated this advice. No one from the delegation asked Stalin or Molotov whether the Hungarian claims would be supported by them. Nevertheless, the atmosphere of the conversations was so friendly and Stalin's attitude so benevolent that the delegation took Soviet support for granted. There was another reason that Moscow's apparent goodwill toward Hungarian claims appeared credible. As mentioned, Voroshilov and Pushkin had encouraged Gyöngyösi and Tildy time and again that Hungary should raise territorial claims against another former satellite country, Rumania. In reality, both before and after the Moscow visit of the Hungarian delegation, Molotov opposed most resolutely in the Council of Foreign Ministers an American proposal favoring a slight modification in the Transylvanian boundary line in favor of Hungary.

The Hungarian delegation returned from Moscow in an optimistic mood. Some confident politicians concluded that Stalin seemed to be a reasonable man of goodwill with whom the Smallholder politicians would be able to negotiate without the mediation of the Hungarian Communists. (It should be noted parenthetically that Stalin made similar favorable impressions on several Western politicians).

After the Moscow visit, the Communist party in Hungary made a full turn-about and began to support Hungarian territorial claims. One of the leading Hungarian Communist authorities in foreign affairs, József Révai, delivered such an irredentist speech on April 26 that it would have satisfied even the League of Revision of the Horthy regime. Révai demanded that all territory along the Rumanian borders inhabited by Hungarians should be returned to Hungary, together with such cities as Arad, Szatmárnémeti (Satu Mare), Nagybánya (Baia Mare), and Nagyvárad (Oradea). Moreover, he asserted that the Communists in the emigration between the two World Wars were the true representatives of Hungary's national aspirations but that their efforts were annihilated by the suicidal pro-Nazi and anti-Soviet policy of the Horthy regime. A few weeks before that speech, Révai had wanted every "reactionary" who asked for territory from Groza's Rumania to be brought before the people's court. "We cannot weaken Groza's democracy," he had said at that time.

This reversal of Communist policy concerning Hungary's territorial claims gave a basis for optimistic speculation. Later it became evident that the motive behind the change in Communist tactics was the hope of winning the support of Hungarian public opinion. The change of tactics did not alter their final goal. The Communists apparently did not want to burden the Party by opposing national aspirations; they preferred to ride a popular bandwagon. In all probability, the leaders of the Hungarian Communist party believed that after the Moscow visit the Soviet government would support some Hungarian territorial aspirations. According to my observations, Soviet authorities gave orders and instructions to the Muscovite Communists but did not inform them of the real objectives and tactics of Soviet foreign policy.

On May 5, the prime minister at Székesfehérvár and the foreign minister at Szolnok delivered addresses outlining in vigorous terms the peace aims of Hungary. Public opinion became optimistic all over the country for a short time, although the first disappointment occurred a few days before the delivery of these addresses. In accordance with Moscow's advice, a high official of the Foreign Ministry, Pál Sebestyén, was sent to Bucharest to initiate negotiations. Prime Minister Petru Groza and Foreign Minister Gheorghe Tatarescu gave him a courteous reception, but refused to discuss Hungarian territorial claims. For this reason Sebestyén returned home immediately, and a note was dispatched to the representatives of the major victorious powers in Budapest on April 27.[54] This note was based on the above described proposal prepared in the Paul Teleki Institute and presented in Moscow by the Hungarian government delegation. The Hungarian government requested the return to Hungary of 22,000 square kilometers, that is, twenty percent of the total area of 104,000 square kilometers transferred to Rumania by the Treaty of Trianon.

The optimism that followed the visit to Moscow soon vanished, and uneasiness developed in political circles. One of the reasons for this change was the negative attitude of Rumanian statesmen with regard to Hungarian overtures. The shrewd Tatarescu would not have refused negotiations with Sebestyén had the Rumanian government lacked assurance of full Soviet support. Groza and Tatarescu hinted as much to the Hungarian envoy.

The coalition parties became disappointed when it appeared that the members of the government delegation to Moscow could not support with facts the optimism they had expressed in public speeches. The warm reception and the small concessions gained at Moscow had not warranted such optimism. Even the economic concessions gained were of small value.

Because of dissatisfaction and reproaches from many quarters, the foreign minister decided to send me to Paris, where at the time the Council of Foreign Ministers was in session preparing the drafts for the peace treaties. Pushkin refused to grant me permission to leave the country, saying that peace preparation would not be needed in Paris. Gyöngyösi—under attack at that time even in the Smallholder party—remained adamant. He told Pushkin that if he was not allowed to send a high official of the Foreign Ministry to Paris to make contacts and preparations for the peace conference, he would no longer consider himself as foreign minister. Pushkin, not wanting to make a political issue of this trifle, told Gyöngyösi that he could give me the necessary permit to leave the country if I would be appointed to the Hungarian Legation in Paris. The foreign minister promptly appointed me minister-counselor to the Hungarian Legation, and I left for Paris on May 9. Shortly before my departure news arrived from Paris like a bombshell about the decision of the Council of Foreign Ministers reestablishing the Trianon boundary between Hungary and Rumania.

Finale in Paris and New York

When I arrived in Paris, the Hungarian minister to France, Paul Auer, received me in a pessimistic mood because of the unfavorable decision of the Council of Foreign Ministers, a body established by the Potsdam Conference to prepare the peace treaties with Italy, Finland, Bulgaria, Hungary, and Rumania. The Council was composed of the foreign ministers of the five victorious great powers, but only those nations that had signed the armistice agreement with a particular enemy state prepared the peace treaty for it. This meant in the case of the three Danubian states, Britain, the United States, and the USSR.

In Budapest, we were forced to live behind a diplomatic iron curtain and knew little of the Council activities, but in Paris I gradually reconstructed the chain of events in the Transylvanian question. I understood that at the first session of the Council in London, in September, 1945, the American secretary of state, James Byrnes, had proposed the consideration of a modest boundary revision along ethnic lines to decrease the Hungarian minority in Rumania. When Molotov heard this proposal, he turned to one of his advisers and asked: "Are there Hungarians in Transylvania?" The Soviet delegation refused to discuss the American proposal, and the British delegation supported the Soviet position. The situation was similar in March, 1946, when at the session of the deputy foreign ministers the Soviet delegation submitted draft treaties for Bulgaria, Hungary, and Rumania. These sketchy documents were briefer than the armistice and did not mention frontiers with the exception of the restoration of northern Transylvania to Rumania. The United States delegation proposed that the Council either make a direct investigation of the boundary problem or request the Rumanian and Hungarian governments to discuss the dispute directly. The Soviet delegation refused again even to discuss the matter. After these antecedents, Secretary Byrnes at the Paris session of the Council of Foreign Ministers abandoned the fruitless attempt to take up the revision of the the Hungarian-Rumanian boundary and proposed the restoration of the frontier between Hungary and Rumania as it existed on January 1, 1939.[55] This meant that the American delegation gave up its endeavors for a modest revision on ethnic grounds of the boundary between Hungary and Rumania. Byrnes wanted to expedite the convocation of the Paris conference and for this purpose he wanted to eliminate as many conflicts as possible between the United States and the Soviet Union. Since the Council of Ministers made all decisions unanimously and the Russians were unwilling even to discuss any boundary rectification between Hungary and Rumania, this seemed to him a hopeless case.

For Hungarians it was impossible to accept this verdict as final, and we brought up the Transylvanian question through all possible channels. This was one of our major topics when I visited along with Auer the ambassadors of most countries participating in the Paris Conference. Such visits brought a few surprises. At the Polish Embassy, the ambassador interrupted our presentation to tell us that our colleague from London had visited him recently and had given him all the information about the Transylvanian problem. We suggested that this was impossible because the Hungarian envoy to Britain would have informed us of his visit to the Polish Embassy. We continued to explain the intricacies of the conflict between Hungary and Rumania. The ambassador interrupted us again and said, "Gentlemen, I will call my secretariat and will prove to you that your colleague from London visited me a few days ago and gave me the same information." He went to the telephone and after a brief conversation said, "I apologize. My visitor was the Rumanian ambassador from London." We witnessed such lack of knowledge about Danubian affairs on several occasions.

Despite hopeless political conditions, we wanted to raise the Hungarian-Rumanian frontier question at the Paris Conference and for this we needed American support. Auer and I visited the foremost Eastern European expert of the American delegation, Philip E. Mosely, on May 17. He told us that at the London meeting of foreign ministers Secretary Byrnes "had not advanced any proposal for a revised frontier but had merely pointed out that the question existed and should be studied to see if the boundary could be improved over that established in 1920 and of which the United States government had been critical at that time." Mosely pointed out that "the Soviet delegation had been unwilling at all times to admit even that the question deserved study." To the question whether Hungary would have an opportunity to raise the question at the Paris Conference, Mosely stated his personal understanding that "Hungary would be free to present its view on any aspect of the treaty which affected its position or interest." Concerning various Hungarian suggestions for boundary readjustment, Mosely avoided detailed discussion but stated that the concept of a numerical balancing of minorities on opposite sides of the frontier "might seem somewhat mechanical in approach and might be interpreted to imply a willingness to provide for large-scale exchanges of population." He stated as his strictly personal view that "a moderate suggestion for rectification based mainly on ethnic and economic factors might have a better hearing."[56]

Mosely's cautious statements reflected accurately the American position, of which he had been one of the major architects. The Hungarian government decided to ask for a hearing. The Soviet bloc countries opposed even a debate about the frontier between Hungary and Rumania, but the strong American support prevailed.

When Foreign Minister Gyöngyösi visited most heads of delegations, he discussed with them Hungary's major political and economic problems, our conflict with Czechoslovakia, and the frontier dispute with Rumania. Gyöngyösi in a plenary session of the conference was permitted to present the views and proposals of the Hungarian government. In his address on August 14, he asked the reattachment to Hungary of 22,000 square kilometers of Rumania; that is, he repeated the request expressed in the Hungarian note of April 27.[57] As Mosely told us in cautious diplomatic terms three days later, this proposal had no chance for consideration.

At the meeting of the Political and Territorial Commission for Rumania on August 29, Mr. Officer from the Australian delegation proposed that the Commission hear the views of Hungary on Article 2 of the draft treaty. This article dealt with the boundaries of Rumania. Ambassador Alexander Bogomolov (USSR) saw no need to consult the Hungarian government since the text of Article 2 had been agreed to by the Council of Foreign Ministers. After a long debate, a Czechoslovak motion for adjournment was defeated by eight-to-four vote, and the Australian proposal was carried by a vote of eight to four.[58] The Commission decided that both the Hungarian and Rumanian delegations should be invited to appear before it to express their views on Article 2, the Hungarian delegation speaking first.

On August 31, Auer in a joint session of the Hungarian and Rumanian Territorial and Political commissions delivered an address. In view of the unfavorable decision of the Council of Foreign Ministers, he asked the reattachment to Hungary of only 4,000 square kilometers along the boundary; this would have meant reattachment to Hungary of approximately a half million persons—about two-thirds of whom were Hungarians—and with them the major cities along the boundary. Auer emphasized the necessity of guaranteed international protection of Hungarians remaining in Rumania.[59] The foreign minister of Rumania, Gheorghe Tatarescu, in his address delivered in a joint session of the Hungarian and Rumanian Territorial and Political commissions on September 2 opposed Auer's proposals and argued for the maintenance of the boundary established by the Trianon Treaty.[60]

Such addresses had mainly symbolic significance, because the Conference could not have changed the decision of the Council of

Foreign Ministers. When we asked the Soviet delegation for support in the Transylvanian question, we received the answer that they could not do anything because Secretary Byrnes had withdrawn his proposal concerning revisions of the boundary between Hungary and Rumania. Technically, this was true, because Byrnes proposed on May 7 in the Council of Foreign Ministers the reestablishment of the Trianon boundary between Hungary and Rumania. He acted this way because the Soviet Union was not willing even to discuss a boundary change and he wanted to eliminate a point of friction between the United States and the USSR. In view of the fact that both Hungary and Rumania were occupied by Soviet troops and in the Council of Foreign Ministers unanimity was necessary for all decisions, American diplomacy had little clout in the matter.

At the meeting of the Political and Territorial Commission for Rumania on September 5, the Australian delegate, Mr. Officer, wanted to hear from the representative of one of the states responsible for drafting Article 2, so that the Commission would know the reasoning that guided the Council. Averell Harriman, responding to the Australian request, said that

> the United States had not been a strong supporter of the proposed text but wished to make it clear that he would vote for it since it had been agreed by the Council. He said that during the discussions in the Council the United States Delegation had made certain proposals for a study of possible modification of the frontier which might, by reducing the number of persons under alien rule, contribute to stability and to mutual cooperation between Hungary and Rumania. The other members of the Council of Foreign Ministers had not shared this view and, in view of the desirability of reaching unanimous agreement, the U.S. had not insisted on its position. Mr. Harriman reiterated his statement that he would vote for Article 2 as drafted but wished to take the occasion to say that, in view of the differences on various subjects evident in the statements of the Hungarian and Rumanian representatives, the United States hoped that progress might be made through direct negotiations between them toward a mutually satisfactory settlement of the outstanding questions.[61]

After statements by the Soviet, British, and French delegates, Officer proposed that "Article 2 be adopted with a rider in the form of a recommendation that the Council of Foreign Ministers, before putting it into the final treaty, make a further effort to secure, in cooperation with the two interested parties, an adjustment by which some additional Hungarian centers might be incorporated in Hungary." This proposal was not accepted, and eventually Article 2 was adopted by ten votes and two abstentions.[62] Thus the Australian attempts to reopen the Transylvanian question failed.

The American position concerning the dispute between Hungary and Rumania was reiterated on September 23 in the Political and Territorial Commission of Hungary (heretofore Hungarian Committee) by General Walter Bedell Smith. He read into the record a statement similar to that made by Harriman in the Rumanian Commission "regarding the desire of Rumania to sign a protocol with Hungary or any bilateral arrangement which the United States Delegation felt would tend to improve relations and good understanding between the two countries."[63]

The Hungarian territorial claim presented by Auer on August 31 was evaluated by the Rumanian specialist of the American delegation, John C. Campbell, in a memorandum of September 2.[64] He pointed out that this territorial claim was based purely on ethnic consideration; it was about the same as the hypothetical ethnic line worked out in the Department of State. Campbell discussed the pros and cons of the Hungarian proposal and concluded that if there was any disposition on the part of the other members of the Council of Foreign Ministers to make any change in the frontier, "we might give as our view that the Hungarian claims appear reasonable with the exception of the claim for Arad and the immediate vicinity." Campbell also raised the possibility of direct Hungarian-Rumanian negotiations along these lines. Since the Council's attitude was negative, these ideas were not submitted to further discussion.

At the plenary meeting of the Conference on October 10, Molotov stated that "the treaty with Rumania was a matter of great importance for the peace of Europe. Rumania was now a democratic state and it was essential that the questions of Transylvania be settled to the satisfaction of the Rumanian people."[65]

As a last endeavor, the Hungarian government addressed a note to the Council of Foreign Ministers, which was in session in New York in November–December, 1946, to draft the final text of the peace treaties. This note proposed that the third article of the Rumanian draft peace treaty should be supplemented by a clause, according to which the rights of the Hungarian minority in Rumania would be defined through direct negotiations between Hungary and Rumania. "Should these direct negotiations between Hungary and Rumania result in failure, the Hungarian government should be given an opportunity to apply to the Council of Foreign Ministers for a final adjustment of this problem."[66] The Council disregarded this proposal.

Minority Protection and Human Rights

One of the major tasks of the peace preparatory work in Hungary was to defend the vital interests of the Hungarian population in neighboring states. The Hungarian government informed the victorious great powers and the Paris Conference in aide-memoires of the grievances of the Hungarian minority in Transylvania and pointed out that redressing of these grievances and securing of satisfactory conditions of existence for the Hungarians were the sine qua non of a reconciliation between Hungary and Rumania. A booklet submitted to the Conference gave an overall view of the situation of Transylvania since 1918 and enumerated the anti-Hungarian discriminations and atrocities between August, 1944, and May, 1946.[67]

For the future, the Hungarian government proposed the application of the principles of self-determination of peoples and the institutionalization of the protection of minorities under the aegis of the United Nations. On one occasion, I pointed out to the Soviet ambassador to France, Alexander Bogomolov, that according to our views, a lasting peace must be based on self-determination of peoples. I quoted Lenin, who had taken a stand for this principle and condemned the injustices of the peace settlement after the First World War. Bogomolov replied that Lenin was right in his time but times and conditions had changed.

A Hungarian memorandum of June 11, 1946, addressed to the members of the Council of Foreign Ministers emphasized the importance of reviving and strengthening provisions for the international protection of minority rights.[68] Later the Hungarian delegation submitted an elaborate draft treaty for the protection of minority rights, with a system of mixed commissions and tribunals to enforce them under the supervision of the United Nations.[69] Such proposals for the modernization of the minority protection system were disregarded because the Council preferred provisions concerning human rights and fundamental freedoms. True, these provisions obligated the defeated states to take all measures necessary to secure to all persons under their jurisdictions, "without distinction as to race, sex, language or religion, the enjoyment of human rights and of the fundamental freedoms including freedom of expression, of press and publication, of religious worship, of political opinion and public meeting." But an international control for the enforcement of these rights was not established. An Australian proposal aiming at the creation of a European Court of Human Rights was rejected by the Paris Conference. The British, United States, and French delegations proposed that any dispute concerning the execution or interpretation of the peace treaties, which could not be settled by direct negotiations, might be referred at the request of any party to the dispute to the International Court of Justice. This proposition, strongly opposed by the Soviet delegation, was accepted at the Conference by a vote of fifteen to six. But the Council of Foreign Ministers eliminated all reference to the International Court of Justice from the final draft because of Soviet opposition.

Events proved later that a weak legalistic system inserted into the peace treaties was not a workable arrangement in the face of the obstructive tactics of the Soviet Union and the Danubian Communist countries.[70] When Great Britain and the United States charged Bulgaria, Hungary, and Rumania with having violated their obligations under the respective Peace Treaty provisions requiring them to secure to all persons under their jurisdiction the enjoyment of human rights and the fundamental freedoms, they simply refused to recognize the existence of a dispute. Moreover, the Danubian countries denounced the English and American notes as illegitimate interference in their domestic affairs and stated that they had fully complied with the human rights provisions of the peace treaties. Subsequent proceedings before the General Assembly of the United Nations and the International Court of Justice were fruitless.[71]

In the absence of an effective enforcement procedure, the provisions concerning human rights and fundamental freedoms have become dismal examples of the kind of peacemaking that occurred after the Second World War.

NOTES

1. Excerpts from Kristóffy's report of July 11, 1940 (113/pol.-1940).

2. Hungary recognized the U.S.S.R. in April, 1934. The Soviet government severed diplomatic relations in February, 1939, because Hungary adhered to the Anti-Comintern Pact.

3. *The Ciano Diaries 1939–1943,* ed. Hugh Gibson (Garden City, N.Y.: Doubleday, 1946).

4. Ibid., Jan. 6–7, 1940.

5. Csáky requested Ciano to inform the Rumanians of the following: "If Russia attacks Rumania and Rumania resists sword in hand, Hungary will adopt an attitude of benevolent neutrality towards Rumania. On the other hand, Hungary would immediately intervene should one of the three following cases arise: (1) the massacre of the minorities; (2) Bolshevik revolution in Rumania; (3) Cession by Rumania of national territory to Russia and Bulgaria without fighting." Csáky added that even in that case "nothing will be done without previous consultation and agreement with Italy." *Ciano's Diplomatic Papers,* ed. Malcolm Muggeridge (London: Oldham Press, 1948), p. 331.

6. *The Ciano Diaries,* Mar. 25, 1940.

7. Ibid., Mar. 28, 1940.

8. Ibid., Apr. 8, 1940.

9. Ibid., Apr 9, 1940.

10. For details, see András Hóry, *Még egy barázdát sem* [Not Even a Furrow] (Vienna: Hóry András, 1967). Hóry was the Hungarian negotiator in Turnu-Severin.

11. Before the occupation of Bessarabia and Northern Bukovina, Molotov assured the German government that the Soviet Union "simply wished to pursue its own interests and had no intention of encouraging other states (Hungary, Bulgaria) to make demands on Rumania." *Nazi-Soviet Relations 1939–1941,* (Washington, 1948), p. 160.

12. According to Hungarian documents, Hitler made statements in this regard to Sztójay on February 1, 1941, and to Bárdossy on March 21, 1941. Hitler told Bárdossy that the Rumanians asked for a quick German intervention because of the preparations of the Red Army to cross the Danube. Cf. Petru Groza, *In Umbra Celulei* (Bucharest, 1945), p. 276.

13. *Ciano Diaries,* Aug. 28, 1940.

14. Ibid., Aug. 29, 1940.

15. An area of 43,492 square kilometers with a population of 2.6 million was reattached to Hungary. According to the Hungarian censuses of 1910 and 1941, the number of Hungarians exceeded the Rumanians in this territory, while the Rumanian census of 1930 indicated a slight Rumanian majority. Following the delivery of the Vienna Award, Csáky and Ribbentrop signed a treaty assuring special rights to the German minority in Hungary. With the conclusion of this treaty the problem of the German citizens of Hungary ceased to be exclusively within the domestic jurisdiction of the Hungarian state. For the text of the treaty, see, Matthias Annabring, "Das ungarländische Deutschtum," *Südost-Stimmen* 2 (March, 1952): 13–14. For detailed discussion and bibliography, see Béla Vágó, "Le Second Diktat de Vienne: Les Preliminaires," *East European Quarterly* 2, no. 4, (1969): 415–37 and idem, "Le Second Diktat de Vienne: Le Partage de la Transylvanie," *East European Quarterly* 5, no. 1 (1971): 47–73.

16. Molotov considered the Italo-German guarantee to Rumania, with respect to its national territory, as a justification for the supposition that this action was directed against the USSR. For the pertinent exchange of notes see, *Nazi-Soviet Relations 1939–1941,* pp. 178–94.

17. It is a curious historical parallel that Article 22 of the peace treaty of February 10, 1947, authorized the Soviet Union "to keep on Hungarian territory such armed forces as it may need for the maintenance of the lines of communication of the Soviet army with the Soviet zone of occupation in Austria."

18. The government was violently attacked by the opposition in both houses of parliament because of this step. Count István Bethlen and Tibor Eckhart, leader of the Smallholder party, strongly criticized this move. The Hungarian minister to Washington, John Pelényi, resigned in protest.

19. Cf. A. Ullein-Reviczky, *Guerre Allemande Paix Russe: le Drame Hongrois,* (Neuchâtel, 1947), pp. 71–73.

20. Winston S. Churchill, *The Grand Alliance* (Boston: Houghton Mifflin Company, 1950), p. 168. For Teleki's way of thinking during the critical events in 1940 and 1941, see Richard V. Burks, "Two Teleki Letters," *Journal of Central European Affairs,* 7 (1947): 68–73. Cf. Loránt Tilkovszky, *Teleki Pál—Legenda és Valóság* [Paul Teleki—Legend and Reality] (Budapest, 1969).

21. According to a German diplomat, Erich Kordt, the German General Staff arranged the bombing. *Wahn und Wirklichkeit* (Stuttgart, 1948), p. 308. At the Nuremberg trials General István Ujszászy stated that he was convinced "that the bombarding was carried out by German planes with Russian markings." The Kassa incident is still a much debated question. See for the intricacies involved N. F. Dreisziger "New Twist to

an Old Riddle: The Bombing of Kassa (Košice), June 26, 1941," *Journal of Modern History* 44 (1972): 232–42; "Contradictory evidence Concerning Hungary's Declaration of War on the USSR in June 1941," *Canadian Slavonic Papers,* vol. 19, no. 4. (Dec., 1977), pp. 81–88. Regarding the political influence of military leaders in these crucial years, see Dreisziger, "The Hungarian General Staff and Diplomacy, 1939–1941," *Canadian-American Review of Hungarian Studies,* 7, no. 1 (Spring 1980); 5–26.

22. *Trial of the Major War Criminals Before the International Military Tribunal,* vol. 7 (Nuremberg, 1947), p. 335.

23. The British note was handed to Bárdossy on November 29, 1941, by the American minister to Hungary. It read as follows: "The Hungarian Government has for many months been pursuing aggressive military operations on the territory of the Union of Soviet Socialist Republics, ally of Great Britain, in closest collaboration with Germany, thus participating in the general European war and making substantial contribution to the German war effort. In these circumstances His Majesty's Government in the United Kingdom finds it necessary to inform the Hungarian Government that unless by December 5 the Hungarian Government has ceased military operations and has withdrawn from all active participation in hostilities, His Majesty's Government will have no choice but to declare the existence of a state of war between the two countries."

24. The British ultimatum was delivered to Finland, Hungary, and Rumania as a result of Stalin's repeated and pressing appeal. Prime Minister Churchill tried in vain to convince Stalin that the declaration of war against these countries would not be beneficial to the Allied cause. Churchill explained to Stalin in his telegram of November 4, 1941, that these countries "have been overpowered by Hitler and used as a cat's-paw, but if fortune turns against that ruffian they might easily come back to our side. A British declaration of war would only freeze them all and make it look as if Hitler were the head of a grand European alliance solid against us." Winston S. Churchill, op. cit., p. 528. Bárdossy's record of his conversation with Pell and Travers is among the files of the Hungarian Foreign Ministry.

25. Bárdossy's instructions sent to the Hungarian ministers in Berlin and Rome on December 11 and 12 show how he tried to avoid involvement in war with the United States. For the text of the instructions see Stephen D. Kertesz, *Diplomacy In a Whirlpool* (Notre Dame: University of Notre Dame Press, 1953), pp. 234–36.

26. Cordell Hull, *The Memoirs of Cordell Hull,* vol. 2 (New York: Macmillan, 1948), pp. 1114, 1175–76. Cf. *Documents on American Foreign Relations,* vol. 4 (1942), pp. 123–24. Senator Vandenberg suggested that the declaration of war on Hitler's Danubian satellites was done in response to Russian demand. *The Private Papers of Senator Vandenberg,* ed. Arthur H. Vandenberg, Jr. (Boston: Houghton Mifflin Co., 1952), pp. 31–33.

27. Filippo Anfuso, *Du Palais de Venise au Lac de Garde* (Paris, 1949), p. 221.

28. Hungary's military participation in the war against the Soviet Union was limited. The number of combatant Hungarian divisions in Russia was five in 1941, ten in 1942, none in 1943, and fourteen in 1944. During the same period, the number of divisions for occupation duties varied between two and six divisions. The number of combatant Rumanian divisions was twelve in 1941, thirty-one in 1942, and twenty-five in 1943 and 1944. There were only three Rumanian divisions for occupation duties in 1942 and 1943. For details see *La Hongrie et la Conférence de Paris,* vol. 1, Publié par le Ministère des Affaires Etrangères de Hongrie (Budapest, 1947), pp. 86–90. It should be noted that during this period, the population of both Hungary and Rumania was around 14 million.

29. See about my assignment, Dániel Csatári, *Forgószélben: Magyar-román viszony*

1940–1945 [In the Path of a Tornado: Hungarian-Rumanian Relations 1940–1945] (Budapest: Akadémiai Kiadó, 1968), p. 123.

30. Memorandum of the conversation between the Führer and the Duce, with Ribbentrop and Ciano also present, at Klessheim near Salzburg, April 29, 1942. *Bulletin of the State Department,* 15 (1946), no. 367, p. 59.

31. For the activities and report of this commission, see Csatári, op. cit., pp. 124–32. This book with some abbreviations was published in French under the title: *Dans la Tourmante. Les relations Hungaro-Roumaines de 1940 a 1945.* (Budapest: Akadémiai Kiadó, 1974). For the Italo-German Commission see pp. 114–18.

32. The Hungarian government inquired and found out that the German and Italian governments did not know of this Rumanian allegation.

33. For details see Csatári, *Forgószélben,* pp. 229–51 and *Dans la Tourmante,* pp. 209–24. Cf. Elemér Illyés, *Erdély változása* [Transformation of Transylvania] (Munich: Aurora könyvek, 1976), 2d, expanded edition, p. 101.

34. He indicated his feelings frankly to the Rumanian foreign minister, G. Gafencu, on April 19, 1939. "They say that I want to restore the grandeur of Hungary. Why should I be so ill advised? A greater Hungary might be embarrassing for the Reich. Besides, the Hungarians have always shown us utter ingratitude. They have no regard or sympathy for the German minorities. As for me, I am only interested in my Germans. I said so frankly to Count Csáky . . . And I have said so without equivocation to the Regent Horthy and to Imrédy: the German minorities in Rumania and Yugoslavia do not want to return to Hungary; they are better treated in their new fatherland. And what the German minorities do not want, the Reich does not want either." Grigore Gafencu, *Last Days of Europe, A Diplomatic Journey in 1939* (New Haven, Conn.: Yale University Press, 1948), pp. 68–9.

35. Paul Schmidt, *Hitler's Interpreter* (New York, 1951), pp. 205–06.

36. Ibid., p. 244. As to Hitler's encouragements given to Antonescu concerning the ultimate fate of Transylvania, see *Trial of the Major War Criminals,* vol. 7 (Nuremberg, 1947), p. 322. Hitler and his underlings juggled with promises and threats to keep Hungary and Rumania in line. This was especially the case when political leaders of these countries visited Hitler. Ibid., pp. 320–23.

37. *Ciano Diaries,* Aug. 25, 26, 27, 29, 1942. Mussolini considered the Hungarian plan as part of an anti-German conspiracy that would have caused a crisis in Italo-German relations. For the details of the affair, see Filippo Anfuso, *Du Palais de Venise au Lac de Garde* (Paris, 1949), pp. 230–31.

38. *Ciano Diaries,* Nov. 5, 1942.

39. Nicholas Kállay, *Hungarian Premier* (New York: Columbia University Press, 1954), p. 147.

40. For the entire exchange of views, see ibid., pp. 146–61.

41. *Colloqui con Due Dittatori* (Roma: Ruffolo Editore, 1949).

42. Ibid., pp. 102–08.

43. Ibid., p. 109.

44. Ibid., p. 112–14.

45. For the wartime period many Hungarian, Rumanian, German, British, American, and Italian documentary sources and memoirs are available. For further readings see some monographs that used such sources: C. A. Macartney, *October Fifteenth, A History of Modern Hungary, 1929–1945,* 2 vols., (Edinburgh: Edinburgh University Press, 1961); Nandor A. F. Dreisziger, *Hungary's Way to World War II* (Toronto, Canada: Hungarian Helican Society, 1968); Andreas Hillgruber, *Hitler, König Carol und Marschall Antonescu, 1938–1944,* (Wiesbaden: Franz Steiner Verlag, 1954); Mario D. Fenyő, *Hitler,*

Horthy, and Hungary: German-Hungarian Relations, 1941–1944. (New Haven, Conn.: Yale University Press, 1972); Csatári, *Dans la Tourmante*; Gyula Juhász, *Magyarország Külpolitikája, 1919–1945,* [The Foreign Policy of Hungary, 1919–1945] (Budapest, Kossuth könyvkiadó, 1975) idem., *Magyar-brit titkos tárgyalások 1943-ban* [Hungarian-British Secret Negotiations in 1943] (Budapest, Kossuth könyvkiadó, 1978).

46. Churchill, *Triumph and Tragedy,* pp. 222–27.

47. See Albert Resis "The Churchill-Stalin 'Percentage' Agreement on the Balkans," *American Historical Review,* (April 1978), pp. 368–87; Sir Llewellyn Woodward, *British Foreign Policy in the Second World War,* vol. 3 (London: Her Majesty's Stationery Office, 1971), pp. 149–53; Daniel Yergen, *Shattered Peace* (Boston: Houghton Mifflin Co., 1977), pp. 58–61; Geir Lundstestad, *The American Non-Policy Towards Eastern Europe, 1943–1947* (Tromso: Universitetsforlager, 1978), pp. 89–92.

48. Anthony Eden, Earl of Avon, *The Memoirs of Anthony Eden, The Reckoning* (Boston: Houghton Mifflin Co., 1965), p. 560. Elisabeth Barker, *British Policy in South-East Europe in the Second World War* (New York: Barnes & Noble Books, 1976), pp. 140–47, 220–22.

49. Eden, op. cit., p. 559.

50. For details see *Cordell Hull,* op. cit., vol. 2, pp. 1451–57.

51. For description of the delegation's Moscow trip and its aftermath, see Ferenc Nagy, *The Struggle Behind the Iron Curtain* (New York: Macmillan Co., 1948), pp. 204–19.

52. Actually Hungarian manpower and Hungarian experts were used for this work performed under the direction of the Red Army. Some of the railroad lines for which Hungary was required to pay were situated in the neighboring countries. Ibid., p. 208.

53. Article 19 of the Rumanian armistice agreement set forth: "The Allied Governments regard the decision of the Vienna Award regarding Transylvania as null and void and are agreed that Transylvania (or the greater part thereof) should be returned to Rumania, subject to confirmation at the peace settlement, and the Soviet Government agrees that Soviet forces shall take part for this purpose in joint military operations with Rumania against Germany and Hungary." The parenthetical phrase was used by the Russians as a club held over the Rumanians and as encouragement to the Hungarians in Budapest. The British and Americans proposed the expression "subject to confirmation at the peace settlement." They thought that this insertion would keep the whole question for reconsideration at the peace table after the war. By handing all of Transylvania to the Groza regime in March, 1945, the Soviets played their trump card to consolidate that puppet regime in power. They refused to discuss at inter-Allied meetings the meaning of the parenthetical phrase. And "subject to confirmation at the peace settlement" thereafter meant to the Soviets automatic confirmation of what they had done. The important thing to them was control over Rumania. Stalin was not secretive about his aims during the war. When the British foreign secretary, Anthony Eden, visited him in December, 1941, Stalin explained his ideas concerning the postwar territorial and political settlement. He stated that "Rumania should give special facilities for bases, etc., to the Soviet Union, receiving compensation from territory now occupied by Hungary." Winston S. Churchill, *The Grand Alliance,* p. 629.

54. *La Hongrie et la Conférence de Paris,* vol. 1, pp. 108–11. For the English text of this note, see Appendix C.

55. *Foreign Relations of the United States, (FRUS),* 1946, vol. 2, pp. 309–10; John C. Campbell, *The United States in World Affairs, 1945–1947* (New York: Harper & Brothers, 1947), pp. 67, 115, 117, 123, 142; idem., "The European Territorial Settlement," *Foreign Affairs,* 26 (1947): 211–13; Philip E. Mosely, "Soviet Exploitation of National Conflicts

in Eastern Europe," Waldemar Gurian, ed., *The Soviet Union* (Notre Dame, Indiana: Notre Dame University Press), p. 75.

56. *FRUS,* 1946, vol. 2, pp. 441–42.

57. See note 54.

58. The following delegations supported the Australian motion: Australia, Canada, France, Great Britain, Greece, New Zealand, Union of South Africa, U.S.A. The following delegations voted against it: Byelo-Russia, Czechoslovakia, Ukraine, USSR. See for details *FRUS,* 1946, vol. 3, pp. 311–12.

59. Ibid., pp. 330–31. For the text of his address see Appendix D.

60. Ibid., p. 339. For the text of his address see Appendix D.

61. Ibid., pp. 375–76.

62. Ibid., pp. 376–77.

63. Ibid., pp. 528.

64. *FRUS,* 1946, vol. 4, pp. 851–53.

65. *FRUS,* 1946, vol. 3, p. 761.

66. *FRUS,* 1946, Council of Foreign Ministers, pp. 1074–75.

67. *Le Problème Hongrois par rapport à la Roumanie, Publié par le Ministère des Affaires Etrangères de Hongrie* (Budapest, 1946). For the grievances of the Hungarian minority in Transylvania, see notes of May 20, 1946, and of July 15, 1946, Appendix C.

68. See Appendix C.

69. *La Hongrie et la Conférence de Paris,* vol. 1, pp. 142–71.

70. Cf. Martin Domke, "Settlement-of-Disputes Provisions in Axis Satellite Peace Treaties," *American Journal of International Law,* 41 (1947): 911–20; Stephen D. Kertesz, "Human Rights in the Peace Treaties," *International Human Rights: Part II,* Symposium published as the Autumn, 1949, issue of *Law and Contemporary Problems,* Duke University Law School, Durham, N.C., pp. 627–46.

71. Cf. Yuen-Li Liang, "Observance in Bulgaria, Hungary and Rumania of Human Rights and Fundamental Freedoms: Request for an Advisory Opinion on Certain Questions," *American Journal of International Law,* 44 (1950): 100–17; Kenneth S. Carlston, "Interpretation of Peace Treaties with Bulgaria, and Rumania, Advisory Opinions of the International Court of Justice," *American Journal of International Law,* 44 (1950): 728–37.

VIII. TRANSYLVANIA AND THE MAGYAR AUTONOMOUS REGION, 1952-1960

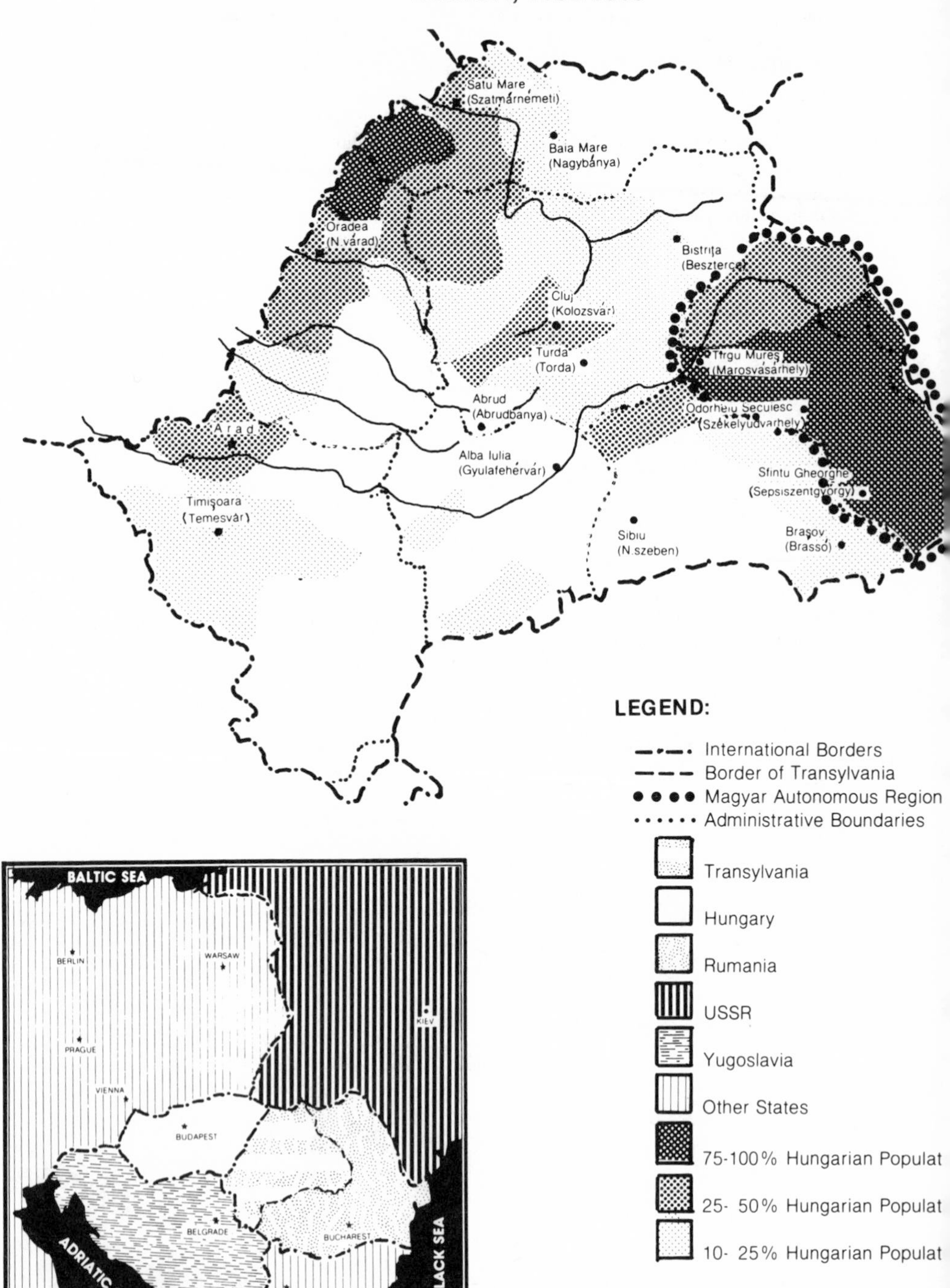

*Anuaral Statistic al RPR, (Bucharest: Direcţia Centrală de Sta[illegible] 1959, 1961, 1969)

Contemporary Rumanian Policies in Transylvania 4

In the twentieth century, Transylvania has been under Rumanian jurisdiction for most of the time. As the essays of the previous section demonstrate, international events and the shifts of power both regionally and globally have enabled Rumania to retain its hold over this area. In the present section, Andrew Ludanyi, Elemér Illyés, and Bulcsu Veress present and discuss some of the implications of Rumania's control over the destiny of Transylvania's inhabitants.

The three essays focus on Rumanian control as it has manifested itself since 1945. Although each of these studies deals with a different overall theme, all of them examine Rumanian nationality policies as these have evolved in a Communist-controlled setting. In a sense, the studies examine the extent to which a Communist regime has overcome or failed to overcome the legacy of the "bourgeois nationalist" regime that preceded it. In Rumania, as in other socialist states, the claim has been made—just as the promise was held out before the seizure of power—that the persecution and oppression of national minorities has been terminated. The Rumanian Communists contend that they have overcome the negative nationalist excesses of the past by conscientiously implementing Marxist-Leninist nationality policies.

At the heart of Marxist-Leninist nationality policy is the claim that all real problems are a reflection of class conflict. It is even maintained—although in recent years with less conviction—that national and nationality conflicts are merely a ploy of the ruling classes to keep the proletariat divided and to ensure their continued exploitation. The interwar treatment of Rumania's minority nationalities is even held up as the epitome of "reactionary chauvinism," but it is claimed that the abuses and oppressive policies of the reactionaries were swept away with the last bourgeois caretaker government and the abdication of King Michael.

Three areas in which the interwar Rumanian governments have been extensively—and rightly—criticized by their contemporary successors are those of minority education, minority political rights and participation, and the unequal status of minorities within the legal order. The three essays that follow examine these sensitive questions and evaluate the performance of the present regime. Although the analyses make reference to the abuses of the past, their main concern is to present Rumania's contemporary policies, which define the existence of the "coinhabiting nationalities" within a socialist setting.

The study by Andrew Ludanyi focuses mainly on the present Rumanian regime's self-definition. His study describes the Daco-Roman state-myth and points out how it has been adapted to the new ideological commitments. At the same time, it sheds light both on the pervasive role of the state-myth for the nationalist legitimation of the current Rumanian leadership and on the extensive effort on their part to propagate it. Finally, the study analyzes the impact of the prevailing state-myth on the minority nationalities.

Elemér Illyés examines a specific aspect of the second-rate citizenship of the minorities, their educational opportunities or lack thereof. He traces the pattern of Rumanian policies from the interwar years to the end of the 1970s, describes the different phases in Rumanian minority education policies, and provides an effective summary of the process of Rumanianization.

Bulcsu Veress sets out to examine not only the status of minority educational opportunities, but the whole area of minority rights in contemporary Rumania. His approach is to examine the existing international legal order's definition of basic human, civil, social, economic, and political rights and to compare these rights to the conditions of the minorities in Rumania. He contends that violations of these rights are a day-to-day phenomenon and that within a state controlled by the principles of Lenin's "democratic centralism" it is inconceivable that the government would not be the major culprit.

Although the following essays provide a very pessimistic profile of Rumania's contemporary minority policies, they may also contain a glimmer of hope. If after so many years of overt pressure the Hungarians, Germans, and other minorities are still conscious of their identities and unique destinies, then perhaps even a state based on democratic centralism is incapable of permanently "solving" the nationality question.

IX. TRANSYLVANIA AND THE MUREŞ-MAGYAR AUTONOMOUS REGION, 1960-1968

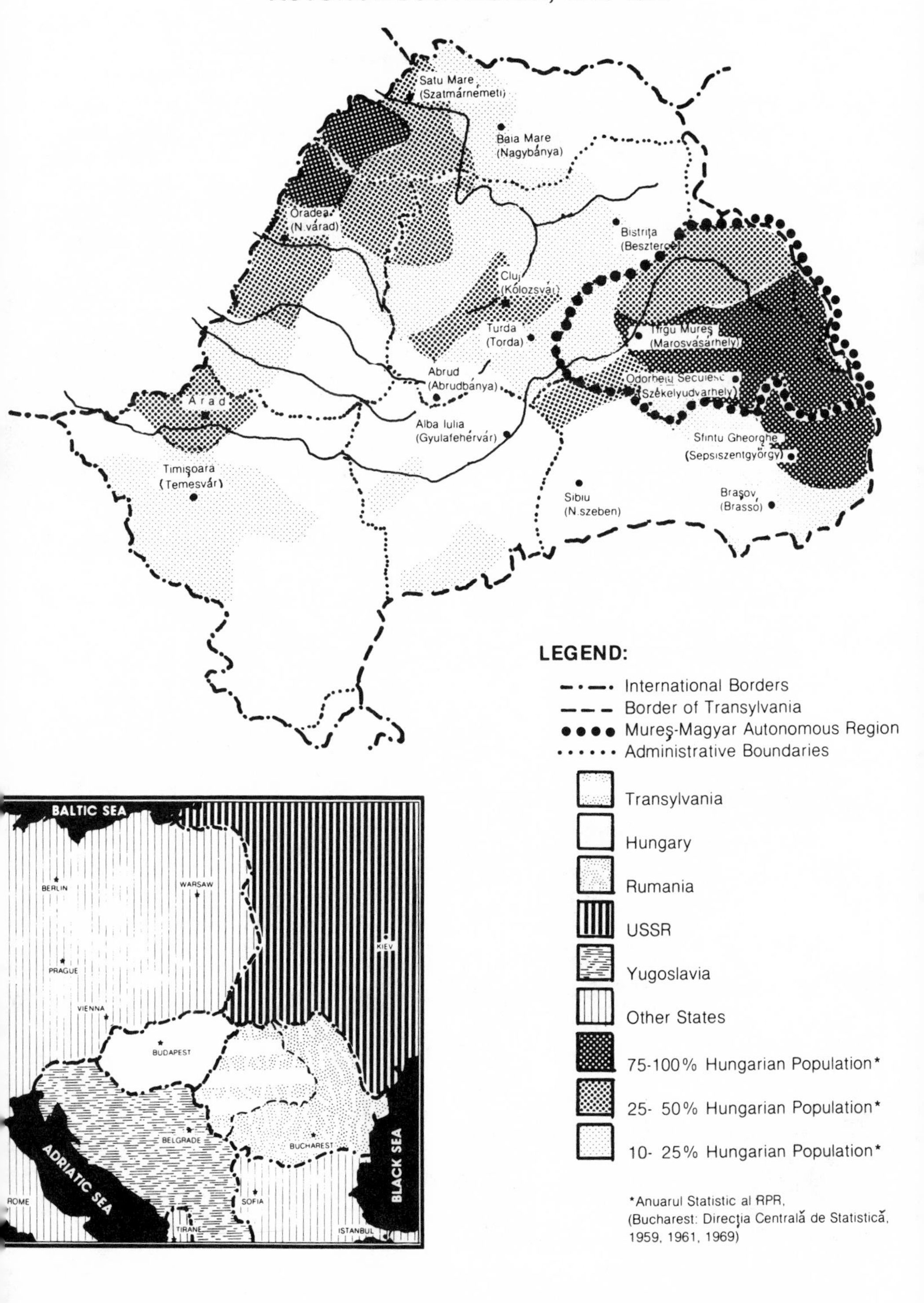

Satu Mare
(Szatmárnemeti)
Baia Mare
(Nagybánya)
Oradea
(N.várad)
Bistrița
(Beszterce)
Cluj
(Kolozsvár)
Turda
(Torda)
Tîrgu Mureş
(Marosvásárhely)
Abrud
(Abrudbánya)
Odorheiu Secuiesc
(Székelyudvarhely)
Arad
Alba Iulia
(Gyulafehérvár)
Sfîntu Gheorghe
(Sepsiszentgyörgy)
Timişoara
(Temesvár)
Sibiu
(N.szeben)
Braşov
(Brassó)
LEGEND:
International Borders
Border of Transylvania
Mureş-Magyar Autonomous Region
Administrative Boundaries
Transylvania
Hungary
Rumania
USSR
Yugoslavia
Other States
75-100% Hungarian Population*
25- 50% Hungarian Population*
10- 25% Hungarian Population*
*Anuarul Statistic al RPR,
(Bucharest: Direcția Centrală de Statistică,
1959, 1961, 1969)
BALTIC SEA
BERLIN
WARSAW
KIEV
PRAGUE
VIENNA
BUDAPEST
BELGRADE
BUCHAREST
BLACK SEA
ADRIATIC SEA
ROME
SOFIA
TIRANE
ISTANBUL

X. TRANSYLVANIA AND ITS ADMINISTRATIVE COUNTIES FROM 1968 TO THE PRESENT

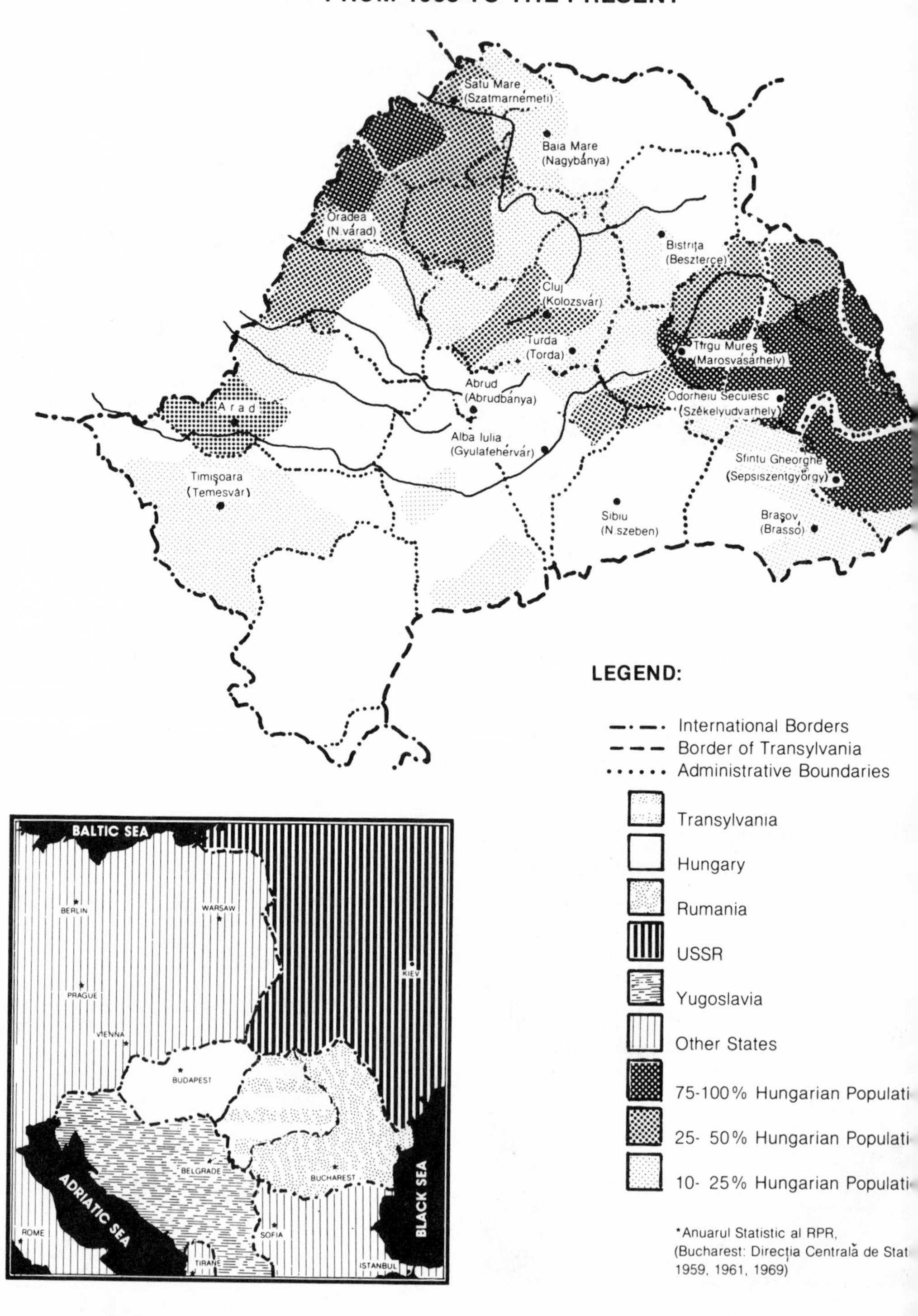

Ideology and Political Culture in Rumania: The Daco-Roman Theory and the "Place" of Minorities

ANDREW LUDANYI

In his collected essays on Rumanian-Hungarian relations, Zoltán I. Tóth provides a concise summary of the dangers and the promises inherent in the settlement patterns of these two peoples. Tóth writes:

> If we examine a topographical map of Eastern Europe, our attention is immediately drawn to the imposing curve of the Carpathian mountains. If on the other hand, we turn our examination to an ethnographic map of Eastern Europe, we will be struck by the mixture of colors which designate the different nationalities. The large sploches of color which stand for Rumanians and Hungarians respectively are linked by a zone in which the colors representing the two peoples are extensively intertwined. Inadevertantly the question comes to mind: surely these two peoples must have many things in common, they most certainly have many more related concerns than is the case with peoples who live in compact settlements separated from one another by clearly distinguishable ethnographic frontiers. It would seem that nature itself has predestined these two peoples to a common destiny. Hungarians—primarily the Csángó Hungarians—can be found living east of the Carpathians, in Moldavia. Rumanians, on the other hand, may be found even west of Transylvania on the periphery of the great lowlands, beyond the present Hungarian-Rumanian state frontiers. What would be more natural than to expect these two peoples—living side-by-side, and even intermingled—to appreciate and to respect one another, and that peace, understanding and a spirit of good will would prevail between them?[1]

Unfortunately during the past two centuries, in an age of extreme nationalism, peace and understanding, respect or appreciation in general have failed to prevail between these two peoples. Nor do such sentiments prevail between them at present. Instead, they are divided from one another by suspicion, misunderstanding, jealousy, and on occasion even by military confrontation and struggle, which has too often resulted in bloodshed, destruction, and mutual recriminations. Although outside forces incited, nurtured, and played on these animosities, the sources of conflict must be sought also in the cultural realm, in the mutually exclusive self-definitions of these two peoples.

The nationalist orientations of the past two centuries have provided justification for the establishment and exercise of monopolistic and exclusivistic "nation-state" hegemony. The present exploitation and oppression of the Hungarians in Transylvania is based on this same nationalist orientation. Rumania's assertion that Transylvania is the communal property, sphere of interest, and inheritance exclusively of the Rumanian people makes the existence of Hungarians and other minorities an inconvenience that must be overcome in some fashion, via emigration, assimilation, exclusion, or deportation.

Today, Transylvania is part of the Rumanian Socialist Republic. The objective of this paper is to discuss the present Rumanian national self-definition in terms of its evolution to the present and its consequences for the Hungarian and other minority nationalities of Transylvania. This analysis requires an examination of the official state myth of Rumania and the socialization process that the state utilizes to preserve, develop, and propagate it. The questions that need answers: What is the official Rumanian *Kulturpolitik*? What is the official state myth? What is the origin and content of this myth and what are its consequences for the national minorities? (The goal is not to prove or disprove the accuracy or validity of the state myth. The latter task is the responsibility of historians.)[2]

Every self-conscious political community has myths that are basic to its self-definition. A myth, at least as the term will be used in the present study, is a world-view that explains political and social existence and justifies activities and struggles central to a particular community. A people or community derives self-consciousness and self-definition from such a world-view. Therefore, a myth is, as it were, a script that defines the roles and objectives of a group, community, people, or state and determines its relations with the outside world. A myth may be naive or fictitious, grounded in extant facts and images or consciously manufactured in part or whole.[3] The myth may be significant whether it is naive or fictitious (or both). Its political significance is that it strongly influences the functioning of political systems; it molds the relationships and guides the behavior of members of the community who adhere to the myth, and it also affects that community's relationship with and behavior toward other communities.[4]

The content of a myth-system, however, is rarely admitted to be mythical; instead the system is called an ideology, or political philosophy.[5] Here it is important to distinguish carefully the mythical patterns of thought from the actual ideological modes of self-definition. The latter are usually rational and logically consistent interpretations of social, economic, cultural, and political relationships. The myth-system and its corresponding thought-processes, by contrast, are composed mainly of irrational, mystical, and, in large part, emotional elements. Otherwise, the function of both is basically the same, to provide a world view that establishes guidelines for behavior and that outlines and explains the major goals of the community. Both are basically social and political "maps," or "blueprints," to give a community a sense of purpose and direction.

The concern of the present analysis is to examine how the Daco-Roman theory has been transformed into a state myth-system. In this context it is useful to restate the difference between theoretical thinking on the one hand and mythical or ideological thinking on the other. Theory stands for an abstract model. It is an explanation, or a frame of reference, that provides a guide to the systematic collection and analysis of political or other data. Ideology and myth are also, of course, guides to behavior but on a different level; examples might be the research work of nationalist or Communist groups. What distinguishes the theorist is the tentativeness of his assumptions, his willingness to discard hypotheses that prove fruitless or false after conscientious examination. The theorist also attempts to maintain a dispassionate stance toward the subject of inquiry, unlike the ideologist or myth-maker, who claims that his basic assumptions are proven gospel.

This mythical game plan, or myth-system, is manufactured and propagated by the political leaders of a particular society. The manufacturing and socialization process used to instill it in the masses is what can be called *Kulturpolitik*. The French *"mission civilizatrice,"* the Soviet "proletarians of the world unite," the American "manifest destiny," or "make the world safe for democracy," the English "white man's burden," and the German Third Reich's *"Übermensch-Lebensraum"* myths are examples. In Rumania's history, the Daco-Roman theory occupies a similarly central place as a national myth. What are the roots and major assumptions of this myth?

Elemér Illyés, in his study "Rumanian Historiography," notes that "The later a nation acquires political, economic and cultural independence, the later it becomes a national state with a developed national consciousness, the more pronounced will be the nationalist character of its historiography."[6] The less developed, the less politically mature, the more likely is nationalist assertion to become a cover for a sense of uncertainty or even inferiority.[7] The above observations can be amended by pointing out that the quest for a "great" historical past is in part due to frustrations and failures within a national context. The relatively young United States of America has a record of success that obviates the need to focus on a semimythical past. Rumanians and

Hungarians, on the other hand, for different reasons, seem to make a habit of escaping into the past.

Rumanian national consciousness and its Daco-Roman justification emerged in Transylvania in the seventeenth century in the writings of Uniate Catholic priests. The three outstanding individuals representing this national awakening were Samuil Micu, Petru Maior, and Gheorghe Şincai. Although they did have one or two predecessors who discussed the theory,[8] these three developed its foundations systematically and made it into a doctrine that could be used for instilling pride of the Rumanian past into the masses. According to Emil Niederhauser, all three were:

> Vatican educated with a broad European perspective, whose education in Latin enabled them to recognize the Latin origin of the Rumanian language and that the ancient past of the Rumanians was in some way linked to the Roman Empire. They reasoned that if their language ties the present-day Rumanian language to the Romans, then obviously this also determines the question of origins: the Rumanians are the descendants of the ancient Romans. For the Rumanian intelligentsia living in Transylvania—and barred from political life—this naturally meant that their people were directly descended from the Roman inhabitants of ancient Dacia, therefore making them the oldest among all the inhabitants in Transylvania. They were, in other words, the ancient and indigeneous inhabitants of this area. This trio with the help of other intellectuals—now no longer drawn just from priestly ranks—exerted a great deal of effort and enthusiasm to prove the Roman origins and character of the Rumanian people. They began the process of renewing the vocabulary of the Rumanian language which had borrowed extensively from other languages. To emphasize the Latin origins of their language the reformers abandoned the Cyrillic alphabet inherited from the Orthodox Church and now began to use the Latin alphabet. They compiled dictionaries and through them they popularized the new Latinized words. They also wrote historical studies to prove the Roman origins of their people.[9]

The results of this work were so successful that by 1791 they turned to Leopold II, Habsburg emperor, in the *Supplex Libellus Valachorum* for the recognition of their equality with other nations in the empire. In this Rumanian petition, they already referred to the Daco-Roman theory to back up their request for equal treatment by the emperor.[10]

In terms of content, the Daco-Roman theory ties the Rumanian people to a glorious Roman and Dacian past. Through this theory Rumanian historians since Micu, Maior, and Şincai, have focused primarily on three themes: (1) the origin of the Rumanians as Transylvania's "autochton," or indigenous and ancient inhabitants; (2) the uninterrupted and continuous settlement of Transylvania (the center of the ancient Dacian kingdom) by Rumanians; and (3) Rumanian priority of settlement in Transylvania as opposed to the "later" settlement of Hungarians and Saxons.

Briefly summarized, during the course of the reign of Emperor Trajan (A.D. 98–117) the Romans conquered the Dacians after two bloody wars (A.D. 101–02 and 105–06). From this time until c. A.D. 271–75 Dacia remained under Roman control.[11] These 165–170 years are the basis of the Daco-Roman theory. These years of Roman rule allegedly resulted in the "Romanization" of the native Dacian population. Rumanian historians contend that the Romans settled many of their own people and people from the Roman provinces on the newly acquired Dacian territories together with the Roman legionaires. Between the Romans and Dacians this led to rapid intermarriage and amalgamation. Earlier explanations also stress that the Dacian menfolk were, for the most part, exterminated in the two bloody wars fought against Roman expansion. Between the widowed Dacian women and the Roman legionaires physical and not merely cultural mixing took place.[12] Furthermore, this intermarriage made the remainder of the Dacians so Romanized that when the Romans were forced to evacuate Dacia between A.D. 271–75, the population was already a homogeneous people who became the ancestors of present-day Rumanians. This people, "in spite of adversity, oppression and conquest" remained in its areas of settlement and survived the rule of all "foreign" peoples, until between 1859 and 1918 they finally achieved their national independence and finally united all the "Rumanian countries."[13]

This theory was popularized and even forged into a dogma by Nicolai Iorga, one of the most prolific of Rumanian historians.[14] His work contributed immensely to the gains made by the Daco-Roman theory even on international forums. Iorga's influence is everywhere in evidence even in Western works on Eastern Europe. Thus, the Daco-Roman theory has been successfully disseminated on the international level and in many cases has even been adopted by some Western historians.[15]

Iorga's historical legacy was temporarily abandoned when the Communist-dominated Rumanian People's Democracy was brought into being after World War II. As in the other Eastern European states, an attempt was made to eradicate nationalist elements from the country's history. From 1947 to the middle of the 1950s, Rumanian historians stressed only the "progressive," "revolutionary," and "workers' movement" aspects of history.[16] The content of their writings was always supposed to be guided by the principles of Leninist-Stalinist nationality policies. Accordingly, class solidarity would overcome national antagonisms, which were simply the remnants of bourgeois efforts to turn Rumanians, Hungarians, and other nationalities against one another. Therefore, the purpose of historians was to reveal the common struggles of all exploited peoples, without regard to nationality, against their exploiters. In this scheme of things, the "coinhabiting nationalities" were always at the side of the Rumanian people in combating reaction. This perspective enhanced the importance of the great peasant uprisings (Bábolna [Bobîlna], 1437; Dózsa, 1514), the strike of workers at Grivița, and above all else the "switch in time" of August 23, 1944, which belatedly linked Rumania's destiny to the anti-Axis coalition.

Yet even this "revolutionary and workers' movement" emphasis included a mixed legacy. There was already a premonition of things to come, when the "progressive elements" of historical writings could be utilized to support certain nationalist objectives. Thus, the peasant rising led by Antal Budai Nagy at Bábolna and the peasant war of 1514 under the leadership of György Dózsa became not merely social revolutions, but at the same time were viewed also as the manifestations of discontent among oppressed nationalities.[17] The August 23 switch and its symbolic significance was also reevaluated in this light by Rumanian historians. This event provided the opportunity to stress the role of Rumanian military units as allies of the Red Army in the struggle against "fascist" German and Hungarian contingents. The new Rumanian state, the Rumanian People's Republic, came into being as a consequence of Soviet-Rumanian joint effort. (This achievement also had immediate practical consequences, since Northern Transylvania was again incorporated into Rumania.)

While this Hungarian-inhabited area now was put under Rumanian sovereignty, Stalin wanted to restrain the Rumanian quest for revenge. Therefore, he demanded of the Rumanian authorities the guarantee of nationality rights. At the same time, he also demanded that a damper be placed on nationalist sentiments, particularly in the sensitive area of majority-minority relations. It is because of this that the Daco-Roman theory was left out of Rumanian historical studies. Only after Stalin's death did the nationalist elements creep back into the Rumanian national self-definition. This revived nationalism was already evident by 1955–56 in Rumanian travel guides and popular, nonscholarly historical articles and interpretations.[18]

The Hungarian Revolt of 1956 signaled the real return to the unfettered symbols of Rumanian nationalism. Two years after that event, the Soviet Union withdrew its forces from Rumania as a reward for its assistance—providing a staging ground—in crushing the Hungarian revolt. From then to the present, Rumanian nationalism has been undergoing a constant revival. Parallel to this, the Daco-Roman theory has received a new lease on life and has been transformed into the official state myth. The rehabilitation of this interpretation—and of Nicolai Iorga—has been the task primarily of the historical revisionists Daicoviciu, Pascu, Constantinescu and Giurescu,[19] through whose efforts the myth has acquired new strength, although it has undergone some slight alterations in content.

The new Daco-Roman myth places much more stress on symbols that link it to the "peoples' struggles" to overcome oppression through the ages. The roots of the workers' movement are intertwined with the whole theory of national origins. If a comparison of the Daco-Roman myth of the interwar years is made with its postwar counterpart, the first and most striking difference is the extensive discussion of the Dacians and the relatively more modest role of the Romans. There are probably three explanations for this. First, the Dacians have more "folk," or "peoples', " appeal, while the Romans are the representatives of a form of world "imperialism." In this context, the Dacians can be more easily fitted into the ideological prerequisites of present-day Rumania. Thus, the discussions of national origins focuses more on the roles of the Dacian leaders Burebista and Decebalus than on the role of the conquering Roman emperors Hadrian or Trajan. A second reason for the Dacian emphasis is that their settlements preceded those of the Romans on Transylvanian soil.[20] In fact, most references to the Dacians give the impression that they had been the inhabitants of the environs of the Carpathian Mountains from time immemorial.[21] The third reason is that the Dacians are known only indirectly via Greek or Roman written sources. Remnants of the Dacian language and culture are scarce indeed. Hardly any Dacian words have been preserved. (According to the historian László Makkai, only some sixty names have been identified as "Dacian" by the Rumanian historian C. C. Giurescu out of some 3,000 names that remain from inscriptions of the Dacian period.)[22] The relative lack of evidence about the culture, history or language of the Dacians provides a field day for those who like to write history on the basis of assumptions and theoretical speculation. Too much is known about the Romans to be able to trace direct Rumanian descent to them. This is not the case with the Dacians, and via speculative theories the Rumanians can be linked to them without too much difficulty.

In the fashion indicated above, the Daco-Roman myth pervades all aspects of life in Ceauşescu's Rumania. The people who can appreciate this most are those who systematically follow Rumanian historical research and historiography. An average history of Rumania or Rumanian historical chronology, without regard to number of pages or overall length, will devote c. one-fourth of its content to ancient history, i.e., to the elaboration and proof of the Daco-Roman theory. Another one-fourth of the book will be devoted to the period between A.D. 275 and 1700, mainly concerning the question of Rumanian "continuity" in Transylvania and the efforts of Wallachian and Moldavian voivodes to realize the unification of the Rumanian-inhabited "countries." The last half of the content is devoted to the period since 1700. In this way, approximately the same number of pages are devoted to the first 165 years as to the next 1425 years, while intense attention is again provided for the last 280 years.[23] It would be hard to duplicate the distortion of events that results from this strange allocation of attention to only a selected part of historical time. The feverish archeological activity in present-day Transylvania attests to this same skewed perspective. Almost everywhere digs are in progress that attempt to find the evidence that will conclusively link the Rumanians to the early history of Transylvania. The latter is indeed a thankless task, since the tangible evidence in written documents, architecture, and art testifies primarily to a Székely, Magyar, and Saxon past. The archeological finds within the Carpathian Basin—including Transylvania—reveal at least as many traces of the Celts, Huns, Avars, Goths, or Romans as of the Dacians.[24] The theories and assumptions are nonetheless reasserted and the finds are claimed for their support. Many of these finds have even been "Rumanianized."[25]

Contemporary Rumanian historians do not question the validity of the Daco-Roman myth. For them it is a matter of faith and the official interpretation of the origins of their people. Its acceptance as the official position is demonstrated in the recently published article of Ilie Ceauşescu—the historian brother of Nicolae Ceauşescu—who contends that we can trace the Dacian civilization back at least 4,000 years and that: "The Dacians and their industrious descendents, the sons of the Romanian people, were the predecessors and contemporaries of the great civilizations of antiquity."[26] He goes on to state in this same essay that the Rumanian Communist party's Central Committee also affirms this thesis and that: "As the reality of history over its multimillenia existence [*sic*] attests, the Romanian people has itself retained its distinct traits. Never was it dislodged from its ancestoral [*sic*] lands and never did it merge or mix with other peoples which moved into the Carpathian Danubian-Pontic region."[27] Even the "migratory populations" (i.e., Huns, Goths, Avars, Magyars, etc.), which were "at a lower level of civilization . . . could not budge the Romanian people from the ancestoral [*sic*] homeland. . . ."[28]

The Daco-Roman myth also finds its way into history textbooks. It is presented as unchallengeable fact rather than as tentative theory that still requires substantiation. In a history textbook translated for Hungarians in Rumania we encounter the following:

> The emergence of the Rumanian language and people was the result of a long evolutionary period of about a thousand years, and it lasted from the first to the tenth centuries.
>
> The Daco-Roman population, which came into being under Roman rule in Dacia, sustained itself even after Roman authorities evacuated Dacia. During this time period the indigenous population underwent a process of Romanization, in the course of which most of the population adopted the Latin language. Romanization—a process begun even before the actual conquest—continued under the influence of the Romanized provinces on the right bank of the Danube also after the evacuation of Dacia. Almost constant contact between the peoples on both sides of the Danube perpetuated the Roman influence at least to the beginning of the seventh century. . . . The emergence of the Rumanian people is closely related to the development of the Rumanian language. For this reason, the evolution of the Rumanian language corresponds closely to the development of the Rumanian people. Thus, the period between the first and fourth centuries is from a linguistic perspective characterized by the Daco-Roman Latin phase and corresponds to the blending of the Dacian and Roman peoples, while the seventh to tenth centuries witness the close existence of Slavic and Daco-Roman peoples which produced the Rumanian language and the Rumanian people.[29]

The myth is mirrored in all aspects of cultural life, not just in historical studies and the contents of school curriculum and textbooks. Elements of the myth find their way into the everyday existence of the people via the channels of popular education. As recently as the summer of 1976, visitors noted that museums with a historical character, without exception, had a large area set aside to prove the Daco-Roman theory. At the same time, the past of the minorities, particularly the Hungarians, is now presented in Rumanianized fashion with all the key heroes receiving Rumanian names (e.g., Iancu de Hunedoara for János Hunyadi, Gheorghe Doja for György Dózsa, etc.) The film industry also follows suit. Three of the most advertized and popularized films have been "Decebalus," "The Dacians," and "The Column," all dealing with the Dacian past.[30]

In the historical interpretation of events and the role of individuals, top priority is also given to those that have in any way contributed to the "reestablishment" of the Daco-Roman "state-system" or "country." In this way, great importance is attached to every voivode of Moldavia or Wallachia who contributed to the struggles against Turkish, Habsburg, Hungarian, or Polish control of their destinies. The role of Mihai Viteazul is considered particularly significant. He is presented as the first successful reunifier of the "Rumanian countries" (Moldavia, Wallachia, Transylvania) in the course of the chaotic power vacuum of 1599–1600.[31] From this point onward, each event is evaluated by Rumanian historians in terms of its contribution to the instinctive struggle of their people against oppression and for the independence of a reestablished Daco-Roman state. Thus, the peasant rising of Horea, Cloşca, and Crişan in 1784, the activities of Bishop Şaguna and of Avram Iancu in 1848–49, the "mass meeting" at Blaj (Balázsfalva), all the way to the events of 1918–20, are all considered to be links in a chain of events that re-create the Daco-Roman state.[32] In fact, these historians claim that the realization of this ideal is only now reaching full fruition under the leadership of Nicolae Ceauşescu within the context of the Rumanian Socialist Republic.

The leaders of the Rumanian Communist party and the Rumanian government consistently and consciously propagate and utilize the Daco-Roman legacy. Under Ceauşescu's leadership, the myth-making process has even been accelerated.[33] While between the two world wars it was popular to give Roman names like Victor, Trajan, or Ovid to children, so at present Dacian names are being popularized. This change is also apparent in the displacement of old monuments and the erection of new ones. The monuments or artifacts that remind people of the Hungarian and Saxon past are all but eliminated. At the same time, the Romulus and Remus statues, so popular in the interwar years, are now being eclipsed in popularity by the statues of the Dacian heroes Decebalus and Burebista.[34] Street names and even city names are being "re-Dacianized." Thus, Turnu-Severin is now called Drobeta and Cluj (Kolozsvár) has been renamed Cluj-Napoca.[35]

With Ceauşescu this process of myth-making occupies such a central position that the names of Burebista and Decebalus even made their way into the Rumanian Communist party program of 1974.[36] Even more significant was Ceauşescu's pronouncement on cultural and political education at the June, 1976, Congress deliberating issues relative to education and national consciousness. Both at this meeting and at the October, 1976, meeting of the cadres involved with political and social education, he revealed his impatience concerning the shortcomings and delays encountered in the propagation of the state's myth-system. According to Ceauşescu, the origins and development of the Rumanian people is not dealt with enough or treated adequately in existing educational programs.[37] The general secretary of the Rumanian Communist party felt that the historians had an obligation to demonstrate the importance of the Thracian-Dacian civilization on the "nomadic peoples" and "immigrant peoples", i.e., Hungarians, Saxon-

Germans, and other non-Rumanians, who settled "here" later. He contended it to be a well-known fact that these peoples did not bring with them a developed civilization, but, on the contrary, adopted the civilization existing "here," thereby to enable them to reach a higher level themselves. A realistic understanding of history demonstrates, Ceaușescu continued, that the nationalities' cultural debt to the Thracian-Dacian civilization strengthens and links more closely the "coinhabiting nationalities" to the destiny of the Rumanian people.[38] To phrase it another way, the use of the past in this fashion will contribute to the "homogenization" of contemporary Rumanian society, i.e., the absorption of the minority nationalities.

Ceaușescu's pronouncements reveal not only the close link between political objectives and the role of history in Rumania, but also that the state's myth system, or at least some of its elements, are given different prominence depending on circumstances. As was already pointed out, the myth-system's original formulation emphasized the role of the Romans in the Rumanian ethnogenesis. After World War I, historians began to write more about a Dacian-Roman synthesis. In the new "Socialist" Rumania, on the other hand, the Dacians receive more and more attention. And now, at the behest of Ceaușescu, the Thracian-Dacian-Roman synthesis receives ever increasing consideration. In addition to ideological factors, these alterations in the development of the myth-system are probably due to the inability of historians and archaeologists to prove the myth's contentions. Therefore, it is constantly necessary to amend the myth-system and to provide it with new life as it begins to grow stale, via new theoretical assumptions. It is difficult to find something new to say about the Dacians that would reinforce the myth, so it is now important to expand the Rumanian connection to all the Thracian tribes. The data supportive of the myth-system must be gathered with all due haste since Ceaușescu is feverishly preparing Rumania for the celebration of the foundation of the Dacian state's 2050th year anniversary.[39]

Besides Cluj-Napoca (Kolozsvár) and Turnu-Severin, other cities have also held renaming and myth-generating mass meetings and celebrations. Not very long ago Ceaușescu was present in Satu Mare (Szatmárnémeti) and Alba Iulia (Gyulafehérvár) to celebrate the alleged 2000th anniversary of their existence.[40] The myth is present in reference to every other phase of existence as well. From problems of industrialization to military preparedness, the party and government leaders are not wont to exercise restraint in reference to the examples set by the heroic Dacian forefathers. Almost every larger city has a hotel named "Dacia" to serve the tourist trade. The automobile manufactured in Rumania is also called "Dacia." Whenever party leaders discuss agriculture, they inevitably make references to the flowering of agriculture in "Dacia Felix" (Happy Dacia). Whenever military training and preparedness are discussed, talk about the struggles and wars of Decebalus and Burebista is also inevitable.[41]

What are the consequences of the Daco-Roman myth-system for the existence of Rumania's minority nationalities? The official designation for the Hungarians and the other nationalities is "coinhabiting nationalities." On this basis: "The coinhabiting nationalities—organically part of the unified Socialist people—associate themselves with the aspirations and destiny of the Rumanian people forever, and take part in a creative manner in the Socialist construction of Rumania."[42]

By associating themselves "forever" with the destiny of the majority, the Hungarians are assured a second-rate citizenship status, at least within the context of the Daco-Roman myth system. Both the Hungarians and the Saxon-Germans are labeled "latecomers" and are considered "colonists" who have been settled in the land later than the Rumanians. Furthermore, they are considered to be the instruments of exploitation of previous regimes. They have even been excluded from Socialist Rumania's major mythicized event, the switch of sides on August 23, 1944. This event, establishing the new Rumania, pitted the Rumanians against both the Hungarians and the Germans. Thus, contemporary Rumania came into being through a struggle against Germans and Hungarians, rather than on the basis of joint struggle with them. The myth, at any rate, labels them as the fascist forces that had to be overcome. With this interpretation, the "coinhabiting nationalities" are effectively excluded from the recent past as well. Being deprived of any role in the myths defining Rumania's past and present, the minorities receive protection against the abuses of nationalism only in the context of Communist ideological commitments and certain domestic and international political alignments.

The existing ideological and political restraints do not guarantee, however, that the rights of the minorities will be defended "forever" in perpetuity. The official myth of Rumanian self-definition implies instead that the Hungarian and other minorities are only temporarily tolerated. Under Ceauşescu's leadership, the Rumanian self-definition is closely linked to two other conceptions: first, to a unitary and centralized state and government order and, second, to a society that is undergoing a process of "homogenization." Within these parameters, minorities cannot have a history of their own, nor can they have developmental opportunities that are uniquely tailored to their own needs. At the same time, they are excluded from the Rumanian national myth-system until they abandon their own minority consciousness and become "homogenized" with the majority. If they melt down, blend in, and become absorbed in the majority, then of course they too can become part of the Daco-Roman self-definition of present-day Rumania.

In spite of the pressures, the latter development is not likely to take place, since the Hungarians are a large minority and possess a rich and hardy culture of their own. Rumanian pressure to "homogenize" the minorities seems to have the opposite effect and makes the Hungarians even more conscious of their Hungarianness. The monopoly enjoyed by the Daco-Roman myth-system does not really contribute to the assimilation of the minorities. On the contrary, the childish simplicity of the myth-system and its aggressive propagation have only led to the alienation of many Hungarians from their Rumanian "coinhabitants."

In the long-run, this polarization of Transylvania's peoples can serve only the interests of those major powers that want to dominate Eastern Europe. It perpetuates the divisions of Eastern European peoples and thereby fosters the likelihood that outsiders will continue to play the old game of divide and conquer. The Daco-Roman myth is tailored to the nation-state system; as such, it tends to encourage divisions, since it has an exclusive trait that provides only the Rumanian *Staatsvolk* with a historical role. It is tragic that the leaders of contemporary Rumania do not realize that this scheme of reference can only feed the illusions of the past and the interests of the interventionist powers of the present.

Inadvertently, the Daco-Roman myth-system may be providing concerned and thinking people in Eastern Europe with an opportunity to rethink the consequences and ramifications of the Ceauşescu-sponsored new chauvinism. Its patently primitive formulation and destructive repercussions may help to discredit the remnants of the nation-state as a means to govern multiethnic societies. It may contribute to the demise of the very state it has tried to rationalize. Instead of an exclusivist Rumania, the bankruptcy of exclusivist myths may very well convince Rumanians as well as Hungarians, Saxon-Germans, and others that Eastern Europe needs a supraethnic, tolerant, and pluralistic myth-system that legitimizes a new multinational and federalistic state-system based on the appreciation of both diversity and uniqueness.

NOTES

1. Zoltán I. Tóth, *Magyarok és románok: Történelmi tanulmányok* [Hungarians and Rumanians: Historical Studies] (Budapest: Akadémiai Kiadó, 1966), p. 61. Quote in text translated by author.

2. For some historians' challenges of the Daco-Roman theory see László Makkai, "Egy kis szakmai ördögűzés," [A Minor Professional Exorcism] *Történelmi Szemle* [Historical Review] 985 (1975): 751–54, and Gyula Kristó, "Rómaiak és vlachok Nyesztornál és Anonymusnál," [Romans and Vlachs in Nyestor and Anonymous] *Századok* [Centuries] 112, no. 4 (1978): 623–58.

3. Péter Szabó Szentmihályi, "Az irodalom negyedik dimenziója," [The Fourth Dimension of Literature"] *Valóság* [Reality] 19, no. 8 (1976): 94, contends: "Belief in myths and the creation of new myths appears to be a basic and ancient human trait, and while this need is probably in an inverse relationship to the growth of civilization, the scientific-technological revolution of our century, the nuclear threat, environmental pollution and the dependence on machines can be made manageable and understandable to the masses only in a simplified, even 'naive' way. Science has overcome myth, and in the place of 'naive' myths, it has established newer, not any less naive scientific myths." Quote in footnote translated by author.

4. The definition of "myth" used in the present study is based on a previous attempt to define the concept. See "Jugoslávia válsága és Közép-Európa jövője," [The Future of Central Europe and the Crisis in Yugoslavia] *A XII. Magyar Találkozó Krónikája* [The Chronicle of the 12th Hungarian Assembly] (Cleveland: Árpád Könyvkiadó, 1973), pp. 72–74.

5. Within the context of this study, "myth" refers to the general phenomenon while "myth-system" refers to the specific set of mythical categories and symbols that have been elaborated for the national self-definition of the present-day Rumanian state.

6. Elemér Illyés, "Román történetírás," [Rumanian Historiography] *Transylvania* 17, no. 3 (1976): 6.

7. Ibid., pp. 6–7.

8. Elemér Illyés, *Erdély változása: Mitosz és valóság* [Transylvanian Metamorphosis: Myth and Reality], 2d ed. (Munich: Aurora, 1976), pp. 354–89. Illyés points out that the Transylvanian School (Şcoală Ardeleana) was preceded by certain humanists who also speculated about the Roman relationships. An outstanding example is Nicolaus Olahus (1493–1568).

9. Emil Niederhauser, *Nemzetek születése Kelet-Európában* [The Birth of Nations in Eastern Europe] (Budapest: Kossuth Kiadó, 1976), pp. 199–200. Quote in text translated by author.

10. D. Prodan, *Supplex Libellus Valachorum: The Political Struggle of the Romanians in Transylvania During the 18th Century,* Bibliotheca Historica Romaniae Monographs 8 (Bucharest: Academy of the Socialist Republic of Romania, 1971), pp. 10–12.

11. Constantin C. Giurescu and Dinu C. Giurescu, *Istoria Românilor I: Din Cele Mai Vechi Timpuri Pina la Intemfierea Statelor Românesti* [History of Rumania I: From the Earliest Times to the Earliest Rumanian State Systems] (Bucharest: Editura Ştiinţifică Enciclopedica, 1975), pp. 72–203.

12. For the shortcomings of the theory see Illyés, *Erdély változása,* pp. 360–64.

13. Ibid., 375–76.

14. An excellent example is the following selection from his portrayal of Hunedoara (Hunyad) county. It is, if anything, a fantastic reconstruction and a vision rather than an effort to present the past objectively. Consider the following excerpt: "Yet it is the Dacians who won, the onetime lords of this land who have prevailed in spite of the chains and the bloodletting imposed on them by their foes. Their invincible courage and patient perseverance triumphed in the end. Look around you now, here are the true Dacians, the new Dacians of 2,000 years past, who carry with them as a sign of their triumph the language of a Rome long consigned to dust. The peasants here are indeed

Dacians, with their tough and reserved features, their tight-lipped and ancient custom of paying everyone their due with a sense of justice and not the vengeful 'an eye for an eye and a tooth for a tooth'." This literary reconstruction of the past is characteristic of his other works as well. See Nicolai Iorga, *Válogatott írások* [Selected Writings] (Bucharest: Kriterion, 1971), pp. 167–69. Quote in footnote translated by author.

15. Excellent examples of this impact are Richard Todd's review of Adolf Armbruster's *La Romanité des Roumains: Histoire d'une Ideé* in the *Slavic Review* 38, no. 1 (March, 1979): 150, and Paul MacKendrick, *The Dacian Stones Speak* (Chapel Hill: The University of North Carolina Press, 1975).

16. Michael J. Rura, *Reinterpretation of History as a Method of Furthering Communism in Rumania* (Washington, D.C.: Georgetown University Press, 1961), pp. 1–2, 8–9, 17–22.

17. Lajos Jordáky, *Szocializmus és történettudomány: Tanulmányok* [Socialism and Historiography: Studies] (Bucharest: Politikai Kiadó, 1974), pp. 167–68, 178–79.

18. Ştefan Pascu, et al., *Kolozsvár,* trans. József Debreczeni (Cluj-Kolozsvár: Kolozsvár Nyomdaipari Vállalat, 1957).

19. For example, Giurescu and Giurescu, op. cit.; Ştefan Pascu, *Voievodatul Transilvaniei* [The Transylvanian Principality] (Cluj: Editura Dacia, 1972); Ştefan Pascu, ed., *Istoria Clujului* [The History of Cluj] (Cluj: Consiliul Popular al Municipiului, 1974); and in English, Constantin C. Giurescu, *The Making of the Romanian People and Language* (Bucharest: Meridiane, 1972).

20. Gheorghe Ştefan, *Mozzanatok a román nép történetéből* [Events in the History of the Rumanian People] (Bucharest: Politikai Kiadó, 1967), p. 4

21. Ilie Ceauşescu, "Transylvania from the Dacians to 1918: Two Millenia of Struggle and Work to Maintain and Affirm National Being and Dignity" *Anale de Istorie* [Annals of History] 6 (Nov.-Dec., 1978) as translated in JPRS (Joint Publications Research Service) (Washington, D.C.) no. 073103, International Affairs, p. 3.

22. Makkai, op. cit., p. 752.

23. A concrete example of this is Andrei Oţetea, ed., *The History of the Romanian People* (originally *Istoria Poporului Român,* 1970), trans. Eugenia Farca (New York: Twayne Publishers, 1972). It spends 159 pages on the formation (Daco-Roman phase) of the Rumanian people, c. 150 pages on the "medieval period" (c. 800 years) and c. 300 pages on the period from 1821 to the present. Also see Constantin C. Giurescu, ed., *Chronological History of Romania* (Bucharest: Editura Enciclopedica Română, 1972), which devotes pp. 11–20 to the "Pre-Historic Age," pp. 21–46 (100 B.C.–A.D. 900) to the "Ancient Epoch," pp. 47–153 (A.D. 900–1821), 154–269 (1821–1918) to the "Modern Epoch," and pp. 270–406 (1919–71) to the "Contemporary Epoch."

24. For a popular archeological survey of all these ancient peoples see particularly Gyula László, *Emlékezzünk régiekről: A Kárpát-Medence egykori népeinek története és a magyar honfoglalás* [History of the Former Peoples of the Carpathian Basin and the Hungarian Conquest] (Budapest: Móra Ferenc könyvkiadó, 1979).

25. Good examples of this "Rumanianization" can be found in Razvan Theodorescu, "Old Romanian Art in European Museums," *Rumanian Review,* 30, no. 1 (1976): 87–90.

26. Ceauşescu, op. cit., p. 4.

27. Ibid., p. 5.

28. Ibid., p. 6.

29. Ştefan, op. cit., pp. 10–13. Quote in text translated by author.

30. "A New Romanian Film: The Column," *Documents, Articles and Information on Romania,* 22–23 (Dec. 5, 1968): 19; Manuela Gheorghiu, "Birth and Evolution of a

Film Epic," *Romanian Review* 31, no. 2 (1977): 92–93.

31. St. Ştefanescu, "Michael the Brave—The First Ruler of All Romanians," *Romanian Bulletin,* June, 1975, p. 4.

32. Illyés, *Erdély változása,* pp. 374–77, 388–93. Some Rumanian examples are Ceauşescu, op. cit., pp. 11–23; Constantin Daicoviciu, et al., *Romania: Geography, History, Economy, Culture* (Bucharest: Meridiane Publishing House, 1966), pp. 15–35; L. Bányai, *Pe Făgaşul Tradiţiilor Fratesti* [Continuity of Traditional Fraternal Struggles] (Bucharest: Institutul de Studii Istorice se Social-Politice, 1971), pp. 22–117; Vasile Netea, *The Union of Transylvania with Romania* (Bucharest: Meridiane Publishing House, 1968), pp. 4–13.

33. Donald Catchlove, *Romania's Ceausescu* (London: Abacus Press, 1972), pp. 23–37.

34. See for example the new (1976) equestrian statue of Decebalus by Ion Jalea at Deva. "Ion Jalea: Sculptor," *Romanian Review,* 31, no. 4 (1977): 56.

35. George Cioranescu, "The Political Signifiance of the Thracians," *Radio Free Europe Research RAD Background Report* no. 218 (Oct. 22, 1976), p. 6.

36. Ibid., p. 1.

37. Ibid., pp. 1–2.

38. Ibid., p. 2.

39. Ibid., pp. 1, 7.

40. Ion Ionescu, "Alba Iulia: A Two Millenium Old Town," *Romanian Bulletin* June, 1975, p. 3. Even more recently, Nicolae Ceauşescu visited Arad to celebrate the 2000th anniversary of the establishment of the Dacian city of "Zirdava." See "Lelkesítő találkozások," [Inspirational Meetings] *A Hét* [The Week] (Bucharest), Mar. 30, 1979, pp. 1, 3.

41. Stan Newens, ed., *Nicolae Ceausescu* (Nottingham: Spokesman Books, 1972), p. 94.

42. Ecaterina Deliman, *A román dolgozók és az együttlakó nemzetiségekhez tartozó dolgozók testvéri barátsága* [The Fraternal Friendship of the Rumanian Workers and the Workers of the Coinhabiting Nationalities] (Bucharest: Politikai Kiadó, 1973), p. 21. Quote in text translated by author.

Education and National Minorities in Contemporary Rumania

ELEMÉR ILLYÉS

Historical Development

The existence of educational institutions teaching in the national minority languages, in accordance with the minorities' numerical strength, geographical location, and levels of cultural development, has been indispensable to the survival and development of the national minorities. In the long run, education only in the language of a national majority has meant the absorption of national minorities, but documentation of this rate of assimilation has had to rely heavily on numerical comparison. At the same time, statistical data often have not provided an accurate picture of the level, quality, and content of education for minorities in their mother tongue, and the figures frequently have served propagandistic objectives.

Consequently, an awareness of the historical background and the motives of a nation's cultural policy has to precede the analysis of statistical figures. If, for example, a minority language has barred one from occupations requiring a higher level of education, then national minorities have been compelled to send their children to majority-language schools. This in turn has led the state organs to the conclusion that there has been no demand for minority education in the mother tongue. Or if, for example, the schools teaching in minority languages have not for any reason competed with the majority schools in the quality of education they have provided, parents will have to send their children to those schools that offer better prospects. Furthermore, in many instances institutions termed nationality schools have been such in name only, with instruction carried out only partly or not at all in the minority language.

In light of the above considerations, when studying the educational position of the national minorities, two aspects of the question have to be kept in the forefront: first, educational policy as it has affected the national minorities and, second, as it has related to the framework of the country's entire educational system. On the basis of the former, the laws, which have guaranteed teaching in the mother tongue of the national minorities, have to be analyzed to see how far the educational institutions actually have contributed to the maintenance of national equality and to what extent these institutions really have served "national minority" existence. This analysis must include examination of such conditions of educational activity as the levels of instruction in the mother tongue, the character and content of textbooks and syllabi, particularly regarding the teaching of literature and history, the training and composition of the teaching staff, and the other assorted ways and conditions that circumscribe the transmission of the cultural inheritance of national minorities.

Before discussing the education of the national minorities in Rumania and the Rumanian educational system at present, it is necessary to provide a brief outline of the historical developments in this sphere. The beginnings of the independent Transylvanian Saxon and Hungarian school networks go back to the fourteenth–sixteenth centuries, and the scholastic traditions of the Transylvanian nationalities have been inseparable from the historic role of the nationality churches. The first Transylvanian Saxon and Hungarian schools, in the Middle Ages, were ecclesiastical institutions functioning along with monastic communities or at the seats of bishoprics. The Saxon Lutheran and the Hungarian Catholic, Calvinist, and Unitarian churches had the oldest ecclesiastical schools in Transylvania. On the other hand, the educational history of the Rumanian Uniate and Orthodox churches began later with less developed institutions.[1]

Ecclesiastical education for the national minorities in Transylvania acquired an additional significance after the first and second world wars in providing continuity in the education of the national minorities in their own language. The survival of the Hungarian and Saxon schools and the necessary intellectual leadership between the two world wars were secured by the churches.

Education for the National Minorities between the Two World Wars

The social structure of the Hungarians and Germans of Transylvania at the time of Transylvania's annexation by Rumania differed significantly from the social composition of the Rumanian Regat (Old Kingdom). At the conclusion of World War I, the nationalities in Transylvania had already developed a modern bourgeois social stratum. The bourgeois transformation and economic-intellectual growth were particularly noticeable in the German and Hungarian cities of Transylvania, which also contained a third urban element, the Jews, who contributed significantly to intellectual and economic development as well. At the same time their different historical development enabled the Hungarian, German, and Jewish populations of Transylvania to attain a relatively higher economic and cultural level than the Rumanian population of either Transylvania or of pre-World War I Rumania.[2]

Between the two world wars, the nationalities in Rumania waged a hard struggle for the survival of their centuries-old educational institutions. In the three periods between 1919–25, 1925–34, and 1934–40, the tactics in the educational struggles showed marked differences. As successive governments followed one another, the status of the various schools was affected differently. Perhaps Rumania's Peasant party exhibited somewhat more patience than the Liberal party; however, all the political parties that attained power during these years could be described as antiminority.

New laws and decrees were enacted in the sphere of education practically every academic year, with the result that within a short space of time the number of the Hungarian schools was reduced by sixty-two–ninety-three percent, depending on the type of school involved. The Rumanian state abolished more than half of the Hungarian-language schools between 1919 and 1924; it also abolished the Hungarian university in Cluj (Kolozsvár).

The Position of National-Minority Education after 1945

Between the two world wars, the oppression of the national minorities involved a more or less open struggle. The nationalities had their defenders and also, even if only to a limited extent, the means to defend themselves. They were supported in this not only by their political, social, and cultural organizations, but by the school network as well.

After the Second World War, the national-minority ecclesiastical schools were nationalized by the Decree of August 3, 1948; thus the protection offered by the churches was eliminated. The Decree also removed the possibilities for defending nationality cultures and languages through nonstate institutions. With the introduction of state monopoly over education, the educational system has not been a means for minority protection but for repression and denationalization.[3]

The Rumanian national-minority educational system attained its present character through complex and complicated changes, which were adopted in the legal framework after the Second World War. These changes appeared to make concessions, while in reality they brought restrictions and a state of permanent uncertainty. However, the negative repercussions were not apparent immediately in the post-war period, because the official educational policy did not aim, in the beginning, at the forced leveling of the more-developed Transylvanian educational system to the status of that of the less-developed Regat. Furthermore, educational development of the national minorities in Transylvania was not yet curbed to favor the Rumanian population.

After the Second World War, the first Rumanian regulation affecting the education of the national minorities was the Nationality Statute of February 6, 1945.[4] This, however, only represented a temporary stage. It was superceded by the Decree of March 15, 1946, of the Groza government, which partially secured the continued functioning of the still existing Hungarian school network and facilitated the foundation of more schools, colleges, and cultural institutions. At this time the Catholic church still represented a considerable force.

Within the sphere of educational policy, the 1946–47 academic year was characterized by two factors, which were seemingly contradictory but in reality organically complemented each other. Rumanian administrative organs at the national level were compelled for reasons of external and internal politics to make concessions in favor of the Hungarians, while at the lower and local levels they allowed nationalist manifestations against the minorities.

An old demand of the Hungarians of Rumania was realized when in 1945 the government issued a decree concerning the establishment of a Hungarian-language state university possessing the faculties of arts, law, economics, and natural sciences, which was the Hungarian Bolyai University of Cluj. At this time there were several other higher education institutions teaching in Hungarian. This period created the foundations for a school network teaching in the mother tongue, in accordance with the proportion of the numbers of Hungarians in Rumania. It also seemed to begin the process of providing equal opportunities for the nationalities within the sphere of education.

National Minority Education in the Rumanian People's Republic

The first Constitution of the people's democracy, enacted on April 13, 1948, and the August 3, 1948, decree[5] on educational reform, whose principles have remained the foundations for the present Rumanian educational system, brought about a radical change of direction in the educational system of Rumania. The latter is the concern of the remainder of this study, which has focused on the history of national-minority education from August 3, 1948, to the present. The frequent and contradictory changes in nationality policy and the misleading nature of the available official statistics has posed significant difficulties in the analysis of this topic. The official use of statistical data for propaganda purposes by the Rumanian state has also posed some problems.

Article 24 of the first People's Democratic Constitution, published on April 13, 1948, has guaranteed the "free use of the mother tongue for all the 'coinhabiting nationalities,' as well as the organization of education in their mother tongue." The law on educational reform enacted on August 3, 1948, did not bring about a genuine reform and deviated from democratic commitments. As was the Constitution, the law also was based on the Soviet model; it introduced the ideological foundations of the educational system of the future and prescribed the nationalization of all the ecclesiastical and private schools as well as the expropriation of the landed and other properties of the churches and of the religious and private organizations that served the maintenance of the earlier educational institutions (Article 35). This measure destroyed the link between the churches and the school systems, which had played such a great part in the education of national minorities in Rumania. This law created an absolute state monopoly in the sphere of education.

Following the 1948 educational reform, class considerations gained priority, and the workers and peasantry were given privileged treatment regarding educational opportunities. But the real purpose of the law was the introduction of Marxist ideology in the new school system and the development of a new intellectual elite (i.e., teachers) acquainted with Marxist-Leninist ideas. The objective was also to exclude the influence of the churches, which were the protectors of the nationality ecclesiastical schools. They endeavoured to achieve this by removing a large proportion of teachers in church-related schools, and by the ideological reeducation of the teaching staff left at their posts. Simultaneously, new syllabi replaced the old ones. The decree also guaranteed the education of the nationalities in their mother tongues from the primary to the university level. However, the 1948 educational reform had two other striking characteristics from the point of view of the national minorities: the introduction of the teaching of Rumanian in all educational establishments, including the Hungarian university, and the radical reinterpretation and rewriting of the history syllabus. The negative Hungarian reaction in Transylvania led Party leadership to claim that these measures served the cause of "Hungarian-Rumanian fraternity." After 1948, in effect, only the language of instruction remained in the national-minority educational system, since the entire educational system was redirected to serve the realization of "proletarian internationalism." At the same time, in the course of nationalization, a large number of national-minority institutions were converted into Rumanian institutions.[6]

Almost parallel with these directives, other kinds of nationality institutions were simply abolished. The regime used this period of reshaping and reorganization to carry out changes and purges among the teaching staff and the students.

The year 1948 brought additional and significant changes in Rumanian nationality policy. From this year onward, the national minorities have been subjected to serious infringements in many spheres of life. Several of the measures, which have limited national equality, were particularly adverse for education. According to statistical data, education in the major nationality languages has been increasing, but the number of independent national-minority schools has been constantly decreasing. In fact, this process had already begun in the early 1950s, as illustrated in the following table:[7]

	Academic Year			
	1948–49	*1951–52*	*1957–58*	*1958–59*
Total number of schools with national-minority education	2,289	2,515	2,514	2,534
Of the above, number of majority schools with "sections" for minority education	111	189	457	475
Independent national-minority schools	2,178	2,326	2,057	2,059

In 1956, the Hungarian Revolution contributed greatly to the reorganization of higher education in Rumania. Higher education was put under more rigid control. The July 26, 1957, reform of higher education confirmed the intentions of Bucharest: the ideological reeducation of the future entrants into the ranks of the new intellectual elite.[8]

At the end of the 1950s, the nationalistic atmosphere became even more manifest. The ideology, which claimed that the nationality question had been solved, called for an ideological struggle against "national isolation" in 1959. The merging of the national-minority schools and Rumanian schools, their "parallelization" at the end of 1959, indicated the roundabout way in which the Rumanian authorities endeavoured to nullify equal rights for the national minorities in education. The hidden purpose of the so-called parallelization, or unification (*un-*

ificarea), was the abolition of independent national-minority schools and the acceleration of a general Rumanianization.

"Parallelization" has meant that, parallel with the nationality-classes, Rumanian-language classes have been established even in those areas where there were only very few Rumanian pupils. In schools possessing Hungarian instruction, a request by three Rumanian pupils has been enough to start a Rumanian-language section. The purpose of establishing the parallel classes, the so-called *secţie* (sections), has been to persuade with carefully chosen methods the pupils belonging to the national minorities to enter the Rumanian-language sections. The result of this policy has been that, lacking a suitable number of pupils belonging to the minority nationalities, their schools have been abolished one after another.[9]

Unification, or parallelization, began with the merger of the independent Hungarian Bolyai University of Cluj with the Rumanian Babeş University (1959), under the name of Babeş-Bolyai University.[10] Just as in the Bolyai University, instruction in Hungarian has been gradually phased out in the other Hungarian-language institutions of higher education as well. The Institute of Medicine and Pharmacology, which in the beginning had had an exclusively Hungarian character, was moved from Cluj to Tîrgu Mureş (Marosvásárhely) and transformed from 1962 onward into an institution with a majority of Rumanian students, drawn from the Regat. Only a reduced portion of the Hungarian teaching staff has remained at their posts.[11] Instruction in Hungarian has been maintained only in the College of Dramatic Art of Tîrgu Mureş, which has a special character and by its nature has catered only to a few students, and at the ecclesiastical institutions of higher education. The training of teachers for the general schools has been provided in the minority languages, in the form of a section, at the Teacher Training College of Tîrgu Mureş.

There has been little available data concerning the number of college students belonging to the national minorities during the 1950s. In the 1957–58 academic year, the number of Hungarian students enrolled in the Hungarian-language institutions of higher education was 4,082, with an estimated 1,000–1,500 students in technical training or attending Rumanian universities. This makes a total of 5,500, 10.75 percent of all Hungarian students, as compared with 51,094 students enrolled in full-time higher education in the whole country.[12]

After the absorption of the Bolyai University, the process of eliminating teaching in national-minority languages—particularly in Hungarian—was accelerated.[13] The method, which has remained to this day as the means for denationalization, has been the same as that employed in the case of the universities:[14] combining the Rumanian and the national-minority schools into a single school with nationality sections. This has made it possible at a later date to reduce the number of the nationality sections.

Another method generally employed has been to persuade parents to send their children to Rumanian classes. Since instruction in the languages of the nationalities has been almost completely eliminated from two highly important areas, higher education and vocational education, parents have been more easily persuaded. Among the methods used to convince them has been pressure exerted within the Party and also in various offices and at the workplace. On top of this, administrative barriers serving the same aim were employed. All this was justified by the argument that insistence on teaching in the mother tongue is a form of nationalism.

As a result of the educational policy of mergers, all technical education in the minority languages has been abolished, even in the apprentice schools. Finally, in the wake of the reorganization of the general or elementary schools, the number of schools teaching in the languages of the national minorities has been reduced by half.[15]

The unification process, or parallelization, of the schools meant in practice that in the vast majority of cases the educational institutions were given Rumanian directors, the language of staff conferences became exclusively Rumanian, and from this time onward school ceremonies were conducted in Rumanian. These measures have been intended to hinder the education of intellectual leadership belonging to the national minorities and to limit the number of skilled workers and foremen from the ranks of the minorities.

After 1960, from the time when uniformization of the schools had been completed, the Rumanian statistical yearbooks discontinued publishing data regarding the education of the national minorities. Since then, educational data relative to minorities has been more and more difficult to obtain.

According to the 1966 census, in relation to the total population the proportion of the Rumanians in general schools (seventh–eighth primary grades) was 84.11 percent, of the Hungarians 11.61 percent, of the Germans 2.80 percent, of the Jews 0.30 percent, and of the Gypsies 0.06 percent. In secondary technical and special schools, there were 86.75 percent Rumanians, 9.88 percent Hungarians, 3.29 percent Germans, and 0.66 percent Jews. In secondary academic schools, 86.58 percent were Rumanians, 8.94 percent Hungarians, 2.15 percent Germans, and 1.25 percent Jews. In institutions of higher education, 88.72 percent were Rumanians, 6.10 percent Hungarians, 1.83 percent Germans, and 2.13 percent Jews.[16] Thus, the two largest nationalities, Hungarians and Germans, were relatively better represented in the primary and intermediary levels, but underrepresented in secondary academic schools and higher educational institutions. The Jewish minority has been better represented in secondary academic schools and institutions of higher education, while Rumanians have a distinct overrepresentation at all levels of the educational system.

The Present System of National Minority Education

Besides the ideological (Marxist-Leninist) factors, the dominant characteristic of education in Rumania has been the stress on the "national," which has been manifested primarily in the disproportionate emphasis on Rumanian national history, as well as Rumanian language and literature. The question of national-minority education has to be approached with an awareness of these two considerations as well as of the internal and external political factors that shape nationality policy.

The 1965 Constitution of the Rumanian Socialist Republic referred in several places to the equal rights possessed by the nationalities. Section II, Article 22, dealing with the fundamental rights of citizens, guaranteed the free use of the mother tongue in education. According to the text of the Constitution, "education for the nationalities is in their own languages at all levels." The Education Act of May 13, 1968, also stipulated, in accordance with the guaranteed rights of the Constitution: "Education at all levels for the coinhabiting nationalities is in their own languages." The measures connected with this have been regulated in the spirit of the Constitution by Education Act No. 11/1968 and by Decree No. 6/1969, relating to the status of the teaching staff. The former states that education for the "coinhabiting nationalities" has to be in their own languages at every level (Article 9, Paragraph 2). School textbooks have to be written for instruction in the languages of the "coinhabiting nationalities" in the languages concerned (Article 45, Paragraph 3). The former stipulated that in those schools and sections where teaching is to be in the languages of the coinhabiting nationalities the teaching and auxiliary staff have to be selected from among those who are familiar with the language in question (Paragraph 9). In these schools or sections, principals or assistant principals have to be selected from the nationality in question or from among those who speak the language of that nationality (Article 40, Paragraph 2). In those counties with schools in which teaching is to be carried out in the languages of the coinhabiting nationalities, the staff of the directing and controlling organs is to be appointed from among the members of these nationalities (Article 46, Paragraph 4).[17]

However, the rights contained in the Constitution have not been put into practice. This was due in part to the lack of clarity in the formulation of the text of the Constitution and in part to the failure to realize the rights enshrined in the text. In guaranteeing the free use of the minority languages in education, the constitutional text spoke of education "at all levels" and not "of all types." This did not exclude the possibility of there being schools within secondary education, such as the secondary specialized technical schools, where education was exclusively in Rumanian. Further, the Constitution does not guarantee schools based on the mother tongue but only "teaching in the mother tongue."

National-minority education has not been stabilized nor normalized since the 1968 events in Czechoslovakia. After this crisis, a policy of delay as well as a degree of relaxation developed, partly as a result of internal pressure by the nationalities and partly in response to external pressures caused by the Soviet intervention. Certain concessions were made that, although only of secondary significance and not an alteration of the fundamental political line, were nonetheless sufficient to reassure the national minorities and to raise hopes abroad. Once the danger of Soviet invasion was over, as far as Rumania was concerned, the system of national discrimination and cultural suffocation was reasserted. The temporary gains made by the network of minority schools during the crisis where thereby allowed to atrophy.[18] In fact, newly developed policies took a form that far surpassed in severity the conditions between the two world wars. The aim was to restrict the nationalities merely to the right to use the mother tongue, without allowing any nationality content whatever. This goal has received an official formulation in the designation "Rumanian writers writing in Hungarian or German." However, Rumanian nationality policy, employing the well-established pattern of concessions and relaxation alternating with deprivation, led to new concessions in 1969 and even in 1971 after the plenary session of the Council of Workers of Hungarian Nationality. In the regions inhabited by the Hungarian nationality, secondary specialized and technical schools and Hungarian-language parallel classes and vocational schools were established. However, these concessions were short-lived.

In the 1973–74 academic year, new educational laws[19] were adopted with the objective of completely eliminating instruction in the mother tongue by way of universal Rumanianization. In accordance with the new law, the secondary academic schools, which correspond to the old gymnasium or the arts and science (human and real) gymnasiums of Western Europe, were reorganized: seventy percent became secondary specialized, or technical or vocational schools, with Rumanian as the medium for instruction, and thirty percent were retained as secondary academic schools, some of them possessing nationality sections. In order to maintain classes in the national-minority sections at the elementary level—spanning the fifth to the tenth years—at least twenty-five applicants were needed, otherwise the school could provide only the first four grades and even this required at least seven applicants.[20] An exception to this limitation required the approval of the Ministry of Education. As a result of this measure, the widely scattered elements of the national-minority population or those living in smaller settlements do not have a "legal" right to instruction in their own languages. In the secondary academic and specialized or technical schools, for grade levels nine to ten, the minimum number of students required was thirty-six. By contrast, there was no minimum number stipulated for setting up classes taught in Rumanian. The law in the latter case prescribed that in those secondary and elementary schools where there were classes taught in the languages of the national minorities, Rumanian sections had to be established, independently of the number of Rumanian pupils attending the school.[21] The discriminatory character of the law was not even disguised.

It has already been noted that there exists only incomplete data concerning the education of the national minorities in Rumania for the past two decades. Furthermore, the selected statistical data that has been published by the Rumanian authorities failed to reflect the real situation. The available data on the nationality educational institutions and the comparisons that could be made based on them do not provide an accurate picture of the nationality populations' educational needs in line with their geographical distribution. Additionally, these statistics do not depict the quality of education provided in the mother tongue, the spirit underlying it, or the direction of new developments.

Official and detailed data on national-minority education in the Rumanian Socialist Republic is available from the 1966 census, as well as from various other scattered sources. According to some of these sources, during the 1966–67 academic year, there were 376 German-language schools or sections attached to Rumanian schools in the whole of Rumania, consisting of 354 general schools or sections with one to eight classes; 19 secondary schools or sections with one to twelve classes; and 3 pedagogical schools, with a total of 314 students, two of which trained teachers and one of which trained nursery-school instructors.[22] According to other sources, in the 1967–68 academic year, there were 1,944 minority-language schools and sections in all of Rumania. Of these, 1,480 were Hungarian and 386 German; the other

78 offered instruction in Serbian, Slovak, Ukrainian, and Czech.[23] In the 1969–70 academic year, 225,618 pupils attended Hungarian-language educational institutions: of these 35,177 attended kindergartens, which corresponded to 7.9 percent of all the children in kindergartens in Rumania. In the general grade schools, 168,218 pupils studied in Hungarian, which corresponded to only 6 percent of all general grade-school pupils in Rumania. Moreover, in higher-level Hungarian-language education, 21,568 students attended secondary academic schools, 665 attended teacher-training colleges, 1,425 attended secondary specialized, or technical schools, and 6,308 attended vocational schools.[24]

In the 1970–71 academic year, Hungarian was the language of instruction for 157,000 pupils in 1,337 general grade schools and for 21,106 pupils in 91 secondary academic schools; altogether for approximately 178,000 pupils. In the 1971–72 academic year, 955 Hungarian kindergartens functioned, attended by approximately 50,000 children.[25]

In the 1973–74 academic year, significant changes occurred in secondary education for the national minorities regarding the number of schools and sections. The educational institutions of the nationalities were considerably reduced in number, while in compensation the number of sections functioning within the framework of Rumanian schools increased. According to the official statistics, the number of general grade-school and secondary pupils belonging to the Hungarian nationality during this academic year was 190,000, and 2,383 Hungarian-language schools and sections functioned with 220,000 pupils. Of the kindergartens and general schools, 1,230 were still independent Hungarian schools, while 1,062 functioned as Hungarian sections within Rumanian schools. At the same time, during the 1973–74 academic year, 60,992 German pupils were enrolled in German-language schools or sections; of these, 16,130 were enrolled in kindergartens, 40,071 in general schools, and 4,791 in secondary academic schools. The total number of German-language schools was 711, including both independent schools and sections.[26]

German-language secondary technical education was expanded numerically in the 1974–75 academic year. In this academic year, there were 340 kindergartens and sections with 16,087 children, 355 general schools and sections with 41,661 pupils, and 28 secondary academic schools and sections with 4,696 pupils. The total number of German-language schools was 723, with a total of 62,444 pupils.[27]

German was the language of instruction during the 1975–76 academic year in 324 kindergartens or sections attended by 14,878 children, 338 general schools or sections with 42,043 pupils, and 30 secondary academic or technical schools or sections with 6,272 pupils. The total number of schools was 692, with 63,193 pupils.[28] In the academic year 1976–77, there were 13,748 children enrolled in 309 kindergartens and sections, 41,737 pupils in 335 general schools and sections, and 5,689 pupils in 33 secondary academic schools and sections. The total number of German-language schools and sections was 677, with 61,174 pupils.[29]

According to official figures during the 1976–77 academic year, there were only 4,666 Hungarian students in the third year of the secondary academic schools entitled to grant degrees, in contrast to the 8,300 who had completed the second year in the system during the previous academic year. Hungarian was the language of instruction in a total of 128 secondary academic schools. Out of a total of 34,738 secondary-school pupils whose mother tongue was Hungarian, 15,591 attended technical secondary schools where the specialized subjects were taught exclusively in Rumanian, because there was no Hungarian-language specialized education available for them.

In the academic year 1977–78, there were 1,393 Hungarian-language general schools and sections and 112 lycees, of which 12 were independent and 100 were sections within Rumanian schools. If these figures are compared with data for 1947, the decline in numbers is quite clear: in 1947 there were 186 Hungarian secondary schools in Rumania; in Cluj (Kolozsvár) alone there were fourteen Hungarian-language secondary academic schools in operation in 1947.[30]

These figures related to the relevant data on Rumanian education, as well as to the overall national statistics, indicate the following: In the 1948–49 academic year, 217 secondary academic schools functioned in the country, whereas in 1968–69 there were 568, to which one has to add 53 art, 415 specialized or technical schools, and a further 191 vocational schools, making a total of 1,227.[31]

According to the official statistics for the academic year 1976–77, about a third of the Hungarian pupils attended Rumanian general schools;[32] by comparison, in the academic year 1977–78, 70 percent of German pupils attended Rumanian general schools.[33] However, if the proportion of the Hungarian pupils in relation to the various counties is considered, it becomes clear that the figures in the official statistics have falsified the situation. In reality, the actual proportion of Hungarian pupils attending Rumanian schools was approximately 30–40 percent; this proportion increased by 1977–78 to 47–83 percent.[34] According to another official source, 24 percent of the Hungarian pupils went on to further studies after completing the eighth year of their general education, in comparison with the national average of 19 percent.[35] This figure was used by the official authorities to laud their program in Hungarian-language education and their nationality policy in general. However, this figure obscured the fact that a considerable proportion of Hungarian students attended Rumanian schools. Thus the purpose of this statistical datum veiled the actual state of affairs. Furthermore, the figure itself has to be regarded as a distortion since the proportion of Hungarians gaining a secondary education in Rumania was estimated at only between 7 and 8 percent.

After analyzing the statistical data of elementary and secondary education, it can be concluded that all minority nationalities in Rumania faced a constant decrease in the number of educational institutions during the 1969–79 decade. While, for example, 3,479 minority schools or sections existed in 1978, by 1980 their number was reduced to about 3,000.[36] The most drastic reduction has been felt by the Hungarians; a continuous decline was evident in the instruction of Hungarian especially in secondary education. The Germans were somewhat better represented in secondary academic schools, but they were underrepresented at the lower and higher educational levels. Almost to try to prove the contrary, in 1978 elementary schools were established for the numerically small Turkish, Polish, Czech, Bulgarian, and Greek national minorities.[37]

Regarding higher educational opportunities for the national minorities, instruction in the mother tongue has been indispensable to their development, and the Hungarian national minority of 2.5 million has to have several branches of higher education for its educational needs. The existence of Hungarian higher educational institutions would provide the necessary foundation for scientific life, for growth of the general cultural-technological participation, and for the maintenance of a viable minority intellectual leadership. For the Rumanians as a whole, the intellectuals have multiplied as compared to the period before the First World War. While during the 1937–38 academic year Rumanian universities had 26,498 students, by the 1978–79 academic year their numbers increased to 190,560.[38]

The development of higher education for the national minorities in Rumania has shown a very different and at the same time a contradictory picture: the largest nationalities, like Hungarians and Germans, were underrepresented in the higher educational levels, while smaller ethnic groups for a tactical-political reason were enjoying considerable support in this educational category.

Utilizing the favorable political conditions in 1968, Hungarian intellectuals and the Hungarian public in Transylvania did everything possible to obtain the reestablishment of the Bolyai University of Cluj

(Kolozsvár). On this point, however, the Rumanian party leadership was adamant and uncompromising, and the Hungarian university was not revived.

In the academic year 1978–79, the Rumanians had seven universities and ten technical, four agricultural, four medical, seven art, five pedagogical, and four mixed colleges with 134 faculties. There were also four theological institutes of university rank and two theological seminaries.[39]

In contrast, already by the end of the 1960s Hungarian-language higher education was reduced to a minimum in Rumania. Yet, party leader Nicolae Ceauşescu made a promise at the March 12, 1971, plenary session of the Workers of Hungarian Nationality that higher education would be expanded.[40] At the same time, the deputy rector of the Babeş-Bolyai University also emphasized that "there were setbacks, mistakes . . ." in providing higher education for the national minorities in the mother tongue.[41] However, these statements were not followed by increased Hungarian study opportunities. Instruction in the languages of the national minorities in Rumania in the academic year 1978–79 was carried out only in some sections at the following institutions of higher education: the Babeş-Bolyai University of Cluj-Napoca, the Institute of Medicine and Pharmacology at Tîrgu Mureş, and the István Szentgyörgyi Institute of Dramatic Arts at Tîrgu Mureş; lectures were given in German by the Sibiu (Nagyszeben, Hermannstadt) faculty belonging to the Babeş-Bolyai University and in German Studies at the Universities of Bucharest, Iaşi, and Timişoara (Temesvár). At the same time, despite the high number of students belonging to the national minorities, there was no instruction in their languages at the ten technical, four agricultural, five pedagogical, and four other colleges. The situation was the worst in the sphere of technical training. During the 1977–78 academic year, all the arts-oriented secondary academic schools were reorganized into specialized or technical schools.[42] Consequently, a large percentage of the teachers belonging to the national minorities lost their jobs. At the same time, lacking technical training at the college level, the reorganized secondary schools do not have instructors who can teach in the minority languages.

The Babeş-Bolyai University has been, on the whole, dominated by a Rumanian administration. There has been no institutional arrangement to ensure the dual Rumanian and Hungarian character of the university, and there have been no separate Rumanian and Hungarian sections in the individual subjects. This has had an adverse effect on national-minority university enrollments.

The trend has been against the minorities in this area. In the

1974–75 academic year, of a total of 108,750 students attending full-time courses in higher education, there were only 6,188 Hungarians,[43] or only 5.7 percent of the total. Comparing these figures with the data relating to the 1957–58 academic year—when the Hungarian-language higher education institutions were attended by 4,082 Hungarian students and an additional 1,000–1,500 Hungarian students attended technical courses at Rumanian universities as compared with the national total of 53,007 students in full-time higher education—demonstrates the drastic reduction in minority higher education. Thus, while in the 1957–74 period the number of university students in Rumania doubled, the number of the Hungarian students went up by only approximately 10 percent.

In the Babeş-Bolyai University, approximately 6,000 students were enrolled at the beginning of the 1976–77 academic year. Of the above, 1,206 were first-year students, which included 269 Hungarians. However, not all of the Hungarian students were able to attend lectures given in Hungarian. The Hungarian lectures were attended only by 8 percent of the students. Thus, the majority of the Hungarians attended courses given entirely in Rumanian. The teaching staff, which totaled approximately 900 academic personnel, included 210 Hungarians, but most of them taught their courses in Rumanian.[44] The number of German students at Rumanian colleges and universities in the 1976–77 academic year was 1,966.[45]

The further development of secondary education was also dependent on and determined by the existing system of university education. The fact that specialized subjects in higher education have been taught in Rumanian, together with the difficulties of passing the university entrance examinations, which have been given in Rumanian, has meant that those attending a Rumanian secondary school stood a much better chance of getting into a university than those who attended a Hungarian secondary school. Thus, the university has served the purpose of deterrence: deterring the national minorities from insisting on having their children attend secondary schools that teach in their own languages. Furthermore, this pressures them to transfer their children to Rumanian schools already at the secondary level. In any case, very few schools teaching in the languages of the national minorities have been permitted in each town or city to set up an eleventh and twelfth year to complement the secondary level of education. Therefore, large numbers of students from the national minorities have been forced to complete the last two years of their schooling prior to university admission in a school where instruction is in Rumanian. In other words, as the educational process progresses towards the higher levels, it has become increasingly Rumanian.

The career opportunities for graduates from colleges and universities has also played an important role, which has complemented the above policies. The state has placed graduates in jobs, which they have been obliged to accept, and has done this in such a way that members of the national minorities—particularly those who have demonstrated their attachment to their nationality by attending classes in their own language—inevitably find themselves in comparatively less desirable positions. For example, a high proportion of Hungarian graduates have been given jobs in Rumanian areas. If they have been fortunate and have obtained employment in areas inhabited by Hungariains, and if they are teachers, they have been in general appointed to teach in primary and not in secondary schools.

Two specific local examples provide additional support for the above delineated characterization of Rumanian educational opportunities for the minorities. At the end of the Second World War, there were eleven Hungarian-language secondary schools in Cluj; of these, seven were entitled to issue matriculation certificates. There were three additional Hungarian-language secondary schools in the county outside of Cluj, for a total of fourteen altogether. By the beginning of the 1973–74 academic year, only nine secondary academic schools taught in Hungarian in the city of Cluj, with a further five in the rural areas; these, together, provided a total of fourteen. At the beginning of the 1976–77 academic year, seven secondary academic schools existed in Cluj having classes with instruction in Hungarian. Another four existed in the countryside, making a total of eleven. The deterioration is quite clear and it becomes even more manifest if the fact is taken into consideration that the educational system had in the meantime been reorganized. Under the new system, the objective was no longer restricted to the narrow task of training the future teachers and intellectuals; it was now given a more general role. In 1973, at the beginning of the academic year, there were thirty-two secondary academic schools teaching in Rumanian in the city of Cluj and a further twenty-nine in the county, making altogether sixty-one. By 1976, of the secondary academic schools in the county as a whole, seventy-four had Rumanian-language classes.[46] Thus, while education in the languages of the national minorities declined, the development of Rumanian-language education was constant and rapid. It is worth noting that at the beginning of the 1970s almost half of the population of Cluj was of Hungarian nationality, and it was only the large-scale settlement of

Rumanians there that succeeded in changing the national composition of this traditionally Hungarian-inhabited city.

In Cluj, education in the languages of the national minorities is now below the level attained between the two world wars. Rumanian-language education has in the meantime increased severalfold compared with interwar figures. Taking the number of pupils in first-year secondary classes to be the compulsory thirty-six, and working out the proportions on this basis, the number of pupils being taught in Hungarian in Cluj County is approximately 12–13 percent of the total, which is less than half of the proportion of Hungarians in the population of the county as a whole.

The school system in Tîrgu Mureş (Marosvásárhely) presents a similiar picture. At the end of the war, there were three independent Hungarian-language secondary schools teaching up to the matriculation level, while at present there are three Rumanian-language schools that also have Hungarian classes. In 1974, there were still three independent Hungarian-language secondary schools in the city and two in the countryside. The present proportions are as follows: in Tîrgu Mureş there are twelve Rumanian and eight Hungarian sections at the secondary level. If all the schools are taken into account, including the general schools that pass for academic schools, there are eight teaching in Hungarian, as opposed to thirty-six teaching in Rumanian. Of the three secondary schools possessing parallel Rumanian and Hungarian classes, the principal of one is Hungarian, while the other two principals are Rumanian. The direction of development is also indicated by the decline of the number of Hungarian primary and secondary school teachers during the past ten years corresponding with the increase of the number of Rumanian teachers from 110 to more than 1,000.[47] This process has had no relation to nationality needs, since, according to the official census of 1956, 73.8 percent of the population of Tîrgu Mureş belonged to the Hungarian nationality.

The Administration of National Minority Education: The Question of Supervision

In the administration of the educational system for the national minorities, after the mergers were realized at the end of the 1950s, the nationality organs for supervision, the school inspectorates, also ceased to exist. Furthermore, the administrative reorganization of the counties led to the rapid exclusion of members of the national minorities from this area of responsibility.

Within the framework of the Ministry of Education, in 1970 a section was reactivated called the Directorate for Nationality Schools. The responsibility of this section was to deal with the special problems of nationality education. This organ, however, has been limited to dealing with the problems arising in individual classes within the school system. It has not had general jurisdiction over minority educational problems. In a country like Rumania, inhabited by several nationalities, a directorate would be justified in having general jurisdiction over nationality education.[48]

At the county level, the supervision of education has been the responsibility of the county school inspectorate, which has been under the direct control of the county council and the Ministry of Education. Professional supervision has been within the framework of the individual school inspectorates.

With the abolition of the national-minority organs responsible for education, the number of educational specialists belonging to the national minorities has been significantly reduced for the county school inspectorates, particularly outside the compact nationality areas.[49] The national-minority schools, which have included the nationality sections, have been generally directed by Rumanian principals or chairmen, with the members of the minorities filling only subordinate posts. Rumanian teachers have also frequently taught in national-minority schools. Abuses and arbitrary measures have been frequent. After the 1968 Czechoslovakian event, for some time articles appeared in the Hungarian-language press complaining about circumstances that made teaching in the languages of the nationalities almost impossible in certain parts of the country having a mixed population. These articles referred to meager financial provisions, out-of-date school buildings, and inadequate instructional equipment and supplies, as well as the arbitrariness of Rumanian district superintendents and school inspectors.[50]

The number of Hungarian principals and assistant principals of general schools was 1,430 in 1971. In the overwhelming majority of cases, the Hungarian principals directed only the independent Hungarian schools. In the jointly directed institutions, or mixed schools, the general practice has been for the principal to be Rumanian and his assistant to be a member of a national minority.

Textbooks

In Rumania, the publication of textbooks for the national minorities has been the responsibility of the Textbook and Educational Publishing House. The great majority of minority-language textbooks for the various school grades have been poor translations of Rumanian textbooks, using vocabulary and modes of expression that have been often incomprehensible to the pupils. The situation has been the same as regards methodological handbooks. Consequently, the standards in the teaching of the history of national-minority literature has left a lot to be desired. The situation has been even worse regarding the teaching of history. The pupils belonging to the national minorities have not been taught either the history of their people or the factual history of Transylvania. Instead they have been provided with a falsified history reflecting the spirit of Rumanian nationalism.[51] In this way an attempt has been made to break the ties of the minority pupils with their historical and cultural roots.

As in the case of history books, the depiction of the literary history of the national minorities also has left out, apart from the private endeavors of a few lecturers, the national historical connections. It has been impossible for pupils to form a realistic picture of their national development over the centuries. The student teachers in the teacher-training colleges have only been able to obtain books that have been prescribed by the educational plan as "compulsory matter" in accordance with an arbitrary and nationalistic view. Books in the national-minority languages in school libraries have not been adequate in content or quantity. The shortage of reading material in the minority languages has also hindered the work of the primary and secondary school teachers in the outlying areas. Because of the prescribed and inadequate quotas, the Kriterion Nationality Publishing House has only very rarely published specialized works or enough copies.[52] While textbooks for the Hungarian minority living in Yugoslavia have been printed in Hungary, in Rumania it has been forbidden to use books from Hungary in the classroom. Specialized education for the national minorities has to rely on the poor translations of Rumanian publications. It has been characteristic, for example, that textbooks in Hungarian literary history have not been available in secondary schools for a long time. The textbook for the first year was prepared only for the 1972–73 academic year, and, as has been the case for Hungarian-language publications in general, so few copies were printed that they could not even come close to filling existing needs.

Conclusion

From the point of view of minority education, on a relative scale, qualitatively better conditions have existed in towns and cities that have strong Hungarian and/or German cultural traditions and where the proportion of Hungarian or German inhabitants has remained considerable (e.g., Cluj-Napoca, Oradea [Nagyvárad] Satu Mare [Szatmárnémeti]). Conditions have been worst of all in areas where relatively few Hungarians or Germans live in relation to the total population. For example, beyond the Carpathians, where about 300,000–350,000 Hungarians live, only in Bucharest do they have a Hungarian school.[53]

At the beginning of the 1970s, the network of Hungarian-language academic secondary schools came close to meeting the existing needs in areas inhabited by a compact Hungarian population, such as the Székely region. At the same time, the majority of pupils in the Rumanian-language classes also belonged to the Hungarian nationality in that region. At the beginning of the 1970s, slightly more than half of the Hungarian-language general schools and kindergartens were independent institutions under Hungarian direction. In the sixteen Transylvanian counties, and in the capital, Bucharest, 1,230 general schools and kindergartens taught exclusively in Hungarian and 1,060 functioned as nationality sections.[54]

However, national-minority education in Rumania reached the stage in the second half of the 1970s where only the nameplates outside of their schools indicated the existence of instruction in the language of the minorities ("Hungarian school," "German school," etc.). In practice, the purpose of education has been no less than the creation of the "unified, socialist nation" whose language is Rumanian. The slogan "national in form and socialist in content" has been given lip-service by government officials, but its application has been inconsistent at best.[55] The objective in the areas inhabited by the national minorities has been Rumanianization and the eventual elimination of the school network of the national minorities, from elementary-level to higher-level education as well.

The compulsory teaching of the Rumanian language in the national-minority schools, at the expense of their languages, has become one of the major issues concerning national-minority education. It is imperative that states inhabited by several nationalities consider that *all* the peoples should be encouraged to learn each other's language. At the same time no member of any nationality should be discriminated against for not speaking any other language but his own. At a time when equal rights in language usage has become an international issue, linguistic intolerance is an anachronism beyond understanding in Central Europe. The national minorities living in Rumania do not possess equal opportunities either in the sphere of vocational training or in securing their future by having the institutions and organs of society support their right to existence and development. It is in the interests of the national minorities to acquire the language of the national majority; however, to make this compulsory and to employ sanctions to punish those who do not speak the language of the national majority is irreconcilable with the spirit of the present age.

NOTES

1. For more detail on this, see Ernst Wagner, *Historisch-statistisches Ortsnamenbuch für Siebenbürgen* [Historical-Statistical Place-Name Directory of Transylvania] Studia Transylvanica, (Cologne-Vienna, 1976), pp. 84–88; see further T. Gilberg, *Modernization in Rumania Since World War II* (New York, 1975), p. 210. In the so-called Obere Vorstadt of Braşov [Scheii Braşovului] a Rumanian school of the Orthodox church was founded during the fifteenth century.

2. Among others Gilberg, op. cit., p. 209.

3. For more detail see T. Gilberg, "Ethnic Minorities in Romania Under Socialism," *East European Quarterly* 7 (Jan. 1974): 439.

4. Decree-Law No. 86/1945, *Monitorul Oficial* [Official Gazette] (Bucharest), pt. 1, no. 30/1945, Feb. 7, 1945, p. 819 ff.

5. *Monitorul Oficial*, pt. 1, no. 177, Aug. 3, 1948, p. 6322 ff.

6. Alfred Bohmann, *Menschen und Grenzen* [Men and Frontiers] (Cologne, 1969), p. 200.

7. *Anuarul Statistic al R.P.R. 1959*. [The Statistical Yearbook of the Rumanian People's Republic 1959] (Bucharest, 1959), pp. 288–93.

8. Constantin Sporea, "Probleme des Hochschulwesens in Rumänien" [The Problems of Higher Education in Rumania], Special Number of *Wissenschaftlicher Dienst Südosteuropa*, no. 3 (1959): 7.

9. Randolf L. Braham, *Education in the Rumanian People's Republic*, U.S. Department of Health, Education and Welfare. (Washington, D.C.: U.S. Government Printing Office, 1963), p. 75.

10. For additional details see Stephen Fischer-Galaţi, "Rumania," in *East Central Europe and the World*, ed. Stephen D. Kertesz (Notre Dame: University of Notre Dame Press, 1962), pp. 158–66. The history of the present-day Babeş-Bolyai University began in the sixteenth century with the foundation of the Hungarian Jesuit-Academy in Kolozsvár by the Transylvanian Prince Stephen Báthori in 1581. This institution obtained university status in 1872 with the name Ferenc József University; in 1919 this university was expropriated by the Rumanian state and renamed Ferdinand I. University. Between 1940 and 1958 it again became a Hungarian institution.

11. George Bailey, "Trouble Over Transylvania," *The Reporter* 31 (Nov. 19, 1964): 27.

12. Quoted from the Memorandum of Lajos Takács, former Deputy-Rector of the Babeş-Bolyai University, Cluj (Kolozsvár) [Manuscript].

13. Bohmann, op. cit., p. 180.

14. Bailey, op. cit., pp. 26–27; see also David Binder, "Rumania's Minorities Pressed by Nationalist Drive," *The New York Times*, July 14, 1964, p. 4; J. F. Brown, "The Age-Old Question of Transylvania," *The World Today* 19 (Nov., 1963): 503–04.

15. George Lázár, "Jelentés Erdélyből" [Report from Transylvania] in *Irodalmi Ujság* [Literary Gazette] (Paris), Mar.-Apr., 1977.

16. Information based on Gilberg, *Modernization in Rumania*, p. 227, Table 8.10.

17. Imre Mikó, "Az együttélő nemzetiségek jogegyenlősége" [Equality Before the Law of the Coinhabiting Nationalities], *A Hét* [The Week] (Bucharest), 1972, vol. 3, no. 16.

18. Report by János Demeter, Deputy Rector of the Babeş-Bolyai University of Cluj, *Korunk* [Our Age] 1970, no. 11; *Buletinul Oficial,* July 9, 1973.

19. Decretul nr. 278 din 11 mai 1973 privind stabilirea normelor unitare de structură pentru instituţiile de invăţămînt [Decree no. 278 of May 11, 1973 Concerning the Regularization of Standard Structural Units of Educational Institutions] in *Buletinul Oficial,* no. 67, May 13, 1973, p. 818. See further the June 18–19, 1973, Resolution of the Central Committee of the RCP in *Buletinul Oficial,* pt. 1, no. 100, July 9, 1973.

20. Decree no. 278, art. 3, pars. 2, 3.

21. Ibid.

22. Bohmann, op. cit., p. 202.

23. Nicolae Ceauşescu, *România pe drumul desăvîrşirii construcţiei socialiste* [Rumania on the Road of Completion of Socialist Construction], (Bucharest, 1976), vol 3, p. 700.

24. János Demeter, *Korunk* [Our Age], 1970, no. 11, p. 1627.

25. *Tanügyi Ujság* [Educational Journal], 1971, no. 31; *A Hét,* 1971, no. 37.

26. Eduard Eisenburger, *Wegzeichen der Heimat* [Signposts of the Homeland] (Cluj, 1974), p. 163. See further information provided by the Rumanian Ministry of Education, March, 1977.

27. Walter König, *Die gegenwärtigen Schulverhältnisse der Deutschen in Rumänien* [The Present-day Educational System of the Germans in Rumania] (Cologne, Vienna, 1977), pp. 124–25.

28. *Sächsisch-schwäbische Chronik* [Saxon-Swabian Chronicle], ed. E. Eisenburger and M. Kroner (Bucharest, 1976), p. 194; see also data issued by the Rumanian Ministry of Education, vols. 1947–76.

29. König, op. cit., pp. 124–25.

30. From data issued by the Ministry of Education, March, 1977.

31. Ibid.

32. Ibid.; Árpád Debreczi, *Előre* [Forward] (Hungarian-language daily, Bucharest), Mar. 31, 1972.

33. *Invăţămîntul liceal şi tehnic profesional* [Education in Lycees and Technical-Occupational Schools], (Bucharest), Apr., 1978.

34. Ibid.

35. Data from speech given by N. Ceauşescu at the March 14, 1971, session of the Council of Workers of Hungarian Nationality, *Előre,* Mar. 14, 1971.

36. Information from Mihnea Berindei, "Les minorités nationales en Roumanie," vol. 2, in *L'Alternative,* (Paris) May-Aug., 1980, p. 41.

37. Ibid.

38. *Anuarul Statistic al R.S.R. 1979,* p. 568.

39. *Wissenschaftlicher Dienst Südosteuropa,* no. 10, 1975, pp. 207–08; see also *Anuarul Statistic al R.S.R. 1979,* p. 557 ff.

40. From speech given by N. Ceauşescu at the March 12, 1971, session of the Council of Workers of Hungarian Nationality, *Előre,* Mar. 14, 1971.

41. Statement by János Demeter, *A Hét,* 1971, no. 28.

42. Decree No. 207/1977 "Concerning the Organization and Function of the Lycees," *Buletinul Oficial,* no. 67, July 12, 1977, and Decree No. 208/1977 "Concerning the Organization and Function of the Vocational Schools."

43. *The Hungarian Nationality in Rumania.* Institute of Political Science and the Study of Nationality Question, (Bucharest, 1976), p. 17.

44. Data issued by the Ministry of Education.

45. König, op. cit., p. 110.

46. Data provided by the Rumanian Ministry of Education, 1974–77.

47. George Lázár, "Jelentés Erdélyből" [Report from Transylvania], *Irodalmi Ujság* [Literary Gazette] (Paris), Mar.-Apr., 1977.

48. *Tanügyi Ujság,* 1971, no. 11.

49. Ibid.

50. Elemér Illyés, *Erdély változása: Mitosz és valóság* [Transylvanian Metamorphosis: Myth and Reality] (Munich: Aurora, 1976), p. 203.

51. *Istoria României, Manual pentru clasa a XII-a, partea a II-a* [The History of Rumania, Textbook for the 12th class, pt. 2], ed. Florea Dagne. (Bucharest, 1968).

52. *Ifjumunkás* [Young Worker] (Hungarian-language organ, Bucharest), 1972, no. 15.

53. The territory beyond the Carpathians ("Old Kingdom") has a Hungarian population of about 150,000 Csángó Hungarians in Moldavia and about 200,000 Hungarians in Bucharest and the other urban centers of the Regat. Already at the end of the 1920s the Hungarian population of the Regat was estimated at 200,000. *Erdélyi Magyar Évkönyv 1918–1929* [Transylvanian Hungarian Yearbook 1918–1929], vol. 1. (Kolozsvár, 1930), p. 3. For data on the one Hungarian school in Bucharest see the data issued by the Rumanian Ministry of Education for Bucharest during 1974–77.

54. István Bántó, "Együttélés, testvériség" [Coexistence, Fraternity], *Tanügyi Ujság,* 1971, no. 11.

55. Hans Bergel, "Die Entwicklung der Siebenbürger Sachsen seit 1945 als Problem der Volksgruppen im Donauraum" [The Development of the Transylvanian Saxons since 1945, as a Problem of the Ethnic Groups in the Danube Region], *Der Donauraum* (Vienna), 1976, pp. 151–60; see further Wolfgang Oberleitner, "Exodus 78: Rumäniens Volksdeutsche geben auf: Assimilierungspolitik und ethnische Isolation signalisieren den Aufbruch" [Exodus 78: The Ethnic Germans of Rumania Give Up: The Migration is Signalled by the Policy of Assimilation and Ethnic Isolation], *Die Presse* (Vienna), Jan. 14–15, 1978, p. 5.

The Status of Minority Rights in Transylvania: International Legal Expectations and Rumanian Realities

BULCSU VERESS

In examining the ways in which the international system works or does not work to protect the rights of national minorities, my underlying assumptions are that the institution of human rights is a good thing; that ethnicity, mother tongue, and native culture are some of the most powerful elements of identification and self-definition and that they are likely to remain so for the foreseeable future. Furthermore, the deprivation of one's ethnic identity is in itself a deprivation, if not of life, at least of liberty, and certainly of the pursuit of happiness. Oppression of minorities in the long run is inimical to the interest of majorities also, and only pluralism and tolerance will provide a solution to this problem that is consistent with progress and human dignity.

Many other scholars in the field probably hold similar commitments. The research on the subject of human rights is so interwoven with normative commitments that it is wise to summarize the underlying assumptions at the outset.

The study is mainly concerned with so-called positive minority rights and only to a limited extent with the right to nondiscriminatory treatment. Nondiscrimination is the first step, of course, but is not peculiar to national minorities. It is forbidden to discriminate because of race, sex, religion, color, or social origin. Minority protection proper involves a further step: granting minorities the right, as well as the suitable means, to preserve and develop their national identity, traditions, and culture.

This paper takes into consideration the actual conditions and status of Rumania's national minorities, most of whom are concentrated in the region of Transylvania, as compared to the standards of international law. There is unfortunately no comprehensive international code of minority rights, which still suffer the consequences of the collapse of the League of Nations system. Minority protection was part of that interwar system, shared its weaknesses, and went down with it amidst the general disintegration that led to World War II. The cynical manipulation and abuse of the minority question by Hitler cast a shadow over the whole idea for many years, and recovery has been very slow. Even today mistrust remains. Conor Cruise O'Brien, who spent many years at the United Nations working on this problem, described this phenomenon in the following manner:

> As a matter of experience I have found . . . that people who are all in favor of human rights generally speaking are very likely to sit up and look suspicious where there is any question of *minority* rights. Human rights is a pleasing abstraction impregnated with our notion of our own benevolence. But *minority rights* evoke a sudden sharp picture of "that lot" with their regrettable habits, extravagant claims, ridiculous complaints, and suspect intentions. Special rights for *them*? Not likely. Governments are representative, of course, either of majorities or more often of ruling minorities which of course do not think of themselves as minorities ever. It is therefore unlikely that an international association on the scale of the United Nations will promulgate an effective code giving protection to minorities.[1]

In spite of these pessimistic, even slightly bitter words, there is very slow, very incremental, but continuous progress in "international legislation" concerning minority rights. It works in many ways. It is very interesting to observe, for instance, the transformation that the "Universal Declaration of Human Rights" is undergoing. There is the ever growing consensus that by now the Declaration has solidified into an international code of conduct instead of just a declaration of intention. Its specific rules have the weight of legal obligations. More importantly, while originally it was thought that the Universal Declaration did not include any reference to the rights of national minorities beyond the prohibition of discrimination, some recent interpretations strongly disagree with this view.[2] They argue that the idea of freedom of choice pervades the entire Declaration, and that Article 26 on the right to education or Article 27 on the right to participate in the cultural life of the community can have no interpretation other than that which includes the right to education in the mother tongue and the right to one's native culture, and all that it involves. It is very difficult to argue against this interpretation. This change in interpretation is similar to what happened to the American Constitution: even where the language did not change, it is a very different document from the one accepted almost 200 years ago.

Beside the reinterpreted Universal Declaration, there are numerous other documents defining international standards for treatment of minorities. Without going into the details, the "International Covenant on Civil and Political Rights" should be mentioned, especially its Article 27, which explicitly provides for the cultural, religious, and linguistic rights of minorities. The "International Covenant on Economic,

Social and Cultural Rights" is also relevant, as well as the "International Convention on the Elimination of All Forms of Racial Discrimination." The UNESCO "Convention Against Discrimination in Education" includes provisions recognizing the right of national minorities to their own educational system. Finally, the Helsinki Agreement contains three paragraphs on the rights of national minorities. While it is understood that the latter agreement is not legally binding on the parties, its political significance is beyond doubt in light of the parties' accountability for its implementation.

The sources consulted for this study include official Rumanian publications, often propaganda material intended to demonstrate the enlightened nature of Rumania's minority policies.[3] Also utilized are the few published studies on the subject, particularly the one by Robert R. King and the one by George Schöpflin.[4] Personal discussions with the above authors provided additional information and insights. A third source has been provided by the *samizdats* written by Hungarian officials within Rumania who became dissatisfied with the treatment of their fellow nationals and let their views be known in letters of protest against what they perceive as mistreatment of the minorities. The personal risks they took by protesting these conditions is a sufficient guarantee of the veracity of their accounts. One such *samizdat,* a document of about 16,000 words, was written under a pseudonym but was found highly reliable by Western experts and commentators.[5] Other sources are articles in the Western press[6] and, finally, interviews with well over 100 present and former residents of Rumania about their personal experiences. The most interesting of these interviews is one with a Rumanian sociologist who, as a member of a Rumanian government research institution, was one of the authors of a little propaganda booklet on the situation of the Hungarian nationality in Rumania. This booklet was published in several languages in 1976 and distributed around the world. The sociologist subsequently defected and today lives in New York City. His account on the factual basis of that booklet and the methods employed in writing it are highly enlightening.

For the illustration of the problems of minority protection, few examples could give as complete a picture as that of the Hungarians in Rumania. They are the largest national minority in Europe. They are an ethnic, linguistic, and religious minority at the same time, very distinct from the majority in all three aspects. In some parts of Rumania their population is concentrated in compact settlements, while in other areas they are interspersed with the Rumanians and the German minority population. Just across one border they do have a so-called mother country, which might be a source of protection and comfort, but is instead often a cause of further friction and tension. Finally, Rumania is a totalitarian country where the government exercises full control over every aspect of the life of the population. Since the life of the minorities is under total government control, the intentions of government interference cannot be misinterpreted. Thus, the Hungarian minority situation is a classroom example of minority conditions, like the proverbial horse at the veterinary school, which has all the illnesses a horse might possibly have.

Given the geographical, ethnographical, historical factors, the multinational region of Transylvania could be a model for the coexistence of diverse nationalities in an atmosphere of mutual tolerance and understanding. Unfortunately, the Rumanian leadership seems to have chosen a different path.

Before reviewing several aspects of the Hungarian minority's existence, the overall pattern should be outlined. The individual elements of Rumania's minority policies can not be viewed as distinct or isolated phenomena. The evidence is overwhelming that they are the interrelated components of a planned and consistently executed policy, which is more than the mere sum of its parts. This policy is based on a deep sense of insecurity that the Rumanian leadership feels about the problem as a whole. They are clearly uncomfortable with the existence of 3 million non-Rumanian inhabitants in the country. There is no room for these people in the neo-fascist mythology of the new Rumanian nationalism. The expression "neo-fascist" is used advisedly, not just as an expletive. A recent article on Rumanian history by a very authoritative source, President Ceauşescu's brother, Ilie Ceauşescu, borrowed a great deal of its vocabulary from Alfred Rosenberg's *Der Mythus des. 20. Jahrhunderts*. Ceauşescu claims that the Rumanian people "had to fulfill a heroic, uneasy and glorious historical destiny during an existence of nearly two millenia." He also assures his readers of the racial purity of the Rumanian people by asserting that they "never did merge or mix with other peoples which moved into the Carpathian-Danubian-Pontic region."[7] This basic insecurity, reflected in the fabrication of history, has cultural and political roots. At the time of their merger, Transylvania and the Old Kingdom had fundamentally different cultural orientations, and they differed also in their degrees of cultural development. These differences made it difficult for Rumania to digest the new acquisition. The political root of this insecurity is the dubious legitimacy of the acquisition of Transylvania, and of the right of sovereignty over millions of people who belong to other nations. In spite of all the efforts of Rumanian historians to pretend that some sort of divine justice was done at the close of World War I, the fact remains that an imperialist peace was written in Versailles by world leaders who were ignorant about local conditions and likely could not have cared less anyway. Allies, as well as those who timed their switch to the side of the victors, were rewarded well, while the people who were thrown to an alien sovereignty were ignored. Not that all this was necessarily unjust; even justice may accidentally prevail when territorial adjustments are made at the conclusion of a major war. But it was done in a manner that has raised serious doubts about its legitimacy ever since. If legitimacy is missing at the outset, it can be acquired subsequently; it depends only on the consent of the ruled. A case in point is Yugoslavia, which not only treats its minorities fairly but plays an effective leadership role in trying to bring about an international code of minority protection. Rumania, on the other hand, regards its minority citizens as living question marks of the legitimacy of its rule over territory and population acquired sixty-five years ago. As a consequence, every aspect of minority existence is totally politicized and controlled. The government looks at Hungarian volumes of innocent poetry as time bombs and confiscates them at the border as contraband. Throwing the purity of the race so cherished by Ilie Ceaușescu to the wind, it attempts to force its minorities to assimilate into the Rumanian population by gradually curtailing and eliminating the cultural opportunities and institutions of the minorities and by any other means at its disposal.

The minority situation in Rumania is examined here in the following areas of concern:

1. Recognition
2. Political rights
3. Cultural and linguistic rights
4. Religious rights
5. Economic rights
6. Legal remedy

Recognition

The obvious first condition for the fair and just treatment of national minorities is the government's recognition of their existence. Some governments try to preempt the problem by denying that minorities exist within the jurisdiction of the state. While the Rumanian government recognizes the existence of its minorities, it does this with some qualifications. One is the obvious underrepresentation of the minority population in the official census statistics.

According to these figures, between 1956 and 1966 the non-Hungarian population of Rumania grew by 9.9 percent, at a rate almost five times greater than the alleged Hungarian growth rate of 2.0 percent. Similarly, between 1966 and 1977 the total population of Rumania, excluding Hungarians, supposedly grew by 13.5 percent, while the growth rate of Hungarians was only 5.4 percent.[8] In reality, aside from statistical juggling, there is no circumstance that can be cited to justify such vast differences in growth rates.

One tactic involves the demographic questionnaire used to compile census data, of which the most recent was gathered in January, 1977. The form contains three spaces requiring identification as to "citizenship," "nationality," and "mother tongue," in that order. The census taker is instructed not to complete the "nationality" blank, as if he had forgotten to pose that question. As "citizenship" is obviously Rumanian, where "mother tongue" is Hungarian, the blank is later filled in as follows: "Nationality: Hungarian-speaking Rumanian." This artificial distinction between nationality and mother tongue, together with the "correction" of census returns, thus serves the dual purposes of understating the size of the Hungarian population and increasing the number of Rumanians. This practice was uncovered by the International Commission of Jurists[9] and confirmed by an interview with a former census taker.[10]

There is considerable pressure on minority persons who achieve international fame in arts, sports, or other endeavors to change their names to Rumanian-sounding ones. The domestic press often Rumanianizes these names even without the permission of those involved. Persons of achievement from among the minorities are often denoted as Rumanians who speak and write in Hungarian. Hungarian writers are deeply offended by being referred to as "Hungarian-speaking Rumanian writers" in the press. Even the official name of the minorities, "coinhabiting nationalities," strikes many minority individuals as implying their secondary dependent status to the "inhabiting nationality," the only really legitimate inhabitants of the country.[11] This may be just semantics, but this secondary, dependent, appendix status is powerfully demonstrated by the way the whole network of cultural institutions is set up in Rumania, which is discussed later.

Political Rights

One of the most sensitive areas of international relations concerns the political rights of national minorities. It strikes at the core of the existence, sovereignty, and legitimacy of regimes. In descending order, the right of self-determination has to be dealt with first. If all United

Nations resolutions, declarations, and covenants were to be taken literally, the minorities in Rumania would have the right to determine under what sovereignty they want to live; for instance, that they might want to secede from Rumania and join Hungary. However, self-determination is not a right, it is hardly more than a political slogan that has two functions. It has given legitimacy to the decolonialization movement, as well as to secession movements, not necessarily to those whose claim was justified, but to those that had superior firepower and—like Bangladesh—prevailed. The other function is to send chills up the spines of majority regimes and thereby serve as a bargaining tool in the hands of recalcitrant minorities. Political science still owes the world the answer to whose claim to secession is justified and whose is not. International politics not only can afford hypocrisy, it is one of the major currencies of the trade. Scholarship, however, cannot afford it. This paper does not have the answer, but secession is certainly a breakdown that results in the minority being driven to the point of desperation. It is hardly to be recommended as a general solution. A gradual depolitization of ethnicity, dissolution of borders, is a much more attractive alternative. Formerly very "hot" European borders are hardly noticeable today, in terms of the life of the peoples they divide.

Secession, of course, is only the most extreme result of the exercise of the right of self-determination. A minority may well be satisfied with political rights it can exercise while remaining part of a given state. The right to autonomy with a federal system is one of the strongest of such rights but it does not apply in the present case, Rumania not being a federal state. The right of local autonomy, however, is relevant. The Hungarian minority is fairly concentrated in some areas and could support an autonomous political structure. A Hungarian Autonomous Province existed for almost two decades until 1968, but it was autonomous in name only. It never had a statute and it hardly differed from the other provinces. Since its abolition, every succeeding reorganization of the administrative structure gerrymandered the provinces to deprive most of them of a Hungarian majority.

Even the simple right of representation, perhaps the most fundamental among the political rights of a minority, is completely missing for the Hungarians. Minorities obviously have to have representation as minorities, not only as individual elements of a heterogeneous population, in order to be able to articulate their special concerns. Although there are officials of minority extraction at every governmental level, they are permitted no meaningful voice in representing their own ethnic groups.

The Hungarian Nationality Workers Council was established in

1968 as the only body capable of serving the interests of the Hungarian minority. But the very document establishing this council exposes it as an instrument of the state, acting to undermine minority interests. The Council's stated purpose is "to assist the Party and the state, on both the central and local levels, in mobilizing the nationalities to assume their responsibilities in the building of socialism, in researching particular questions concerning the respective populations and in implementing the nationality policies of the Party."[12]

Károly Király, vice president of the Council for ten years until his removal in March, 1978, furnished ample evidence of the Council's abject ineffectiveness. In his letters to Party leaders, Király charged that the Council's activities "have declined to zero";[13] repeatedly, but to no avail, he called upon the government to "guarantee the proper organizational framework"[14] as a precondition to treating minorities in the proper fashion. Hungarians are proportionately represented, but only in those state and Party organs that are not allowed to exercise any real power, such as the showcase "Grand Assembly" and the 500-member Party Central Committee. Hungarians are virtually excluded from any body that is granted an effective role in matters affecting their own interests. Of the seven secretaries of the Party Central Committee, who are the holders of real power aside from Ceauşescu, not one is of minority origin. The Secretary for Nationalities in the Party Central Committee cannot speak any minority language, only Rumanian. In the leadership of such vital organs as the Department of Culture and the Department of Education, not one Hungarian is to be found, even among the deputy ministers. On the county level, the ineffectual People's Councils and Party Committees by and large do maintain proportional representation. But where the real power lies, within the seven–eleven member Executive Comittees and Party "Bureaus," Hungarians are grossly underrepresented. Indeed, in several heavily Hungarian-populated counties, such as Banat (Bánság), Arad, and Maramureş (Máramaros), they are completely excluded from the Party "Bureaus." "In the same way," Károly Király pointed out, "it is nothing new that in cities where the majority of the population is Hungarian—such as Nagyvárad, Marosvásárhely Szováta, etc.—Rumanians who speak no Hungarian are being appointed as mayors."[15]

Of course, this deprivation of political rights has to be viewed in the context of a tightly controlled Communist dictatorship. The Rumanian majority cannot exercise self-determination either. They are also deprived of any possibility of making a political choice. What adds to the burden of the minority, however, is that even the Communist leadership of that minority does not have any decision-making authority in their own affairs. For the minorities, therefore, nationalistic oppression comes on the top of the general political oppression, which victimizes every Rumanian citizen regardless of ethnic background.

Cultural and Linguistic Rights

In the absence of some form of political self-administration, a measure of cultural autonomy is simply indispensable for the well-being of a minority. This means a cultural self-administration, an independent decision-making role in their own cultural and educational affairs. It can function only if it has a strong institutional basis under the control of the minority.

In Rumania, there is no trace of cultural autonomy for the minorities, and even independent institutions have been eliminated almost completely. The ingenious method of accomplishing this consisted of attaching almost every institution to a Rumanian counterpart, in the name of brotherhood. For example, the Hungarian university in Cluj (Kolozsvár) was made a section of its Rumanian counterpart; Hungarian schools have been merged into Rumanian schools as sections; four out of the six formerly independent theaters are now just sections of Rumanian theaters; and so on. The result is the complete destruction even of the elements—not to mention the superstructure—of an independent hierarchy of Hungarian institutions. The clear purpose of such arrangements is to have a Rumanian official to look over the shoulder of even the most insignificant contributors to Hungarian culture. It makes the dependence total and prevents even the most routine decisions from becoming the internal business of the Hungarian community.

As was mentioned above, only two independent Hungarian theaters remain now, where there were six a few years ago. No association of Hungarian writers, poets, artists or musicians is permitted to exist, despite the rich living heritage of Transylvanian Hungarian creators in those areas. Hungarian poets have stated that within the Rumanian Writers Association they have to conduct even their poets' workshops in Rumanian—out of "courtesy" to the ever-present Rumanian officials. In other words, they have to analyze each other's poems—written in Hungarian—in another language. Even knowing the methods of the Rumanian government one found this hard to believe—until it was confirmed by several independent sources.[16]

The volume of Hungarian-language books published in Rumania is clearly insufficient. According to official statistics, 2,423,000 copies were published in 1977,[17] meaning only one book per Hungarian for the entire year. And, of course, this figure includes children's books and an inordinately heavy share of translations from the Rumanian, including the collected works of Nicolae Ceauşescu.

The number of Hungarian-language newspapers, frequency of publication, and number of pages have all been forcibly curtailed in the past years. Six Hungarian newspapers, formerly published daily, are now allowed to appear only weekly. There is no journal on drama, music, or the other arts in Hungarian, even though the demand for these items is high. Nor are there any technical, medical, and other professional journals in the minority languages.

To provide detailed data on the elimination of folk ensembles and orchestras, the grossly inadequate number of radio and television programs, the shortage of Hungarian books in public libraries, and the total lack of training facilities for theater directors, drama, art, and music critics would overload this paper. Education, however, has a crucial role in ensuring the survival of an ethnic community and thus warrants particular attention.

Official Rumanian statistics[18] indicate that while twenty years ago the number of students allowed to attend Hungarian classes was roughly proportional to the size of the Hungarian population, more recent figures show an alarming decline. Attendance in Hungarian classes has fallen in each category far below the levels that even the official population statistics would warrant.

Since 1956, independent Hungarian schools have been systematically attached to Rumanian schools as mere sections, which, in turn, have been gradually phased out. The process of totally eliminating these Hungarian sections was legitimized by enactment of the clearly discriminatory Decree/Law 278 of May 11, 1973.

This unprecedented piece of legalized discrimination requires the presence of a minimum quota of twenty-five students at the grade school level and thirty-six students at the high school level in order to maintain or establish a class in one of the minority languages. If a given Hungarian community contains, for example, only twenty-four Hungarian students for a given elementary school class, these children are forced to complete their studies in the Rumanian language. As most villages in Transylvania have only between 500 and 1,000 inhabitants, the number of Hungarian students very often falls short of the required quota, and the Hungarian classes must be terminated.

What makes this decree still more offensive is that the provisions applicable to Hungarians and other minorities do not apply to Rumanian sections or classes in areas inhabited predominantly by Hungarians. In such towns or villages, a Rumanian section must be maintained regardless of demand, i.e., even if a given Hungarian village contains only one Rumanian student. The wording of Decree/Law 278 makes this requirement perfectly clear: "In those communities where schools function in the language of the coinhabiting nationalities, Rumanian language sections or classes shall be organized regardless of the number of students."

The fact that Decree/Law 278 was repealed in the fall of 1978, due largely to Western pressure, did not change the situation at all. The same policy is being continued as administrative practice. In Rumania, the system of secret instructions, existing parallel with written laws and often overriding them, is particularly prevalent, especially in the field of nationality policy. Written constitutional guarantees therefore exist on paper only, and that is the reason this paper neglects dealing with them.

Even in the remaining Hungarian schools and sections, not just the Rumanian language but the general subjects of literature, geography, and history must also be taught in Rumanian. In many Hungarian sections, there are so many Rumanian-language courses that the section is Hungarian in name only. This is especially the case in Hungarian vocational and technical schools, where only Hungarian literature and physical education are actually taught in Hungarian.

Matters have taken a sharp turn for the worse since the fall of 1976, when a drive was initiated to reorganize Rumania's entire educational system, placing greater emphasis on technical and vocational training and reducing the number of high schools, or lyceums, which provide instruction in the liberal arts. As an outgrowth of this drive, Hungarian lyceums that had been in continuous existence for the past 300–400 years have been summarily eliminated. They were not, however, replaced by Hungarian vocational schools. As Károly Király, former high-ranking party leader who became a dissident, pointed out in a letter to the Party leadership:

> We were promised new secondary vocational and technical schools in which studies were to be conducted in the languages of the nationalities, but in reality we have witnessed a decline in the number of these schools. Each year there are fewer and fewer of them. Children cannot study in their native tongue; compulsory instruction in the Rumanian language has been introduced even at the kindergarten level.[19]

Finally, through discriminatory admissions policies, the government makes it difficult for graduates of Hungarian schools or sections to enter the the next higher educational level. The government, in the meantime, alleges that it is due to lack of popular demand that Hungarian-language courses are closed. Thus, as in the many illustrations provided above, the discriminatory cycle is complete and the outcome for the Hungarian minority is devastating.

Higher education has a great historical tradition in Transylvania. The Bolyai University of Cluj (Kolozsvár), for instance, can be traced to the Jesuit academy founded in 1581. On March 5, 1959, the Bolyai University was forced to merge with the Rumanian Babeş University. In his book *Minorities Under Communism,* Robert R. King calls the elimination of this Hungarian institution "the most serious blow to intellectuals among the Hungarian minority."[20] Three professors, including the celebrated writer László Szabédi, committed suicide out of despair at this arbitrary act.[21] It is characteristic that the document of unification, which lists the existing faculties of the two universities at the time of the merger, has been concealed ever since, so as to hide any official evidence of the extent to which the Hungarian faculties have been eliminated. King further states that after the merger "the 'Rumanianization' of the unified university was gradually carried out."[22] He cites numerous examples of this ruthless process.

Present conditions at this allegedly bilingual university are dismal. In the 1976–77 academic year, of all the students, which numbered approximately 6,000, only 480 (eight percent) had the opportunity to attend Hungarian classes.[23] A meaningful indicator of the total volume of Hungarian-language education that occurs at the University can be computed by multiplying the number of Hungarian courses by the number of students attending those courses. In recent semesters, the resulting figure has fluctuated between five and ten percent of the comparable figure at the time of the merger.[24]

The extent to which a minority has to be provided with its own educational system always depends on several factors, such as the size of the minority, the degree of general development in the country, or the extent to which the government interferes with, subsidizes, administers, or monopolizes education. None of these factors is relevant here, however, in the sense that it would justify, in any manner, the refusal to provide something that does not exist, let alone the systematic destruction of something that did exist. The Hungarian minority in Rumania forms the largest national minority in Europe. One third of all the countries in the world have fewer inhabitants than there are Hungarians in Rumania.[25] It is grossly discriminatory that this population is not allowed to have a single university of its own.

In addition to the Bolyai University, all other Hungarian institutions of higher education have been systematically curtailed or eliminated. Károly Király wrote about the fate of institutions of higher education in the following manner:

> In 1976 a decision was born to eliminate Hungarian institutions of higher educaton. After the "Bolyai" University in Kolozsvár came the Institute of Medicine and Pharmacology at Marosvásárhely, and then, by special order from above, a Rumanian section was established at the István Szentgyörgyi School for the Dramatic Arts, thereby liquidating in effect the last "island" of higher education in a nationality tongue.[26]

One final comment on this topic seems appropriate. The severe restriction on those subjects that may be taught in Hungarian is not without serious impact on the lower levels of education. As indicated earlier, the various elements of discrimination in Rumania cannot be isolated, for they act to reinforce one another. Thus, the relentless decline in the number of subjects that may be pursued in Hungarian beyond high school undoubtedly serves to pressure aspiring Hungarian students to study these subjects in Rumanian during their earlier years of schooling.

The content of the education, even when it is conducted in Hugarian, is another matter. According to Article 26 of the "Universal Declaration of Human Rights," education ". . . shall promote understanding, tolerance and friendship among all nations, racial or religious groups . . ."[27] In Rumania today, textbooks in history stigmatize minority groups as "intruders" who upset the social and cultural order of the "original inhabitants," the Rumanians. In many cases, textbooks, travel guides, and other literature actually re-christen Hungarian historical figures and make them into Rumanian national heroes having no connection with the Hungarian people. The same materials contain an almost absolute silence on the centuries of Transylvania's Hungarian history. The unproven hypothesis of Daco-Roman origin has been elevated to the level of state ideology, to prove the Rumanians' historical "precedence" in the area.[28]

At this point it should be noted that arguments concerning the historical priority of peoples living many centuries ago have no relevance whatsoever to the rules of international law governing the treatment of national minorities; still less can such arguments be used as an excuse for the oppression of minorities.

By the assertion of "prior settlement," the dynamism and superiority of the Rumanian people becomes "historically proven," while national-minority inhabitants, lacking historical or cultural roots of comparable brilliance, are considered less than second-class citizens. One devastating practical effect of this process in Rumania today is that minority children are taught that the cultural richness of the area is solely the result of Rumanian creativity, thereby making those children ashamed of their ethnic identity. The remaining schools that still educate children in Hungarian must use official textbooks that teach these children that their nationality has no past in the area. Without a past, by implication, this nationality can have no future—unless, of course, it assimilates into the resplendent Rumanian people.[29]

Language rights are also limited and circumscribed. Rumanian is the official language spoken everywhere in Rumania; it is the exclusive language at all levels of government bureaucracy. Use of the native tongue by the nationalities has been completely eliminated from all areas of official activity. As Károly Király pointed out: "Use of the native tongue is severely restricted at meetings of the Party, the Young Communists League, the trade unions, and in the various workers' councils; indeed, *use of the native tongue is prohibited even at meetings of the Nationality Workers Councils*."[30] (Emphasis added.)

Traffic safety signs, bureaucratic forms, menus, postcards, and tourist literature are all in Rumanian. In addition, there is an increasing tendency to appoint Rumanian personnel to all positions that involve contact with the public in Hungarian areas.

According to Article 109 of the Rumanian Constitution, judicial proceedings throughout the country must be conducted in the Rumanian language. The only right a Hungarian defendant or litigant has before the court of his own native community is to be provided with an interpreter. This "right," however, is no more than the right granted to any foreigner brought to trial in any country.

Due to this complete absence of any degree of bilingualism and the chauvinism encouraged by governmental policies, members of minorities are often forced to endure derision and threats for using their mother tongue, even in private conversations at public places.[31]

At every border checkpoint on the Hungarian-Rumanian border the visitor is greeted by a huge sign, "Welcome to Romania!" in English, in French, in German, in Russian, and in Rumanian.

This leads us to the sensitive question of contacts with the "mother country." Unfortunately it is only a moral claim that minorities should have unhindered contacts with related groups of the same national, ethnic, or linguistic character, who may constitute a majority or minority in another country. The often existing mutual jealousies and territorial suspicions have made it so far impossible to insert such a provision in any of the above-mentioned multilateral agreements. On the bilateral level, there are many fine examples of cooperation, though none of these involves the Rumanian government.

Book imports from Hungary are severely restricted. This applies equally to classical literature, specialized scientific and technical texts, and phonograph records, even those containing only folk and Gypsy music. Subscriptions to periodicals published in Hungary can be obtained only with official permission. Eighty to ninety percent of such requests are rejected, including those of schools, libraries, and other institutions, as well as individuals.[32]

Hungarian books and periodicals are routinely confiscated from private travelers at border checkpoints, no matter how innocent or nonpolitical they may be. Several Western reporters made a test run last year with totally innocent volumes of Hungarian literature, to find out about this practice.[33] Their books, too, were confiscated.

To cut off personal contacts between Hungarians on the two sides of the border there are two further restrictions. According to Rumanian law, citizens of Rumania can travel to Hungary only once every two years. The law does not give the right actually to make the trip every two years, but only to apply for permission. Applications by Hungarians have a less than 50 percent chance of being approved, and no reasons are given for their rejection.[34]

The same purpose is served by Decree/Law 225 (1974), which prohibits the accomodation of any foreign citizen, except most immediate family members, in private homes. Fines equivalent to $1,200 are imposed on the unfortunate hosts even where no alternative hotel accomodations are available.[35] It is the Hungarians who have the greatest number of relatives and potential visitors abroad. There are 11 million Hungarians in neighboring Hungary and several million in other countries.

While the above interference with contacts with Hungary does not violate any international agreements on minorities, it specifically and clearly violates the following provisions of the Helsinki Agreement:

—point (a) in the "Information" chapter of Basket III;

—most of the rules in the chapters "Cooperation and Exchanges in the Field of Culture" and "Cooperation and Exchanges in the Field of Education" of Basket III;

—the "Promotion of Tourism" chapter of Basket II; and

—the "Human Contacts" chapter of Basket III, especially points (a), (d), (e), and (f).[36]

Religious Rights

There are no specific rules in international law concerning religious minorities. Noninterference by the government, freedom of conscience, and freedom of worship should satisfy any religion, minority or majority. However, in Rumania no religious freedom exists.

The Rumanian government, through its Ministry of Cults, exercises a policy of total interference in ecclesiastical matters regardless of their administrative, social, or theological nature. No decision can be implemented by the churches unless it is thoroughly reviewed and approved by the Ministry of Cults. For instance, any social or religious gathering, with the exception of Sunday worship, must be approved by the state. The same condition applies to the right of churches to use their material resources. Religious instruction is also subject to debilitating government intrusion. While the state does allow religion classes to be held during certain prescribed hours, school authorities are instructed to organize compulsory school activities at precisely the same hours.

It should be emphasized that these restrictions harm especially the minority populations. Religious affiliation generally corresponds with nationality in Rumania. The church then is the only remaining institution that could fulfill the minorities' needs and permit them to nurture their ethnic heritage. In this sense, therefore, harassment of churches assumes a far greater meaning for minorities than simply the curtailment of religious freedoms.

Hungarian minority Protestant churches are dependent to a great extent on donations from sister communities in the West to support their charitable work. Clergymen, however, are forbidden to receive gifts from abroad, and such donations, if intercepted, are confiscated, even, as happened in 1977, when they were sent to repair churches damaged by an earthquake.[37] Freedom to publish theological books, periodicals, and other religious material is extremely limited.

Some of these difficulties are shared equally by Rumanian believers. But it was clearly an attack on the heritage of the minorities that during the years 1974–75, on the pretext of "protection of the national cultural treasury," church archives were summarily confiscated and trucked into warehouses. Since then, part of this material has been destroyed due to neglect, and none is accessible for researchers.[38]

Religious persecution of individual believers has also been documented by Amnesty International in its 1978 report on Rumania.[39]

Economic Rights

In the economic sphere, in questions of employment and compensation, minorities are entitled to nondiscriminatory treatment. In Rumania, however, economic tools, such as the total government control over industry and the labor and housing markets, are used to break up homogeneous ethnic Hungarian communities.

Rumanian citizens are not permitted to resettle in another city without official approval. At the same time, it is government policy to prevent the minority populations of cities from growing. Accordingly, while Hungarians find it almost impossible to move into the major cities of Transylvania, the influx of Rumanians is not only permitted, but encouraged through offers of favorable housing opportunities and other benefits.[40]

Industrialization, as in all Communist states, is government-planned and used as a tool to achieve the same purpose. Instead of employing the local nationality population, the new factories are staffed mostly by Rumanian settlers imported by the government from compact Rumanian areas like Muntenia or Oltenia.

The breakup of Hungarian communities is further accomplished through the routine assignment of Hungarian graduates of universities and trade schools to jobs outside their native communities. Even though President Ceauşescu himself, speaking on March 14, 1978, before a joint plenary session of the Hungarian and German Nationality Workers councils, cited this practice as a "deficiency" in Rumania's nationality policies, it continues unaltered to the present day. The Hungarian minority is deprived of doctors, lawyers, and other professionals who speak their own language. A complaint heard frequently, especially among the elderly in rural areas, is that they cannot communicate with the local doctor.[41] Rumanian professionals do not have to speak Hungarian in Hungarian areas. Consequently, the local population must either accomodate to the language of the Rumanian professionals foisted on them, or suffer the consequences. The discriminatory nature of this policy is clear. It is also intimately tied to the government's policy on minority schools. The sending of Rumanians into Hungarian areas paves the way for the elimination of Hungarian schools, since the children of these Rumanians are educated in newly created Rumanian sections. The Hungarian sections are then phased out as shown above.

Legal Remedy

Finally, for Rumania's minorities there is no effective legal remedy against abuse. Section 247 of Rumania's Criminal Code, which forbids discrimination on the basis, inter alia, of national origin, is never enforced in criminal trials.[42]

This deficiency clearly violates the "International Covenant on Civil and Political Rights," which states (Article 2, Section 3):

Each state party to the present Covenant undertakes:

(a) to ensure that any person whose rights and freedoms as herein recognized are violated shall have an effective remedy notwithstanding that the violation has been committed by persons acting in an official capacity;

(b) to ensure that any person claiming such a remedy shall have his right thereto determined by competent judicial, administrative or legislative authorities, or by any other competent authority provided for by the legal system of the state, and to develop the possibilities of judicial remedy;

(c) to ensure that the competent authorities shall enforce such remedies when granted.

The lack of legal remedy is, of course, in perfect harmony with the official position that this problem simply does not exist. In Rumania, "there is continuous repetiton of the proposition that the nationality question in our country has been finally, once and for all, solved," wrote Károly Király.[43] While some discussion and even occasional concessions are allowed concerning other social, economic, and political questions, the problems of the minorities is a forbidden subject. Still less is it permitted to propose any improvement in this area. The only task is to combat "nationalism," which means minority nationalism and to neutralize the "troublemakers." According to Károly Király, who has himself experienced the dire consequences of such "troublemaking," "unpardonably extreme methods of intimidation are employed against those who dare to ask for permission to speak in the interest of having the nationality question handled legally and in accordance with the Constitution."[44] In this way, any demand or complaint concerning minority conditions is wholly ignored or, in Király's words, "killed by persistent silence."[45]

Notes

1. Quoted in Georgina Ashworth, ed., *World Minorities* (Sunbury: Quartermaine House, 1977), vol. 1, p. xix.

2. See for instance Myres S. McDougal, Harold D. Lasswell, Lung-Chu Chen, "Freedom from Discrimination in Choice of Language and International Human Rights," *Southern Illinois University Law Journal,* no. 1 (1976): 164; also John Carey, "Editorial Comment: Progress on Human Rights at the United Nations," *American Journal of International Law* 66, no. 4 (Sept., 1972) p. 107.

3. For example, *The Hungarian Nationality in Romania* (Bucharest: Meridiane Publishing House, 1976); also *A Living Reality in Romania Today; Full Harmony and Equality between the Romanian People and the Coinhabiting Nationalities* (n.p., n.d.) distributed by Rumanian diplomatic missions in 1977–78.

4. Robert R. King, *Minorities Under Communism: Nationalities as a Source of Tension Among Balkan Communist States* (Cambridge, Mass.: Harvard University Press, 1973); George Schöpflin, *The Hungarians of Rumania* (London: Minority Rights Group, 1978).

5. Three letters of Károly Király, former alternate member of the politbureau of Rumania and one of the most prominent leaders of the Hungarian minority; a list of demands by Lajos Takács, professor of international law, former university rector, party official; and the anonymous study signed by the nom-de-plume György Lázár were published in *Witnesses to Cultural Genocide: First-Hand Reports on Rumania's Minority Policies Today* (New York: American Transylvanian Federation and the Committee for Human Rights in Rumania, 1979).

6. A list of seventy-nine such articles is provided in "Continuing the President's Authority to Waive the Trade Act Freedom of Emigration Provisions," hearing before the subcommittee on International Trade of the Committee on Finance, U.S. Senate (Washington, D.C.: Government Printing Office, 1978), pp. 85–88.

7. Ilie Ceauşescu, "Transylvania From the Dacians to 1918: Two Millenia of Struggle and Work to Maintain and Affirm National Being and Dignity" *Anale de Istorie* no. 6 (Nov.-Dec., 1978), pp. 69–84, as translated in JPRS (Joint Publications Research Service) (Washington, D.C.) no. 073103, International Affairs.

8. *The Hungarian Nationality in Romania,* p. 8; *A Living Reality in Romania Today,* pp. 3–4.

9. "The Hungarian Minority Problem in Rumania," *Bulletin of the International Commission of Jurists* no. 17 (Dec., 1963). p. 41.

10. Private communication from Dr. András Zsigmond of Toronto, Ont., former census taker in Rumania.

11. See the suggestive title of the second publication in note 3.

12. *Scînteia* (Bucharest), Nov. 16, 1968.

13. *Witnesses to Cultural Genocide,* p. 171.

14. Ibid., p. 167.

15. Ibid., p. 175.

16. Private communication from several noted Hungarian authors living in Rumania. The communications were obtained while they were visiting the West. For obvious reasons they had to remain anonymous.

17. *A Living Reality in Romania Today,* p. 12.

18. "Continuing the President's Authority," p. 63.

19. *Witnesses to Cultural Genocide,* p. 174.

20. King, op. cit., p. 153.

21. For a description of the circumstances of Szabédi's death, see *Witnesses to Cultural Genocide,* pp. 66–69.

22. King, op. cit., p. 154.

23. *Witnesses to Cultural Genocide,* p. 119.

24. Ibid., p. 120.

25. The Official Associated Press Almanac. (New York: Hammond Almanac, 1977).

26. *Witnesses to Cultural Genocide,* p. 174.

27. General Assembly Resolution 217, United Nations Document A/810 at 71–77 (1948).

28. See for example Andrei Oţetea, ed., *The History of the Romanian People* (New York: Twayne Publishers, 1970), pp. 23–159.

29. *Witnesses to Cultural Genocide,* pp. 184–209, contains an informative document on this hate-mongering campaign.

30. Ibid., p. 175.

31. Private communications from members of the Hungarian minority visiting the West; also, *Witnesses to Cultural Genocide,* pp. 32–35.

32. *Witnesses to Cultural Genocide,* p. 99.

33. "After 20 years of Silent Protests, Transylvanians in Romania Are Calling Loudly for Their Rights," *The Christian Science Monitor,* May 25, 1978, p. 15.

34. Private communications from members of the Hungarian minority.

35. F. Kunszabo, "En Moldavie," *Espirit* (Paris) Mar., 1978, p. 83.

36. Conference on Security and Cooperation in Europe, Final Act, Helsinki, 1975.

37. "Continuing the President's Authority," pp. 45–50.

38. *Neue Züricher Zeitung,* February 1/2, 1975, p. 6.

39. "Romania. Forced Labor. Psychiatric Repression of Dissent. Persecution of Religious Believers. Ethnic Discrimination and Persecution. Law and the Suppression of Human Rights in Romania." Amnesty International USA, 1978.

40. *Witnesses to Cultural Genocide,* pp. 110–34.

41. Schöpflin, op. cit., p. 14.

42. All Hungarian minority intellectuals interviewed stressed this point, namely, that to their knowledge section 247 is the only section of the Penal Code of Rumania that has never been enforced even as far as the indictment stage.

43. *Witnesses to Cultural Genocide,* p. 170.

44. Ibid., p. 171.

45. "Vara protestar tigs ihjal" [Our Protests are Killed by Persistent Silence]. *Dagens Nyheter* (Stockholm), Mar. 2, 1978.

Concluding Comments

Any conclusion that attempts to draw together the loose ends in the debate surrounding the fate of Transylvania cannot hope to be "the last word." More likely, it will serve as the preface to the next stage in the discussion. The editors of the present collection of essays seek only to round out the picture by adding some of their own observations and the insights of other scholars who are not represented in the present collection. If by sharing such observations they contribute to a continuation of the Transylvanian debate, their efforts have not been in vain.

The topic of Transylvania needs discussion, debate, analysis, and understanding. Only in this way is it possible to get beyond the vampire-infested fog to reflect on the real place and its peoples. If this fog can be lifted even a little with a continuing discussion, then perhaps the day is not far off when real solutions will be considered for a festering nationality problem that ever threatens to embroil the peoples of Eastern Europe in renewed conflicts.

As Professor Gerald J. Bobango pointed out in his reflections on some of the foregoing studies at the Symposium on Transylvania held at Kent State University on May 19, 1979:

> the most vital observations [regarding Transylvania] . . . are threefold, namely, there is nothing *unique* about our problem, firstly—it beset our ancestors and all those who marched through the generations culminating in 1848 or 1918 or 1940. Secondly, it is not predetermined that Romanians and Hungarians should be implacable opponents—the "clash" of peoples and claims over Transylvania is a product of identifiable historical circumstances, not of deep-seated and irrevocable differences. We continue to engage in polemics today because we remain under the influence of certain powerful 19th-century delusions which made the state coterminous with nationality. Finally . . . [our] discussions ought to convince us that the situation of minorities in Transylvania is and always has been a complex one, defying the simple solutions of official state news organs or the rantings of the American ethnic press.

Still, our scholarly endeavors have to operate in an environment that is dominated not so much by "the simple solutions of official state news organs or the rantings of the American ethnic press," but by the apolitical and antiintellectual escape literature of Count Dracula. Perhaps the distortions of the former have contributed to the popularity of the latter, but this does not excuse us from challenging the assumptions and the conclusions of both sets of primitivism.

The foregoing essays have focused on some of the key events, the turning points, and developmental processes and have thereby contributed to a more accurate portrayal of Transylvanian reality, both past and present. Unquestionably, many gaps remain. These, hopefully, will be treated in future volumes dealing with Transylvania. If the present effort becomes the first in a series, then the problems of all the peoples in Transylvania will have moved one step closer to solution. Dispelling the fog is just the first step. Once an awareness of the real Transylvania supercedes the illusion, its problems will have to be dealt with.

The first problem is, of course, the nationalist posturing that surrounds the entire question of minority-majority relations in Eastern Europe. As Professor Paul Underwood pointed out at the Kent State Symposium on Transylvania:

> . . . [Nationalism] is a far stronger force in Central and Eastern Europe than it is in Western Europe generally. Probably this is so because of a feeling on the part of these people of being relatively small islands in a sea of alien languages and cultures. In this milieu, nationalism is passionate and, with the possible exception of the Poles, nowhere more so than among the Hungarians and the Romanians. This passion fires the essential national ideologies of both peoples, ideologies in which Transylvania has been given a special role. And the problem is that each of these roles is exclusive, in conflict with the other. So there is precious little middle ground on which an observer can find a comfortable footing.

Yet there is some middle ground. It can be provided by responsible scholarship that attempts to deal with Transylvania on the basis of reality rather than nationalistic or Hollywood-inspired mystification. Rumanian, Hungarian, and Saxon or Swabian German scholars—or American scholars, for that matter—need not divest themselves (even if they could) of their passionate commitments to write with relative fairness and objectivity. As long as they adhere to the rigorous demands of their respective disciplines, they should be able to reach at least that "precious little middle ground." Once that has been reached it is not too difficult to realize that Transylvanian Rumanians, Hungarians, and Germans are indeed the victims of their past experiences and that they "remain under the influence of certain powerful 19th-century delusions which made the state coterminous with nationality."

From that point on it is possible to reflect on the problems and prospects of *all* the peoples of Transylvania. In fact, even a dialogue becomes possible among the scholars of the respective nationalities. Then questions are no longer phrased simply in terms of minority versus majority rights or in terms of national interests, but in terms of the long-term interests of *all* Transylvanians. Are the interests of the different nationalities in Transylvania really mutually exclusive? If we find this to be the case, we might suggest a territorial solution: partition, partition with population exchange, or something similar. On the other hand, if the interests of Transylvanians are not mutually exclusive but merely seem so under the constraints of the present-day nation-state, democratic centralism, and nationalism, then we have to define the minimum and optimum institutional changes that will make peaceful coexistence and tolerance a reality instead of an empty promise. Here consideration of individual human rights, corporate minority (group) rights, and the defense of both is indispensable. Territorial autonomy, guaranteed bilingualism, and nondiscrimination in government relations, social intercourse, and economic opportunities are just some of the areas that must be considered. Finally, the vision of a transnational, multiethnic Danubian state committed to cultural pluralism should be given at least intellectual consideration even if the present balance of world power makes its realization unlikely in Soviet-controlled Eastern Europe.

Rumanian, Hungarian, and German Geographic and Historic Place Names in Transylvania[1]

Rumanian[2]	*Hungarian*	*German*[3]
I. REGIONAL, COUNTY, AND OTHER GEOGRAPHIC OR ADMINISTRATIVE SUBDIVISIONS[4]		
Alba de Jos	Alsó-Fehér	
Alba	Fehér	
Ardeal[5]	Erdély[5]	Siebenbürgen[5]
Arad	Arad	Arad
Arieş	Aranyos	Aranyosch
Banat	Bánság	Banat
Bihor	Bihar	Bihar
Bistriţa-Nasaud	Beszterce-Naszód	Bistritz-Nasod
Braşov	Brassó	Kronstadt
Caraş-Severin	Krassó-Szörény	
Ciuc	Csík	Csik
Cluj	Kolozs	Klausenburg
Covasna	Kovászna	
Crasna	Kraszna	Krasna
Crişana[6]	Körösvidék	Kreischgebiet
Harghita	Hargita	Hargita
Hunedoara	Hunyad	
Maramureş	Máramaros	
Mureş	Maros	
Mureş-Turda	Maros-Torda	
Niraj	Nyárád	Nyarad
Odorhei	Udvarhely	
Satu Mare	Szatmár	Sathmar
Sălaj	Szilágy	
Secuime	Székelyföld	Seklerland
Sibiu	Szeben	
Solnoc-Dobîca	Szolnok-Doboka	
Ţara Bîrsei	Barcaság	Burzenland
Timiş	Temes	Temesch
Trascău	Torockó Vidéke	
Treiscaune	Háromszék	
Zona Calatei	Kalotaszeg	
II. CITIES AND TOWNS		
Abrud	Abrudbánya	Gross-Schlatten
Adămuş	Ádámos	

Rumanian	Hungarian	German
Ady	Érmindszent	
Aghireşu	Egeres	
Agnita	Szentágota	Agnetheln
Aiud	Nagyenyed	Gross-Enyed
Alba Iulia	Gyulafehérvár	Karlsburg (Weissenburg)
Anina	Stajerlakanina	Staierdorf
Apahida	Apahida	
Arad	Arad	Arad
Ardud	Erdőd	Erdeed
Ariuşd	Erősd	
Armăşeni	Csíkménaság	
Armeniş	Örményes	Armenisch
Asinip	Asszonynépe	Frauenvolk
Avram Iancu	Felső-Vidra	
Bagara	Bogártelke	
Baia de Arieş	Aranyosbánya	Offenburg
Baia de Criş	Körösbánya	Altenburg
Baia Mare	Nagybánya	Frauenbach
Baia Sprie	Felsőbánya	Mittelstadt
Balan	Balánbánya	
Balda	Báld	
Baraolt	Barót	
Bazna	Bázna	Baasen
Băţani Mari	Nagybacon	
Băţani Mici	Kisbacon	
Beclean	Bethlen	
Beiuş	Belényes	
Belin	Bölön	Blumendorf
Bistriţa	Beszterce	Bistritz
Bixad	Bikszád	
Blaj	Balázsfalva	Blasendorf
Bobîlna	Bábolna	
Bod	Botfalu	Brenndorf
Borsec	Borszék	
Bran	Törcsvár	Törzburg
Braşov	Brassó	Kronstadt
Bratca	Brátka	
Breaza	Beresztelke	Ungersdorf (Breit)
Calaţele	Kiskalota	
Cara	Kolozskara	
Caransebeş	Karánsebes	Karansebesch
Carei	Nagykároly	Karol

Rumanian	*Hungarian*	*German*
Cămăraşu	Pusztakamarás	
Cătina	Katona	
Cehul-Silvaniei	Szilágycseh	
Cernatul de Jos	Alsócsernáton	
Chichiş	Kőkös	
Chieşd	Szilágykövesd	
Ciacova	Csák	Tschakowa
Ciceu	Csíkcsicsó	
Cincul	Nagysink	Gross-Schenk
Cisnădie	Nagydisznód	Heltau
Cisnădioara	Kisdisznód	Michelsberg
Ciucea	Csucsa	
Cîmpeni	Topánfalva	
Cîmpia Turzii	Aranyosgyéres	
Cluj-Napoca	Kolozsvár	Klausenburg
Codlea	Feketehalom	Zeiden
Cojocna	Kolozs	Salzgrub
Coltău	Koltó	
Colţeşti	Torockószentgyörgy	
Copăceni	Koppánd	
Copşa-Mică	Kiskapus	Kleinkopisch
Corund	Korond	
Covasna	Kovászna	
Crasna	Kraszna	
Cristeşti	Maroskeresztúr	
Cristian	Keresztényfalva	Neustadt
Cristurul Secuiesc	Székelykeresztúr	
Cugir	Kudzsir	
Cuzaplac	Középlak	
Dalnic	Dálnok	
Dăbîca	Doboka	
Deda	Déda	
Dej	Dés	Desch (Burglos)
Deva	Déva	Schlossberg (Diemrich)
Ditrău	Ditró	
Dr Petru Groza	Vaskóhsziklás	
Dumbrăveni	Erzsébetváros	Elizabethstadt
Dumbrăvioara	Sáromberke	Scharenberg
Ernei	Nagyernye	
Făgăraş	Fogaras	Fogarasch
Făget	Facsád	Fatschet
Filpişu	Magyarfülpös	Ungarisch-Felps
Floreşti	Földszin	Feisendorf

Rumanian	*Hungarian*	*German*
Frata	Magyarfráta	
Geoagiu	Algyógy	
Gheorgheni	Gyergyószentmiklós	
Gheorgheni	Györgyfalva	
Gherla	Szamosujvár	Armenerstadt
Gilău	Gyalu	
Halmeu	Halmi	
Harghita Băi	Hargitafürdő	
Haţeg	Hátszeg	Wallenthal (Hötzig)
Hărman	Szászhermány	Honigberg
Herculian	Magyarhermány	
Huedin	Bánffyhunyad	
Hunedoara	Vajdahunyad	Eisenmarkt
Ibăneşti	Libánfalva	
Iernut	Radnót	
Ighiu	Magyarigen	Grabendorf
Ileanda	Nagyilonda	
Ilioara	Kisilye	
Izvorul Crişului	Körösfő	
Izvorul Mureşului	Marosfő	
Jibou	Zsibó	
Jidioara	Zsidóvár	
Jigodin Băi	Zsögödfürdő	
Jimbolia	Zsombolya	Hatzfeld
Lenauheim	Csatád	Tschatad
Lipova	Lippa	Lippa
Lisnău	Lisznyó	
Luduş	Marosludas	
Lugoj	Lugos	Lugosch
Lupeni	Farkaslaka	
Lupeni	Lupény	
Măeruş	Szászmagyaros	Nussbach
Malnaş	Málnás	
Marghita	Margitta	
Mănăştur	Kolozsmonostor	Appesdorf
Mediaş	Medgyes	Mediasch
Miercurea Ciuc	Csíkszereda	
Miercurea Sibiului	Szerdahely	Reussmarkt
Mihai Viteazul	Szentmihályfalva	
Mihai Viteazul	Zoltán	Zoltendorf
Mociu	Mócs	
Moftinul Mic	Kismajtény	
Moraviţa	Temesmóra	Morawitza

Rumanian	*Hungarian*	*German*
Nădlac	Nagylak	
Nădrag	Nadrág	
Năsăud	Naszód	
Nimigea Ungurească	Magyarnemegye	
Nireş	Nyires	
Nuşfalău	Szilágynagyfalu	
Ocna Dejului	Désakna	Salzdorf
Ocna Mureşului	Marosujvár	Maroschujwar
Ocna Sibiului	Vizakna	Salzburg
Odorheiul-Secuiesc	Székelyudvarhely	Hofmarkt
Oituz	Ojtoz	
Oradea	Nagyvárad	Grosswardein
Orăştie	Szászváros	Broos
Orşova	Orsova	Orschowa
Panticeu	Páncélcseh	
Petrila	Petrilla	
Petreşti	Péterfalva	Petersdorf
Petroşani	Petrozsény	Petroschen
Piatra-Fîntînele	Forráskő	
Poiana Braşov	Brassópojána	
Praid	Parajd	
Prundul Bîrgăului	Borgóprund	
Pui	Puj	
Racul	Csíkrákos	
Radna	Máriaradna	
Răstoci	Hosszúrév	
Recaş	Temesrékás	Rekasch
Reghin	Szászrégen	Sächsisch-Reen
Remetea	Gyergyóremete	
Remetea	Magyarremete	
Reşiţa	Resica	Reschitza
Rimetea	Torockó	Eisenmarkt (Traschen)
Rîşnov	Barcarozsnyó	Rosenau
Rodna	Óradna	Altrodna
Roşia Montana	Verespatak	
Saciova	Szacsva	
Salonta	Nagyszalonta	
Sarmisegetuza	Várhely	
Satu Mare	Szatmárnémeti	Sathmar
Săcuieni	Székelyhíd	
Sălişte	Szelistye	Grossdorf
Săpînţa	Szaplonca	
Sărate	Sófalva	Salz

Rumanian	*Hungarian*	*German*
Sărmaşul Mare	Nagysármás	
Sărmăşel	Kissármás	
Sebeş	Szászsebes	Mühlbach
Sfîntul Gheorghe	Sepsiszentgyörgy	
Sibiu	Nagyszeben	Hermannstadt
Sic	Szék	
Siculeni	Mádéfalva	
Sighetul Marmaţiei	Máramarossziget	
Sighişoara	Segesvár	Schässburg
Simeria	Piskitelep	
Sîncrăeni	Csíkszentkirály	
Sîngeorgiul de Mureş	Marosszentgyörgy	
Sînnicolau Mare	Nagyszentmiklós	Grossanktnikolaus
Sîntana	Ószentanna	
Sîntimbru	Marosszentimre	
Someşeni	Szamosfalva	
Sovata	Szováta	
Surdoc	Szurdok	
Şimleul Silvaniei	Szilágysomlyó	
Şiria	Világos	Wilagosch
Şoimuş	Sólymos	Scholmosch
Şomcuta Mare	Nagysomkút	
Şura Mare	Nagycsűr	Grosscheuern
Taşnad	Tasnád	
Tălisoara	Olasztelek	
Tămaşda	Tamáshida	
Tămăşeu	Paptamási	
Tărtăria	Alsótatárlaka	
Tătîrlaua	Tatárlaka	Taterloch
Teaca	Téke	Tekendorf
Teiuş	Tövis	Dreikirchen
Tileagd	Mezőtelegd	
Timişoara	Temesvár	Temeschwar
Tîrgu Mureş	Marosvásárhely	Neumarkt
Tîrgu Secuiesc	Kézdivásárhely	
Tîrnăveni	Dicsőszentmárton	
Toplița	Maroshévíz	
Tulgheş	Tölgyes	
Turda	Torda	Thorenburg (Thorda)
Turnu-Roşu	Verestorony	Rothenturm
Tuşnad Băi	Tusnádfürdő	
Urvind	Örvend	
Valceu	Magyarvalkó	

Rumanian	*Hungarian*	*German*
Valea-Drăganului	Nagysebes	
Valea Frumoasă	Szépvölgy	
Valea lui Mihai	Érmihályfalva	
Vărădia	Tótvárad	
Viştea	Magyarvista	
Vîrghiş	Vargyas	
Vulcan	Volkánny	Wolkendorf
Zagon	Zágon	
Zalău	Zilah	Waltenberg
Zamsîncrai	Kalotaszentkirály	
Zetea	Zetelaka	
Zlatna	Zalatna	Grosschlatten

III. Rivers and Lakes

Almaşul	Almás	
Arieşul	Aranyos	Aranyosch
Barcăul	Berettyó	
Bega	Béga	Bega
Bîrzava	Berzence	
Bistriţa	Beszterce	Bistritz
Buzăul	Bodza	
Caraşul	Karas	
Cerna	Cserna	
Cibin	Szeben	Zibin
Crişul Alb	Feher Körös	Weisse Kreisch
Crişul Negru	Fekete Körös	Schwarze Kreisch
Crişul Repede	Sebes Körös	Schnelle Kreisch
Dunărea	Duna	Donau
Hîrtibaciu	Hortobágy	
Iara	Jára-patak	
Îzei	Iza	
Jiul	Zsil	Schyl
Lacul Roşu	Gyilkos-tó	
Lacul S. Ana	Szent Anna-tó	
Lapuş	Lápos	
	Mohos-tó	
Mureşul	Maros	Mieresch
Nera	Néra	
	Nyárád	
Oltul	Olt	Alt
Săsar	Zazár	
Sebeşul	Sebes	Sebesch (Mühlbach)
Secaşul	Szekás	Zekesch

Rumanian	*Hungarian*	*German*
Someşul	Szamos	Somesch (Samosch)
Someşul Cald	Meleg-Szamos	Warmer Somesch
Someşul Mare	Nagy-Szamos	Gross Somesch
Someşul Mic	Kis-Szamos	Kleiner Somesch
Someşul Rece	Hideg-Szamos	Kalter Somesch
Strei	Sztrigy	
Timişul	Temes	Temesch
Tîrnava	Küküllő	Kokel
Tîrnava Mare	Nagy Küküllő	Gross Kokel
Tîrnava Mică	Kis Küküllő	Kleiner Kokel
Tisa	Tisza	Theiss
Trotuşul	Tatros	
Uzul	Uz	

IV. Mountains, Mountain Ranges, and Mountain Peaks

Carpaţii Meridionali	Déli-Kárpátok	Südkarpaten (Transsylvanische-Alpen)
Carpaţii Orientali	Keleti-Kárpátok	Ostkarpaten
Ceahlău	Csalhó	
Ciceului	Csicsói-Hargita	
Cîndrel	Csindrel	
Ciomatul	Csomád	
Cohardul	Nagy-Kohárd	
Dealurile Feleacului	Feleki hegy	
Delhedi	Dél-hegy	
Fîncel	Fancsal-tető	
Ghilcoş	Gyilkos	
Hăsmaşul Mic	Öcsém-tető	
Inăul	Ünő-kő	
Mădăraş	Madarasi-hargita	
Munţeleşes	Réz-hegység	
M.tii Almăjului	Almás-hegység	
M.tii Apuseni	Erdélyi Szigethegység	
M.tii Banatului	Bánsági hegyvidék	
M.tii Baraoltului	Baróti-hegység	Baroter-Gebirge
M.tii Bihorului	Bihar-hegység	
M.tii Bîrgăului	Borgói-havasok	Borgoi-Gebirge
M.tii Bistriţei	Besztercei-havasok	
M.tii Bodocului	Bodoki-hegység	
M.tii Braşovului	Brassói-havasok	
M.tii Breţcu	Háromszéki-havasok	
M.tii Bucegi	Bucsecs-hegység	

Rumanian	*Hungarian*	*German*
M.tii Buzăului	Bodzai-hegység	
M.tii Călimani	Kelemen-havasok	Kelemen-Gebirge
M.tii Cernei	Orsovai-hegység	
M.tii Cibinului	Szebeni-havasok	
M.tii Cindrelului	Szebeni-havasok	
M.tii Ciucului	Csíki-havasok	
M.tii Codrului	Béli-hegység	
M.tii Dognecei	Dognácskai-hegység	
M.tii Făgăraşului	Fogarasi-havasok	Fogarascher Alpen
M.tii Făgetului	Bükk-hegység	
M.tii Godeanu	Godján	
M.tii Gilăului	Gyalui-havasok	
M.tii Giurgeului	Gyergyói-havasok	Gyergyoi-Gebirge
M.tii Gurghiului	Görgényi-havasok	Görgeny-Gebirge
M.tii Gutîiului	Gutin-hegység	
M.tii Harghitei	Hargita-hegység	
M.tii Hăghimaşului	Nagy-Hagymás	
M.tii Locvei	Lokva-hegység	
M.tii Lotrului	Lotru-hegység	
M.tii Maramureşului	Máramarosi-havasok	
M.tii Mehedinţului	Domogled	
M.tii Metaliferi	Erdélyi Érchegység	Siebenbürger Erzgebirge
M.tii Mezeşului	Meszes-hegység	
M.tii Parîngului	Páreng	
M.tii Perşanilor	Persányi-hegység	
M.tii Retezatului	Retyezát	
M.tii Rodnei	Radnai-havasok	Rodna-Gebirge
M.tii Sebesului	Kudzsiri-havasok	
M.tii Semenicului	Szemenik-hegység	
M.tii Sureanului	Kudzsiri-havasok	
M.tii Tarcului	Szár-kő	
M.tii Ţibleşului	Cibles-hegység	
M.tii Vîlcanului	Vulkán-hegység	
M.tii Vîrşeţului	Verseci-hegység	
M.tii Zărandului	Hegyes-Drócsát	
Oştoroş	Ostoros	
Pădurea Craiului	Királyerdő	Königswald
Parîngul Mare	Páreng	
Peleaga	Retyezát	
Piatra Altarului	Oltár-kő	
Piatra Craiului	Király-kő	
Piatra Groznei	Szemenik	

Rumanian	Hungarian	German
Piatra Roşie	Veres-kő	
Piatra Unică	Egyes-kő	
Pietrosul	Pietrosz	
Pietrosul Rodnei	Nagy-Pietrosz	
Poiana Ruscă	Ruszka-havasok	
Racu	Rákosi-Hargita	
Saca	Mezőhavas	
Siculenii	Mádéfalvi-Hargita	

V. Mountain Passes, Valleys, and River Basins

Rumanian	Hungarian	German
Cazanul Mare	Kazán-szoros	Kasan Pass
Cheile Turenilor	Turi-hasadék	
Cheile Turzii	Tordai-hasadék	
Cîmpia Crişurilor	Körösök-síksága	
Cîmpia Someşului	Szamos-síkság	
Cîmpia Tisei	Tiszai-alföld	
Cîmpia Transilvaniei	Mezőség	
Dealurile Someşului	Szamos-hátság	
Depresiunea Almăjului	Almás-medence	
Depresiunea Baia-mare	Nagybányai-medence	
Depresiunea Bilbor	Bélbori-medence	
Depresiunea Bistriţei şi Năsăudului	Beszterce vidéke	
Depresiunea Borsecului	Borszéki-medence	
Depresiunea Braşovului	Brassói-medence	
Depresiunea Ciucului	Csíki-medence	
Depresiunea Făgăraşului	Fogarasi-medence	
Depresiunea Gheorghenilor	Gyergyói-medence	
Depresiunea Haţegului	Hátszegi-medence	
Depresiunea Homorodului	Homoród vidéke	
Depresiunea Mureşului	Maros-Tordai-medence	
Depresiunea Petroşanilor	Petrozsényi-medence	
Depresiunea Sălajului	Szilágysági-halom és dombvidék	
Depresiunea Secaşului	Székás-medence	
Depresiunea Sibiului	Szebeni-medence	Hermannstadter Gelande
Depresiunea Someşului	Szamos-medence	

Rumanian	*Hungarian*	*German*
Depresiunea Trei-Scaune	Háromszéki-medence	
Depresiunea Transilvaniei	Erdélyi-medence	
Pasul Bicaz	Békási-szoros	
Pasul Bran	Törcsvári-hágó	
Pasul Buzău	Bodzai-szoros	
Pasul Craiului	Királyhágó	
Pasul Ghimes	Gyimesi-szoros	
Pasul Oituz	Ojtozi-szoros	
Pasul Predeal	Tömösi-hágó	Predeal Pass
Pasul Prislop	Priszlop-hágó	
Pasul Teleajen	Ósánci-szoros	
Pasul Tîrnavelor	Küküllő mente	Das Gebiet Der Beiden Kokeln
Pasul Tolvaioş	Tolvajos-hágó	
Pasul Tulgheş	Tölgyesi-szoros	
Pasul Turnu-Roşu	Vöröstoronyi-szoros	Törzburger Pass
Porţile de Fier	Vaskapu	Eisernes Tor
Strîmtoarea de la Buru	Borrévi-szoros	
Vadul Crişului	Révi-szoros	
Valea Chintaului	Kajántói-völgy	
Valea Mehadica	Mehádia völgye	
Valea Oltului	Olt völgye	

Notes

Sources: János Ritoók, *Kettős tükör: A magyar-szász együttélés multjából és a két világháboru közötti irodalmi kapcsolatok történetéből* [Double Mirror: From the Past of Hungarian-Saxon Relations and the History of Their Literary Contacts Between the Two World Wars] (Bucharest: Kriterion, 1979), pp. 239-44; Károly Kós, *Tájak falvak, hagyományok* [Regions, Settlements, Traditions] (Bucharest: Kriterion, 1976), pp. 382-386; Vilmos Mátyás, *Utazások Erdélyben* [Travels in Transylvania] (Budapest: Panoráma, 1977); László Ádám, György Belia, et al., *Románia* (Budapest: Panoráma, 1973); and the Central and South East European map collection of the Geography Department at Kent State University.

1. Transylvania includes in the present context not only historical Transylvania, but also the other areas acquired by Rumania from Hungary in 1918–20. These areas are the Banat, Crişana|Partium and the Maramures.

2. The alphabetical listing follows the present Rumanian place names. The editors have assumed that this would be the most practical and useful way to list the designations since most current maps use the Rumanian appellations rather than the historical Hungarian or German names. This listing also includes more than just the place names

mentioned in the individual studies within the volume. It provides a useful reference to the more important names in Transylvania, past and present. (Note: In recent years, the Rumanian government has undertaken the official celebration of the Dacian origin of some of its cities. In most cases this has meant paying tribute to the past in order to stress the present state's "Dacian roots." In some cases, however, it has led to the readopting of the Dacian name of the city or town. Cluj [Kolozsvár, Klausenburg] is an outstanding example; it is now officially called Cluj-Napoca. Other Transylvanian cities or towns that may face similar prospects are Roşia Montana [Alburnus Maior], Zlatna [Ampelum], Vărădia [Argedava], Rîşnov [Cumidava], Orşova [Dierna], and Turda [Potaissa].)

3. German place names do not exist for all locations in Transylvania. Unlike the Hungarian and Rumanian populations, which are located throughout Transylvania, The German population is located overwhelmingly in southern Transylvania. Aside from the small pocket of German-Saxons in the area around Bistriţa [Bistritz, Beszterce] most German-Saxons are located in the regions surrounding Sibiu [Hermannstadt, Nagyszeben] and Braşov [Kronstadt, Brassó], while the German Swabians are located primarily in the Banat [Bánság] in and near the cities of Arad and Timişoara [Temeschwar, Temesvár]. In other parts of Transylvania the Germans have simply followed the place names provided by the official state language (i.e., Hungarian prior to 1918 and Rumanian since then). In the present listing, in certain instances two German designations for the same place have been provided, with the less used designation in parentheses following the more popular name.

4. Including both current county designations and former regional and historical designations.

5. Transylvania (Latin).

6. Crişana also covers the general area of the historic Partium (Latin), which "parts" were attached to Transylvania as a consequence of struggles against the Ottoman Turks, later as a consequence of Habsburg administrative expediency, and most recently, in 1918–20, due to Rumanian acquisition of it together with Transylvania proper.

The Population of Rumania and Transylvania According to Nationality

(in thousands)

Nationality[1]	*1910*	*1920*	*1930*	*1948*	*1956*	*1966*[2]	*1977*[3]
			TRANSYLVANIA[4]				
Rumanians	2,830	2,930	3,208	3,752	4,081	4,559	5,321
Hungarians	1,664	1,306	1,353	1,482	1,616	1,597	1,651
Germans	565	539	544	331	372	372	323
Jews	182	181	178	30	30	14	8
Others	201	337	444	197	170	178	197
Total	5,260	5,112	5,549	5,792	6,232	6,720	7,500
			RUMANIA[5]				
Rumanians	10,524	13,186	11,360	13,598	15,081	16,746	19,207
Hungarians	1,823	1,362	1,553	1,500	1,654	1,620	1,671
Germans	829	593	636	344	395	383	332
Jews	820	873	260	139	34	43	25
Ukrainians	1,032	576	45	38	68	55	52
Bulgarians	340	261	64	14	13	11	9
Turks[6]	222	174	43	29	35	18	21
Slovaks and Czechs	25	32	42	35	25	32	25
Yugoslavs	66	53	47	45	43	44	38
Tatars[6]	32	35				22	21
Gypsies[7]			90	53	67	64	76
Others	126	133	141	78	74	65	83
Total	15,723	17,641	14,281	15,873	17,489	19,103	21,560[8]

NOTES

Sources: Allgemeine Statistik des Auslandes. Landerkurzbericht Rumänien 1978, Statistisches Bundesamt (Wiesbaden, 1978), pp. 57–58; *Anuarul statistic al R.P.R. 1963* [Annual Statistical Yearbook of the Rumanian People's Republic 1963] Tables 16 and 17, pp. 88–89; Robert R. King, *Minorities Under Communism: Nationalities as a Source of Tension Among Balkan Communist States* (Cambridge, Mass., 1973), Table VI, p. 267; Dezső Kopreda, *Mit kell tudni Romániáról?* [What One Must Know About Rumania] (Budapest, 1979), pp. 5–6; *Recensămîntul Populaţiei din februarie 1956; Rezultate Generale* [Population Census of February 1956: General Results] Tables 10, 11, and 12, pp. XIX–XX; *Recensămîntul populaţiei şi al locuinţelor din 5 ianuari 1977* [Population and Settlement Census of January 5, 1977] (Bucharest, 1980), Vol. I–II, Table 17, pp. 614–15; András Rónai, "Románia néprajzi viszonyai," [Rumania's Ethnographic Profile] *Földrajzi köz-*

lemények, [Geographic Proceedings] LXVIII (1940), pp. 86–109; G. D. Satmarescu, "The Changing Demographic Structure of the Population of Transylvania," *East European Quarterly*, vol. 8, no. 4 (Jan., 1975): 425–49; The Mid-European Research Institute (ed.) "Statistical Studies on the Last Hundred Years in Central Europe: 1867-1967," (unpublished manuscript).

1. In this table, "nationality" means either the declared nationality or the mother tongue of the respondent. The two have not been separated, since some of the censuses were based solely on declared nationality, others have been based solely on mother tongue, and still others on both. The census data for 1910, 1930, 1948, and 1956 used in this table are based on mother tongue. The 1920, 1966 and 1977 data are based on declared nationality.

2. Data for the 1966 census in this table is based on "Communique on the Preliminary Results of the Population and Housing Census of March 5, 1966," *Documents, Articles and Information on Romania*, No. 18 (Oct. 15, 1966), pp. 15–16 and Table 6 in Satmarescu, p. 443.

3. The Rumanian data for 1977 is not yet available in Western libraries and depositories. Only the overall population and the percentage share of the minorities are available on the basis of secondary sources. This condition is itself a reflection on the present Rumanian policy relative to national minorities. The refusal to share such information with the scholarly community seems to have become the practice since the 1966 census. The 1977 Rumanian census results were obtained from the Központi Statisztikai Hivatal [Central Statistical Office] in Budapest in January, 1983. A review of the Rumanian statistical yearbooks since 1966 supports the conclusion that the Rumanian policy is to hide the minorities from the outside world. For example, these annual volumes have ceased to publish specific data relative to the minorities either according to declared nationality or mother tongue. While the *Anuarul statistic al R.P.R. 1964* [Annual Statistical Yearbook of the Rumanian People's Republic 1964] (Direcţia Centrală de Statistică, 1964) still contains sections related to nationality and mother tongue (See Contents on p. 5 and also Sections 16 and 17 on p. 88), the post-1966 yearbooks do not have such listings at all. For more recent examples of this gap in data, see *Anuarul statistic al Republicii Socialiste România 1977* [Annual Statistical Yearbook of the Rumanian Socialist Republic 1977] (Direcţia Centrală de Statistică, 1977) concerning the overall population of Rumania in Chapter II (pp. 45–78). The analogous sections in the 1978 and 1979 editions of this yearbook also remain silent on the minorities (See respectively pp. 45–80 and pp. 45–84). This refusal to share information on the minorities is also demonstrated by the crude attempt to censor the summary of statistical results of the 1966 census, which was published in 1969. In *Recensămîntul populaţiei şi locuinţelor din 15 Martie 1966* [Population and Settlement Census of March 15, 1966] (Direcţia Centrală de Statistică, 1969), pp. XLIV–XLV, the original text referring to minorities had been removed and replaced by an edited summary before the volume was made available for general distribution. Because gaps, silence, and distortion are characteristic of Rumanian census results, it is important to go beyond the "official" Rumanian demographic and statistical analyses. While the Rumanian data shows a stagnant Hungarian population growth, which represents a decreasing percentage relative to the overall population of Rumania (i.e., 10 percent in 1930, 9.1 percent in 1956, 8.5 percent in 1966 and 7.9 percent in 1977), the actuality is probably not as dismal. According to G. D. Satmarescu, in his study on the demographic structure of Transylvania (see Sources above), the probable Hungarian population of Transylvania is about 400,000–800,000 more than admitted by the official census, which in 1966 would have meant 2 to 2.4 million Hungarians instead of 1.6 million.

4. Including Maramureş (Máramaros), Crişana (Körösvidék), and the eastern half of the Banat (Bánság).

5. The statistics for 1910 and 1920 refer to the area of Rumania in the interwar years. The statistics of 1930, 1948, 1956, 1966 and 1977 refer to the reduced area of present-day Rumania.

6. For the 1930, 1948, and 1956 censuses, this table enumerates the Tatars and Turks together.

7. The Gypsies have been placed under the category "Others" for the 1910 and 1920 censuses.

8. The data provided for 1977 by the official census is at variance with the data in Monica Barcan and Adalbert Millitz (eds.) *The German Nationality in Romania,* trans. Anda Teodorescu-Bantas (Bucharest: Meridiane Publishing House, 1978), p. 7. The latter source listed 205,000 less Rumanians, 35,000 more Hungarians, and 27,000 more Germans than what appeared in the official census results published two years later. The discrepancy is due to the Barcan-Millitz use of data based on "mother tongue" while the published official figures are based on "declared nationality."

Notes and Aide-Memoires of the Hungarian Ministry of Foreign Affairs, April 27, May 20, June 11, and July 15, 1946

Annex N°7.

Hungarian Ministry for Foreign Affairs.

80/Bé. res.
1946.

Sir,

I have the honour to transmit herewith for kindly furthering to Your Excellency's Government and to the Conference of Foreign Ministers in Paris respectively an Aide-Mémoire of the Hungarian Government concerning the territorial and minority questions arising between Hungary and Roumania.

I avail myself of this opportunity to renew to Your Excellency the assurance of my high consideration.

Budapest, 27th April 1946.

(signed) *Gyöngyösi*

His Excellency
G. M. Puskin
Envoy Extraordinary, Minister Plenipotentiary
Union of Socialist Soviet Republics,
His Excellency
H. F. Arthur Schoenfeld
Envoy Extraordinary, Minister Plenipotentiary
U. S. Minister for Hungary,
His Excellency
A. D. F. Gascoigne, C. M. G.
Political Representative of His Britannic
Majesty's Government and Minister Designate,
Budapest.

AIDE-MÉMOIRE.

Considering that the Conference of the Ministers for Foreign Affairs of the victorious Allied Powers is dealing with the establishment of the provisions of the peace treaty with Roumania, the Hungarian Government feels bound to summarize hereunder its point of view and proposals with regard to the territorial questions and the problem of the nationalities in Hungaro-Roumanian relations.

The establishment of the preliminary conditions of friendly relations and sincere cooperation with the neighbouring countries is one of the basic endeavours of democratic Hungary's foreign policy. But to attain this it seems to be necessary to secure the future of the Hungarian population of those countries. As is generally known, more than one fourth (i. e. more than 3 million souls) of the Hungarian people were placed by the Treaty of Trianon under foreign rule and therefore the reassuring settlement of this question is of great importance to the democratic Hungarian Government.

The unfavourable condition of the Hungarian minorities living in the neighbouring countries, the socially and economically difficult situation of those hundreds of thousands who were driven away to Hungary, and the drawing of frontiers also economically unfortunate was greatly instrumental to the reactionary Hungarian regime in using irredentist slogans to veil the existing social evils and to stabilise its own rule, as well as in attempting to introduce in its foreign policy the revisionist idea.

The treatment extended to the Hungarian minority of Roumania and especially actions intentionally concentrated on its economic impoverishment, as well as the policy of the Roumanian Government directed towards the expulsion of the Hungarians from Transylvania, all necessarily led to the conclusion, that "life in freedom from fear and want" cannot be ensured to the Hungarians in Roumania. No doubt the Groza Government undertook laudable endeavours to ameliorate the fate of the Hungarians but unluckily these endeavours were, in practice, to a great extent frustrated by the conduct of the Roumanian administrative apparatus, inimical to the Hungarians. It is further to fear that after the definitive settlement of the frontier the persecution of the Hungarians will continue in Roumania without any restraint. It is memorable that only the energetic measures taken by the liberating Soviet Russian army saved the Hungarians from the murders and atrocities initiated by the so-called Maniu Guards in autumn 1944.

After the experiences of the past the only definitive reassuring settlement seems to be the transfer to Hungary of the major part of the more than one and a half million Hungarians of Roumania, together with their respective territories.

Article 19 of the Armistice Agreement concluded between the Allied Powers and Roumania offers means to submit territorial claims, when stipulating that—conditioned by the subsequent sanction of the Peace Treaty to be concluded—Transylvania, or her major part, shall be retransferred to Roumania. The question of the Hungarian-Roumanian frontier is, in fact, left open by this provision, the more so because, as known, the Treaty of Trianon attached to Roumania—apart from the

57,000 km^2 of Transylvania—another 47,000 km^2 of territory not forming part of historical Transylvania.

The solution of the Hungaro-Roumanian territorial controversy is rendered more difficult by the fact that a larger number of Hungarians live in Upper Transylvania than in districts situated nearer to Hungary, and that a quite homogeneous block of Hungarians—the 600,000 Székelys—are living in the centre of present day Roumania. The reattachment of the Székelys to Hungary would involve the division proven unlucky of Transylvania, and would, in fact mean the transfer of several millions of Roumanians to Hungary.

In view of this position, the existing difficulties could best be solved by drawing the frontier line in an economically most suitable way, and in such a manner as transferring to Hungary a number of Roumanians approximately equal to that of Hungarians remaining on Roumanian territory. This seems the best way of securing an acceptable treatment for the respective national minorities in both countries.

The Hungarian Government, in order to carry into effect its above proposition, formulates its claims most modestly, requesting the transfer to Hungary of but 22,000 km^2 out of the total of 47,000 km^2 of non-Transylvanian soil. The new frontier line would mostly run along watershed mountains, including several towns with a Hungarian majority. The area in question represents but 20% of the total area of 104,000 km^2 transferred to Roumania by the Treaty of Trianon, though the proportional number of the Hungarians in these districts is one third of the total population.

This solution would create a satisfactory equilibrium also with regard to the national minority problem, because 865,000 Roumanians would be transferred to Hungary, while 1,060,000 Hungarians would continue to remain under Roumanian rule. Considering that these calculations are based on the Roumanian census of 1930, the methods of which were most unfavourable to the Hungarians, the above proposition is in reality even less to the advantage of the Hungarians. This method of proceeding would, if the worst comes to the worst, also offer the possibility of certain subsequent exchanges of population.

This new frontier would also serve the economic interest of both countries, but especially of the population of the "Partium", the districts in question, lying outside of historical Transylvania. It is well known that the frontier line drawn in Trianon between Hungary and Roumania cut in two an area which undoubtedly forms one economic unit, the mutual attraction of which was always evident and perceivable even at the time of severe economic seclusion and artificial customs-walls.

It is also an important circumstance, that from the point of view of communications the "partium" entirely belongs to the Hungarian Alföld (Great Plain), fourteen railway-lines link it—across the Trianon Frontier—to Hungary, while only four lines are running to Transylvania, i. e. to Roumania. Four other railway-lines lead to the Bánság, but these are of but local importance. The situation is just as favourable to Hungary from the point of view of highways.

No doubt, the execution of these proposals would represent, on both sides, the greatest difficulties as to the realisation of the national ideals. The giving up of the Székely-land and of other Hungarian districts and towns would represent an enormous sacrifice to the Hungarians. There would be without doubt similar difficulties on the Roumanian side too.

For this reason, together with the above solution, a wide basis should be created for the Hungaro-Roumanian reconciliation and cooperation. This aim could best be served by securing the rights of the minorities on the basis of the Atlantic Charter and the principles of Lenin and Stalin, following the Soviet model. This could lead to wide cantonal, or other territorial autonomies wherever the minorities are living in compact masses.

Besides guaranteeing mutually the autonomous rights of the nationalities, it would be desirable to extend to the widest possible degree the economic and cultural cooperation of both nations; this would lead to the spiritualisation of frontiers. Thus in fact, the frontiers would practically lose their significance, and Transylvania would no more be a separating wall, but a connecting link between the two countries.

In addition to the above propositions the Hungarian Government expresses its readiness to accept a solution by which a plebiscite under international control would be held within the whole area transferred to Roumania in 1919. The area to be retransferred to Hungary would be fixed in proportion to the votes of the population.

In order to secure an objective settlement of all questions connected with the problems of the new frontier, it would certainly be most desirable, if the powers charged with the preparation of the Treaty of Peace with Hungary would send their experts to the districts in question and would make their proposals after having considered the views of those experts.

Budapest, 25th April 1946.

Hungarian Ministry for Foreign Affairs. **Annex N° 10.**

160/Bé. res.
1946.

Budapest, May 20th, 1946.

Your Excellency

I have the honour to send herewith an Aide-Mémoire of the Hungarian Government concerning the grievances of the Hungarian minority in Transylvania, and beg Your Excellency to kindly transmit the same to Your Excellency's Government, respectively to the Conference of Foreign Ministers in Paris.

I cannot fail to take this opportunity to point out the fact that the redress of these grievances and the securing of adequate conditions of existence for the Hungarian minorities is not only the sine qua non of a sincere reconciliation between Hungary and her neighbours but is also an essential factor of the consolidation and peaceful development of Hungarian democracy.

Sir, I avail myself of this opportunity to renew to Your Excellency the assurance of my high consideration.

(signed) *Gyöngyösi.*

His Excellency
G. M. Puskin
Envoy Extraordinary and Minister Plenitpotentiary,
Union of Socialist Soviet Republics

His Excellency
H. F. Arthur Schoenfeld
Envoy Extraordinary and Minister Plenipotentiary,
United States Minister in Hungary.

His Excellency
A. D. F. Gascoigne, C. M. G.
Political Representative of His Britannic Majesty's
Government and Minister Designate.

Budapest.

In the following pages, the Hungarian Government desires to inform the Governments of the Allied Powers of the grievances of the Hungarians in Transylvania.

The first laws and decrees which appeared in the democratic Roumania are characteristic of the anti-Hungarian intentions of Roumanian official circles, in contradiction to the principles proclaimed by M. Groza. In these measures, if not *expressis verbis* at least in covert form, one can everywhere discern a tendency to oppress and to impoverish the Hungarians.

The Government first of all turned its attention to those who suffered most in the war, the 350,000 to 400,000 Magyars who were driven from their homes by the German army, by the Hungarian fascist authorities or in Southern Transylvania by the fascists of the chauvinistic Antonescu regime. They had hardly been expelled when the troops who drove them out began to plunder their homes. For months they were forced to wander about the country in the greatest distress, finding their way home with difficulty and deprived of everything. These people really suffered more than anyone from the war and its effects. Yet these were the people whom the so-called democratic Roumanian regime characterised as having "voluntarily collaborated with the enemy" and as will be seen later deprived of their citizenship for this reason, sequestrated their goods, confiscated their land and dismissed them from their employment. The so far unheard-of category of "presumed enemies" was invented, and of course it was the Magyars who were meant. The places of those who were dismissed for absence from their posts were given to Roumanians who had taken refuge from the consequences of their crimes against the Russian and Jewish population of Bessarabia and Northern Bukovina. Notaries, teachers and priests who were of Hungarian nationality were declared to be fascists, while the Roumanian officials who took their place, although imbued with the spirit of the Iron Guard, were considered as good democrats. The "purge" was only taken seriously as far as the Magyars were concerned while from the top to the bottom of the Roumanian administration almost all the same people remain at their posts as have been there for the last 27 years, persecuting the Magyars and hindering any democratic development on their part in the spirit of racial prejudice which the Roumanians were most likely the first to proclaim.

Courts-Martial.

Soldiers who deserted from the Roumanian or Hungarian armies, if they are Magyars, are condemned by thousands by the Roumanian military courts, although it was because of their determination not to fight the Russians that they deserted.

Forced Settlements.

With the object of being able to show as many Roumanians as possible in Transyslvania at the time of the peace-conference, people are being forcibly removed, and Roumanian officials from the Old Kingdom and from Southern Transylvania, employees and even pensioners, are being compelled to settle in Transylvania under threat of disciplinary action or loss of employment. In order to make room for them, the Hungarian towns, such as Kolozsvár, Brassó, Temesvár and so on, are being partially cleared of their Hungarian population, with confiscation of their homes. An act has been passed for the protection of the minorities, but nothing whatever has been done to put it into effect. In many official places the Hungarian language is only permitted through an interpreter.

It is especially in the places where there is a mixed population that the defenceless Hungarians are freely insulted, beaten and even murdered, plundered and threatened, usually with the connivance of the Roumanian officials and police.

People's Courts.

Characteristic of the anti-Hungarian feelings of the Roumanian authorities is the discrimination against the Magyars in the people's courts. At the Kolozsvár court Roumanians are often released, and many of the instigators of the atrocities against the Jews are now free. At the same time there has just recently been a large number of accusations against Magyars, and the extreme penalty has been inflicted in many cases. The Kolozsvár court, whose jurisdiction covers the whole of Transylvania, has instituted proceedings for anti-popular acts against 177 persons; of these, 153 are Magyars and 24 Roumanians. The death-penalty was inflicted in 27 cases, all of them Magyars. Penal servitude for life or long terms of imprisonment were given to 69 people, all of whom again were Magyars.

National minorities are always exposed to the dangers of economic oppression, of which the Roumanians have shown themselves masters in the last 22 or 23 years.

CASBI.

One of the most serious grievances of the Magyars of Transylvania now under Roumanian rule is the method in which the act and decree for the establishment and working of the CASBI is applied. The avowed object of this institution is the sequestration and administration of the property of enemy citizens. In practice, it is applied so that most of the Magyars are deprived of everything they possess and reduced to penury. In order to make clear the difference between the spirit and the execution of the decree, some account must be given of the origin of the CASBI and the abuses and arbitrary actions of the authorities in carrying it out, which conflict with its expressed intention.

CASBI is an abbreviation of the Roumanian name for the office for the Administration and Supervision of Enemy Property. It was established and organised by a royal decree which appeared in the Roumanian official gazette on February 10th, 1945.

It was set up in connection with Clause 8 of the Armistice Agreement signed in Moscow on September 13th, 1944 between the United Nations and Roumania, under which the Roumanian Government undertook not to permit the removal or expropriation of property of any description belonging to Germany and Hungary or their nationals in Roumania, and to arrange for it to be secured upon conditions to be laid down by the Soviet High Command.

Clause 19 of the Armistice Agreement stated that the Allied Governments regarded the Vienna Award applying to Transylvania as null and void. It follows from this that all those persons who on August 20th, 1940 were residents of Transylvania, that is, were Roumanian citizens, retained that status. The decision also renders void the act of the Hungarian Government by which all persons who were domiciled and permanently resident in Northern Transylvania became Hungarian citizens. To this must be added the fact that all the provisions and decisions of the Roumanian Government which refer to Transylvania are on the basis of the *restitutio in integrum* principle. According to this, Clause 8 of the Armistice Agreement can only affect two categories:

1. the property of persons with a Hungarian passport who were on territory under Roumanian sovereignty on the day when the Armistice Agreement was signed;
2. property of the Hungarian State or Hungarian capital interests found upon the said territory.

In the event, what happened? The Roumanian authorities considered the great mass of the Hungarians of Transylvania as Hungarian, that is, enemy nationals, sequestrated their property, confiscated their goods, and placed them under the supervision of the CASBI, thus literally reducing enormous numbers of Magyars to complete poverty.

The CASBI decree refers in the first place to Act No. 90 of February 10th, 1945, and instructions for it to be put into effect appeared on April 5th of that year. The Armistice Agreement between the United Nations and the Provisional Government of Hungary, on the other hand, was signed on January 20th, 1945. As from that date therefore Hungary ceased to be an enemy country, both as regards the United Nations and those who had allied themselves with them. It undertook to declare war on Germany and to pay reparations. By doing the latter, Hungary therefore meets her material obligations and thus cannot be obliged to pay double material reparations. It follows from this that the Roumanian Government too cannot issue such decrees as qualify Hungary as an enemy country after the signature of the Hungarian Armistice Agreement.

"Presumed Enemies"

According to paragraph c. of Clause A. of the second section of the decree, citizens who before or after September 12th, 1944 took refuge in Germany, Hungary, or territory occupied by them are to be presumed to be enemies. The clause does not clear up the question of since when a state of war is supposed to have existed between Roumania and Hungary, because those persons who left before such a state of war occurred cannot in any case be considered as presumed enemies, just as going from Northern Transylvania, which had until then been Hungarian territory, to another part of Hungary cannot be a political crime open to reprisals or punishment.

According to Clause c. and paragraph c. of Clause a. of the CASBI decree, all persons who left Roumania before or after September 12th, 1944 are to be presumed to be enemies. Their property and assets are to be confiscated. This is the trickiest point in the whole decree. There is no legal basis for it whatever. Clause 8 of the Roumanian Armistice does not mention this at all. Nor do the various acts which give the CASBI decree its legal basis, apart from Clause 8 of the Armistice Agreement. Act 498 which appeared in the *Monitorul Oficial*, the Roumanian Official Gazette No. 152 on June 3rd, 1942, Act 443 of September 2nd, 1944, Act 453 which appeared in No. 209 for September 11th, 1944, Act 465 in No. 219 for September 22nd, 1944, or even the CASBI decree No. 4501 which appeared in No. 294 for December 19th, 1944. This provision, the category of the presumed enemy, is nothing more than an attempt planned in malice to ruin and pauperise the great majority of the Magyars of Transylvania.

The fact that a person left an area which became the scene of military operations during the war can offer no legal basis for considering or presuming such a person to be an enemy.

In this connection, what happened in Northern Transylvania at the end of August 1944 should also be known. The following facts may be quoted:

1. The German military authorities did everything in their power to get the greater part of the population to leave their homes. This was

mainly so that the evacuated houses could be looted. In many cases these defenceless people were only given a few hours to leave.

2. Posters were put up to the effect that the population was not allowed to remain. People who refused to obey were collected and driven off, or considered as partisans. Cases are also known where people who refused to leave their homes were shot.

3. Before the front got as far as Transylvania, officers of the German and Hungarian armies spread the news that a place would be a bridge-head with hand-to-hand fighting, and was likely to be completely destroyed. This induced the people of many villages to escape.

Of the population who left their homes, 90 per cent did not leave of their own free will, but were partly intimidated or ordered to go, and partly believed that Hungary would surrender the moment the front reached the river Tisza. The population, therefore, left in the belief that they were going to an area which would be occupied by the Red Army without a fight and that they would therefore escape the actual fighting with all its attendant suffering for the civil population.

In such circumstances, the question may be raised of whether the civil population who left their homes in these times and as a result underwent appalling sufferings can be considered as enemies. Did the Roumanian Government consider the thousands of refugees from Bukovina and Bessarabia as enemies? The answer is of course that they did not. It is therefore entirely illegal and also most unreasonable and unjust that these unfortunate Magyars should be called enemies and then be deprived of their remaining possessions and rendered homeless.

There is here a serious conflict between the declarations in principle of Roumanian nationality policy and its practical working.

There are a very large number of complaints about the way in which the CASBI decree is put into effect. It is an interesting point that, by sequestrating the property of those who left Southern for Northern Transylvania, the Roumanian Government recognises Hungarian sovereignty over the latter.

The Union of Magyars in Transylvania has already brought the complaints to the notice of the Roumanian Government, and received promises that they will be attended to. At the same time, however, the Roumanian Minister of Justice published Decree No. 104,005 on October 10th, 1945, which prohibited the Roumanian courts from restoring the rights of refugees.

The Allied Control Commission in Roumania consented to Hungarian citizens wishing to be repatriated to Hungary taking certain of their belongings with them. Since however this can only be done if the Roumanian authorities give a written permit—which they refuse to do—this favour from the Allied Control Commission has only a theoretical value. On May 10th, 1946 the chief Government Commissioner, Oeriu, informed the organs of the CASBI that the sequestrated property of Roumanian citizens was to be held at the disposal of the Government, and it would be decided on the basis of the opinion of local administrative bodies and committees composed of delegates of the political parties whether goods in certain categories should be returned to their owners' possession. Due to the generally known chauvinistic and anti-Hungarian attitude of the Roumanian administrative bodies, it seems certain that the Hungarian minority in Roumania will again have to suffer serious material losses.

It may be stated on the basis of the foregoing that the Roumanian CASBI decree is one of the principal grievances of the Magyars of Transylvania, that it deprives a very large number of completely innocent Hungarians of their material existence, and that when complaints are made the Roumanian Government makes promises which it does not keep.

The Land Question.

Of the Magyars of Transylvania, some 70 to 80 per cent are cultivators of the soil, so that the land question is one of their principal problems. The origins of this go back to the Garofild land reform of 1921, just after the first world war. From the social point of view this reform was justified and might have had the effect of promoting economic and social progress if it had been carried out in a spirit of social and national justice. Its object however was expressly to weaken the position of the Magyars in Transylvania and the strengthening of the Roumanians of the province.

When the Groza Government came to power, the small farmers and peasants of Transylvania believed that they might hope that a Roumanian Government which represented true democracy would see that their claims were met.

Unfortunately their justifiable expectations proved illusory. The second Roumanian land-reform act, which appeared in the official gazette for March 22nd, 1945, and the decree for putting it into effect, combined with a crop of abusive practices in its execution, in fact brought fresh burdens to the Magyars with its injustices, and only a very small amount of land.

At first sight, the land-reform of the Groza Government does not appear to contain any discrimination against the nationalities. In fact however there is very serious discrimination, in that paragraph C. of

Clause 3 of Section II. states that the land of all those who took refuge abroad in countries at war with Roumania, or left after August 23rd, 1944, is to be confiscated as a whole. Paragraph D. goes even further by saying that the agricultural property and equipment of "absentees" is to be confiscated.

These two points in the Roumanian land-reform act affect an approximate number of 300,000 Magyar landowners in Northern and Southern Transylvania, most of them the holders of small farms or a few acres. It is generally known that in the autumn of 1944 the Hungarian Government then in power in agreement with the German military authorities ordered the complete administrative and civil evacuation of Northern Transylvania, and removed the Hungarian population, especially from the Székely country, and also from other parts, by force, and often by brutal methods and threats. Again, between 1940 and 1944 some 200,000 Magyars were forced to flee from Southern Transylvania under the chauvinistic terrorism of the Antonescu regime, most of them again being farmers. A very large number of them were deserters who did not want to help Roumania's campaign against the Soviet Union.

On the intervention of the Union of Magyars in Transylvania, a promise was given in Bucharest that the instructions for the putting into effect of the law would remedy the points to which exception was taken. Instead however of remedying the two points which formed the grievance, the apparently innocent point a. of the fatal Clause 3 was interpreted to the effect that any landowner of Hungarian nationality was to be considered as a "collaborator" and have his property confiscated who had left the country with German or Hungarian troops. To the greater glory of the principle of equal rights for all, the same instruction stated in definite form that this did not apply to Roumanians who had been called up for home defence work and taken to Germany or Hungary. Later, the Central Land-Reform Committee in their circulars of April 21st, May 13th and July 12th, attempted to make this a little less severe on the Magyars, but unfortunately the local authorities whose duty it was to put the decree into effect took no notice. The abuses during the course of the execution of the law were so widespread and so serious that they endangered the basis of existence of the Magyars.

The protests of the Union of Magyars had no effect. There were hardly any Magyar members of the local land-reform committees, and if there were occasional Magyar members of the local organs, naturally there was not a single one on the Central Committee of 9 members in Bucharest. There is no legal or political control of the composition of these committees, so that even notorious members of the Iron Guard can be in influential positions in them. The prefects are generally unwilling to interfere in these matters, and it often happens that Hungarian properties are confiscated by committees among the members of which are persons who have been sentenced for thefts committed on the very owners of the property confiscated.

The main source however of the anti-Hungarian excesses is the process of expropriation. The conception of land which can be expropriated covers all kinds of property, without regard to its purpose. People are considered as refugees if they were bombed out of their homes or left for other reasons connected with the war but returned as soon as circumstances permited; the land even of Magyars who are doing military service with the Roumanian army is confiscated, and even that of disabled men, sick persons, those under medical treatment, in fact everyone who is a Magyar and for any reason is not permanently on his property. The land of Roumanian citizens of Magyar nationality who are in Hungary with a regular passport is taken. It is a regular practice that if any Hungarian property cannot be considered as belonging to a refugee, it is considered as being that of an "absentee". Land has been taken away from many small farmers in Southern Transylvania because their permanent domicile is in Northern Transylvania, where they were sent by order of the Roumanian Government in the autumn of 1940.

The legal limits are respected only in exceptional cases in procedures for expropriation. Not only the land is taken away, but also the dwelling-house; big estates, on the other hand, if the owner happens to be a Roumanian, are left alone.

The committees, in general, do not issue written verdicts. No legal remedy is granted.

From the way in which the land-reform has been put into effect so far one can only draw the conclusion that almost everything has been taken from the Magyar proprietors, while those of the proletariat who would be entitled to receive land have so far received nothing.

The Roumanian Act. No. 645 of 1945 for the invalidation of certain agreements made during the period of occupation.

One of most serious grievances of the Magyars of Transylvania in the economic field is the Roumanian decree No. 645, which appeared in the official gazette for August 14th, 1945 and which nullifies certain agreements made during the period of Hungarian rule.

This law states that transactions done between August 30th, 1940 and October 25th, 1944 are to be cancelled, for various reasons, among which are if the plaintiff suffered loss amounting to 50 per cent, if he fled or was deported and suffered a loss amounting to 25 per cent, if a custodian of his assets was appointed and he suffered loss amounting to 25 per cent, and further if the transaction was made as a result of anti-democratic persecution, under compulsion or under the influence of threats. If the plaintiff suffered loss amounting to 25 per cent, it is assumed that his consent was obtained under duress. Clause 4 of the decree makes it possible to annul expropriations. In Clauses 6–11 of the second part the decree discusses the consequences of annulment, and states that the annulment is effective as regards third parties even if the property has been conveyed by entry in the land-register.

The consequence of the annulment of a transaction is that the object concerned is restored to its original owner. The plaintiff is only obliged to return the purchase price which he received at the time of the transaction.

This decree affects a very large number of Hungarians, and especially "small" men. There were very frequent exchanges of property between Magyars who left Southern Transylvania as a result of persecution by the Antonescu regime and Roumanians who left Northern Transylvania. These exchange agreements can now be attacked by the Roumanians under the decree; they can retain the property they obtained in exchange in Southern Transylvania, and, as prices are at present, recover their former property in Northern Transylvania for a ridiculously low price, a mere fraction of the original purchase price. Since there was no definite scale laid down for price-relations, the establishment of 25 or 50 per cent less depends entirely on the authorities, and as the law does not permit revaluation, small Hungarian farmers are deprived of their very existence. Promises for the repeal or alteration of this decree with its anti-Magyar discrimination, have remained merely promises.

Office of Administrators.

The system of administrators is a serious grievance of the Magyars, and they see in it another attempt to ruin them economically. Administrators are appointed to the commercial and industrial undertakings of citizens of Magyar, and only Magyar, nationality, to banks in which Hungarian capital is interested, to cooperatives and even to agricultural concerns, and they can interfere in the business of the concern of any kind, and collect large sums for their work. It should be emphasized that the origin of these administrators goes back to the Antonescu regime, when Roumanians from Northern Transylvania were given remunerative sinecures with Hungarian firms. The new regime took over the system with Decree No. 448 of October 6th, 1944 and decrees Nos. 644 of December 19th, 1944 and May 29th, 1945 which amplified it. No reply has so far been received to petitions for the suspension of a system which is detrimental also to Roumanian national, political and economic interests.

Special Tax on Signs in Hungarian.

In the period before the war the Roumanian fiscal authorities imposed a triple and even quintuple tax on shop-signs etc. or commercial books in Hungarian. This definitely anti-democratic arrangement which conflicts with the basic principles of the equality of nationalities, and whose object was again to weaken the economic position of the Magyars, has been retained in Groza's Roumania. It need hardly be emphasized that this arrangement too is in direct contradiction to both the letter and the spirit of the nationality law passed in Roumania, and is characteristic of the fact that it remains merely on paper.

Taxes.

Roumanian taxation policy proved in the past one of the most reliable methods of impoverishing and dispossessing the Magyars. There has been no change in this. With the introduction of Roumanian administration to Northern Transylvania a new system of taxation was brought in, and the basis of assessment for the Magyars was revised and put at a much higher figure than that for the Roumanians. The Roumanian system of taxation divides taxpayers into three categories, and Hungarian taxpayers, especially in Southern Transylvania, are consistently placed in the highest category. Thus it can be understood why for example a Hungarian manufacturer pays five times as much in taxes as his Roumanian neighbour who may have a bigger turnover.

Cooperatives.

Hungarian cooperatives developed on a large scale in Transylvania. Today there are about a thousand of them, with one main consumers' and one credit organisation. The Roumanian Government has introduced changes in their statutes which are so anti-democratic and so much in conflict with the cooperative spirit, and has taken such other measures as have almost completely crippled the operations of these

Magyar cooperative societies. They have restricted the sphere of transactions of the central organisations, and forbidden the establishment of school cooperatives in the interests of cooperative education; the Hungarian cooperatives do not get a share of the goods of prime necessity which are blocked by the Government and only distributed by Roumanian cooperatives. When the taxes of these societies, which suffered enormous losses through the war, are assessed it is on the basis of their pre-war working capital, and not one of the Magyar credit cooperatives has received so far a single leu of the millions and millions which have been put at the disposal of the Roumanian societies. Administrative principles which cannot be put into practice are prescribed for the Magyar cooperatives, which have the effect of undermining them completely.

A new Roumanian cooperative law is now being drafted, in the preparation of which, in spite of the promises that have been made, none of the Magyar cooperative leaders have been asked to participate. This is comprehensible in view of the fact that the news which has leaked out is to the effect that the centres of the Magyar cooperatives are to be abolished.

The Question of Citizenship.

The Treaty of Trianon made the acquisition of the rights of citizenship dependent upon permanent domicile (*pertinenza*). In 1924, when the Roumanian authorities were instructed to compile a register of citizens, without regard to how long they had resided in Transylvania, they omitted from the register all those who were unable to prove their permanent residence or *pertinenza* by means of documents.

Thus the names of about 200,000 persons of Hungarian nationality have not been entered in the registers of citizenship. The question of citizenship of these persons is now pending unsettled for over 26 years.

A new decree of citizenship was published in the Roumanian Official Gazette of April 4th, 1945, paragraph 2nd of which provides that those inhabitants of Northern Transylvania shall *not* be regarded as Roumanian citizens who

a) from August 30th 1940 up to the date of above decree opted for a foreign citizenship, further those who

b) voluntarily joined any military formation of a State at war with Roumania, or served in any foreign military or half-military formation.

The provisions of this decree affected the interests of hundred thousands of Hungarians of Transylvania, for several hundred thousand persons asked for Hungarian citizenship since August 30th 1940, after the re-transfer to Hungary of those territories, because the granting of that citizenship was formally necessary to occupy positions in general and especially in economic life and, apart from this, a very great number of Hungarian men had to perform compulsory military service in the Hungarian army, or in half military formations. Apart from the directly interested Hungarians of Northern Transylvania, about 200,000 Hungarians were forced to take refuge in Hungary or to opt for Hungarian citizenship in consequence of the persecutions of the fascistic Antonescu Government.

The executive decree of the law concerning citizenship, published on August 17th 1945, expressly provided that *all those persons shall lose their Roumanian citizenship, "who, on the occasion of the retreat of the enemy army, voluntarily left Northern Transylvania, thus making common cause with the enemy"*. It is thus absolutely left to the interpretation of the authorities, who out of the several hundred thousands of Hungarian refugees of Northern Transylvania may retain their citizenship, because it is very difficult to prove whether the departure was voluntary or not, and therefore ample opportunity is offered to the chauvinistic Roumanian authorities arbitrarily to convict a great number of Hungarians.

Further measures were taken to deprive the Hungarians of their rights by the Roumanian Minister of Justice, Patrascanu, who issued the decree No. 104.005/1945 of October 10th addressed to all Law Courts of Northern Transylvania. The Law Court of Kolozsvár registered that decree on October 13th 1945 under No. 1.879. Its text is the following:

"Those inhabitants of Northern Transylvania who, making common cause with the German and Hungarian enemy army, retreated to Hungary, shall lose their Roumanian citizenship under the provisions of the Law of April 4th 1945. Therefore if those persons should return to Roumania they shall be considered as enemy citizens, and if their property should fall under the provision of Chapter 8th of the Armistice Agreement (CASBI), the Roumanian authorities shall not be entitled to meet any requests of those persons concerning that property; the legal authorities may therefore do nothing to restitute the immovable or movable property of those persons, or to help them to occupy their dwellings again."

Patrascanu thus deprived hundreds of thousands of Hungarian refugees of all legal remedies by the aid of which they could have defended themselves against the arbitrary actions of the authorities.

The new executive decree of the citizenship law, which was issued in December 1945, contains certain mitigations by providing that nobody shall be deprived of his Roumanian citizenship under the title that, as inhabitant of Southern Transylvania, he opted for Hungary on the basis of the Vienna Award, or that as inhabitant of Northern Transylvania, he asked for a Hungarian certificate of citizenship. But it is a great fault also of this decree that it leaves wide scope for arbitrary actions of the authorities. And it is just in the line of the execution of the decrees that Hungarians had the worst experience in the past and even in very recent times.

Public instruction.

After its one year rule the Groza Government is undoubtedly in a position to point to certain measures which prove that somewhat more consideration was shown to Hungarian instruction than before 1940.

The Hungarians of Roumania would be much satisifed with these measures, if only they would not cover grave and apprehensive facts.

There are no legal securities behind these favourable measures, thus the entire Hungarian instruction in Roumania is characterised by a *legal uncertitude*. The gravest of all is that no new public instruction law refers to Hungarian instruction. Consequently Anghelescu's ill-famed private instruction law of 1925 is still in force, under which it would even today be possible to close hundreds of Hungarian schools.

The Royal decree No. 406 was issued as law on May 29th 1945, providing that all Roumanian schools which fled from Northern Transylvania in 1940 shall return to their former domicile. Consequently most of the Hungarian secondary schools were forced to cede their premises to the Roumanian schools, quite irrespective of the proportional number of the Hungarian inhabitants of the respective district.

It is one of the gravest offences that, up to the end of the last year, the Hungarian teachers received only quite inconsiderable advances, which we could hardly even call starvation wages, while the Roumanian teachers got their full salaries. The payment of the differences is now in course, but—compared to April 1945—the depreciation is 3-fold. Regular payments of the salaries are not ensured even today.

University.

The position of the Hungarian University is also a very serious question. In autumn of 1944 the Hungarian University did not obey the evacuation order of the military authorities and continued its work.

Later—after the return of the Roumanian University from Nagysze-ben—the Hungarian University was at once ready to share with them, in a friendly manner, all buildings, clinics, scientific institutions in its possession. An agreement was arrived upon, on April 16th–18th 1945 concerning the two Universities, according to which the Hungarian University kept its full equipment, obtained since August 1940, but—with the exception of two clinics—had to leave all other establishments where it was working up to that date.

On May 26th 1945, about one month and a half after the above agreement, a Decree-Law was issued concerning "the establishment of a State University with Hungarian language of instruction" which, contrary to the provisions of the mentioned agreement, greatly reduced the status of the Hungarian University. According to this Decree the Hungarian University must leave all the 50 buildings of University District and must accept the premises of a former girls' college.

Since that time a new plan was realised, according to which the medical faculty of the Hungarian University has to move to Marosvásárhely, occupying there the public hospital and the building of a military school. The Ministry of National Defence however refused its consent to this arrangement as far as the military school was concerned. If we consider that three Roumanian medical faculties will work in Transylvania, i. e. those of Nagyszeben, Kolozsvár and the newly-established one in Temesvár, we can feel only bitterness in view of that national expansion and oppression which is hardly ready to grant even one medical faculty to serve the health of the one million and a half of Hungarians in Transylvania. The furnishing of the University and its professors is the worst we could imagine. A large scale collection was started amongst the Hungarians of Transylvania to offer some relief to the University, but some results could only be attained if the Government would consent to the collected funds being used for the purposes of the University. The Government did not, however, grant this consent up to now, probably out of propagandistic considerations, fearing that the Hungarians would assert that they have established their University by their own means.

The laws and measures taken by the authorities mentioned above show to what degree those high-sounding and democratic declarations of single members of the Roumanian Government and especially of Prime Minister Groza himself are in fact being realised. These laws, decrees and measures deeply affect the life of the Hungarians, gravely endangering their economic existence, and so it is not to wonder if the

Hungarians of Transylvania see no difference, between the national policy, concerning the settlement of their vital problems, of the reactionary Governments of the past 22, respectively 27 years, and that of the new Government, established since the liberation of the country, bearing high-sounding democratic slogans on its banner. No wonder that—in spite of the promising words, newspaper articles and radio declarations—the Hungarians are unable to find even under the present new rule any effective guarantees for the securing of their democratic nationality rights.

Annex N° 11.

Hungarian Legation.
Hungarian Ministry for Foreign Affairs.

87/B. 1946.
232/Be. res.
1946.

Paris, June 11th, 1946.
Budapest, July 2nd, 1946.

Your Excellency,
Sir,

In its Note No. 130/Be. res.—1946 dated May 8th, the Hungarian Government took the liberty of informing the principal Allied Powers of its views on the reconstruction of South-eastern Europe upon the three principles expressed in that document. On this occasion the Hungarian Government desires to stress the third of the said principles, which has as its object the removal of any factor which might produce friction in international affairs. Dealing with this problem, the Note of the Hungarian Government recalled that one of the objectives of the United Nations is to promote and encourage respect for human rights and freedoms for all, without distinction as to race, sex, language or religion (Article 1 of the Charter). Similarly, my Government referred to Article 4 of the Charter, by which the United Nations bound themselves to see that human rights and fundamental freedoms are respected and honoured for all, without distinction as to race, sex, language or religion, as was also expressed in the first Article.

According to paragraph b. of Article 13 of the Charter, it is within the competence of the General Assembly of the United Nations to initiate studies with the object of promoting the realisation of fundamental human rights and freedoms for all, without distinction as to race, sex, language or religion. It will be seen from paragraph 2 of Article 62 that the Economic and Social Council may "make recommendations for the purpose of promoting respect for and observance of human rights and fundamental freedoms for all."

In the interest of promoting the realisation of the principles mentioned above, the Hungarian Government begs to submit its memorandum concerning the exercise of these rights, with special reference to the peculiar conditions of the Danube region, to the Governments of the principal Allied powers and the members of the United Nations. The Government however desires to retain the possibility of placing a more detailed plan before the principal Allied Powers at a later date, in which it will refer to these rights in the light of the experience gained in the period between the two world wars.

The Hungarian Government is convinced that, in the interests of maintaining respect for the rights of minorities in Southeastern Europe, it would be indispensable either to insert provisions for the protection of national minorities in the text of the peace-treaties in the spirit of the attached memorandum, or to arrange special treaties referring to the protection of such minorities between the permanent members of the Security Council of the United Nations and the countries of Southeastern Europe which are concerned.

The duty of supervising the observance of and respect for the rights of the minorities should be entrusted to the United Nations, and in the first place to the General Assembly, on the authorisation of which the Economic and Social Council should carry out these duties (Article 60 of the Charter). As has been mentioned above, the latter may "make recommendations for the purpose of promoting respect for and observance of human rights and fundamental freedoms for all." (Article 62 paragraph 2).

It follows from the above-quoted provisions of the Charter that if any member of the United Nations reports a breach of the principles expressed in the said Article or laid down in the peace-treaty or special minority treaty, the Economic and Social Council, under the first paragraph of Article 62 of the Charter, will undertake a full examination of the case or take action for the initiation of the necessary enquiry, or make such proposals as it thinks fit.

The provisions outlined above, or those contained in the attached memorandum, might usefully be amplified by special provisions concerning the setting up of mixed commissions or mixed tribunals to operate on the spot under the leadership of a president appointed by the Economic and Social Council of the United Nations in the interests of a pacific settlement in the spirit of paragraph 3 of Article 52 of the Charter, in the event of any dispute of a local or general character which arises from the interpretation or application of provisions concerning the exercise of the rights of national minorities.

The Hungarian Government declares that it is from now on prepared to accept any advice, proposal or decision of the General Assembly or any other organisation or authority of the United Nations regarding the application of minority rights, in accordance with its frequently-expressed desire that Hungary should be admitted to the United Nations Organisation as soon as this becomes possible, in order that this country may contribute to the common work of the democratic nations.

I have the honour to inform Your Excellency that the Hungarian Representation in Paris has already handed this Note and the attached memorandum to the Foreign Ministers of the principal Allied Powers who are now in conference there.

I avail myself of this opportunity to renew to Your Excellency the assurance of my highest consideration.

(signed) Auer
(signed) Gyöngyösi

His Excellency
V. M. Molotov
Minister for Foreign Affairs,
Union of Socialist Soviet Republics.

His Excellency
J. Byrnes
Secretary of State for Foreign Affairs,
United States of America.

His Excellency
E. Bevin
His Majesty's Principal Secretary of State
for Foreign Affairs, Great Britain

His Excellency
G. Bidault
Minister for Foreign Affairs,
France

His Excellency

G. M. Puskin
Envoy Extraordinary & Minister Plenipotentiary,
Union of Socialist Soviet Republics.

His Excellency

H. F. Arthur Schoenfeld
Envoy Extraordinary & Minister Plenipotentiary,
United States of America.

His Excellency

Alexander K. Helm
British Political Commissioner
& Minister Designate.

Monsieur

Robert Faure
Chargé d'Affaires a.i. of France.

MEMORANDUM.

In the years 1919 and 1920, Minority Treaties were signed between the Allied and Associated Powers and the new or territorially increased States of Central and Eastern Europe, namely Czechoslovakia, Roumania and Yugoslavia. The treaties ensured certain minimum rights to the religious, linguistic and racial minorities of these countries, and these rights were placed under the guarantee of the League of Nations. Similar provisions were inserted in Articles 54–60 of the Treaty of Trianon concluded with Hungary.

By these treaties with the new or enlarged countries, the Great Powers confirmed their recognition of them, and the signature of the treaties was a condition of their recognition of the territory acquired. The Great Powers made these treaties because they considered the international protection of the national minorities necessary in the interests of peace in this part of Europe, where there are various national minorities living in all the countries, either in groups or in mixed areas. After the resettlement of territorial questions which is now going forward there will still be the necessity for the international protection of national minorities in this part of Europe, and perhaps in certain respects an increased need of it. There are at present signs which give increasing cause for alarm that the Hungarian minorities which will, as far as can be seen, remain outside the frontiers of the country in considerable numbers, are being deprived of their most elementary economic, social and cultural rights; this makes it the unconditional duty of the Hungarian Government to press for such protection, all the more so because the validity of the provisions contained in the treaties of 1919 has not ceased, and they are in fact still in force. Since it is evidently necessary that the economic and social provisions should be put into practical effect, the legal measures applying to the rights of the minorities should be amplified by certain principles which arise directly from them, and the guaranteeing of them, now that the League of Nations has ceased to function, should be entrusted to the United Nations Organisation.

The principles proposed by the Hungarian Government are as follows:

1. No person should suffer any kind of disadvantage because of the declaration of his or her nationality or language either at a census or on any other occasion. There should be suitable punishment for any person who offends another by using an expression casting an aspersion on his nationality or acts in a manner which does so.

2. The fullest protection of life, health, religion and personal liberty should be assured to every inhabitant of a State regardless of nationality or language.

3. Citizens of a country who belong to a national minority should enjoy both legally and in fact the same civic and political rights as the other citizens. Difference of nationality or language should not place any citizen at a disadvantage in the exercise of these rights. The State in its capacity of a factor controlling economic affairs, e. g. as an employer or contractor, should not be allowed to differentiate between its citizens on the ground of nationality. The distribution of land expropriated under land reforms should be made solely for social and economic reasons, the nationality of those claiming land not being taken into account. Active and pensioned employees of the State and corporations belonging to the nationalities should not receive less favourable treatment than other State or public employees. The right to manual or office work, the right of choice and the right to strike of workers belonging to the nationalities should not be restricted for the benefit of the ruling nation. Any regulation of the unemployment question in such manner that there is a disproportionate decrease in the number of employees belonging to the nationalities is in conflict with the principle of equality. Any instigation of employers not to take on workers from the nationalities, or to dismiss them or exclude them, is inadmissible.

4. The inhabitants of a country may not be restricted in the free use of any language either in private affairs or in business, and especially in religious matters, in the press, in associations or trades unions and in general in economic, cultural and social affairs.

5. If persons belonging to the national minorities apply to a court or administrative authority the competency of which extends to a district in which at least twenty per cent of the population belongs to that nationality, they may use their own language both in speech and in writing, and the said authorities will communicate their decisions to the persons concerned in the language of the latter. In order that this principle may be applied in practice, a sufficient number of administrative officials and magistrates must be employed who can both speak and write the language of the national minority concerned. Within the above limits, local and representative autonomous corporations may choose the language of discussion and business themselves. These principles should also be applied correspondingly to the concerns and undertakings of the State and corporations (railways, postal, telegraphic and telephone services, trams etc.) in verbal and written communication.

6. Persons belonging to the nationalities and also churches must be permitted at their own expense to set up and maintain schools and educational establishments where instruction is given in any language, which are considered as public schools and can issue certificates of equal validity with those issued by the State schools.

7. In all communities where there are at least thirty children of school age who belong to any national minority, the State must maintain an elementary school for them with instruction given in their own language, and employ teachers belonging to that nationality who speak and write the language perfectly. In order that this principle may be applied in practice, the State should see to it that there are a sufficient number of teachers training colleges with instruction in the language of the nationality concerned.

8. Where there are at least fifty thousand citizens of a national minority in the territory of a State, the State shall see to it that there shall be at least one of each type of school giving instruction of higher grade than elementary, with the exception of universities and high-schools, for pupils of that nationality, and one further school of each type for every additional 100,000 people, instruction being given in the language of the minority concerned.

9. The nationality of the pupil is to be established solely by the verbal or written declaration of his or her legal representative, and this may not be revised or questioned by the educational authorities. School books or readers which offend the national feelings of the pupils or stir up hatred between the nations may not be used in the schools established for the national minorities.

10. Persons belonging to the national minorities have the right to foster and develop their own language, to organise and further educational matters, to develop their culture, and for this purpose to es-

tablish and maintain associations, societies and any other kind of cultural institution.

11. In their financial estimates, the State and the local and other autonomous bodies must, out of the expenditure provided for educational purposes, apply such sums to each type of school maintained in accordance with the foregoing as is proportionate to the numbers of the national minority in question as compared with the total population of the State or area concerned, and in the case of representative autonomous bodies to the total number of those concerned. The same principle is to be applied also in the application of sums provided for cultural purposes in the State and corporation financial estimates.

12. It is not permissible to hinder the contacts of citizens belonging to the national minorities with citizens of other countries who are of the same nationality in cultural, social and economic matters. The principle covers the right of attending schools in other countries, including universities and high schools, where the language of instruction is the same as that of the national minority concerned.

13. The States interested should be obliged to enact provisions covering the above principles, and should not be allowed to pass legislation or issue decrees conflicting with them or permit contradictory action by their authorities.

Hungarian Ministry for Foreign Affairs. **Annex No. 12.**

280/Be. res.
1946. Budapest, July 15th, 1946.

Your Excellency,

For kind transmission to the Government of the Union of Socialist Soviet Republics (of the United States of America, of His Britannic Majesty's Government, of the French Republic), I have the honour to enclose herewith a Memorandum of the Hungarian Government concerning the citizenship of Hungarians living in Roumania.

The Roumanian Government intends to solve the question of citizenship of the Hungarian minority living in Roumania by unilateral measures. The recent orders and official declaration of the Roumanian Government are sources of great anxiety as to the future of Hungarians in Transylvania. The Hungarian Government is of the opinion that the just and equitable settlement of this question is the indispensable preliminary condition of the peaceful cooperation of these two neighbouring nations. For this reason I have the honour to ask your Excellency, kindly and urgently to draw the attention of the Government of the Union of Socialist Soviet Republics (of the United States, of His Britannic Majesty's Government, of the French Republic) to this problem requesting their valuable support at the Peace Conference of the proposals detailed in the enclosed Memorandum.

I avail myself of this opportunity to renew to your Excellency the assurances of my high consideration.

(signed) *Gyöngyösi.*

His Excellency
G. M. Puskin
Envoy Extraordinary and Minister Plenipotentiary,
Union of Socialist Soviet Republics

His Excellency
H. F. Arthur Schoenfeld
Envoy Extraordinary and Minister Plenipotentiary,
United States Minister in Hungary.

His Excellency
A. K. Helm
Representative of His Britannic Majesty's
Government.

His Excellency
H. L. Gauquié
Envoy Extraordinary and Minister Plenipotentiary,
French Republic,

Budapest

AIDE-MEMOIRE

concerning the citizenship of Hungarians living in Roumania.

In a memorandum attached to its note-verbale No. 99/res. Be. of October 31st, 1945 regarding certain questions of citizenship which have arisen in Southeastern Europe, the Hungarian Government referred among other things to the fact that there are serious difficulties as regards citizenship in this region, and expressed its opinion that the situation might deteriorate further.

The Hungarian Government emphasized that the position was especially serious in those territories which came temporarily under Hungarian sovereignty under the Vienna Awards and where in consequence the majority of the population acquired Hungarian citizenship for the period that it lasted.

In the said memorandum the Hungarian Government pointed out that from the legal point of view the previous citizenship of the inhabitants of such territories is automatically restored without reserve. At the same time the Government made proposals for a radical solution of the question based upon principles in harmony with the objectives set forth in the Charter of the United Nations.

When the Hungarian Government presented this memorandum, it was already in possession of detailed information concerning the situation as it had developed since 1919 and as it is at present and also offered to make it available.

Since then, the situation of the population of Hungarian nationality in Roumania has further deteriorated, and the speech of M. Lucreţiu Patrascanu*, the Roumanian Minister of Justice, on June 11th of this year at Kolozsvár (Cluj), and the anti-Hungarian agitation which began after that in the Roumanian press has again given the Hungarian Government cause for serious alarm concerning the several hundred thousand Hungarians in Roumania to whom the Roumanian Government continues to deny Roumanian citizenship, and whom it desires in fact to render homeless or to compel them to emigrate.

In connection with the statements of the Roumanian Minister of Justice, the Hungarian Government considers it necessary to point out the following facts:

Roumanian laws passed in the course of the last 25 years and Roumanian governmental and administrative measures have contained the most serious disabilities affecting the question of the citizenship of the large number of Hungarians who live under Roumanian rule in Transylvania. These disabilities have deprived a very large number of these Hungarians of the possibility of making a living, since the question of citizenship is of basic importance in every aspect of public and private affairs.

---

*In his speech on June 11th, M. Patrascanu said in part: "The three or four hundred thousand Hungarians who are still living in Roumania today, illegally and outside our laws, are not only staying here to earn a living. Their presence here, and the continuation of their presence, gives cause for anxiety, because it is these Hungarians who cultivate and spread revisionist tendencies and work to undermine our country. In this matter there is a limit to our patience.

"We are not going to give Roumanian citizenship to those Hungarian citizens who, although born in Transylvania, left the country and refused to do their duty to the Roumanian State, but returned with the occupying troops in 1940. It is not right that they should receive Roumanian citizenship."

As to the antecedents of the present situation, the Hungarian Government would mention first of all that by Articles 3–7 of the Minority Treaty signed on December 9th, 1919 between the Allied and Associated Powers and Roumania, the latter undertook to recognise as Roumanian citizens, legally and without reserve, all persons permanently resident in the territory concerned (Article 3, paragraph 1) or who were born there (Article 4 paragraph 1).

Under Article 1 of the Minority Treaty, Roumania also undertook to recognise as basic laws the provisions contained in Articles 2 to 8, that no law, decree or official measure would be passed in contradiction of their provisions and that no law, decree or official measure should be effective against them (Article 1). Following the enactment however of the Minority Treaty as a law of the country on September 26th, 1920, Roumania did pass laws contravening these provisions and took measures affecting citizenship. Among these are the following:

1. Clause 56 of the Nationality Act of February 24th, 1924 only recognises the Roumanian citizenship of persons who were resident (*pertinenza*) in Roumanian territory on December 1st, 1918. In addition it prescribed forms which even people who had automatically obtained Roumanian citizenship under the Minority Treaty were unable to comply with. The administrative authorities were pronounced competent to make up the lists of persons who obtained citizenship. When this was done, however, the names of some 200,000 Hungarians of Transylvania were omitted, partly as a result of defects in the law and partly owing to arbitrary methods being employed.*

The enormous numbers of Hungarians thus omitted were compulsorily deprived of their most elementary human rights, among them the right to work. It was for this reason that a considerable number of them were forced to leave Transylvania for Hungary as a result of losing their employment, official pressure and often open persecution. Between 1920 and 1940 some 260,000 Hungarians were compelled to leave Transylvania.

2. Article 5 of the Roumanian Constitution of February 28th, 1938

*The correctness of this very modest estimate of the number of Hungarians whose names were omitted from the lists is supported by the preamble to the Roumanian Nationality decree of July 27th, 1939. This decree, which was published in the Official Gazette No. 171 for July 27th, 1939, provides for persons who acquired Roumanian citizenship under the Act of February 24th, 1924 requesting confirmation within three months. According to the preamble of the Ministry, the decree became necessary because it had been proved that the number of heads of families omitted from the lists amounted to nearly a hundred thousand. As an example it may be mentioned that of the 88,000 inhabitants of Nagyvárad 32,000 were not entered in the lists.

states that all Roumanian citizens are equal before the law, regardless of their religion or racial origin. According however to official explanations contained in subsequent legal measures, this provision only applies to the duties of citizens and only secures the equality of all citizens before the law in this respect. (Preamble to Decree No. 2560 published in No. 183 of the Roumanian Official Gazette for August 9th, 1940). The principle of the Roumanian Constitution giving precedence to the Roumanian element is also evident in legislation regarding citizenship. The Nationality Law of January 20th, 1939 ensures the acquisition of citizenship to racial Roumanians (*român de origine*) as against those who are not of Roumanian racial origin.

3. According to the decree of July 27th, 1939, Roumanian origin is sufficiently proved if one of the parents is of Roumanian race (*de origine etnica românesca*). Such persons are granted Roumanian citizenship by the Council of Ministers on the proposal of the Minister of Justice.

These few examples are sufficient documentation of the fact that Roumanian legislation has not complied with the obligations undertaken in the international agreement as regards citizenship.

Mention must further be made of another provision of the Roumanian legislation affecting citizenship, namely the decree of October 20th, 1939, which instead of *pertinenza* makes the person's place of residence the legal basis for the acquisition of citizenship for those who lived in territory annexed to Roumania either on December 1st, 1918 (the date of the meeting of the Roumanian National Assembly at Gyulafehérvár)* or July 26th, 1921, the date of the ratification of the Treaty of Trianon.

The Vienna Award of August 30th, 1940 and the subsequent provisions of the Hungarian Government stated that in principle everyone in the Northern Transylvanian territory which came under Hungarian rule automatically became a Hungarian citizen if they had lived in the territory for five years without a break.

Article 19 of the Armistice Agreement between the United Nations and Roumania returned Transylvania (or the greater part of it) to Roumania, assuming that this would be allowed to stand by the peace-treaty, and declared the Vienna Award null and void inasfar as it applied to Transylvania. Following this, the Roumanian Government began the introduction of legal rules which represent the most serious grievances of the Hungarians of Transylvania. In regard to citizenship

*The so-called National Assembly which met on December 1st, 1918 and consisted exclusively of Roumanians, declared the adherence of Transylvania to Roumania.

too the Roumanian Government issued provisions having the effect of depriving the Hungarians of their rights, though it might well have declared simply that the inhabitants of this territory automatically became Roumanian citizens.

The Groza Government has produced three important laws which regulate the citizenship of the inhabitants of Northern Transylvania:

1. Decree No. 261 of April 2nd, 1945 (a translation of which is annexed to this memorandum), clause 2 of which deprives a considerable section of the Hungarians in Transylvania of their citizenship, and thus of their opportunity to work, and forces them to leave their homes, or prevents them from returning. According to paragraph a. of this clause this applies to inhabitants of Northern Transylvania who opted for foreign citizenship from August 30th, 1940 to the entry into force of the decree, and under paragraph b. to those who voluntarily took military service with a country with which Roumania was at war or joined any foreign military or para-military formation.

This citizenship decree affects the Hungarians of Transylvania because it continues to exclude from citizenship the approximately 200,000 Hungarians who had not yet obtained Roumanian citizenship on August 30th, 1940. Especially disadvantageous however are the provisions of Clause 2 of the decree, which affect further large numbers of Hungarians in that after the Vienna Award several hundred thousand people in Northern Transylvania asked for Hungarian citizenship. Proof of citizenship was a condition of practically every form of employment or economic activity, such as the carrying on of industry or trade and the purchase of property. Roumanian legal practice considers the establishment of Hungarian citizenship or the taking out of a certificate to that effect as "opting for foreign citizenship". A further enormous mass of people is represented by the number of Hungarian men who served in Hungarian military or para-military formations because they were liable to military service. Finally, the fact must also be borne in mind that apart from the Hungarians of Northern Transylvania directly affected there are a further 100,000 Hungarians in Southern Transylvania who were driven out or expelled from that region by the Roumanian authorities under the fascist Antonescu regime.

2. Executive decree No. 12, published as a Royal Decree on August 11th, 1945 concerning the regulation of citizenship for inhabitants of Northern Transylvania increased the grievances of the Hungarians still further. Specially detrimental to them were paragraphs a. and c. of clause 4 of the decree. Under previous regulations, all those who came under the operation of the conditions of clause 40 of Law 33 of

January 19th, 1939 lost their Roumanian citizenship.* According to paragraph e. of clause 4 of the same, persons who "voluntarily" left the territory of Northern Transylvania with the enemy forces and "showed solidarity with them" lose their Roumanian citizenship.

In practice, the above provision means that about 300,000 Hungarians are unable to prove that their departure was forced on them, because the Roumanian authorities do not regard the posters ordering the population to leave as force, and it is hardly possible to prove that force was actually employed to make them leave. There is no doubt that the Roumanian authorities have considerable liberty of action in deciding that as large a number as possible of the Hungarians lose their Roumanian citizenship.

On October 10th, 1945 the Roumanian Minister of Justice took a further step towards depriving them of their rights with Decree No 104.005/1945. K. 10. This decree of the Minister of Justice was sent to every court of justice in Northern Transylvania. The text is as follows:

"Those inhabitants of Northern Transylvania who made common cause with the enemy German and Hungarian troops and withdrew to Hungary lose their Roumanian citizenship under the law of April 4th, 1945; consequently, if these people return to Roumania, they are to be considered as enemy subjects and if their property comes under the provisions of Clause 8 of the Armistice Agreement (the CASBI**) the Roumanian authorities are not permitted to fulfil any request of these people regarding their property; the judicial authorities therefore may do nothing to enable them to recover their movable or immovable property or move into their dwellings."

This provision even deprived hundreds of thousands of refugee Hungarians of the possibility of such legal assistance as would have enabled them to defend themselves against arbitrary action on the part of the authorities.

3. On December 15th, 1945, the Roumanian Minister for Internal Affairs issued instructions under the number 46.886. A. as to the application of the executive decree referring to the regulation of the cit-

*Clause 40: Any person loses all rights to Roumanian citizenship who 1. entered the service of a foreign state without the previous consent of the Roumanian Government; 2. entered any foreign military service or adhered to any foreign military formation without the previous consent of the Roumanian Government; 3. placed himself under foreign sovereignty for any period and as a result of whatever action. The establishment of cases under the above clause will be effected by a decision of the Council of Ministers.

**The Roumanian Government, under Clause 8 of the Armistice Agreement, set up a special organisation for the administration of enemy property, and CASBI is the abbreviation of its Roumanian title.

izenship of the inhabitants of Northern Transylvania.* This provision denotes a certain alleviation in the execution of the citizenship law. It puts an end to the grievance frequently brought up by the Hungarians of Transylvania that opting for Hungary by inhabitants of Southern Transylvania after the Vienna Award, and the acquisition of a certificate of Hungarian citizenship by those of Northern Transylvania does not denote the loss of Roumanian citizenship.

It is a serious error in this decree of the Minister for Internal Affairs that it leaves too much to the discretion of the authorities. The complicated procedure for entering a name on the list of citizens leaves ample room for arbitrary action on the part of minor administrative authorities. It is here that the Hungarians have had the most regrettable experiences in the past, and not so very long ago.

In view of the foregoing, the Hungarian Government requests and proposes that the question of citizenship for persons of Hungarian nationality under Roumanian rule should be settled on the basis of the principles outlined in the memorandum attached to the Note-verbale No. 99/res/Be. of October 31st, 1945. In settling the question of citizenship, the Hungarian Government requests that attention should be given to the principle that all the Hungarians living in Roumania, including their direct descendants, should be granted Roumanian citizenship, if they had a permanent place of residence in that territory on December 1st, 1918 (the day of the National Assembly at Gyulafehérvár), on July 26th, 1921 (the ratification of the Treaty of Trianon) or on August 30th, 1940 (the date of the Vienna Award).

The Hungarian Government further considers it necessary that the explusion of Transylvanian Hungarians deprived of their Roumanian citizenship by the Nationality Act of April 2nd, 1945 or its executive instructions and thus rendered homeless should be suspended by the

---

*Persons who on August 30th, 1940 had a place of residence in another part of the country but subsequently opted for Hungarian citizenship or escaped across the frontier and settled in Hungary may request the declaration of their Roumanian citizenship from their local prefecture.

Persons who figure on the citizenship-register of any locality in Northern Transylvania or requested to be entered thereon within the time limit fixed by Law 62, but who live in another part of the country, may request the declaration of their citizenship in accordance with the decree from the prefecture of their present place of residence.

The "para-military" formations mentioned in paragraph d. of clause 4 refer to such associations as had as their object the giving of pre-military instruction, or armed formations. The phrase "solidarity with the enemy" in paragraph a. of the same clause is to be understood in the sense that this category covers persons who left Northern Transylvania of their own free will with the retreating enemy troops, where they cooperated with enemy troops and carried on operations against the allied and Roumanian troops.

Roumanian Government until the question of citizenship is settled by the peace-treaty.

In conclusion, the Hungarian Government wishes to emphasize that according to its views the peace-treaty alone is competent to order the question of the citizenship of the Hungarians in Transylvania, and not the unilateral proceedings of the Roumanian Government.

Budapest, July 15th, 1946.

ANNEX.

DECREE-LAW
concerning the regulation of the citizenship of the inhabitants of Northern Transylvania.

1. The following are Roumanian citizens and remain so:

a) Those inhabitants of Northern Transylvania who were Roumanian citizens according to the law in force on August 30th, 1940;

b) Children living in Northern Transylvania on August 30th, 1940 or born after that date if their fathers, or in the case of illegitimate children their mothers, remain citizens in accordance with the provisions of paragraph *a*).

c) Children born of an unknown father or mother on or after August 30th, 1940 in Northern Transylvania. Foundlings in this territory are to be considered as having been born there.

2. The following are not to be considered as Roumanian citizens:

a) Inhabitants of Northern Transylvania who between August 30th, 1940 and the entry into force of the present law opted for a foreign citizenship;

b) Inhabitants of Northern Transylvania who voluntarily joined the military service of a country which was at war with Roumania, or adhered to foreign military or para-military formations.

3. Whether persons coming under the provisions of this law reacquire or lose their Roumanian citizenship is to be established by the authorities, by those which undertake the compiling of the lists of such citizens by communities.

The lists are to be displayed for ten days at the perfecture of the locality. One copy of the list is to be sent to the local justices of the peace with a declaration that it has been displayed.

Appeals against the lists may be lodged with the justices of the peace within ten days of the expiry of the time prescribed for their display.

Appeals may be lodged against the decision of the court within ten days from the date of promulgation with the competent court of justice.

All procedure prescribed in this law is to be effected by the authorities.

Petitions and documents of actions are free of stamps and fees.

4. Any provisions or decisions which conflict with this law are to be considered as null and void.

Statement by Paul Auer

Hungarian Minister in Paris, representing the Hungarian Delegation at the joint meeting of the Territorial and Political Commissions for Hungary and Roumania at the Paris Conference, on August 31, 1946.

Mr. President, Gentlemen,

May I first of all express the thanks of the Hungarian delegation to the Conference for having decided to hear us. You can well understand what our feelings would have been if, for reasons of procedure, it would have been impossible to make our voice heard.

The two delegations which today stand before you are not formed of enemies; they represent two countries which, after having passed through grave historical changes, have taken the path of a radical transformation.

In Hungary, after the final collapse of feudal and chauvinist reaction, the democratic parties have come to power, parties which courageously opposed not only the inner policy of the former regime, but also its minority and foreign policies; parties which struggled against the policies of Hitlerite Germany and whose members, victims of the Nazis, had suffered imprisonment and persecution. These parties had always been hostile to the former regime's policy of revision and had always urged the need for understanding with neighbouring peoples, within a framework of friendship and sincere cooperation.

We are not unaware of the fact that at the head of Roumanian affairs are democratic statesmen who likewise desire understanding and friendship between our two peoples.

If we are now here, it is to lay before you a suggestion for the solution of the problem which the former regimes, blinded by their prejudices, were incapable of solving. This problem concerns a territory called Transylvania. Its area of 103,000 square kilometers equals that of Switzerland, Belgium, and Holland together. It considerably exceeds that of present-day Hungary. This province constitutes an integral part of the Carpathian Basin. To the south and east it is the chain of the Carpathian Mountains which forms its natural frontiers, while towards Hungary the Hungarian-Roumanian frontier cuts across the eastern edge of the Great Hungarian Plain. According to the Roumanian statistics of 1930, the total population of Transylvania amounts to 5.5 million people, of whom 3.2 million are Roumanian and 1.5

million Hungarian, the rest being divided among various other ethnic groups.

This territory has played a crucial role in history ever since the eleventh century. It formed part of Hungary until the end of the First World War, after having formerly constituted, for 150 years, an independent province, ruled by Hungarian princes. Transylvania has contributed a large number of eminent statesmen, poets and scholars to the civilization of Hungary and Europe.

After the end of the First World War, by virtue of the Treaty of Trianon, Transylvania was attached to Roumania. This was done without the population concerned being consulted. This treaty is one which was never signed by the Soviet Union nor ratified by the United States of America. These facts confirm that the frontiers, as drawn up, do not coincide with the ethnic boundaries of the population. It is a fact that neighboring states, one after the other, request permission to transfer to Hungary at least a part of the Hungarian population living within and along their borders. No better proof could be asked of the errors committed. It was thus that a population of a million and a half Hungarians was handed over to Roumania, a population whose fate cannot leave us indifferent. The territory in question was conceded to Roumania by the Great Powers only on condition that the racial, religious or language minorities inhabiting it should be granted in compensation certain rights, guaranteed constitutionally and internationally. Thus, on December 9, 1919, a treaty was signed between the Allied and Associated Powers on one hand and Roumania on the other, with a view to ensuring the protection of the minorities under the guarantee of the League of Nations. It is a well-known fact that the former Roumanian governments did not put into practice the measures stipulated for the protection of the minorities. To give a striking example, it is enough to recall that, from 1918 to 1938, 200,000 Hungarians, autochthonous inhabitants of Transylvania, had to leave that province. We thus find ourselves obliged to devote our attention to the Transylvanian problem, not with the intention of increasing the territory of Hungary and for chauvinistic reasons, but certainly with a view to ameliorating the fate of the Hungarians living beyond our frontier, and likewise with the intention of bettering the atmosphere ruling in the Danubian Basin, so as to create the conditions for a collaboration serving the interests of the peoples inhabiting it [and] thereby to further the cause and interests of a lasting peace.

We know perfectly well that nowadays frontier questions should no longer be of any major importance. If everybody could enjoy the full rights of man, in total political, economic, and cultural equality, then the frontiers would, in fact, be only lines of administrative demarcation. Unfortunately, the experience of the last twenty-five years, confirmed by that of today, proves that the fate of the minorities in the Danubian Basin is not an enviable one and that it is impossible to remedy the situation by regulations which remain a dead letter or by high-sounding but empty declarations.

In raising the problem of the Hungarian population of Transylvania, we do not forget two facts of vital importance. The first is that, under the Armistice Agreement concluded between the United Nations and Roumania, Transylvania, or the greater part thereof, will have to belong to Roumania. The second fact which we want to take into consideration is the decision of the Council of Foreign Ministers which declared null and void the Arbitration Decision of Vienna of August 30, 1940, which, although not having been taken on our initiative, had restituted to Hungary some 44,000 square kilometers of the territory of Northern Transylvania. Keeping these two facts in view, all that the Hungarian government asked for, in its memorandum addressed to the Council of Foreign Ministers, as well as in the speech made by the Hungarian minister of foreign affairs before the Plenary Session of the Conference was for a part of the territory of Transylvania, amounting to some 22,000 square kilometers, to be reattached to Hungary. Unfortunately this suggestion has not been accepted by the Council of Foreign Ministers, nor was it favorably received by the Commission. Under these circumstances, and to return to one of the possible solutions, which had already been mentioned in our Memorandum addressed to the Council of Foreign Ministers and outlined in the speech before the Plenary Session of the Conference, we request the rectification of the frontier, corresponding to the ethnic realities.

This would be a question of transfering a territory of 4,000 square kilometers, which constitutes hardly four percent of that area which after the end of the First World War was attributed to Roumania. In these conditions the reattachment to Hungary of this strip of territory, which does not belong to the geographical unity of Transylvania, and which, throughout history, did not form an integral part thereof, would bear the character of a simple readjustment of the frontier. This territory comprises a Hungarian population of sixty-seven percent out of a total population of approximately 500,000 people. This rectification of the frontier would include the towns of Szatmárnémeti, (Satu Mare), Nagykároly (Carei), Nagyvárad (Oradea), Nagyszalonta (Salonta), and Arad.

Permit me, Mr. President, to put at your disposal a map which details the exact lines of the proposed new frontier. This modest solution has the merit of reattaching to Hungary a territory on which the Hungarians form a considerable majority. I must remark here that this suggestion cannot be considered a new one, for our earlier proposals referring to a territory considerably larger necessarily also included the area to which I have just referred.

I must in any case, however, insist that our suggestion only represents a solution if it is closely linked with a settlement of all the required guarantees concerning the rights and the protection of the Hungarian minority of over 1.2 million persons which would still be left within the Roumanian state. The task of seeing the settlement duly respected would fall to the United Nations Organization, as suggested by the Hungarian government in the aide-memoire handed to the Council of Foreign Ministers on last June 11, and quite recently, in the suggestions for a draft treaty laid before the Conference.

If I have considered it essential to insist on the necessity of setting up a statute of local autonomy and protection of the rights of the Hungarian minority of Transylvania it is not only because, as I have indicated above, Transylvanian history teaches us to seek for a solution in this direction, but also because the present situation of the Hungarians in Transylvania has become extremely serious.

In view of the fact that at present, as I have just mentioned, both our countries are ruled by democratic governments, we consider it desirable that the Roumanian and Hungarian delegations, here present, open direct negotiations with each other so as to be able to submit later to the Commission a joint proposal concerning the rights to be guaranteed the Hungarians of Transylvania.

Why is it necessary to have recourse to these means? While recognizing that the democratic government of the Roumania of today, desirous of ensuring to the Hungarian population of Transylvania equality of rights, has already taken certain measures in this connection, we must note, unfortunately, that a large part of these measures is being retarded in application. In theory the Hungarian minority enjoys certain rights, but in practice this minority is the object of numerous discriminatory practices and is not removed from fear and destitution. I would also like to raise here the ever tragic question of the refugees, for whom remedy should likewise be found without delay. Let us recall, as an example, that out of a total population of 1.5 million, the citizenship of some 300,000 Hungarians has been put in question.

The loss of Roumanian citizenship entails disastrous economic consequences, such as the confiscation of property, suspension of salaries, wages, pensions, etc.

The new agrarian law is also no less unfavorable to the Hungarian peasants, who are, in practice, excluded from its benefits. This is all the more serious as more than seventy percent of the Hungarians in Roumania are agriculturists.

It is only in passing that I shall mention the sequestrations and confiscations of property, discriminations mainly in economic life, enforced evacuations, expulsions and arbitrary arrests, the list of which is duly laid down in various sworn statements, but on which I do not want to dwell, so as not to get involved in details. I would not like to appear as accuser at the very moment when I seek reconciliation. But I have had to refer to all this so that you might have an idea of the gravity of the position of the Hungarian minority in Transylvania, and which thus also constitutes a factor which opposes reconciliation.

That is why we have allowed ourselves to ask for a rectification of the frontier, mentioned above, linked to the establishment of a local administrative autonomy and to measures of protection for the minority, under the control and subject to the sanctions of the United Nations Organization. Already the treaty signed in 1919 between the Allied and Associated Nations on one hand and Roumania on the other concerning the protection of the minorities had anticipated an educational and religious autonomy for this compact block of 600,000 Hungarians inhabiting an area of 17,000 kilometers in eastern Transylvania. Even this restricted autonomy was never implemented by the Roumanian governments. In our opinion it would be indispensible for a wide autonomy to be granted to this important homogenous ethnic group, to ensure for it the rights of man and basic liberties.

To conclude, here is a succinct summary of the requests we are respectfully making to the Commission.

First: that the Commission decide to accept our suggestion concerning the rectification of the Hungarian-Roumanian frontier, with a view to reattaching to Hungary the frontier zones with a Hungarian majority.

Second: that the Commission decide to invite the two delegations to open direct negotiations concerning the conclusion of special treaties covering the protection of the rights of the Hungarian minority, under the guarantee of the United Nations and with the assurance of a wide autonomy given to the compact ethnic group of Hungarians inhabiting the eastern part of Transylvania.

Third: In case that, within a fixed period, the two delegations should be unable to reach an agreement on the joint proposal, it is you whom we would allow ourselves to ask to kindly seek for a solution which would best conform to justice and equality, and to recommend it for approval to the Council of Foreign Ministers. We are convinced that this is the direction that can lead to a definite reconciliation between our two countries. The Transylvania of yesterday divided us, but that of tomorrow, in which all the peoples will be free to enjoy their liberty, will serve to unite us. For, gentlemen, you may rest assured, as may Roumania, that what we want is peace. We aspire to it sincerely and with all our hearts. We know that it is in our interest, but we know likewise that it is also in the interest of Roumania. In our ears still ring the words of one of the greatest figures of Hungarian history, those of Louis Kossuth, president of the First Hungarian Republic, who said, when proclaiming his project of a Danubian Union: "In the name of Heaven I adjure the Hungarian, Roumanian, and Slav brothers to throw a veil over the past, to take each other's hands, to rise as a single man in the common struggle for liberty, fighting all for one, and one for all!" But we also recall the words written by one of the best Roumanian publicists of the nineteenth century, Emmanual Gojdu: "I assure the Hungarian Nation that there is no Roumanian thinker who is not convinced that Divine Providence, the God of all the peoples, has established for the Hungarian and Roumanian nations an ordinance that they must live in an eternal alliance. Only thus will they have a glorious future. One against the other, they will both perish." We must take these words to heart, Roumanians, and Hungarians. Through mutual understanding and thanks to your good offices, gentlemen, we shall find the solution which will put an end to the differences separating Hungarians and Roumanians, thus contributing to ensuring peace in Europe.

Index

Place name entries are listed in the language that was the prevalent or official language of the city, county or region at the time of the reference. This means that the same place may in certain instances have two or three separate entries, under two or more names. Place names will be cross-referenced only in exceptional cases since Appendix A provides a listing of all significant locations in the relevant languages.